Constitutionality of Law without a Constitutional Court

This book analyses the problem of the possibility of guaranteeing the constitutionality of law in cases when a constitutional court either has been weakened or does not exist. A starting point of the research is the emergence of the so-called illiberal constitutionalism in several states, namely Poland, Hungary and Turkey, as this phenomenon gravely affects the functioning of constitutional courts. The work is divided into three parts. The first contains contributions of a theoretical nature dedicated to the current shape of constitutional review, in particular in the light of the emergence of 'illiberal constitutionalism'. This part of the book also deals with the collapse of the centralised constitutional review in Poland and the attempts to resolve the constitutional crisis. The second is focused on discussing specific, current problems with constitutional review, on the basis of states such as Hungary, Romania, Turkey and Poland. The third relates to other forms of constitutional review, that is, the so-called dispersed model and the parliamentary one executed in the course of the legislative process. The contributions discuss such forms of constitutional review in the Netherlands and Finland. The book will be a valuable resource for students, academics and policy-makers working in the areas of constitutional law and politics.

Mirosław Granat is a professor of Constitutional Law at the Cardinal Stefan Wyszynski University, Warsaw, Poland, and a head of the Department of Constitutional Law of the Faculty of Law and Administration.

Comparative Constitutional Change

Comparative Constitutional Change has developed into a distinct field of constitutional law. It encompasses the study of constitutions through the way they change and covers a wide scope of topics and methodologies. Books in this series include work on developments in the functions of the constitution, the organization of powers and the protection of rights, as well as research that focuses on formal amendment rules and the relation between constituent and constituted power. The series includes comparative approaches along with books that focus on single jurisdictions, and brings together research monographs and edited collections which allow the expression of different schools of thought. While the focus is primarily on law, where relevant the series may also include political science, historical, philosophical and empirical approaches that explore constitutional change.

Series editors:
Xenophon Contiades is Professor of Public Law, Panteion University, Athens, Greece and Managing Director, Centre for European Constitutional Law, Athens, Greece.

Thomas Fleiner is Emeritus Professor of Law at the University of Fribourg, Switzerland.

Alkmene Fotiadou is Research Associate at the Centre for European Constitutional Law, Athens, Greece.

Richard Albert is the William Stamps Farish Professor in Law and Professor of Government at the University of Texas at Austin, USA.

Also in the series:

Constitutional Law and Politics of Secession
Edited by Antoni Abat i Ninet

A History of the Constitution of Bangladesh
The Founding, Development, and Way Ahead
Edited by Ridwanul Hoque and Rokeya Chowdhury

Constitutionality of Law without a Constitutional Court
A View from Europe
Edited by Mirosław Granat

For more information about this series, please visit: www.routledge.com/Comparative-Constitutional-Change/book-series/COMPCONST

Constitutionality of Law without a Constitutional Court

A View from Europe

Edited by Mirosław Granat

Routledge
Taylor & Francis Group
LONDON AND NEW YORK

First published 2024
by Routledge
4 Park Square, Milton Park, Abingdon, Oxon OX14 4RN

and by Routledge
605 Third Avenue, New York, NY 10158

Routledge is an imprint of the Taylor & Francis Group, an informa business

British Library Cataloguing-in-Publication Data
A catalogue record for this book is available from the British Library

ISBN: 978-1-032-41009-8 (hbk)
ISBN: 978-1-032-41010-4 (pbk)
ISBN: 978-1-003-35579-3 (ebk)

DOI: 10.4324/9781003355793

Typeset in Galliard
by Deanta Global Publishing Services, Chennai, India

Contents

Contributors

Rainer Arnold Professor of Public Law at the University of Regensburg, Germany; head of the Chair of Public Law. In 1999 nominated holder of the Jean Monnet Chair of EU Law and in 2008 holder of the Jean Monnet Chair ad personam 'Legal Relations of the EU with Central, Eastern and Southeastern Europe'. Corresponding Member of the Academy of Sciences of Bologna, Membre de l'Académie internationale de droit comparé, Fellow of the European Law Institute. Former visiting professor at various universities, including University Paris I (Panthéon-Sorbonne), University Paris II (Panthéon-Assas), University of Strasbourg and University of Bologna. Author and editor of many monographs and legal articles.

Leonard F.M. Besselink Professor of constitutional law and head of the Department of Public Law at the University of Amsterdam, the Netherlands, member of the Royal Netherlands Society of Sciences and Humanities, visiting professor of European constitutional law at Libera Universitá Internazionale degli Studi Sociali LUISS, School of Government, Rome, Italy (2015). Author of 250 publications, mainly in the field of Dutch and comparative constitutional law, international law, EU law, as well as mutual interactions between these legal orders, including 'Talking about European Democracy', *European Constitutional Law Review*, 2017, vol. 13(2).

Piotr Chybalski Assistant professor in the Department of Constitutional Law at the Cardinal Stefan Wyszynski University in Warsaw, Poland (since 2017), and expert in legislation in the Bureau of Research of the Chancellery of the Sejm of the Republic of Poland (since 2006). Author of publications and expert opinions in the field of Polish and comparative constitutional law, including '"Chilling Effect" in the Judicial Decisions of the Polish Constitutional Tribunal as an Example of Legal Transplant', *Review of European and Comparative Law* 2022, vol. 1 and *Parliamentary Immunity in Poland*, an in-depth analysis for the Committee on Legal Affairs of the European Parliament (2015).

Marta Derlatka PhD, member of the Warsaw Bar, since 2009 running her own law practice, specializing in constitutional, administrative and labor law. In the years 2000–2008 she was a clerk in the Polish Constitutional Court, then she worked for the Polish Ombudsman (2008–2010); lecturer in constitutional law at Cardinal Stefan Wyszynski University in Warsaw, Poland (2002–2016). Marta Derlatka is the author of numerous publications on constitutional law and protection of human rights. She's been a member of the Polish Association of Constitutional Law from 2001.

Selin Esen Professor of Constitutional Law and chair of the Department of Constitutional Law at the University of Ankara University (Turkey), Faculty of Law and the First Vice President of the International Association of Constitutional Law. She was an academic consultant in the Constitutional Reconciliation Committee formed by the Turkish Parliament to draft a new constitution during 2012–2013. She does research in the field of constitutional adjudication, fundamental rights and freedoms and comparative constitutional law. She has several publications on secularism, political parties, constitutional complaint, internet freedom, freedom of movement, gender equality and emergency regimes in Turkish, English and Spanish languages.

Lech Garlicki Professor emeritus at the University of Warsaw, Doctor h.c. University of Gdansk (2017), since 2017 Visiting Professor at the Washington University in Saint Louis; retired judge of the Polish Constitutional Tribunal (1993–2001) and the European Court of Human Rights (2002–2012). In the past, visiting professor at several universities: NYU, Yale, University of Chicago, Tel Aviv University, IDC Herzliya, Hong Kong University; vice-president of the International Association of Constitutional Law (2010–2018). Author of over 300 publications in the field of constitutional law, human rights law, comparative law, judicial review.

Ewelina Gierach Assistant professor in the Department of Constitutional Law at the Cardinal Stefan Wyszynski University in Warsaw, Poland and expert in legislation in the Bureau of Research of the Chancellery of the Sejm of the Republic of Poland (since 2007). Author of publications and expert opinions in the field of Polish constitutional law (in particular parliamentary law as well as sources of law and review of their hierarchical conformity), including Genesis and significance of the parliamentary control of the constitutionality of law in Poland. Introductory remarks in M. Granat (ed.) *Constitutional Judiciary: Theory and Practice*. Vol. 3, Warsaw 2020.

Mirosław Granat Professor of Constitutional Law at the Cardinal Stefan Wyszynski University, Warsaw, Poland, and a head of the Department of Constitutional Law of the Faculty of Law and Administration. He served as a judge at the Polish Constitutional Court from 2007 to 2016. From 2018 to 2019 he served as a consultant of the Venice Commission of the Council of Europe on the project Advice to the Constitutional Court of Ukraine on the constitutional complaint, and in 2020 as an OSCE advisor to the Constitutional Court of Ukraine. A visiting fellow at several universities, e.g., the University of Copenhagen, Denmark (2018) and the Catholic University of America in Washington, USA (2019), and a member of the Advisory Board in the Demos 2020 Project (the Democratic efficacy and the varieties of populism in Europe). Author of over 200 publications from the field of constitutional law. His research interests include in particular theoretical aspects of constitutionalism and judicial review of the constitutionality of law.

Péter Kruzslicz Assistant professor at the Faculty of Law and Political Sciences (International and Regional Studies Institute) of the University of Szeged, Hungary, director of French-speaking study programmes at the same faculty and director of the Francophone University Centre of the same University. His research is conducted on the field of intersection of the constitutional and European law (national sovereignty, constitutional identity, the relations between national and European law), and in institutional questions, especially democratic challenges in contemporary States in Central Europe and in the institutional and legal system of European integration. He is involved in numerous international research projects and publishes in Hungarian, French and English.

Tuomas Ojanen Professor of Constitutional Law and Director for the Doctoral Programme in Law (2022–2025). He is also Member of the Venice Commission, Council of Europe (2022–9 May 2026); Member of the Management Board of the European Agency for Fundamental Rights (July 2020–June 2025); and Chair of the National Non-Discrimination and Equality Tribunal, an impartial and independent judicial body appointed by the Government and supervising compliance with the Non-Discrimination Act and the Act on Equality between Women and Men both in private activities and in public administrative and commercial activities (1 August 2019–31 July 2023). His main areas of research and expertise include Finnish constitutional law, comparative constitutional law, EU law and international human rights law. He has a track record of over 20 years in directing and participating in multiple research projects and networks that include partners from several European countries.

Aleksandra Syryt PhD in constitutional law, assistant professor at the Faculty of Law and Administration of the Cardinal Stefan Wyszyński University in Warsaw, Poland, Department of Constitutional Law. Her research focuses on the field of constitutional law, including the principles of the system, constitutional review and the protection of human rights, as well as legislation. She has experience in managing and participating in research programmes, including interdisciplinary projects.

Zoltán Szente Research professor at the Institute for Legal Studies of the Centre for Social Sciences in Budapest, Hungary. Since 2013, he has been the vice-chairman of the Group of Independent Experts of the Council of Europe. He is also the co-chair of the Research Group on Constitutional

Interpretation of the International Association of Constitutional Law. His field of interest extends to comparative constitutional law, constitutional theory and European constitutional history. His recent works include The Populist Challenges to Constitutional Interpretation in Europe and Beyond (co-edited with Fruzsina Gárdos-Orosz), by Routledge (2021), Constitutional Law in Hungary, by Kluwer (2023) and The Myth of Populist Constitutionalism in Hungary and Poland: Populist or Authoritarian Constitutionalism? International Journal of Constitutional Law (2023).

Elena-Simina Tănăsescu Professor of constitutional and European law at the Law Faculty of the Bucharest University, Romania. Between 2015 and 2018 she has been presidential advisor for the institutional and constitutional reform of Romania. Previously president of the Romanian Association of Constitutional Law (2014–2019) and of the Franco-Romanian Association of Lawyers (2010–2019), since June 2019 she is a judge at the Constitutional Court of Romania. In July 2018 she was distinguished with the Légion d'honneur by the President of the French Republic.

1 Turbulent times in the constitutionalism of Central and Eastern European countries[1]

Mirosław Granat

1.1 The constitutional crisis. Landscape after the battle

The constitutionalism of Central and Eastern European countries is undergoing major changes. One of them involves a centralised constitutional review of the law carried out by a separate body. This type of judiciary was introduced in the region relatively recently, in the course of the democratic transformation at the end of the 1980s and the beginning of the 1990s. Thirty years ago, we treated constitutional courts like a bridge connecting the democratic states of the then Western Europe with the new democracies of Central and Eastern Europe.[2] They were our guides on the journey from totalitarian regimes to countries implementing the rule of law. The reception of constitutional judiciary took the form of a massive wave of legal changes affected by the German legal culture. It consisted in the adoption of the so-called European model of constitutional judiciary based on Kelsen's theory, albeit subject to a 'realistic adjustment'. At the time, we were unanimous in our opinion that this reception had been extremely successful and that the courts would begin their activities soon.[3]

The constitutional court turned out to be a necessary element of the rule of law. The judicature was instrumental in laying its foundations. Thirty years later, it seems that the path taken by the judiciary of the 'new' European countries, modelled after the system prevalent in Austria and Germany, was the only possible way of transition from a communist regime. It led towards liberal constitutionalism in the form that is at times called 'judicial constitutionalism', that is, one which entails a major role of the judges. Without the active participation of constitutional courts, building a country that observes the rule of law in the existing conditions would probably have been impossible and would have likely ended in failure. Judicial review of the constitutionality

1 This paper has been prepared as a result of the research project no. 2018/31/B/HS5/02667, financed by the National Science Centre (Poland) within the OPUS-15 funding scheme.
2 Cf. M. Granat, *Sądowa kontrola konstytucyjności prawa w państwach Europy Środkowej i Wschodniej*, Warsaw 2003, p. 83.
3 Cf. *ibidem*.

DOI: 10.4324/9781003355793-1

of laws not only stabilised the rule of law, but also restored in particular human rights and freedoms, which had been absent before 1989. The 1990s' constitutions perpetuated the strong position of constitutional courts as a result of the aforementioned practice.

In the 2010s or even earlier (in the period 2005–2007 in Poland), populist tendencies accompanying the emergence of illiberal constitutionalism emerged in Central and Eastern European countries. Many of us assumed that a phenomenon called 'illiberal constitutionalism' did not in fact exist. The term itself seemed to be an oxymoron (such as *wooden iron*), and the threat this trend posed to the judiciary was ignored. For when a lawyer thinks of a constitution, the default form of constitutionalism is always liberal constitutionalism. It has certain flaws and is unable to explain a range of political phenomena, but it appeared to be irreplaceable in the construction of the rule of law. By contrast, the illiberal trend had been known even before it developed in Hungary in 2010 (election won by V. Orban) from countries such as Venezuela. It is sufficiently familiar, so that we know exactly how it uses democratic institutions to undermine the foundations of constitutionalism.[4] Populism contests constitutional courts, because one of its principles is that of the supremacy of the people over law.

However, we can notice both a common denominator and disparities in populism's relationship to judicial review. We can notice that in the cases of, e.g., Hungary, Poland or Romania. The present book demonstrates both. One of the points in common is the launch of a 'carpet attack' against constitutional courts (and the judiciary in general). Its essence is that it is the political power that determines the conditions under which the constitutional court passes judgments. Thus, populism's first strike consisted in blocking the activity of those courts, which took place in various forms, an example being the Polish Constitutional Tribunal (the experience of the Polish constitutional court is a model instance). In contrast, a distinctive feature in the Hungarian case was the replacement of the 'old' constitutional court with a 'new' one. This replacement of one court with another (subordinate to the political power) took place pursuant to the 2011 Basic Law. Finally, the case of the Romanian Constitutional Court is situated in between the above two solutions. It was unique, as the constitutional court was contained without a permanent attack against the rule of law (as in Poland) or a fundamental change to the political regime (as in Hungary). In Romania, the authorities in a way 'tamed' the court, so that it worked hand in hand with the authorities to attack the independence of common courts in the course of the 2018–2019 reforms. The crackdown on the independence of constitutional courts guided by a common goal, that is, subordinating them to the political power, can be compared to chopping off the head of the rule of law. The metaphor may be somewhat

4 Cf. A. Sajó, *Ruling by Cheating. Governance in Illiberal Democracy*, Cambridge 2021, pp. 297 et seq.

drastic, yet it seems justified. The constitutionality of law in the above countries had been based on those courts' judicial decisions. On account of the role they played, they were part of the rule of law's 'critical infrastructure'. They operated at the interface of key elements of the political regime, such as the supreme legal force of constitutional provisions, the principle of separation of powers or human rights. Legal systems turned out to be vulnerable to this attack, as at first glance, it appears impossible to ensure the constitutionality of laws without a judicial body of this kind, at least in Poland.

The changes introduced by illiberal constitutionalism in Central and Eastern Europe are dynamic in nature. We could call this characteristic of the trend its 'voraciousness'. It originates from the principle that politics dominates over law, *ergo*, politics cannot be limited by law. Thus, populism is not limited to attacking constitutional courts alone. It undermines the principles of the independence of courts and judges or strikes against bodies that guard the freedom of the public media. It dismantles the mechanisms of judicial review ('blocks', 'takes over', 'tames' the courts), because they prevent it from 'governing properly'. At the same time, the changes it introduces hinder the comeback of 'normal' (liberal) constitutionalism. One of the distinctive features of the manner in which populism operates turns out to be, as emphasised by A. Sajó, 'systemic deception of the constitutional order as to the validity of the law' while pretending to comply with the constitution.[5] This deception consists in violating the constitution while at the same time pretending it is being adhered to. As a result of such actions, for instance in Poland, we are unable to ascertain the current legal status in a specific field, because the framework of the rule of law in which we are operating is fake. In Poland, a measure of the effectiveness of cheating was the publication by the Council of Ministers in 2018 of the Constitutional Tribunal's 2015–2016 judgments (which aimed to protect the Tribunal's independence of the political power) as the Tribunal's 'rulings'. Despite the violations of the Polish Constitution, many lawyers acknowledged the publication of the 'rulings' as a fulfilment of the constitutional duty to publish judgments. Thus, a practice that was an overt violation of the basic law became a possible interpretation of art. 190(2) of the Polish Constitution. This might be why we say that cheating is the 'secret of illiberal democracy' which ensures its unparalleled effectiveness.[6] The fate of constitutional courts confirms this at least in part.

The case of the Polish Constitutional Tribunal is a model example of building a constitutional judiciary virtually from scratch, yet successfully. Moreover, it is an example of a spectacular collapse of a court of the European type. The example of the Polish Constitutional Tribunal should be noted because this court went perhaps the furthest in jurisprudence aiming at building the rule of law and resisted the political power trying to destroy it, and at the same time

5 A. Sajó, *Ruling*..., p. 281.
6 Cf. A. Sajó, *Ruling*..., pp. 285 and 301.

its decline is rather ominous. The court began to operate in the mid-1980s, chiefly as a fig leaf in real socialism. Under the 1997 Constitution, it became a constitutional court *par excellence*. It performed a wide abstract constitutional review of laws. It acted on the basis of motions filed by political bodies (such as deputies, senators, the government or the president). The Tribunal's case law was of paramount legal significance: it contained the legal system and strengthened the foundations of Polish democracy. This court guided us towards Europe (it was part of the legal infrastructure of Poland's membership of European structures) and served as a mentor with regard to legislation (it set forth the rules of the so-called proper legislation, and its judgments gave the legislature important hints). At the same time, it approved laws that cleared the state and society of their communist past. This was exemplified by both judgments on the constitutionality of the European treaties (from 2005 and 2010) and judgments on the unconstitutionality of the 1981 martial law decrees. The Tribunal was the hegemonic leader in building a democratic rule of law, bringing us closer to Europe and rectifying unconstitutional laws. Its actual role went beyond that of a 'reviewer of the purity of the reproduction of legal rules' (as Kelsen's model provided). But just as the Tribunal gained a strong position in the Polish political system, the destruction of its independence was just as spectacular.

I bring up the example of the Polish constitutional court also because the destruction of the independent position of this type of judicial body was not some backlash by the political class against the 'power of judges' or the 'dictatorship of lawyers', but had a systemic dimension. It began with the introduction of the so-called 'surplus judges' (as discussed further on in the text on Poland) and the enactment of a series of so-called 'remedial laws' (from November 2015 to July 2016), which restricted the Tribunal's work. These actions were a real shock to legal scholars and led to a massive constitutional crisis. A situation arose in which the Tribunal was incapacitated, but at the same time sometimes indispensable to the political power in the pursuit of some of its objectives.[7] An example of this paradox was the series of *ultra vires* judgments from 2021–2022 challenging the place of European (and international) law in Poland. With these judgments, the Tribunal separated Poland from Europe and European law, e.g., with regard to the level of judicial protection of citizens or the independence of courts and judges. A provision is European law in Germany or in France, but not in Poland. Claiming the competences to review judgments of the ECJ or the ECHR, the Constitutional Tribunal won a 'second life', albeit we are aware of its place within the structure of power.

7 For more, cf. M. Granat, *On the Experiences of a Constitutional Court in an Illiberal Democracy. Incapacitated, but Necessary*, (in:) J.M. Castellà Andreu, M.A. Simonelli (eds.), *Populism and Contemporary Democracy in Europe. Old Problems and New Challenges*, London 2022, pp. 137 et seq.

The destruction of an independent constitutional judiciary depicted in this book provides the basis for a series of questions for theory and practice. The foremost of these is whether ensuring the rule of law is possible without a separate constitutional court. This is why we have distilled the questions we ask in this book, which bother many people (not only lawyers), into the book's title: *The constitutionality of law without a constitutional court. A European point of view*. Let us first try to explain what this title means.

1.2 What does 'constitutionality of law without a constitutional court' mean?

To elucidate the sense of 'without' is of fundamental importance. We understand 'without' not in the common sense, as implying a literal lack of a constitutional court; we lend it a functional sense. There are constitutional courts in Poland, Hungary, Romania and Turkey, yet they are dependent on the political power and usually serve its purposes. Thus, 'without' has a deeper meaning. This word makes it possible to reveal the fact that populism has kept constitutional courts (as dummies), but at the same time has hollowed them out. That said, we understand the rule of law as a rule based on the constitution and the constitutionality of law. Independent constitutional review in one form or another is a prerequisite of maintaining the rule of law. This could mean going towards either 'political' constitutionalism or entrusting all courts with constitutional review (the so-called diffuse, or dispersed review).

We could imagine a world 'without a constitutional court' in many ways. The experience of European countries such as Finland or the Netherlands suggests that the constitutionality of laws can be ascertained by the parliament rather than a constitutional court. This type of constitutionalism, which we could probably call 'political' constitutionalism after M. Tushnet, relies not on the courts, but on the parliament to decide whether a law is constitutional.[8] The proponents of this approach maintain that if specific political principles are observed, such as, e.g., political pluralism or representative government, judicial constitutional review loses its significance. As it considers and confronts various points of view, the parliament is predestined to settle great legal disputes. The parliament's deliberative character is a type of rationality resulting from respecting the voice of citizens. It can be more rational than the courts. Consequently, the citizens and their representatives (and not judges) should have the most to say about the constitution. It is namely an act rooted in social life, and not a matter for lawyers to decide. The reaction to a draft provided by 'political' constitutionalism usually consists in pointing out that it is inconsistent (it resembles asking a fox to stand guard over the hen house). Since the parliament enacts a law, why would it declare its own product unconstitutional?

8 Cf. M. Tushnet, *Advanced Introduction to Comparative Constitutional Law*, Edward Elgar 2014, pp. 44 et seq

From the perspective of the present book, it is crucial whether a model solves the problem of the fox and the hen house. The resolution of this contradiction proposed by M. Tushnet is that the constitutional review of a law should be centred around the passing of the law, when its shape is considered. The backers of this solution believe that as long as certain requirements as to the substance of parliamentary review are met, such as maintaining 'constitutional conscientiousness', then passing an unconstitutional law becomes outright impossible. On the other hand, sceptics argue that a law-making body, even a 'constitutionally conscientious' one, could easily overlook an unconstitutional provision. In some countries, this danger is reduced by creating institutions within the parliament that are tasked with minimising the risk of a law being unconstitutional.[9] Lacking M. Tushnet's extensive legal-comparative skill set, let us rely on his assessment that parliamentary review of the constitutionality of laws is a 'serious alternative to judicial constitutional review'. That being said, according to the above author, based on an analysis of the experiences around the world, this mechanism is 'practically unattainable' under contemporary conditions. For instance, political constitutionalism is efficient in terms of debating the legislature's rationality, yet unreliable when it comes to determining the proportionality of the legislature's actions.[10]

When considering the 'constitutionality of law without a constitutional court', an interesting matter of sorts is the 'amendment' to the above model in the form of 'dialogic review'. This improvement to the concept of 'political' constitutionalism is the following: the constitutional court declares a law unconstitutional, but the legislature can 'react' to the judgment by enacting the law again with a specific majority of votes. 'Dialogic review' entails an interaction between the constitutional court and the legislature at the individual stages of work over a new law. It takes the form of a reasonable difference of opinions as to the concretisation of abstract constitutional concepts, e.g., regarding the understanding of human freedom or of vague provisions. M. Tushnet perceives the advantage of 'dialogic review' in the attitude towards the model resulting from 'political' constitutionalism (when the fox guards the hen house), which is to mitigate the so-called counter-majority difficulty. This difficulty is based on the fact that the law reflects the views of the majority of the people expressed in the election, while constitutional review performed by the court consists in overturning the legislature's decision. The constitutional judges' position with regard to the law is then explained somewhat idealistically (they do all in their power to promote good governance) or realistically (they derive benefits, mainly psychological in nature, from their power).[11] To recapitulate, the 'dialogic' character of review enables the legislature to re-

9 For more cf. M. Tushnet, *Advanced...*, p. 47; see also E.-W. Böckenförde, *Państwo prawa w jednoczącej się Europie*, Warsaw 2000, pp. 63 et seq.
10 Cf. M. Tushnet, *Advanced...*, p. 47.
11 M. Tushnet, *Advanced...*, p. 59.

evaluate its position, taking into account the findings of the court. This model can be implemented in the so-called Canadian (the court has the final say) or British (the parliament has the final say) style. A common defect of these solutions is that they assume good faith from all participants of the dialogue, and in particular from the legislature.[12]

Thus, the model of review based on 'political' constitutionalism is mistrustful of the judiciary, but this mistrust differs from the one we encounter in populism. It seems to cover solutions we know from countries whose political regimes we analyse in the present book, such as Finland and the Netherlands. It should be noted that the above-mentioned model has nothing to do with the practice that used to be applied in some Central and Eastern European countries in the 1980s, when bodies – surrogates of constitutional review – operated in Poland or in Hungary (e.g., political bodies monitored the constitutionality of law). These solutions are too archaic to discuss. A real review performed by the parliament was under those conditions logically impossible. This was due to the position of the 'supreme representative body' (and not the parliament) in the state on the one hand and to the role played by the communist party on the other. This matter is discussed further on in the book, when the sense of 'without' with regard to Poland is considered.

Another way to explicate the meaning of 'constitutionality of law without a constitutional court' is related to the performance of constitutional review by common and administrative courts. This perspective seems most appealing. However, it requires that the Kelsenian model, which we are attached to and which involves constitutional review centralised in one court (the 'negative legislature'), be revised. Is an adjustment of this model possible for us? The answer to this question is both affirmative and negative. Firstly, is it possible to abandon Kelsen's idea that common court judges are incapable of reviewing the constitutionality of the law? As remarked by M. Tushnet, this is not about their legal skills, but about a lack of political experience and 'political sensitivity', which is indispensable in the performance of such review. These are attributes of judges in the centralised model of review, or of judges who perform judicial review in the United States, but not of civil or criminal law judges in Europe. Secondly, a factor that favours or even encourages dispersed review is the fact, pointed out by M. Tushnet, that the focus of review shifted in the 20th century from problems with the principles of the political system to the protection of human rights. The observation about shifts in this respect is largely valid with regard to Central and Eastern European countries. Sometimes, laws violate people's fundamental rights only when applied to very specific situations. Such a change to the object of scrutiny would have implications for the Kelsenian model. For example, citizens' access to the constitutional court becomes important. It cannot be limited mainly to state bodies or

12 Cf. M. Tushnet, *Advanced*..., p. 60.

other authorised actors.[13] Such a 'Kelsenian adjustment' requires further that the relationship between common courts, which undertake the review of the constitutionality of the law, and the supreme court or constitutional court (if it is preserved) be rethought. M. Tushnet vividly calls this relationship a 'battle of the courts'. We are familiar with conflicts of this kind from the experience of, for example, Poland, where we have been attempting to apply dispersed constitutional review since 2016, as discussed later on in the book.

However, the constitutionality of law 'without a constitutional court' may not be construed in the manner that it is done in the American judicial review model (or in other countries which apply it). The mechanism is well known and there is no need to describe it here. In this system, review is performed continually as an element of ordinary practice of applying private law. I rely on M. Tushnet's assessment that judicial review is not some extraordinary theory, but a practice without 'any specific political component'.[14] The adoption of judicial review in Central European states is impossible, as our legal systems are not based on precedent, especially as we are not familiar with the culture of case law, which plays a great role in this model. The judicial review model remains available, but its adoption is completely unrealistic.

Ensuring the constitutionality of law seems to be a necessary condition for overcoming the constitutional crisis in Central and Eastern European countries, such as Poland and Hungary. It must be stated clearly that it is impossible to restore the rule of law without restoring the position of the constitution as the supreme law.

It is necessary to consider at least three factors in analysing the issue of judicial review. First of all, conclusions should be drawn from the collapse of the activity of constitutional courts as institutions independent from political bodies (as was the case first in Hungary and now in Poland). In the Polish case, a comprehensive and fair analysis of the position of the Constitutional Tribunal is complicated by the fact that the majority of constitutional judges were legally elected by the parliamentary majority. Their terms of office (lasting nine years) expire in the distant future. For this reason, in my opinion, removing legally elected judges (despite doubts concerning their independence or the substance of their judgments) is out of the question, unless it is formally preceded by a constitutional amendment. The question whether legally dubious means can be used in order to restore the rule of law is currently a subject of heated debate in Poland. Some scholars even argue that radical measures are necessary with regard to the composition of the Tribunal.[15]

13 For more about the consequences of introducing the individual application to the Kelsenian model, see M. Tushnet, *Advanced*..., p. 53.

14 M. Tushnet, *Advanced*..., p. 49.

15 Cf. W. Sadurski, *Trybunał do wyzerowania*, Gazeta Wyborcza, 08.07.2022, https://wyborcza.pl/magazyn/7,124059,28665135,trybunal-do-wyzerowania.html (accessed: 8.02.2023)

J. Zajadło, T. Koncewicz, *Niektórzy mówią: nic nie robić z Trybunałem Konstytucyjnym, poczekać aż sam spadnie. Z wirusem też byśmy czekali?*, Gazeta Wyborcza, 27.01.2023, https://

However, just as it is impossible to remove legally elected judges from the Tribunal (despite the criticism of this body and its decisions), so is it impossible to 'return to the past' by restoring the pre-2016 *status quo ante*, i.e., by restoring the Constitutional Tribunal in exactly the same form in which it functioned in the years 1989–2016. In that period, the foundations of the rule of law were laid and the majority of basic legal constructions were created. The Tribunal played a key role in these processes. This importance of the constitutional court (perhaps slightly exaggerated) was necessary to establish the standards of the rule of law. The Tribunal acted as a 'sheriff' supervising the transition from the communist system of lawlessness. Is such a 'cowboy' (using M. Tushnet's terminology) necessary in the present conditions, several decades after the collapse of communism? It seems that in a situation of the proliferation of projects aimed at 'restoring the Tribunal from before 2016', we need a sort of 'awakening from a dream'. In any case, an examination of the current situation of the constitutional court merely opens up the possibility of discussing what judicial review in Poland may look like after overcoming the crisis. Let us then emphasise that thinking about the future of judicial review includes both the 'destruction' phase (referring to the current situation) and the 'reconstruction' phase (projection of new solutions).

The second moment in the reflection on the shape of judicial review in Poland after overcoming the constitutional crisis is the phase of 'reconstruction'. We cautiously argue that the practical experience gained after 2016 (discussed in more detail in subsequent chapters) necessitates a hybrid model of constitutional review, located somewhere between centralised and dispersed review. In this model, centralised review (exercised by one central court) would be complemented by dispersed review (exercised by judges of common and administrative courts), with the latter obviously not in the form of traditional judicial review. The majority of judges in common and administrative courts remain independent of the government. They apply the provisions of the constitution on a daily basis, protecting human rights through their decisions. Since 2016, on numerous occasions the judges themselves have undertaken to review the constitutionality of the provisions applied in particular cases. This practice, which is not approved by the government, cannot be treated merely as a temporary solution which stems from the fact that the constitutional court is dysfunctional; on the contrary, it deserves to be institutionalised. The idea of 'complementing' one type of review with the other is of key importance here. It is a broad term which allows for various relations between the constitutional court and common and administrative courts.

---

wyborcza.pl/magazyn/7,124059,29387384,niektorzy-mowia-nic-nie-robic-z-trybunalem-konstytucyjnym.html (accessed: 8.02.2023)

M. Matczak, *PiS unieważnił wybór 5 sędziów, opozycja chciałaby unieważnić wybór 15?*, Gazeta Wyborcza, 02.08.2023, https://wyborcza.pl/magazyn/7,124059,28748399,marcin-matczak-pis-uniewaznil-wybor-5-sedziow-opozycja-mialaby.html (accessed: 08.02.2023)

Several institutional solutions are possible here, the detailed examination of which is beyond the scope of our work. Contrary to appearances, the hybrid solution has its advantages. Hybridity will force the legislator to balance the role of solutions from two models of review, originating in different legal traditions. There may be more dispersed review than centralised review, or vice versa. It may contain more features of judicial constitutionalism than political constitutionalism, or vice versa. It may go in the direction of 'thin' or 'thick' constitutionalism, as described by M. Tushnet and B. Bugarcič.[16] In particular, the hybrid model can open up possibilities within the Kelsenian review system, allowing for a kind of relaxation or dilution of centralised review, with dispersed review exercised by courts under the supervision of the Constitutional Tribunal. The hybrid model may also facilitate great disputes concerning judicial activism and the role of judges. The model can be perceived as a kind of chance to rebuild the constitutional judiciary both in Poland and possibly in other countries of the region. It may be considered a temporary solution, but legal historians rightly note that temporary solutions often become permanent in this part of Europe. Obviously, there are global solutions which could restore constitutional review, such as judicial review or the German concept of the rule of law, but as has already been stated, their straightforward reception is not possible due to the circumstances related to legal culture.

The third factor concerns the relations between the legal culture of a given country or region and the model of constitutional review. The legal culture is manifested in various ways, including the adoption of specific legal institutions. This idea can be illustrated by recalling the role of the German legal culture, which developed on the basis of the models proposed by Kant or Hegel (or other thinkers), in relation to the Kelsenian model of review. Presumably, similar remarks would be true for the relation between the legal culture of common law and judicial review. It was Montesquieu who drew attention to the cultural basis of the institutions of constitutional law. Comparative constitutional law scholars emphasise that the type of constitutionalism functioning in individual countries allows for various institutional solutions in the field of judicial review. For example, in Australia and Canada, judges of the highest courts are appointed by the Prime Minister, who acts independently in this regard. In the United States, Supreme Court justices are appointed by the head of the executive branch and are confirmed by the upper chamber of parliament. In contrast, in individual American states, judges are elected by judiciary committees composed of politicians and representatives of civil society.[17] In turn, our findings indicate that the culture of compromise which characterises public life in countries such as the Netherlands or Finland leaves its mark on the approach to constitutional review. All these examples show

16 Cf. M. Tushnet and B. Bugarič, *Power of the People. Constitutionalism in the Age of Populism*, Oxford 2021, p. 9 onwards.

17 *Ibidem*, p. 27.

that there is more to constitutionalism than just institutions. According to Tushnet and Bugarič, 'Constitutionalism, again whether thin or thick, can be sustained only if there's something like a pro-constitutional culture behind it, a commitment by most of a nation's people to the idea of constitutionalism itself'.[18] The legal culture, and in particular the pro-constitutional culture, is sustained by practice which guides the behaviour of politicians and ordinary citizens. Its most important feature is that people with whom we disagree on political matters are not treated as enemies.[19] The arguments concerning the significance of legal culture in constitutionalism can be described as 'only as much, and yet so much'. There is no doubt that societies in countries such as Poland, Hungary or Romania (despite all the differences between them) did not have enough time to consolidate legal culture as a component of constitutionalism. In the case of Poland, with traditions of legal culture dating back to the Constitution of 3 May 1791, the legal culture underwent a revolutionary change in the post-WWII period. However, it was able to develop after the collapse of communism, thanks to the introduction of the constitutional judiciary (among others), primarily with regard to the importance of the case law on human rights. At the same time, it has not become established enough to stabilise and defend the rule of law, including the constitutional court that promoted this culture. Therefore, we take into account the state of legal culture in the countries of Central and Eastern Europe, considering the chances of rebuilding such a sensitive legal instrument as constitutional review in any form. Its essence is the core of legal culture, good practices and reasonable institutions. There is some optimism in this respect, which is related to the fact that the legal culture has been preserved, to a certain extent, by universities or professional circles of lawyers. These bodies are able to respect this culture, so they can pass it on to the next generations of lawyers, despite the degradation of the institutions.

1.3 What is the purpose of this book?

The reason for writing this book is the desire to take a stand on the crisis of the constitutional judiciary in Central and Eastern Europe. We are not content with an attitude of bemoaning the collapse of the judiciary or with dreaming that 'things should be as they used to be'. In Poland, in discussions among lawyers, one sometimes encounters the attitude that 'the authorities have suppressed the Constitutional Tribunal', which caused 'the end of the world'. Certainly, we realise that liberal constitutionalism is faltering before our very eyes. Yet we will not succumb to this sense of helplessness. The purpose of the present book is to see how the collapse of those constitutional courts came about and how legal systems are dealing without such bodies. Thus, we regard

18 *Ibidem*, p. 32.
19 *Ibidem*, p. 33.

the containing of constitutional courts not as 'the end of the world', but as a piece in the constitutional mosaic of the modern world, in whose arrangement we are trying to take part. The collapse of constitutional courts, institutions that are key to liberal constitutionalism, comes to us as a shock. Nevertheless, its effects are interesting to lawyers.

The concept of the present book is that each author writes about their country, yet all of us together explain a shared problem. We ask ourselves numerous questions, which we divide into two categories of issues: what has happened to constitutional justice and which direction should be followed to preserve the rule of law. We are not in a position to offer full answers to those questions. It seems, however, that judicial constitutional review in Central and Eastern Europe performed by courts was a huge construction, yet built upon weak foundations (it was insufficiently rooted in the newly restored democracy). Meanwhile, we associate the maintenance of constitutional review of law, in one form or another, seen as a prerequisite of the rule of law, mainly with the need for a certain dispersion of this review (between common and administrative judiciary) and with the importance of the binding force of European Union law.

We look upon the ruin of the constitutional courts in Poland, Hungary, Romania, Slovakia or Turkey in light of the experiences of countries that have no judicial constitutional review and yet are democratic. Finland and the Netherlands are undoubtedly such countries. The models of constitutionalism they employ are relatively less familiar in Central and Eastern Europe, but no less valuable than the models known from Britain, France or elsewhere. Thus, we look at the constitutional issues that have emerged in our part of Europe from the wider perspective of constitutionalism around the globe. Certainly, Central and Eastern European countries are no lonely isle on the sea of constitutionalism. The Finnish and Dutch experiences we present in this book are helpful, because those countries have been testing types of review that we could find significant. Therefore, in a way, we confront 'crisis' Europe with 'crisis-free' Europe, which is watching the developments. Moreover, it is worth asking: Can the transformations in Central and Eastern European countries be of interest to constitutionalists from other countries? Can the developments in the region be seen as a symptom of a disease of contemporary democracy, which poses a threat to the constitutionalism in Finland and the Netherlands? Is the collapse of constitutional judiciary in our region significant only locally, or is it a lesson also for other European countries and for constitutionalism in general? What does this collapse of the judiciary mean for liberal constitutionalism? These are the questions that gave rise to the design of this book and its title, which boils down to the question of what constitutionality of law means 'without a constitutional court'.

The questions we pose in the book are therefore sometimes harsh. However, we want, through this work, to contribute to the great discussion on constitutional justice that is taking place in world literature on this subject. In describing the crisis of constitutionalism in Central and Eastern Europe and its aftermath, we are perhaps also addressing the problems of other states' systems, although we see these problems from different perspectives.

1.4 Presentation of the individual articles

The book opens with articles on the shape of constitutional review and its foundations. Under the German Basic Law, the repeal of an unconstitutional law is the prerogative of the constitutional court alone. Common court judges have no power to rule on the unconstitutionality of legal rules (they disapply an unconstitutional rule in a specific case). To interpret the law in accordance with the constitution is, in this case, the court's responsibility. In the case of Poland, on the other hand, the authors answer the question of what type of constitutional review must be maintained in order to preserve the rule of law 'without' a constitutional court. Based on the findings of both legal theory and practice, the prevailing view is that all courts exercise dispersed review – under certain conditions. It is treated as an exception to centralised review, resulting from an emergency situation, or as a complement to centralised review. The ultimate shape of such review is not determined. Another view is that the Polish Constitution provides for centralised review, and it is the constitutional court that retains the exclusive right to rule on the constitutionality of law. At the same time, the authors take the position that the case of review in each state must be analysed separately. This is because dispersed review is a complex legal mechanism and in order to discuss it, we must take into account the circumstances of the particular legal system.

The second part of the book is devoted to the crisis of constitutional courts in Hungary, Romania and Turkey, and to the way the legal systems function 'without' these bodies. These courts have followed their own path: from inception, through development, to crisis. Occasionally, our opinions are divided, as is the case of the Hungarian constitutional court. Particularly dramatic is the fate of the Turkish constitutional court and its judges following the 2016 coup attempt. The exercise of the office of judge can entail all sorts of dangers. In Romania, in turn, the regression of the rule of law was shown against the backdrop of the constitutional court rejecting European standards, including the case law of the European Court of Justice. In this situation, we can see the importance of questions referred by judges for a preliminary ruling to the ECJ as an institution of 'last resort', preventing the degradation of the rule of law. This part of the book closes with an interesting analysis by L. Garlicki and M. Derlatka. It is, on the one hand, a summary of changes in our part of Europe, referring to the category of 'abusive constitutionalism', and on the other hand, the authors' proposed solution for the future. The authors reject the model of review offered by 'political' constitutionalism, pointing out that it carries the risk of a new wave of populism (for a parliament can easily be overrun by populist parties). This warning appears to be justified. According to L. Garlicki and M. Derlatka, the model of review proposed by 'political' constitutionalism is 'unworkable', as it requires an extremely well-developed political culture. Without it, politics will always prevail over law. Under such conditions, the cited authors advocate the dispersion of constitutional review.

The third part of the book provides a kind of counterpoint to the earlier considerations. The points made by L. Besselink and T. Ojnanen highlight the importance of 'safety valves' in preserving the rule of law in Finland and the Netherlands, which have no constitutional courts. As they explain, a great role in maintaining the constitutionality of law is played in these countries by international and European law, which is in fact part of their constitutions. Moreover, the culture of compromise and even the shape of the party system play such a role as well. The Europeanisation of national law thus leads to the fact that common courts can rule on the law's compatibility with human rights treaties (which are the main source of Dutch constitutional law). In this dimension, constitutional review is decentralised (performed by all courts). In contrast, the guarantor of the constitutionality of acts of the parliament is the parliament itself. It is therefore the guarantor of the constitutionality of the law it makes. Therefore, the common denominator in the case of both countries, which have no constitutional courts, appears to be weak judicial review and strong parliamentary review.

It should be stressed that articles prepared by M. Granat, E. Gierach, A. Syryt and P. Chybalski have been prepared as a result of the research project no. 2018/31/B/HS5/02667, financed by the National Science Centre (Poland) within the OPUS-15 funding scheme.

References

Bień-Kacała A., *Kontrola konstytucyjności prawa w Holandii: Mit czy rzeczywistość?*, "Państwo i Prawo" 2019, vol. 12.

Blokker P., *Populism as a Constitutional Project*, "International Journal of Constitutional Law" 2019, vol. 17, pp. 536–553.

Blokker, P., *Varieties of Populist Constitutionalism: The Transitional Dimension*, "German Law Journal" 2019, vol. 20, pp. 332–350.

Blokker P., Bugarič B., Halmai G., *Introduction: Populist Constitutionalism: Varieties, Complexities, and Contradictions*, "German Law Journal" 2019, vol. 20, pp. 291–295.

Böckenförde E.-W., *Państwo prawa w jednoczącej się Europie*, Instytut Studiów Politycznych PAN, Warszawa 2000.

Bugarič B., *The Two Faces of Populism: Between Authoritarian and Democratic Populism*, "German Law Journal" 2019, vol. 20, pp. 390–400.

Bugarič B., Ginsburg T., *The Assault on Postcommunist Courts*, "Journal of Democracy" 2016, vol. 27(3), pp. 69–82.

Drinóczi T., Bień-Kacała A., *Illiberal Constitutionalism in Poland and Hungary*, (in:) *The Deterioration of Democracy, Misuse of Human Rights and Abuse of the Rule of Law*, Routledge London 2022.

Granat M., *A Weapon the Government Can Control: Non-Final Final Judgments of the Polish Constitutional Court*, *VerfBlog*, 25.01.2021, https://verfassungsblog.de/a-weapon-the-government-can-control/, DOI: 10.17176/20210125-191350-0.

Granat M., *On the Experiences of a Constitutional Court in an Illiberal Democracy. Incapacitated, but necessary*, (in:) J.M.C. Andreu, M.A. Simonelli (eds.), *Populism and Contemporary Democracy in Europe. Old Problems and New Challenges*, Palgrave Macmilian Cham 2022.

Granat M., *Sądowa kontrola konstytucyjności prawa w państwach Europy Środkowej i Wschodniej*, Wydawnictwo Sejmowe, Warszawa 2003.

Sadurski W., *Constitutional Democracy in the Time of Elected Authoritarians*, "International Journal of Constitutional Law" 2020, vol. 18(2), pp. 324–333.

Sajó A., *Ruling by Cheating. Governance in Illiberal Democracy*, Cambridge University Press, Cambridge 2021.

Scheppele K.L., *The Opportunism of Populists and the Defense of Constitutional Liberalism*, "German Law Journal" 2019, vol. 20, pp. 314–331.

Tushnet M., *Advanced Introduction to Comparative Constitutional Law*, Edward Elgar, Cheltenham, UK, 2014.

Tushnet M., *Taking the Constitution Away from the Courts*, Princeton University Press, Princeton 2000.

Tushnet M., *Varieties of Populism*, "German Law Journal" 2019, vol. 20, pp. 382–389.

Tushnet M., Bugarič B., *Power of the People*, (in:) oni są autorami całej ksiazki nie musisz cytowac nazwy rozdzialu, *Constitutionalism in the Age of Populism*, Oxford University Press: Oxford 2021.

Wyrzykowski M., *The Vanishing Constitution*, (in:) C. Strohal, S. Kieber (eds.), European Yearbook on Human Rights, Intersentia, Cambridge 2018, pp. 3–44.

ZiółkowskiM. Wyrzykowski M., Ziółkowski M., *Illiberal Constitutionalism and the Judiciary*, (in:) A. Sajó, R. Uitz, S. Holmes (eds.), *Routledge Handbook of Illiberalism*, Routledge, London 2022.

Part I

Basic problems of activity of constitutional courts in an illiberal constitutionalism

2 Constitutional jurisdiction and primacy of the constitution

Rainer Arnold

2.1 The primacy of the Constitution as the fundament of constitutionalism

Constitutional jurisdiction ensures the validity of the constitution. The supremacy of the constitution and constitutional jurisdiction are closely linked, indeed they are mutually dependent.

The first consideration is: what is the origin of the primacy of the constitution?

a. Explicit regulation in some constitutions – written provision not constitutive for primacy

Some constitutions, such as the German Constitution, the Basic Law (BL), in Article 1(3) for fundamental rights and Article 20(3) in general for all public authority, express this principle clearly. Such statements can also be found in other constitutions,[1] but not in many of them. However, the written fixation of the primacy of the constitution is by no means constitutive for this, but primacy results from the nature of the constitution.

This also leads to the fact that the rule of law, as it is understood today, encompasses the constitutionality of state action and is not only based on legality, as was the case in the beginning. Today's constitutionalism lives from the primacy of the constitution.

b. Primacy to be derived from the nature of the constitution as the basic legal order

The essence of the constitution can be deduced from its function: it is the basic legal order of the state (which does not exclude the existence of constitutional

1 See, e.g., art. 1 § 5 Romanian Constitution, art. 8 § 1 Polish Constitution, art. 5 of the Croatian Constitution.

DOI: 10.4324/9781003355793-3

law in a functional sense outside the state, for example, in the legal order of the EU).[2]

The constitution-maker, the people, intends to create such a basic order. Let us take as our starting point the Rousseau model of society as a sum of individuals who are free by birth but who must necessarily organise themselves in order to exist and survive in a community.[3]

This organisation is achieved through the creation of institutions and the establishment of common values of orientation. The value orientations must reflect freedom. From today's perspective, we emphasise that they must reflect freedom as the most important expression of human dignity, which is granted to all members of the community by virtue of their being human. These orientations are necessarily the value triad of human dignity, freedom and equality.

It is the will of the constitution-maker to unite society into a state community through a constitution, in the words of Rousseau: a social contract.

This shows that there is a fundamental difference between the act of making a constitution as the *basic* democratic act, and the legislation as an expression of the political majority decisions, special democratic acts that correspond to everyday practiced democracy.

In order to maintain the basic act of constitution-making, the constitution must stand above the legislation, above the special acts of democracy.

Constitution-making comprises the will to uphold the constitution for an indefinite time, which is not to be endangered by politics, in particular by the legislation, but is only subject to amendment through a designated procedure. The will of the constitution-maker is therefore to give the constitution priority over all other acts of public power. A constitution remains in force until it is superseded by a new constitution and retains its regulatory form insofar as it is not amended by the procedure provided for by the constitution itself.

c. The substantive meaning of the basic order

The statement that the constitution is the basic legal order of the state implies that with the constitution the foundations of the state are laid down, the *organisational foundation* in the form of the institutions, their competences and functioning and the *value foundation*, which fulfils the institutional building with the basic ideal orientations. Both, the institutional and the ideal organisation of the state, belong together; one is not conceivable without the other.

It should also be borne in mind that the institutional organisation of the state is (to a certain extent) at the discretion of the constituent power, and

2 See R. Arnold, *Begriff und Entwicklung des Europäischen Verfassungsrechtes*, (in:) M.-E. Geis/D. Lorenz (Hrsg.), *Staat – Kirche – Verwaltung, Festschrift für Hartmut Maurer*, München 2001, pp. 855–868.

3 J.-J. Rousseau, *Du Contrat Social ou Principes Du Droit Politique*, *Livre premier*, chapters I and VI, re-edited by Flammarion, Paris 1966.

subsequently of the legislator amending the constitution, while the ideal organisation must necessarily correspond with the universal values linked to the human being.

It is the result of historical development that the highest power in the state belongs to the people, i.e. the sum of the individuals in the community of the state. The human being is at the centre of law, and in particular of constitutional law the aim of which is to protect and promote the human beings in the community, to protect their dignity, to recognise their freedom as a principle and to do so on the basis of equality, i.e., on the basis of the humanity of all members of the community.[4]

Thus, we can say that the constitution as a basic order forms the foundation of the state system of values and institutions. The constitution thus contains, in written or unwritten form, all statements necessary for the institutional organisation and the value system. The associated details can be developed by the legislature on the basis of authorisation by the constitution, or the constitution itself contains detailed regulations in this regard.

d. The functional meaning of the basic order

If the constitution is a basic order, this means that the other norms of the system must adhere to this basic order. Otherwise, the function of a basic order would not be achieved.

The special norms of the legal system must develop from the basic norms of the constitution and be in harmony with them. This can be described with the classic dictum of the French *Conseil constitutionnel* in the *Nouvelle Calédonie* case:[5] the general will of the people is expressed by legislation when it is in harmony with the constitution. Legislation as a specific democratic act is subordinate to the constitution, and the will of the people is only realised when it conforms to this basic order.

The sovereignty of the people is expressed in the adoption of the constitution as well as in legislation, through the representatives of the people in Parliament or directly by the people in a referendum. As a basic democratic act of a people, the constitution must be observed by all other special normative acts of the people and their representatives in the organs of the state.

4 See R. Arnold, *Struttura ed interpretazione della Costituzione: alcune riflessioni*, (in.) *Scritti in onore di Fulco Lanchester*, Naples 2022, pp. 41–56.

5 See Décision n° 85-197 DC of 23 August 1985 '27. Considérant donc que la procédure législative utilisée pour mettre en conformité avec la Constitution la disposition déclarée non conforme à celle-ci par le Conseil constitutionnel a fait de l'article 23 de l'ordonnance du 7 novembre 1958 portant loi organique une application ne méconnaissant en rien les règles de l'article 10 de la Constitution et a répondu aux exigences du contrôle de constitutionnalité dont l'un des buts est de permettre à la loi votée, qui n'exprime la volonté générale que dans le respect de la Constitution, d'être sans retard amendée à cette fin'.

e. Integration by primacy of the Constitution

A further argument can be made: the constitution has the important function of integrating the whole of the state. The task of integration can only be fulfilled if the fundamental value orientations of the state are also binding for daily politics, i.e. the legislator. Similarly, the structure and functioning of the institutions must be normatively secured. Institutions must reflect the value orientations, realise them and act in accordance with the principle of equality in order to bring about integration. However, all this is only possible if the constitution enshrines this with binding effect for policy and legislation.

We can therefore state that the primacy of the constitution results from its nature as a basic legal order and also from its function of integrating the state as a whole.

2.2 The rare example of the absence of a formal constitution

As one of the few examples, as is well known, Great Britain does not have a formal constitution. The supreme source of law there is the Act of Parliament. The doctrine of the sovereignty of Parliament, developed by the courts in the 19th century, is still valid.[6]

This principle means that parliament cannot be bound, that there can be no higher-ranking norms such as a constitution. Certainly, international law binds Great Britain as a subject of international law, but it is not hierarchically superior to parliamentary law. Nor does EU law take precedence over national law by virtue of a constitutional norm and of itself, but has been introduced into English domestic law through the mechanism of ordinary law, by the European Communities Act 1972.[7] In this way, the link to EU law has also been removed by Brexit.

It should also be mentioned that the doctrine of parliamentary sovereignty has been relativised in many ways: through the devolution of powers to the regions Scotland, Wales and Northern Ireland, through the introduction of the mechanism of the Human Rights Act,[8] or through membership of the EU, as demonstrated in particular by the *Factortame* case law.[9] Nevertheless, this doctrine is still present in its basic idea, although it is more theory than political reality.

Despite the absence of a formal constitution that takes precedence over the law, there is constitutional law, precisely in the form of legislation that is important for the running of the state, jurisprudence on such issues and

6 See G. Marshall, *The Constitution: Its Theory and Interpretation*, (in:) V. Bogdanor (ed.), *The British Constitution in the Twentieth Century*, OUP 2003, reprinted 2005, pp. 42–51; A.W. Bradley, K.D. Ewing, *Constitutional and Administrative Law*, 13th ed. 2003, pp. 49–77.

7 1972, c.68, https://www.legislation.gov.uk/ukpga/1972/68/contents/enacted (repealed).

8 1998, c.42, https://www.legislation.gov.uk/ukpga/1998/42/contents.

9 See https://publications.parliament.uk/pa/ld199899/ldjudgmt/jd991028/factor-1.htm.

so-called constitutional conventions,[10] politico-legal rules on the functioning of state organs, which, however, do not have any binding force to be observed by the court.

The courts also exercise constitutional jurisdiction, even if they are not institutionally constitutional courts and do not review formal laws in accordance with the aforementioned doctrine.

In terms of constitutional theory, we must conclude that no constitution-making has taken place, that it is rather a matter of functionally decentralised constitutional law. The ordinary legal order is used constitutionally in matters that are important for the state and the individual. The legislator becomes the everyday constitutional legislator, the everyday constitution-maker.

This creates a substantive basic order without increased validity. Although this order is normatively binding, it is not capable of asserting itself against amendments by the parliamentary majority. It is a kind of political constitution that can be changed at any time with the will of parliament. It depends essentially on the good will and the insight into the importance of human values on the part of politics.

What is relevant is the hierarchy that applies in the ordinary legal order, namely legislation as the supreme norms, subject to *lex posterior* rule, legislation prevailing over common law, to which the rules of precedent apply, and international law binding the state and introduced into the internal legal order by legislation.

2.3 Primacy of EU law over the law of the Member States and primacy of the national constitution

The following question arises for the Member States of the European Union: can we speak of primacy of the national constitution when EU law claims primacy over national law?

A first observation is necessary: EU law and national law are two different autonomous legal systems, which are integrated in themselves. If we speak of supremacy of the national constitution, this means supremacy over national law. If, on the other hand, we look at the relationship between EU law and the legal systems of the Member States, this is a question of the conflict of legal systems. According to today's understanding, this is resolved in favour of the primacy of EU law, with reference to ordinary national law, and also to national constitutional law.[11] However, the national constitutional courts impose limitations on the position of the EUCJ, which advocates absolute primacy.[12]

10 See G. Marshall, *The Constitution…*, pp. 37–42.

11 See in particular the judicial origins of primacy: ECLI:EU:C:1964:66; ECLI:EU:C:1970:100.

12 See M. Claes, *The primacy of EU law in European and national law*, (in:) A. Arnull, D. Chalmers, *The Oxford Handbook of European Union Law*, OUP 2015, pp. 178–211.

The German Federal Constitutional Court assumes that the limit for the application of EU law in Germany is the so-called constitutional identity of Germany.[13] This is derived from the eternity clause of Article 79 § 3 of the BL, which excludes certain matters (the guarantee of human dignity, Article 1 § 1 of the BL, and the fundamental principles of the state as laid down in Article 20 of the BL) from constitutional reform. This is also applied to the competences of the EU, since the integration norm of the German constitution, Article 23 § 1 BL, refers to this eternity clause. The transfer of sovereign rights to the EU also constitutes a substantive constitutional amendment, to which the limits of the formal constitutional amendment also apply.

In summary, we can say that the primacy of EU law over national law does not prevent us from affirming the primacy of the national constitution over national law; on the contrary, this kind of primacy stands alongside the primacy of EU law over national law. Both run parallel and do not prevent us from speaking of the primacy of the constitution in German law.

2.4 Primacy of the constitution and constitutional jurisdiction

The supremacy of the constitution is the inner reason for constitutional jurisdiction. Constitutional jurisdiction, it should be noted at the outset, is institutionalised constitutional jurisdiction through a special constitutional court, known as the Hans Kelsen model,[14] or functional constitutional jurisdiction through the normal courts, often referred to as the American model.[15] Basically, every court is called upon to exercise constitutional jurisdiction.

However, it is possible, and often the case, that constitutional jurisdiction is concentrated in a specialised constitutional court. In Germany, this is the case due to the allocation by Article 93 § 1 BL.

Let us turn to the basic question of what function constitutional jurisdiction performs. It is important to note that the constitution and the legislation belong to two different spheres. It must be emphasised that legislation is a product of politics, produced by majority decision in parliament or, in plebiscitary systems, by referendum. Clearly distinguished from this is the act of constitution-making, which unites society and integrates it into the state. Constitution-making

13 FCC 123, 267–437; http://www.bverfg.de/e/es20090630_2bve000208.html (German version), http://www.bverfg.de/e/es20090630_2bve000208en.html (English version), §§ 218, 219, 239, 240, 332, 336.

See also R. Arnold, *La Cour de Justice de l'Union européenne comme gardienne de l'identité constitutionnelle des États membres, Mélanges en l'honneur de Pierre Bon*, Dalloz 2014, pp. 49–56.

14 See H. Schambeck, *Hans Kelsen und die Verfassungsgerichtsbarkeit*, (in:) R. Arnold, H. Roth (eds.), *Constitutional Courts and Ordinary Courts: Cooperation or Conflict?*, Regensburg 2017, pp. 10–21.

15 See G. Haase, K. Struger, *Verfassungsgerichtsbarkeit in Europa*, Vienna 2009, pp. 22–24.The decisive case is *Marbury v. Madison*, 5 U.S. (1 Cranch) 137 (1803).

is also a political act, usually also a decision by the majority. However, this act of constitution-making is a basic act in which the general will of the people is expressed. Both constitution-making and legislation are democratic processes: the constitution is created by the people and by a constitutional assembly commissioned by the people, legislation by the legal representatives of the people in Parliament or, only very partially, in a referendum by the people themselves. However, the aim of the constitution and the law is, as already pointed out, functionally different: the constitution is intended to create a basic order that unites society; the law transforms the policy into law by majority vote, but is a special act that creates a special normative order, not a basic order.

We can therefore recognise two spheres:

The sphere of the constitution and the sphere of politics, especially the legislation as an expression of politics transformed into law. The spheres are separate from each other. However, the constitution provides the framework for politics. The latter may not exceed this framework as a limit. Politics must remain within its sphere, and may not intrude into the sphere of the constitution. Politics keeps within its own sphere, as far as it observes the constitution. If it does not observe the constitution, it crosses the border into the sphere of the constitution. The political act, especially the legislation, is then unconstitutional. The intended order of the relationship between the constitution and politics is then not respected. The judge, in the state governed by the rule of law the independent authority that judges only in accordance with the law, is called upon to restore this order. Constitutional jurisdiction therefore means restoring the intended order, correcting the fault.

Constitutional jurisdiction is therefore not politics itself; it acts on politics in order to correct it in the case of non-observance of the constitution.

2.5 The task of the judge applying legislation

It is the task of the judge to apply the law. In principle, the judge is obliged to comprehend the entirety of the legal order in its hierarchy and to apply it in the concrete case of dispute.

A distinction must be made here: the examination of the conformity of the legislation to be applied to the constitution, and, if there is no conformity, the reaction of the judge.

Every judge is obliged to examine whether the law to be applied is in harmony with the constitution. If the law is contrary to the constitution, it is, at least in the German perspective, void, and this *ex tunc*. In this case the judge cannot apply a void and therefore normatively not existing law.

However, also in systems where an unconstitutional law is not to be regarded as null and void *ex tunc*, but the nullity is only *ex nunc*, i.e., it only becomes null and void and normatively ineffective, for example, by the decision of a constitutional court, the judge must examine it and ascertain whether the applicable law is in harmony with the entire legal order, i.e., also with the constitution.

In order to carry out this examination, the judge must interpret the law, i.e., the relevant piece of legislation and also the constitution.

In doing so, the rules of interpretation also include interpretation in conformity with the constitution.[16] The judge has the obligation to bring the law into conformity with the constitution, insofar as this is possible through interpretation, and thus to establish the unity of the legal order.

Even in systems in which the general correction of the norm, i.e., its rejection on grounds of unconstitutionality, is reserved for a central body (in Germany in the form of the centralised, concentrated review of norms at the Federal Constitutional Court),[17] interpretation in conformity with the constitution is obligatory on the part of the court specifically dealing with the matter. The judge is always obliged to apply the 'correct' law. Therefore, the duty of review and the relative duty of correction through interpretation lies with him.

If unconstitutionality is established and cannot be avoided by constitutional interpretation, the possible reactions of the judge are different: as a rule, the judge would not have the power to declare the non-existence of the law with effect *erga omnes* or to repeal the law constitutively.

However, the judge can leave the law *unapplied* in a specific dispute if it contradicts the constitution. This is a *decentralised* control of norms, which in some systems (in Greece[18] or Portugal[19]) is the responsibility of all courts. History also shows that in numerous states (in Germany in 1925,[20] also in Scandinavian countries[21] and so on) the power of the judge to disapply unconstitutional laws has been affirmed.

Let us summarise: there are various possibilities, which are determined by the national legal system.

On the one hand, there is the possibility that the court itself examines the constitutionality of the law to be applied and also decides itself, i.e. in the case of unconstitutionality, it does not apply this law.

Furthermore, it is possible for the court to review the law to be applied, but then, in the event that the unconstitutionality is affirmed or, as in some systems, there are doubts about the constitutionality, to refer the question of constitutionality to the central instance, i.e., to the Constitutional Court (or, depending on the legal system, also to a supreme court of ordinary jurisdiction or administrative jurisdiction), which examines the constitutionality and then reacts to this. This means, to take the example of Article 100(1) of the Basic Law, that if the court is convinced that the applicable law is unconstitutional,

16 See for German law: K. Schlaich, St. Korioth, *Das Bundesverfassungsgericht*, 11th ed., Munich 2018, pp. 347–350, §§ 449–451.
17 See art. 100 § 1 BL.
18 See art. 93 § 4 Greek Constitution.
19 See art. 204 (and art. 280) Portuguese Constitution.
20 RGZ (Reichgericht, civil law matters), vol. 111. 320.
21 See G. Haase, K. Struger, *Verfassungsgerichtsbarkeit*..., p. 229 et seq.

it must refer the matter to the Federal Constitutional Court. If the Federal Constitutional Court finds the law unconstitutional, it declares it null and void (or in some cases only unconstitutional, whereby the court can order the legislature to amend the law within a certain period of time, so-called appeal decision).[22]

Depending on the legal system, however, it is also possible that the court to which the case was referred will rule that the law is unconstitutional, but will only leave it unapplied and not annul it *erga omnes.*

However, there is also a combined method, as in Portugal, whereby the court of dispute can review the constitutionality of the law itself and apply it or not apply it because it is unconstitutional (see art. 204 of the Constitution), against which an appeal can be made to the Constitutional Court with regard to both cases (see art. 280 of the Constitution).

2.6 Conclusion

The primacy of the constitution is the basis of constitutionalism. The fundamental task of the judge is to give effect to the constitution. When applying simple laws, the judge must always check their constitutionality. The judge may only apply laws that are in accordance with the constitution. Unconstitutional laws must be disregarded. In some systems, a central authority, regularly the Constitutional Court, must be called upon to do this, if this is expressly provided for in the constitution. However, there are also systems in which constitutional review of laws by the courts of dispute exists in parallel with constitutional review by the constitutional courts. The annulment of laws *erga omnes* is usually reserved for the constitutional court, while in other courts the power remains not to apply a law on the grounds of unconstitutionality which this court assumes. Only if the constitution itself makes it compulsory to refer to the Constitutional Court in any case of doubt or conviction of the unconstitutionality of the law to be applied, this parallel possibility of reaction to unconstitutional laws by the ordinary court does not exist.

The effective protection of the constitution by the courts is a postulate of the rule of law and the core of contemporary constitutionalism.

References

Arnold R., *Begriff und Entwicklung des Europäischen Verfassungsrechtes,* (in:) M.-E. Geis, D. Lorenz (Hrsg.), *Staat – Kirche – Verwaltung*, Festschrift für Hartmut Maurer, München 2001.

Arnold R., *La Cour de Justice de l'Union européenne comme gardienne de l'identité constitutionnelle des États membres, Mélanges en l'honneur de Pierre Bon*, Dalloz, Paris 2014.

22 See K. Schlaich, St. Korioth, *Das Bundesverfassungsgericht*, pp. 338–342, §§ 431–439.

Arnold R., *Struttura ed interpretazione della Costituzione: alcune riflessioni*, (in:) *Scritti in onore di Fulco Lanchester*, vol. I, Jovene Editore, Naples 2022.
Bradley A.W., Ewing K.D., *Constitutional and Administrative Law*, 13th ed. Longman Harlow, England 2003.
Claes M., *The Primacy of EU Law in European and National Law*, (in:) A. Arnull, D. Chalmers (eds.), *The Oxford Handbook of European Union Law*, Oxford University Press, Oxford 2015.
Haase G., Struger K., *Verfassungsgerichtsbarkeit in Europa*, Verlag Österreich, Vienna 2009.
Marshall G., *The Constitution: Its Theory and Interpretation*, (in:) V. Bogdanor (ed.), *The British Constitution in the Twentieth Century*, Oxford University Press, Oxford 2003, reprinted 2005.
Rousseau J.-J., *Du Contrat Social ou Principes Du Droit Politique, Livre premier*, Chap. I et Chap.VI, re-edited by Flammarion, Flammarion, Paris 1966.
Schambeck H., *Hans Kelsen und die Verfassungsgerichtsbarkeit*, (in:) R. Arnold, H. Roth (eds.), *Constitutional Courts and Ordinary Courts: Cooperation or Conflict?*, Universitätsverlag, Regensburg 2017.
Schlaich K., Korioth St., *Das Bundesverfassungsgericht*, 11th ed., C.H. Beck Munich 2018.

3 Constitutionality of law without a constitutional court in the Polish setting[1]

Mirosław Granat

When reflecting on the issue of the constitutionality of law in Poland – in light of the changes that occurred after 2016 – we have come to a moment when the question arises: is the constitutionality of law possible *without* a constitutional court? I admit this doubt is somewhat ambiguous, as *without* is confronted with the fact that the Constitutional Tribunal continues to exist, our opinion about its composition or judgments notwithstanding. Despite the air of paradox (as in 'unsweet sugar'), the above question generates considerable scholarly possibilities. Certainly, it opens a debate on the issue of the constitutionality of law.

I realise that the expression 'without a constitutional court' requires further explication in order to be understandable. Let me point out that this wording of the research question is inspired by the surprising situation of constitutional review in Poland. Namely, the Constitutional Tribunal issues decisions in extremely sensitive matters, such as the criteria for performing abortions (the relevant judgment sparked off social protests of a magnitude not seen in Poland for years), while at the same time lawyers emphasise that 'there is no Constitutional Tribunal' or that it 'has ceased to exist'. I explain these contradictions in the perception of judicial review by the fact that the court's function changed after 2016. Before 2016, it acted as a safety net for the legal system or even, in Polish conditions, a safety net for the implementation of the rule of law as such. Since this landmark year, the Tribunal – while retaining all its current competences[2] typical of a modern constitutional court – has not served to protect the constitution: its role has been to support the decisions taken by politicians. The change of its function transformed the Tribunal into a political body.

1 This paper has been prepared as a result of the research project no. 2018/31/B/HS5/02667, financed by the National Science Centre (Poland) within the OPUS-15 funding scheme.

2 The competences are stipulated in art. 188 of the Polish Constitution. For more on the position and the competences of the Constitutional Tribunal see M. Granat, K. Granat, *The Constitution of Poland. A Contextual Analysis*, Oxford-London-New York-Sydney 2019, chapter 6.

DOI: 10.4324/9781003355793-4

I find the question posed in the title significant in both the descriptive and the normative plane. Specifically, I would like to reconstruct the framework of constitutionalism in which the constitutional court was destroyed as well as to consider a crucial matter: what type of constitutional review can still be performed under the current conditions so as to preserve the constitutionality of law? Perhaps it can be carried out only to a certain extent or only in certain cases in order to protect individuals' rights. This calls for a certain diffusion of constitutional review so that it is exercised by ordinary and administrative courts.

There is no space in this chapter for a comprehensive breakdown of the conceptual network I am using here. I only wish to explain in advance that I will generally refer to the extraordinarily rich content that the doctrine infers from art. 8(1) of the Polish Constitution of 1997 as the principle of constitutionalism (or just as constitutionalism) or use – for the purposes of the present work – the term 'constitutionality of law'.

I am aware that these concepts are not equivalent, yet they are essentially related. Precise distinctions in this regard are drawn by theorists of constitutional law.[3]

The analysis carried out in Section 3.1 of the present chapter concerns the understanding of the principle of constitutionalism as it existed before 2016. In Section 3.2, I recall certain moments in the process of destruction of the Constitutional Tribunal's independence by the authorities in order to better explain the present situation with regard to constitutional review. Section 3.3 consists of two parts. In the first part, I reconstruct the meaning of the expression 'the constitutionality of law *without* a constitutional court' in the period before the 1997 Constitution was enacted, while the second part is devoted to the understanding of 'without' in the legal situation after 2016. Section 3.4 deals with the possibility of diffuse constitutional review in Poland.

3.1 The principle of constitutionalism

The notion of supremacy of the constitution means that the constitution is superior to all other laws. Thanks to its supremacy, the constitution is not subject to ordinary legislative actions or the majority's whims. The notion of supremacy could be perceived conversely, as well: an act that can be amended by the will of the ordinary legislature does not possess the qualities of a constitution. Next, I understand the principle of constitutionalism as the legal realisation of the above concept. It means that the constitution is a 'standard for other legal standards'. It is the supreme law and, being a legal act, has characteristics inherent only in a fundamental law; i.e., it has its own particular

3 Cf. N.W. Barber, *The Principles of Constitutionalism*, Oxford 2018; J. Limbach, *The Concept of the Supremacy of the Constitution*, "Modern Law Review" 2001, vol. 64, no. 1; M. Tushnet, B. Bugarič, *Power to the People. Constitutionalism in the Age of Populism*, Oxford 2021, chapter 1.

form and content. This is why the constitution is the act that determines the legal system and renders it non-contradictory. A consequence of the principle of constitutionalism is some form of review of the constitutionality of law, because it introduces the derogatory effect on provisions that violate the constitution. From the perspective of the notion of supremacy, the constitution would remain something like an Enlightenment declaration or a profession of faith, as it was treated at the end of the 18th century. In turn, the principle of constitutionalism, through the mechanism of derogation, gives the constitution a normative significance. The derogation of unconstitutional provisions requires, as Kelsen would say, that the institution of a 'guardian' be established. Typically, this role should be played by a constitutional court.

The principle of constitutionalism is stipulated explicitly in art. 8(1) of the Polish Constitution: 'The Constitution shall be the supreme law of the Republic of Poland'. The provision was designed in such a manner as to cover a guarantee that the supreme authority of this law be enforced. It stipulates not only that the constitution shall be observed, but also that it shall be guaranteed by the activity of the Constitutional Tribunal. This understanding of the principle of constitutionalism is confirmed by the history of work on the provision in the Constitutional Commission of the National Assembly. Sometimes, we say that judicial guarantees are the 'procedural' side of this principle.[4] In particular, we refer to the independence of the courts and the independence of judges, since without such a complement, the principle of constitutionalism, presumably, would not hold.

Thus, the above interpretation of the principle of constitutionalism entails the activity of an independent constitutional court with specific competencies. In my research approach, the term 'constitutional court' carries a very precise meaning. It means namely that the Constitutional Tribunal is the only court that reviews the constitutionality of legislation (it holds a monopoly on such review) and that it is authorised to derogate norms that are unconstitutional. It follows from the way it is situated in the legal system that the judges of ordinary courts have no right to review the constitutionality of legislation (they have to apply the procedure of legal questions to the constitutional court). Therefore, what characterises the principle of constitutionalism under art. 8(1) is that it involves a centralised model of constitutional review, including an independent court. The essence of the model is to provide the court with the authority to derogate laws and to guarantee its position as the sole guardian of the law's constitutionality.

The understanding of the principle of constitutionalism outlined above prevailed in Poland before 2016 and was axiomatic. I understood it to mean that if the constitutional court ceases to be one of the guarantees of this principle, then the principle essentially no longer applies. Thus, we interpreted

4 Cf. K. Działocha, *Komentarz do art. 8*, (in:) L. Garlicki (ed.), *Konstytucja Rzeczypospolitej Polskiej. Komentarz*, vol. 5, Warszawa 2007.

the principle of constitutionalism in a radically Kelsenian manner: the operation of the Constitutional Tribunal means we are dealing with the principle of constitutionalism. And conversely: the principle of constitutionalism hinges upon the functioning of the Tribunal. The principle of constitutionalism and the position of the constitutional court were connected by a sort of a logical machine; i.e., the more we weaken the position of the Constitutional Tribunal, the harder we strike against the principle of constitutionalism. As we can see, the understanding of the principle of constitutionalism in Poland was not arbitrary: it referred to Kelsen's model and was decisive in the approach to constitutional review under the 1997 Constitution.

The above explanation of the principle of constitutionalism might not be quite exhaustive. First, Kelsen probably would not have used the term 'legal principle'. Second, a doubt arises: why would the principle not cover a weak version of constitutional review? Could its requirements not be met by a constitutional court in a form more or less as it is now, when it is referred to as 'Julia Przyłębska's Tribunal'? Is such an institution incapable of defending the principle of constitutionalism? All these questions should be answered in the negative, mainly on account of the interdependence between the principle of constitutionalism and such a valuable structure as the identity of the 1997 Constitution. The mutual influence of these categories was explained by the Constitutional Tribunal in its 2010 judgment concerning the Lisbon Treaty, when it described constitutional identity based on the 1997 Constitution.[5] This is why a Tribunal dependent on politicians cannot be condoned, as it would move constitutionalism back to the political categories known from the period of so-called real socialism in Poland. Such a solution full of loopholes resemble concepts known from the communist period in Poland's history, such as compound chocolate or cereal coffee, which were supposed to substitute the original products. I will therefore emphasise it again: the Polish Constitution requires that an independent constitutional court be maintained as a condition for the implementation of the principle of constitutionalism, which harmonises with the meaning of constitutional identity. Consequently, the destruction of the Tribunal after 2016 may affect constitutional identity and certainly does affect the implementation of other legal principles enshrined in the Polish Constitution. Breaking up the above-mentioned interdependences, removing just one element from the set, has consequences that resemble the domino effect. In particular, the dismantling

5 Cf. Judgment of the Polish Constitutional Tribunal of 10 November 2010, ref. no. K 32/09. My task here is not to reflect on constitutional identity on the basis of the Polish Constitution, its content and interdependences. See on this matter M. Granat, *Tożsamość konstytucji*, (in:) D. Dudek (ed.), *Zmieniać Konstytucję Rzeczypospolitej Polskiej czy nie zmieniać?*, Lublin 2017; M. Granat, *Rozumienie zmiany Konstytucji RP a tożsamość konstytucyjna*, (in:) R. Chruściak (ed.), *Problemy zmiany konstytucji*, Warszawa 2017, pp. 255 et seq. On constitutional identity from a broader perspective see G.J. Jacobsohn, *Constitutional Identity*, Cambridge-London 2010.

of an independent constitutional court puts into question the implementation of principles such as judicial independence.

When following the ruling party's destructive actions against the Constitutional Tribunal, it is worth noting – without repeating the known facts – the moments that are relevant to our further considerations.

First, when explaining the concept of 'constitutionalism without a constitutional court', I do not assign significance to the matter of the judges who were elected to the Tribunal to take places that had already been filled. Using the argument of the so-called stand-ins would be too easy and would overly simplify my research task. I realise that the election of persons dependent on politicians to sit on a constitutional court must affect the way they fulfil their duties. Nevertheless, stressing the importance of the stand-in judges would reduce the issue of 'without' to a matter of the wrong composition of the Tribunal. I will therefore point out once again that if a person sits on a court illegitimately, then their position depends not on the law, but on political factors. A so-called stand-in judge is protected not by the provisions of the constitution, but by political connections and circumstances – and those are, after all, subject to change.[6]

I do, however, ascribe importance to the effects of a series of laws concerning the Constitutional Tribunal, referred to by the authorities as 'repair laws', that were enacted by the Sejm in the years 2015–2016. Their role involved shifting the Tribunal's position within the system from that of an independent court – which it had occupied pursuant to the constitution – towards that of a body dependent on the executive. These laws changed the situation of the Tribunal within the system of checks and balances characteristic of the separation of powers. Rather extraordinary amongst them was the act of 22 December 2015,[7] which stipulated numerous solutions that paralysed the operation of the Tribunal. At this point, it is no longer vital to recall these provisions, also on account of their exotic character. Suffice it to say that according to the Venice Commission, the aggregate of these novelties paralysed the Tribunal's operation and resulted in the court 'existing only theoretically'.[8] More centrally, the authorities used the 'repair laws' to bring the Tribunal under their control by the end of 2016.

Thus, the Constitutional Tribunal was subjected to the control of the ruling party with the use of both illegal means (stand-in judges) and acts legally

6 On the so called stand-in judges, see more in W. Sadurski, *Poland's Constitutional Breakdown*, Oxford 2019; see also https://www.batory.org.pl/wp-content/uploads/2020/02/Jak-przywrocic-panstwo-prawa_Interaktywna.pdf (accessed 31.03.2022).

7 Cf. Judgment of the Polish Constitutional Tribunal of 9 March 2016, ref. no. K 47/15, in which the Tribunal declared the law unconstitutional in its entirety. See P. Radziewicz, P. Tuleja (eds.), *Konstytucyjny spór o granice organizacji i zasady działania Trybunału Konstytucyjnego. Czerwiec 2015 – marzec 2016*, Warszawa 2017.

8 Cf. https://www.venice.coe.int/webforms/documents/?pdf=CDL-AD%282016%29012-e (access 31.03.2022).

passed by the Sejm ('repair laws'). Many provisions of these laws raised doubts as to their constitutionality, yet their review was no longer possible. As a result of all these actions, the ruling party took over the Tribunal and then, in 2020, overpowered it. What is the difference between taking over and overpowering a constitutional court? Thanks to overpowering the Tribunal, the authorities gained direct influence on its judgments, including on their effectiveness (their entry into force). For instance, in December 2020, the Council of Ministers rendered the official publication of the Tribunal's judgment on abortion mentioned above dependent on the statement of reasons.[9] Thus, what I mean by overpowering is gaining control over the Tribunal's case law, and in particular on the finality and effectiveness of its judgments. As a result, the authorities were able to use the constitutional court's judgments for their own purposes, and they eagerly availed themselves of this possibility (as will be discussed later).

I am heading towards the conclusion that both the Tribunal and politicians even gave up playing a certain game of appearances related to the existence of a constitutional court. They omit to maintain at least some decorum inherent in the system of checks and balances. The Tribunal's case law began to satisfy or meet the authorities' needs. The Tribunal acquiesces in provisions passed by the ruling majority (e.g., judgment with file ref. no K 12/18, which condones the lack of possibility to appeal to the administrative court against the resolutions of the National Council of the Judiciary).[10] At times, the Tribunal's judgments anticipate the legislature's intentions (e.g., judgment with file ref. no K 5/17 on the amendments to the Act on the National Council of the Judiciary).[11] The main point of the actions aiming to dismantle the constitutional judiciary was that the Constitutional Tribunal was incapacitated by the authorities or, we could say, that it incapacitated itself.

These moments in the process of dismantling the Constitutional Tribunal bring my considerations to the conclusion that the majority that gained power in autumn 2015 was not interested in rectifying the flaws of constitutional review or in a 'new model' of the Tribunal. It could have considered for instance how to improve the institution of constitutional complaint in order to more effectively protect civil rights, or whether to shorten the too-broad list of institutions and bodies entitled to initiate abstract judicial review of laws. The truth is, it intended to take over the Tribunal, to overpower it and, consequently, to incapacitate it. The ruling party's policy statements cover the existence of a constitutional court, yet a very weak one. This objective has been achieved. The Constitutional Tribunal ceased to be an institution of the

9 Cf. the Position of the Council of Ministers of 1 December 2020, Official Journal of the Republic of Poland 'Monitor Polski' of 2020, item 1104.

10 Cf. Judgment of the Polish Constitutional Tribunal of 25 March 2019, ref. no. K 12/18.

11 Cf. Judgment of the Polish Constitutional Tribunal of 20 June 2017, ref. no. K 5/17.

rule of law and became a sham, a pretence, which however serves purposes that will be discussed further on.

Finally, I would like to explain that I do not appreciate the idea which can sometimes be found in subject literature, namely that in practice, there are two tribunals. The first one is the Constitutional Tribunal subject to analysis in the present chapter. The other is the Tribunal which issues its judgments in minor matters with no political aspect, parallel to the first one. In my view, such a distinction between judgments and, consequently, areas of review does not stand up to criticism. The implied duality in the evaluation of the Tribunal would be similar to the actions of the Kelsenian guardian, who is assessed based on the fact that he settles for checking the places which pose no danger, but omits to look into the dark or dangerous places on the street. The constitutional review of law covers the entire cognition of the court and therefore should be assessed in its entirety.

3.2 Constitutionality of law without a constitutional court

'The constitutionality of law without a constitutional court' carries two meanings in my scholarly approach. The first one entails that, rather than constitutional review by the court, we were dealing with a situation where the review concerned the correct enactment of a law by the Sejm. It covered two situations: when a constitutional court still existed (Section 3.2.1) and when there was no such body (Section 3.2.2).

3.2.1 The position of the Constitutional Tribunal before 1997

Prior to the passing of the 1997 Constitution, the position of the Tribunal, established in 1986, was characterised by weak derogation powers. Derogation pertained not directly to unconstitutional statutes, but to subordinate regulations. In the case of a statute, the Tribunal could be outbid by the parliament.

A rather unconventional solution used in the period 1989–1997 was that the Tribunal's judgments declaring the unconstitutionality of statutes were not final and were subject to review by the Sejm.[12] The Sejm could dismiss a declaration of unconstitutionality of its legislation with a 2/3 majority, thus acting as the politically driven supreme state authority. A legal construction in which the Sejm gave legal effect to unconstitutional provisions cannot be considered axiologically neutral. It is not possible to legally express that a provision is unconstitutional, but by a majority vote reject a ruling declaring it so. I recall this solution, which had its roots in the period of Communism – it was introduced during martial law and directly after it was lifted and continued to be used also during the period of democratic transformation up until

12 Cf. art. 6 of the Act of 29 April 1985 on the Constitutional Tribunal (Journal of Laws of 1985, No. 22, item 98).

1997, all the more because E.-W. Böckenförde gave it significance from the point of view of constitutionalism as such. In his opinion, it was possible for unconstitutional acts to function within a legal system, and a defect of law is not tantamount to its unconstitutionality. If the representative body accepted the unconstitutionality of a law, such law in a manner became legal.[13]

As we can see, not so long ago we had constitutionalism that allowed the development of unconstitutional laws. The constitutionality of a law was defined by the position of the Sejm and not by the supreme legal force of constitutional provisions. An unconstitutional law could keep its place in the legal system. According to this understanding of constitutionalism, not every statute had to be strictly bound to the constitution. Furthermore, in the opinion of some theoreticians, this solution met the standards of the rule of law.[14]

I would like to recall the solutions in the March Constitution from 1921 (modelled on the Constitutional Laws of the Third French Republic), as that constitution declared its own supremacy, albeit this obviously involved no derogation rights. As we know, political thought dating back to J.J. Rousseau rejected the concept of judicial review.[15]

Article 38 of the March Constitution, pursuant to which 'no statute may be in opposition to this constitution or violate its provisions', in some respects resembled art. 8 of the 1997 Constitution currently in force. However, the regulation under the March Constitution was toothless. Article 38 namely did not specify at which point unconstitutional laws would be blocked. It provided for no court or derogation of unconstitutional acts, nor did it introduce any automatic invalidity of such laws. Thus, under the March Constitution, statutes decided about themselves. Under these circumstances, the principle of constitutionalism was a declaration, as it did not provide for any means of dealing with unconstitutionality of law.

To sum it up, the discussed meaning of the expression 'the constitutionality of law without a constitutional court' was that the institution which determined the constitutionality of a statute was not the constitutional court, but the Sejm. Thus, 'without' was synonymous with a version of constitutionalism in which there was no Tribunal or in which its role could be ignored on account of the significance of the Sejm. The constitutionality of statutes was determined by the legislature itself and by the presumption of parliamentary enactment, which they enjoyed under the constitution. This type of 'constitutionality without a constitutional court' existed under the March Constitution (in pure form) and later in the period 1986–1997. At that time,

13 Cf. E.-W. Böckenförde, *Państwo prawa w jednoczącej się Europie*, Warszawa 2000, pp. 82–83.
14 Ibidem.
15 Cf. R. Carré de Malberg, *La loi, expression de la volanté générale. Étude sur le concept de la loi dans la Constitution de 1875*, Paris 1931; M. Granat, *Od klasycznego przedstawicielstwa do demokracji konstytucyjnej (ewolucja prawa i doktryny we Francji)*, Lublin 1994, chapter I.

the Constitutional Tribunal's role was purposefully limited by the provisions of the fundamental law dating back to the Soviet times, i.e., 1952.

3.2.2 The dependence of the Constitutional Tribunal on politicians

The second sense of 'constitutionalism without a constitutional court' refers to the situation when there is a body authorised to carry out judicial review, yet it is not independent of politicians. The content of this relationship justifies speaking of a change in the function performed by such a court. This is the type of constitutionalism I wish to demonstrate by analysing the post-2016 case law of the Constitutional Tribunal. The examples I consider are: the status of the Tribunal's judgments (subsection 1), the presumption of the constitutionality of law (subsection 2) and some judgments of the Tribunal which showcase the function it serves (subsection 3).

The paradox of the Constitutional Tribunal's judgments after 2016 consists in the fact that they are promulgated in the Journal of Laws,[16] which means they take effect, albeit at the same time as being formally defective. No one can treat them as non-existent, and yet their legal force is questioned. They are binding on the one hand, but ignored by the courts on the other.[17] Judges of ordinary and administrative courts describe this phenomenon by saying that 'the judgments of the Tribunal do not possess the characteristics of judgments'.[18] In addition, the decisions are challenged by the Court of Justice of the European Union and the European Court of Human Rights, which typically entails interim measures granted by those institutions as well as Poland's liability for damages.[19] An example of the drastic effect of the double standard of the Tribunal's judgments can be the judgment of the CJEU from December 2021 issued in a matter concerning Romania: it committed national courts to disapply the case law of national constitutional courts which is contrary to

16 Cf. art. 190(1–2) of the Polish Constitution of 1997.

17 Cf. e.g., Judgment of the District Court in Gorzów Wielkopolski of 24, ref. no. IC 1326/19, in a case for compensation for damages caused by wild game in a carrot plantation. When ruling on the matter, the judge had to apply the Hunting Law. The constitutionality of the statute had been reviewed by the Constitutional Tribunal. Yet the judge disapplied the Constitutional Tribunal's decision: 'An ordinary court cannot base its ruling on a judgment of the Constitutional Tribunal if the panel contained a so called stand-in judge, who had been incorrectly elected by the Polish Sejm and appointed by the Polish President to take a seat that had already been filled', legal database Lex, ref. no. 3184543.

18 Cf. the stance of A. Zoll, https://www.rp.pl/sady-i-prokuratura/art19007971-zoll-polskie-sady-powinny-ignorowac-wyrok-trybunalu-konstytucyjnego (access 31.03.2022), as well as positions of A. Rzepliński, J. Matras, https://www.rp.pl/sady-i-trybunaly/art19029331-setki-sedziow-zapowiadaja-ze-zignoruja-wyrok-tk (access 31.03.2022). See also M. Granat, *A Weapon the Government Can Control. Non-Final Final Judgments of the Polish Constitutional Court*, https://verfassungsblog.de/author/miroslaw-granat/ (accessed 31.03.2022).

19 Cf. Judgments of the European Court of Human Rights of 6 May 2021, Xero Flor vs. Poland (Application no. 4907/18), 22 July 2021, Reczkowicz vs. Poland (Application no. 43447/19).

EU law. Obviously, the decision is significant from the perspective of Polish courts, as well.[20]

In this sense of the notion of 'the constitutionality of law without a constitutional court', the presumption of the constitutionality of law has gained importance. This presumption is the reverse of the principle of constitutionalism. Since namely the constitution is the supreme law, then all the other provisions of law must comply with it. The presumption is a component of the principle of constitutionalism. The relation between the principle of constitutionalism and the presumption does not rule out the latter being inferred from other constitutional standards, such as for instance the principle of the rule of law (art. 2). In a country where the rule of law is observed, state bodies act on the basis of and within the boundaries of law, which implies that the law issued by those bodies should comply with the constitution.

In the period 1997–2016, when the principle of constitutionalism was observed, there was a tight relationship between the constitutionality of law and the presumption. It was not possible to separate the presumption from the principle of constitutionalism. Following the changes aimed at containing the Constitutional Tribunal, the presumption of constitutionality became independent of the principle of constitutionalism. At present, when we speak in Poland about the law's compliance with the constitution, the emphasis shifts to the source of the act; i.e. it is pointed out that it was passed by a democratically elected Sejm. The source of the statute is perceived as decisive in terms of its constitutionality. When it comes to the legislative changes that were crucial to the ruling party achieving its goals (such as the Supreme Court Act from 2018 or the 2019 amendment to the Act on the National Council of the Judiciary), the presumption of constitutionality became autonomous to such extent that it was treated as tantamount to recognising the statutes as constitutional. Thus, what determined the constitutionality of a law was its source, as it was not possible to review its constitutionality before the court.

Since 2016, the presumption has sufficed, as referring to it renders the discussion about the statute's constitutionality pointless. This attitude to the presumption and its role both weakens the principle of constitutionalism and marginalises the position of the Tribunal. We are looking at a self-regulating system: weaker derogation capacity of the Tribunal results in increased significance of the presumption of constitutionality of statutes. The weaker the Tribunal, the greater the role of the presumption, because the relationship is not counterbalanced by the action of a court. Consequently, the weakening of the principle of constitutionalism has manifested itself in the legal enactment of unconstitutional law. A classic example could be the Supreme Court Act of 8 December 2017, which shortened the six-year term of the First President of the Supreme Court (while art. 183(3) of the Constitution stipulates that the

20 Cf. https://wydarzenia.interia.pl/zagranica/news-tsue-sady-nie-musza-wdrazac-wyrokow-tk-naruszajacych-prawo-u,nId,5722150 (access 31.03.2022).

term of office lasts six years). The same can be said for statutes intended to paralyse the Constitutional Tribunal (the so-called repair laws from the period 2015–2016 mentioned above) or the so-called muzzle law of 20 December 2020 (also referred to as the repression act), which was an attack against the independence of judges of ordinary and administrative courts.

After 2016, the function of the Constitutional Tribunal has changed: it is now to support decisions made by politicians rather than to protect the constitution. This transformation is best demonstrated on the basis of the below presented well-known decisions of the Tribunal:

In its judgment of 15 April 2021, the Tribunal ruled that art. 3(6) of the Act on the Commissioner for Human Rights, under which the Commissioner could perform his duties after their term ended – until the successor took office, was unconstitutional.[21] Despite the fact that the Act on the Commissioner for Human Rights permitted the performance of duties until a successor was appointed – which remains legitimate in the case of other state authorities – the judgment rendered it possible to remove from the office a person famous for his commitment to defending the rule of law. The stake was not to protect the position of this or another person serving as the Commissioner but to ensure the continuous protection of human rights in the event that the parliament failed to elect a new ombudsman on time. The judgment affected the citizens, as, thanks to the parliament, the vacancy in the office of the Commissioner was extended. The Tribunal's ruling was a measure of its dependence on the one hand and of the recognition of the incumbent Commissioner's achievements in the area of human rights protection on the other.

The order issued by the Constitutional Tribunal on 20 April 2020 on the matter of the alleged dispute over powers between the Sejm and the Supreme Court and between the President and the Supreme Court[22] showed that the Tribunal had ceased to play the role of an arbitrator between the state's constitutional bodies organised in a system of checks and balances. The pseudo conflict was created by the Speaker of the Sejm in reaction to the resolution of three chambers of the Supreme Court of 23/01/2020 concerning the defective composition of court panels. The composition was defective whenever the panel included a person appointed by the politicised National Council of the Judiciary (KRS) in the form created under the 2017 act (the so called neo-KRS). The defective composition has specific legal effects, depending on the instance and the date of the adjudication, which bring disadvantages to the parties to the relevant dispute. The arguments presented by the Speaker were based on an erroneous interpretation of the notion of dispute over powers under art. 189 of the Constitution. In fact, the application concerning this dispute was filed in bad faith.

21 Cf. Judgement of the Polish Constitutional Tribunal of 15 April 2021, ref. no. K 20/20.
22 Cf. Judgement of the Polish Constitutional Tribunal of 20 April 2020, ref. no. Kpt.1/20.

There never was a dispute over powers between the Sejm and the Supreme Court or between the President and the Supreme Court, and the Tribunal's decision was unacceptable. A dispute overpowers is essentially possible only within one branch of government and not between powers as different as, e.g., the legislature and the judiciary.[23]

From the point of view of the ruling party, the Constitutional Tribunal plays an instrumental role: it enables the law-making body to omit the law-making process that should take place in the parliament in socially significant matters. A good example is the judgment on abortion of 22 October 2020.[24]

I believe that decisions about the condition of abortion consisting in the 'likelihood of a severe and irreparable impairment of the foetus or of an incurable, life-threatening disease' (art. 4a(1) and art. 4a(2) of the 1993 act) and its interpretation as a provision that legitimises eugenic practices should be taken by the Sejm itself (by means of appropriate amendments to the 1993 act). The Constitutional Tribunal must not aid or replace the parliament's deliberation in search of the right solutions to social problems. When a constitutional court adjudicates on the legal system, then in principle it should have the last word with regard to the actions of the legislature. Consequently, this last word should not be uttered at the very beginning of the debate over adopting an appropriate legal regulation in a sensitive matter such as the conditions for performing abortions.

From the perspective of the authorities' political agenda, the Constitutional Tribunal's case law in European matters is particularly critical. Its purpose is to block the effects of decisions issued by both the Court of Justice of the EU and the European Court of Human Rights. There is no need to recount the content of the Tribunal's relevant judgments, which have been widely commented on by legal scholars. Still, I would like to emphasise the importance of two of them.

In its judgment of 7 October 2021, the Tribunal declared some of the provisions of the Treaty on the European Union unconstitutional.[25] Then, in its judgment of 14 July 2021 concerning the Member States' obligation to enforce interim measures orders of the Court of Justice of the EU – regarding the structure and functioning of the constitutional bodies of the judiciary – the Tribunal denied the binding effect of these orders in Poland.[26] The rulings have no impact on the effectiveness and validity of CJEU decisions at all. Their essence is rather to guarantee the government's immunity from the effects of CJEU judgments in Poland. Thanks to the above rulings, Polish

23 *Nie ma żadnego „sporu kompetencyjnego". Adam Bodnar do TK: umorzyć sprawę z wniosku Marszałek Sejmu*, https://bip.brpo.gov.pl/pl/content/rpo-nie-ma-sporu-kompetencyjnego-sprawa-tk-do-umorzenia (accessed 31.03.2022).

24 Judgement of the Polish Constitutional Tribunal of 20 October 2020, ref. no. K 1/20.

25 Cf. Judgement of the Polish Constitutional Tribunal of 7 October 2021, ref. no. K 3/21.

26 Cf. Judgement of the Polish Constitutional Tribunal of 14 July 2021, ref. no. P 7/21.

law on judicial independence is supposed to become gradually immune to the influence of EU law. The Constitutional Tribunal's case law treats the Polish legal system as a lonely island independent of European standards. In practice, these decisions are tantamount to Poland rebelling against EU law on judicial independence and effective legal protection. Following these judgments of the Constitutional Tribunal, the European Commission launched an infringement procedure against Poland. It stated that it had 'serious doubts on the independence and impartiality of the Constitutional Tribunal', which 'no longer meets the requirements of a tribunal previously established by law'.[27]

To recapitulate, the second understanding of 'the constitutionality of law without a constitutional court' denotes a constitutionalism which does include a functioning Constitutional Tribunal, yet one whose case law is treated as politicians' instrument of wielding power.

3.3 The consequences of the destruction of the Constitutional Tribunal

In light of the dismantling of the Constitutional Tribunal as an independent court, scholars who study the compatibility of laws with the constitution should stop lamenting and wringing their hands over the lack of judicial review. Rather than take on the role of Cassandra, experts on constitutional law should find an answer to the following question: what is the way out of a situation in which the Constitutional Tribunal has ceased to be an independent court, and how else can the constitutionality of law be protected? The current crisis should therefore be perceived as an invitation to debate the transformation of judicial review in Poland.

What solutions are compatible with the principle of constitutionalism stipulated in art. 8(1) of the 1997 Constitution? Is it possible to transform constitutional review by accepting its diffusion, so that it can be carried out by ordinary and administrative courts? Or, conversely: would it be possible to centralise it by establishing, e.g., a Constitutional Chamber within the Supreme Court?[28] The point of this discussion about 'the constitutionality of law without a constitutional court' is not just to fill the gap after the missing independent constitutional court. What matters here is namely the requirement to implement the principle of constitutionalism under art. 8(1) of the Polish Constitution, which provides for an independent judicial review of the constitutionality of law within a centralised model.

In this regard, the following question should be considered: are ordinary and administrative courts authorised to review the constitutionality of statutes?

27 Cf. https://www.prawo.pl/prawnicy-sady/procedura-przeciwnaruszeniowa-ke-wobec-polski-po-wyroku-tk,512489.html (accessed 31.03.2022).

28 Cf. A. Strzembosz, *Trzecia władza w projekcie Konstytucji RP*, (in:) J. Krukowski (ed.), *Ocena projektu Konstytucji* RP, Lublin 1996, pp. 87 et seq.

Their review of law subordinate to statutes has namely been and continues to be legitimate. It was possible as early as under the March Constitution, and it raises no doubts now. But can statutes be reviewed in this manner?

Before 2016, legal scholars spoke against constitutional review by courts consisting in disapplying provisions of acts that, according to the courts, were unconstitutional. It was argued in subject literature that the principle of constitutionalism under art. 8(1) provides only for review by the Constitutional Tribunal. Consequently, a judge of an ordinary or administrative court who had doubts about the constitutionality of a statutory provision they were supposed to apply was de facto obliged to refer a question of law to the Tribunal (art. 193 of the Constitution). Thus, they were not free to disapply the law as long as the Tribunal had not declared it unconstitutional. A judge could not by themselves declare a statute unconstitutional. According to the views presented in subject literature of the time (as well as case law of the Constitutional Tribunal), judges adjudicating on the constitutionality of laws would have violated the Tribunal's monopoly on the competence to rule on the constitutionality of law.

In my opinion, the destruction of the independent Constitutional Tribunal naturally necessitates a reinterpretation of the hitherto understanding of the principle of constitutionalism consisting in accepting review by ordinary and administrative courts. The departure from the earlier understanding of this principle is sometimes treated as a one-time, temporary operation resulting from the emergency in which Polish constitutionalism has found itself[29] – but it could become permanent, too. This is not the principal matter at this point. The reinterpretation of the principle of constitutionalism, regardless of whether it results from an emergency or a permanent need, is supported by the principle of direct applicability of the constitution by the courts stipulated in art. 8(2) of the Polish Constitution ('The provisions of the Constitution shall apply directly, unless the Constitution provides otherwise'). This turnabout in the understanding of the principle of constitutionalism means that if a judge of an ordinary or an administrative court finds it impossible to interpret a statutory provision so that it conforms to the constitution, they decide to disapply said provision in a specific matter (without denying the law the presumption of constitutionality). This judicial approach to disapplying unconstitutional statutes is happening in practice, despite the fact that the relevant judges are accused by the ruling party of 'politicising' judgments or of 'violating the rule of law'. This attitude manifested by the judges results in their facing disciplinary proceedings or being arbitrarily prevented from adjudicating.

An example of constitutional review of statutes performed by judges of ordinary courts is the judgment of the Court of Appeal in Wrocław of 2017 concerning evidence – 'fruit of the poisonous tree' – in which the Court

29 So argues P. Mikuli, *Doktryna konieczności jako uzasadnienie dla rozproszonej kontroli konstytucyjności ustaw w Polsce*, "Gdańskie Studia Prawnicze" 2018, vol. 40.

refused to apply art. 168a of the Code of Criminal Procedure.[30] The same was true for numerous ordinary court judgments concerning the provisions of the 2016 act aiming to dismantle the legacies of the Communist Ministry of Public Security.[31]

As can be seen, the doctrine has come a long way in terms of its attitude to the application of the constitution by judges of ordinary and administrative courts. I have emphasised already that it was the March Constitution of 1921 that separated the judges from the constitution. A form of this distancing of judges from the basic law in the March Constitution was the provision that judges were subject only to statutes (rather than the constitution and statutes) and that they were prohibited from 'reviewing the validity of statutes duly promulgated' (art. 77). Under classical constitutionalism, the judge was in no position to apply the constitution – in one form or another. Then, the interpretation of the principle of constitutionalism under art. 8(1) put the entire burden of constitutional review upon the Constitutional Tribunal. And after 2016, the legal basis on which the courts challenge statutes is found in the Constitution's provision about its direct application (art. 8(2)), which means that the courts are obliged to interpret laws in accordance with the constitution. Thus, I reach the conclusion that under the principle of constitutionalism, direct applicability of the basic law cannot be reserved exclusively to the constitutional court equipped with a monopoly on judicial review and the power of derogation. That is because art. 8(2) of the Constitution orders all institutions, and certainly the judiciary, to apply the Constitution directly.

Yet as I call for constitutional review carried out by ordinary and administrative courts, I mean its complementarity with regard to centralised review performed by the Tribunal. Review by the courts should complement review by the Tribunal, since the principle of constitutionalism under art. 8(1) provides for centralised review, which seems to be the boundary value problem in the approach to this principle. Still, the division of work between the Constitutional Tribunal and the courts would be so that the Tribunal is the body that 'cleans' the system of law, while the courts, by 'suspending' a provision of the law, intervene in individual cases pending before them. Such review does not fix the legal system, but it is aimed to defend individual rights. The fantastic repertoire of constitutional interpretations at our disposal could allow us to avoid collisions between these mechanisms of constitutional review. A certain kind of subsidiarity of the review exercised by the courts does not mean that it should stop at sub-legislative acts, but would include statutes and the suspension of their provisions. Therefore, I do not reduce the issue of the diffuse review in Poland to a discussion on whether the monopoly of the Constitutional Tribunal is good or bad. More important are the questions:

30 Cf. the judgment of the Court of Appeal in Wrocław of 25 May 2017, ref. no II AKa 213/16.

31 Cf. the list of such judgments: https://www.seirp.pl/korzystne-wyroki-sadow-okregowych (accessed 31.03.2022).

what does centralised review mean? Does it cover certain diffuse constitutional review? How does it relate to the principle of constitutionalism considered in the present conditions?

3.4 Conclusion

The question about 'the constitutionality of law without a constitutional court', around which I have centred my reflections on the constitutionality of law in Poland, turned out to be more important than I had initially assumed. It is a helpful tool in analysing this issue after 2016, since 'without' covers various situations in which such review can exist. It is relevant to both recounting facts and reflecting on what can be done in order to protect the constitutionality of law. As a category, it outlines a field of study over the conformity of law with the constitution adequate to the requirements following from both the principle of constitutionalism and the situation in which Poland has found itself after 2016.

In the first sense, 'without' means a constitutionalism in which there is no constitutional court or in which the court's role is secondary to that of the representative body (the parliament). In this type of system, the constitutionality of a statute was determined by the Sejm and the presumption of constitutionality of law enjoyed by a passed act. The resultant question therefore is: can constitutionalism be maintained if the constitutionality of law is not determined by an independent court? It seems that, in the case of Poland, this question has to be answered in the negative, even if we take into account the specific political regime we experienced in the past. In turn, 'without' in the second sense has revealed the extent to which the constitutionality of law has been dismantled over the last years. Certainly, the Constitutional Tribunal continues to exist, yet its role morphed from that of an arbiter – which it played under the 1997 Constitution – into that of a player who can affect the weight of political decisions taken by the ruling party. It is described as an institution that 'helps to exercise power' and 'govern well', that 'defends Poland's sovereignty',[32] but not as a body that exercises hierarchical supervision over the constitutionality of law. It has become a sham institution, although, as I have mentioned above, this expression is highly imprecise, since it fails to express the fact that the functions served by the Constitutional Tribunal are of utmost importance from the perspective of the ruling party. At some point, I described the position of the Tribunal as that of 'an incapacitated yet indispensable' body.[33] The decisions issued at the end of 2021 and the beginning of 2022 in matters

32 Cf. https://www.gazetaprawna.pl/magazyn-na-weekend/artykuly/8266128,wyrok-tk-prawo-krajowe-unijne-trybunal-konstytucyjny-mateusz-morawiecki.html (accessed 31.03.2022).

33 Cf. M. Granat, *On the Experiences of a Constitutional Court in an Illiberal Democracy. Incapacitated but Necessary*, (in:) J.M. Castellà Andreu, M.A. Simonelli (eds.), *Populism and Contemporary Democracy in Europe*, Heidelberg 2022.

concerning European law reveal that the Tribunal – from the perspective of achieving the objectives of the authorities – has become far more necessary than ever before. Through the change in its function, the Tribunal has become a nuclear weapon at the disposal of the ruling party.

So what is the future of the principle of constitutionalism in Poland? I see a possibility to maintain it in such a reading of 'the constitutionality of law without a constitutional court' which allows for diffuse constitutional review so that the review is carried out also by ordinary and administrative courts. This reconstruction of the principle of constitutionalism must take into account the fact that judges of ordinary and administrative courts are competent to review the constitutionality of laws, with suspensive – and not derogatory – effect on a given provision. The success of this approach – despite the pressure from the Minister of Justice to prohibit judges from exercising such review – offers the possibility to defend both the constitution and human rights. This kind of proposition seems to show that, from the theoretical point of view, the close relationship between the principle of constitutionalism and the constitutional court that we assumed before 2016 is not tenable. Diffuse constitutional review, exercised by all courts, breaks the monopoly of the Constitutional Tribunal and at the same time preserves this court as a boundary value for the understanding of the principle of constitutionalism. Does it merely play the role of a sticking plaster (due to the lack of derogation) or is it only an ad hoc solution to a given situation (state of emergency)? Such doubts should be irrelevant, as the supremacy of the constitution may be protected by a different vision than the strict constitutional review exercised by a single court. The possibility of reinterpreting the principle of constitutionalism has the additional advantage that it fits within the existing paradigm set by liberal constitutionalism, which defines the conceptual framework of the present chapter.

However, a front of political change has swept through Poland, as it has swept through other Central European countries, resulting in a departure from the tenets of liberal constitutionalism. These changes manifest themselves in amendments of constitutions by means of ordinary laws or attempts to subordinate the courts to the influence of the executive power. They are also reflected in the atrophy of a certain understanding of the principle of constitutionalism of law, rooted in Kelsen's theoretical model.

Looking at the experience of democratic states, we observe that the constitutionality of law can be ensured not by a mechanism of hierarchical constitutional review, but by institutions of a political nature. In some countries, such as Finland and the Netherlands, there are no constitutional courts. However, even though these countries are not familiar with the concept of judicial review, they are counted among those that respect the principle of constitutionalism, as they ensure the constitutionality of law in a different manner. Explaining the absence of judicial review of the constitutionality of law and at the same time upholding the principle of constitutionalism is the subject of separate considerations in this book. The experience of other states would suggest that there are functioning forms of existence in a world without a constitutional court in which the rule of law is preserved. Moreover, according to well-known American theorists, it is even the case that the constitutionality of law should not depend on the court as an 'undemocratic institution', but rather on a democratically constituted parliament. I realise that American authors carry out their argument largely in Platonic heaven, whereas the object of my analysis is the practice of judicial review after 2016. Nevertheless, in view of the destruction of an independent constitutional court such as the Constitutional Tribunal, one would have to ask J. Waldron or M. Tushnet: is this better? Does hollowing out the Tribunal and depriving it of its functions serve to protect human rights? Are minority rights now more effectively protected? I think that the Polish case may make a certain contribution to the global discussion on the constitutionality of law, as it is a certain testing ground for contemporary constitutionalism.

***

When posing the question about 'the constitutionality of law without a constitutional court', I believed that rather than wringing hands over the Constitutional Tribunal, it is more valuable to look at the meaning of the principle of constitutionalism in the present conditions and at the possibility of its implementation. It turns out that ensuring the constitutionality of law remains a value, regardless of the form in which it is done.

References

Barber N.W., *The Principles of Constitutionalism*, Oxford University Press, Oxford 2018.

Böckenförde E.-W., *Państwo prawa w jednoczącej się Europie*, Instytut Studiów Politycznych PAN, Warsaw 2000.

Drinoczi T., Bień-Kacała A., *Illiberal Constitutionalism: The Case of Hungary and Poland*, "German Law Journal" 2019, vol. 20, pp. 1140–1166.

Garlicki L. (ed.), *Konstytucja Rzeczypospolitej Polskiej. Komentarz*, vol. 5, Wydawnictwo Sejmowe, Warszawa 2007.

Granat M., *Constitutional Judiciary in Crisis. The Case of Poland*, (in:) Z. Szente, F. Gárdos-Orosz (eds.), *New Challenges to Constitutional Adjudication in Europe*, A Comparative Perspective, Routledge, London 2018.

Granat M., *On the Experiences of a Constitutional Court in an Illiberal Democracy. Incapacitated but Necessary*, (in:) J.M.C. Andreu, M.A. Simonelli (eds.), *Populism and Contemporary Democracy in Europe*, Palgrave Macmillan, Heidelberg 2022.

Granat M., *Rozumienie zmiany konstytucji RP a tożsamość konstytucyjna*, (in:) R. Chruściak (ed.), *Problemy zmiany konstytucji*, Wydawnictwo Sejmowe, Warszawa 2017a.

Granat M., *Tożsamość konstytucji*, (in:) D. Dudek (ed.), *Zmieniać Konstytucję Rzeczypospolitej Polskiej czy nie zmieniać?*, Wydawnictwo KUL, Lublin 2017b.

Granat M., Granat K., *The Constitution of Poland. A Contextual Analysis*, Hart Publishing, Oxford 2019.

Halmai G., *Illiberal Constitutionalism? The Hungarian Constitution in a European Perspective*, (in:) S. Kadelbach (ed.), *Verfassungskrisen in der EU*, Nomos, Baden-Baden 2018.
Jacobsohn G.J., *Constitutional Identity*, Harvard University Press, Cambridge-London 2010.
Jacobsohn G.J., *Constitutional Review*, "The Review of Politics" 2006, vol. 68, pp 361–397.
Limbach J., *The Concept of the Supremacy of the Constitution*, "Modern Law Review" 2001, vol. 64(1), pp. 1–10.
Lustig D., Weiler J.H.H., *Judicial Review in the Contemporary World: Retrospective and Prospective*, "International Journal of Constitutional Law" 2018, vol. 16(2), pp. 315–372.
Mikuli P., *Doktryna konieczności jako uzasadnienie dla rozproszonej kontroli konstytucyjności ustaw w Polsce*, "Gdańskie Studia Prawnicze" 2018, vol. 40, pp. 635–648.
Mikuli P., *Zdekoncentrowana sądowa kontrola konstytucyjności prawa. Stany Zjednoczone i państwa europejskie*, Wydawnictwo Uniwersytetu Jagiellońskiego, Cracow 2007.
Sadurski W., *Poland's Constitutional Breakdown*, Oxford University Press, Oxford 2019.
Sadurski W., *Rights Before the Courts*, Springer, Baden-Baden 2014.
Szafnicka M., *Trybunał Konstytucyjny á rebours*, "Państwo i Prawo" 2020, vol. 5, pp. 25–45.
Tushnet M., *Advanced Introduction to Comparative Constitutional Law*, Edward Elgar, Cheltenham 2014.
Tushnet M., *Authoritarian Constitutionalism*, "Cornell Law Review" 2015, vol. 100, pp. 391–462.
Tushnet M., *Weak Courts, Strong Rights. Judicial Review and Social Welfare Rights in Comparative Constitutional Law*, Princeton University Press, Princeton 2008.
Tushnet M., Bugarič B., *Power to the People*, Constitutionalism in the Age of Populism, Oxford University Press, Oxford 2021.
Waldron J., *The Core of the Case Against Judicial Review*, "Yale Law Journal" 2006, vol. 115(6), pp. 1346–1406.

4 The problem of the so-called dispersed judicial review of parliamentary acts in Poland – traditions and current perspectives[1]

Piotr Chybalski

4.1 Introduction

The purpose of the present text is to analyse the acceptable extent of the development of the so-called dispersed model (sometimes known as the 'diffuse(d)' or 'decentralised' model) of constitutional review of parliamentary statutory acts (Polish: 'rozproszona kontrola konstytucyjności ustawodawstwa') in Poland. This matter has been a major subject of considerations by Polish experts in constitutional law, especially since the November 2015 outbreak of the crisis concerning the composition of the constitutional court (the Constitutional Tribunal, TK), which was established in 1986.[2] The case law of the ordinary or administrative courts has likewise included some attempts at developing a new, dispersed model of constitutional review – as a sort of substitute for the review that used to be and formally continues to be performed by the TK. Importantly, those attempts are made in a situation where the applicable constitutional provisions continue to be the original stipulations of the 1997 Polish Constitution, that is, where no formal amendment to the basic law has taken place.

Before we begin with the actual considerations, it is necessary to specify the concept of dispersed constitutional review. In the subject literature, the model of dispersed review is understood as 'review of the constitutionality of law by courts regardless of their instance';[3] yet this description should be complemented with two elements. First, the model concerns specific constitutional review, i.e., assessment performed in connection with a case pending before a

1 This paper has been prepared as a result of research project no. 2018/31/B/HS5/02667, financed by the National Science Centre (Poland) within the OPUS-15 funding scheme.

2 The newest papers dedicated to this matter are: P. Radziewicz, *Judicial Change to the Law-in-Action of Constitutional Review of Statutes in Poland*, "Utrecht Law Review" 2022, vol. 1 (18), as well as A. Rytel-Warzocha, *Jak nie Trybunał Konstytucyjny to co? O rozproszonej kontroli konstytucyjności prawa w Polsce*, "Przegląd Prawa Konstytucyjnego" 2022, vol. 3.

3 P. Mikuli, *Zdekoncentrowana sądowa kontrola konstytucyjności prawa. Stany Zjednoczone i państwa europejskie*, Kraków 2007, p. 11.

DOI: 10.4324/9781003355793-5

court. Second, declaring a reviewed provision unconstitutional results not in its derogation, but in refusal to apply it in the relevant case. The above outlined model of the constitutional review of statutes by courts is commonly referred to as the American model, as it originates from the United States of America. It is historically older than the second of the currently prevailing models, i.e., the centralised or Kelsenian (or European) model, which first took shape upon the establishment of the Austrian constitutional court in 1920.[4]

The present text has been divided into several sections. In the first section, I present previous Polish political solutions in terms of the admissibility of dispersed constitutional review of statutes, from the inter-war period (1919–1939) until the entry into force of the 1997 Constitution. Next, I analyse the legislation and disputes concerning the concept in the period 1997–2015, that is, until the beginning of the above mentioned crisis concerning the Constitutional Tribunal. Finally, in the third section, I discuss the issue of introducing this form of constitutional review as a substitute after 2015 and close with conclusions summarising the whole text.

4.2 The problem of dispersed constitutional review of statutes in Poland between 1919 and 1997

Poland's political system in the inter-war period was defined first by the provisional and additionally laconic so-called Small Constitution of 1919, and then by the March Constitution of 1921 and the Constitutional Statute of 1935, commonly known as the April Constitution. Albeit the issue of constitutional review was considered in the course of the work on the March Constitution,[5] the political system it established very much resembled classic French constitutionalism, which affected the admissibility of assessing laws enacted by the parliament. In the French tradition, a statute was an expression of the 'common will'. Consequently, it was unacceptable for any extra-parliamentary body to review and as a result possibly derogate or refuse to apply it. This solution was typical for the model of the so-called political review of constitutionality, i.e., review carried out exclusively by the parliament itself in the course of legislative work.[6]

Pursuant to art. 38 of the March Constitution, 'No statute shall conflict with or violate this Constitution'. This provision, which seemed to open up broad possibilities to review the constitutionality of laws, was in a manner counterbalanced by art. 81, according to which 'Courts shall have no right

4 M. Granat, *Sądowa kontrola konstytucyjności prawa w państwach Europy Środkowej i Wschodniej*, Warszawa 2003, p. 248.

5 For instance, one of the drafts provided for the possibility of constitutional review of statutes by the Supreme National Court. See R. Jastrzębski, *Sądownictwo konstytucyjne w państwie polskim w XX wieku*, "Zeszyty Prawnicze Biura Analiz Sejmowych" 2021, vol. 2, p. 56.

6 P. Tuleja, *Stosowanie Konstytucji RP w świetle zasady jej nadrzędności (wybrane problemy)*, Kraków 2003, p. 59.

to examine the validity of duly promulgated statutes', and by the principle of subordination of judges to statutory laws, which was stipulated in art. 77(1). These provisions met with considerable reservations of legal scholars, who underlined that art. 81 rendered the prohibition of enacting unconstitutional laws under art. 38 in fact purely declarative as an instance of *lex imperfecta*.[7] As a result, a major part of the contemporary constitutional experts began to gradually back the – initially rarely put forward – idea to establish in Poland a constitutional court modelled on the recently founded courts in Austria or Czechoslovakia.[8] A view that stood out in the subject literature was that of M. Starzewski, who – despite art. 81 of the March Constitution – saw a possibility for the courts to assess the constitutionality of laws. He believed that, in the light of the then applicable basic law, constitutionality was one of the defining characteristics of a statute, which led him to the conclusion that an act passed as a statute but with unconstitutional content in fact was no statute. Furthermore, he argued that courts were supposed to examine whether statutes met the requirement of constitutionality, and that the prohibition to 'examine the validity of laws' under art. 81 referred only to those statutes that, in the opinion of the courts, met this requirement.[9]

M. Starzewski's position remained isolated in constitutional subject literature. Moreover, mindful of art. 81 of the March Constitution, the courts tried to refrain from reviewing the constitutionality of statutes, although tendencies appeared in the judicature to rely on a strict interpretation of the prohibition. For instance, it was applied unconditionally only to statutes enacted by the Polish parliament (the Sejm and the Senate) after the March Constitution entered into force. When it comes to earlier legislation, including that passed before Poland regained its independence (which means, depending on the territory, Russian, Prussian, or Austro-Hungarian legislation), the courts occasionally tried to cite art. 126(2) of the March Constitution, which stipulated that: '[a]ny legal provisions and instruments now in existence which are incompatible with the provisions of the Constitution shall, not later than one year after its enactment, be submitted to the legislature for legislative reconciliation with the Constitution'. The Supreme Court developed in its case law the position that, in the light of the discussed stipulations, with the promulgation of the March Constitution, provisions contrary to the basic law, that is, those that could not be 'reconciled' with it under art. 126(2), were *ipso jure* (by virtue of the directive of *lex posterior derogat legi priori*) derogated, and that the role of the courts would be to assess whether there was such a contradiction in a particular case (and thus whether to disregard those provisions in

7 See W. Komarnicki, *Polskie prawo polityczne*, Warszawa 2008 (reprinted issue of 1922), p. 471.

8 R. Jastrzębski, *Konstytucyjność aktów ustawodawczych w judykaturze II Rzeczypospolitej*, "Przegląd Sejmowy" 2010, vol. 2, pp. 84, 85.

9 M. Starzewski, *Środki zabezpieczenia prawnego konstytucyjności ustaw*, Warszawa 2009 (reprinted issue of 1928), pp. 235-241.

adjudication). This view corresponded to the beliefs expressed in the subject literature at the time, but was challenged by the other chief judicial authority of the time, the Supreme Administrative Tribunal (NTA).[10]

The entry into force of the 1935 April Constitution did not alter the previous legal status, which – along with the already mentioned restriction of court independence – precluded any attempts at reviewing the constitutionality of laws. Pursuant to art. 64(5), '[c]ourts shall not be authorised to examine the validity of duly promulgated legislative acts'. This regulation unequivocally ruled out the possibility of judicial review of statutes and regulations having the force of statutes (a specific Polish form of decrees), where the latter counted together with statutes as legislative acts (art. 49(1)). As a result, the reaffirmation of the earlier reservation that '[n]o legislative act shall be in contravention of the Constitution' in art. 49(2) of the April Constitution served a merely ornamental purpose.

In the period between the end of World War II and the 1989 democratic breakthrough, during most of which the Constitution of the People's Republic of Poland applied, any judicial review of the constitutionality of statutes was out of the question. The Constitution dismissed the principle of the separation of powers and stipulated in art. 15(1) that '[t]he supreme body of public authority shall be the Sejm of the Polish People's Republic'. Therefore, the Sejm 'as the supreme speaker of the will of the working people of town and country' exercised 'the sovereign rights of the people' (art. 15(2)), and its primary tasks were to 'pass laws' and 'supervise the activity of other bodies of state authority and administration' (art. 15(3)). With that definition of the Sejm's political and legal position, any extra-parliamentary review was inadmissible. It was believed that to authorise the courts to perform such review or to establish a specialised constitutional court would be tantamount to 'constraining national representation by a body which would thus be superior to the body of the people's supreme authority', and to introducing a 'reactionary' institution.[11]

The fundamental opposition against extra-parliamentary constitutional review of law began to diminish at the beginning of the 1970s, if only because constitutional courts had been established already in the 1960s in two countries associated with the so-called Eastern Block, that is in Yugoslavia and Czechoslovakia. The change in attitude found its expression in 1976, when the Council of State (i.e., a body serving as a collective head of state, subordinate to the Sejm) was granted the competence to 'watch over the constitutionality of law' (amending art. 30(1)(3) of the Constitution of the Polish People's Republic). This provision, however, had no practical significance, if only because no legal regulations apart from the above were introduced

10 L. Garlicki, *Konstytucja a ustawy przedkonstytucyjne*, (in:) Z. Witkowski (ed.), *Wejście w życie nowej Konstytucji Rzeczypospolitej Polskiej*, Toruń 1998, p. 41.

11 S. Rozmaryn, *Kontrola konstytucyjności ustaw*, "Państwo i Prawo" 1948, vol. 12, p. 13.

that would specify the procedure of exercising this competence.[12] It was not until the establishment of the specialised Constitutional Tribunal under the 1982 amendment to the Constitution of the Polish People's Republic that a turning point was reached (the Tribunal began to adjudicate in 1986). Yet it should be remembered that originally, judgments declaring the unconstitutionality of statutory provisions could be rejected by the Sejm with a two-thirds majority vote. Still, there was no mention of the courts being granted the right to review the constitutionality of legislation.

The situation began to change after the democratic breakthrough in Poland in 1989, which resulted in, among others, the judiciary being granted a character typical of modern democracies, i.e., independence from other powers (formally, the principle of the separation of powers was restored in Poland under the so-called 1992 Small Constitution). In addition to the rapid development of the Constitutional Tribunal's case law, some symptoms indicated that the courts also saw the possibility to undertake independent constitutional review of laws, in addition to the TK. It must be stressed, however, that in principle, these attempts were made almost exclusively by the Supreme Court, i.e., a judicial authority supervising the ordinary, military and, until 2002, administrative courts. Moreover, analyses of the jurisprudence of the time reveal that the judgments in which we could recognise readiness to refuse the application of a statute that was found unconstitutional were incidental. Furthermore, the Supreme Court expressed itself in an oblique way, i.e., no court made an unequivocal statement that, when ruling on a given case, it refused to apply a provision of a law because it had found it unconstitutional. For example, in the resolution of the Supreme Court of 10 May 1996, file ref. I PZP 11/96, which has been cited in the subject literature, the court claimed that it was only interpreting the statutory provision applicable at the time, while in practice, as noted by P. Tuleja, the provision's constitutionality had been reviewed with a negative result and, consequently, the court refused to apply it.[13] The actual significance of the nascent jurisprudence of the Supreme Court in the period from 1989 to 1997, i.e., until the present constitution entered into force, is demonstrated in the fact that it was further developed after 1997, contributing to bolder attempts at reviewing the constitutionality of statutes, which is discussed in more detail in the next section of the present article.

12 See for instance Z. Witkowski, *Zagadnienie zgodności aktów Sejmu z Konstytucją PRL w świetle doktryny*, "Ruch Prawniczy, Ekonomiczny i Socjologiczny" 1981, vol. 1, pp. 40–44.

13 P. Tuleja, *Stosowanie...*, pp. 341–346.

4.3 Dispersed constitutional review between 1997 and 2015

The entry into force of the current Polish Constitution of 2 April 1997 ended the temporary stage of the Polish constitutional system introduced in 1989.[14] The new basic law comprehensively regulated the entirety of typical constitutional matters. Among other things, it provided a fairly detailed description of the organisation and competences of the judiciary, in particular in the extensive Chapter VII 'Courts and Tribunals'. Despite its wide scope, especially in comparison to the earlier legislation, a controversy arose in both constitutional case law and among constitutional scholars concerning the question whether judicial bodies other than the Constitutional Tribunal could review the constitutionality of statutes or, strictly speaking, whether a court could refuse to apply statutory provisions it found unconstitutional. The controversy occurred mainly soon after the Constitution entered into force, only to fade away later, prompting K. Działocha to state (not long before the outbreak of the constitutional crisis in 2015) that the doctrinal conflict had been 'virtually removed'.[15] The axis of these discussions was the interpretation of several provisions of the new constitution, some of which were novel in relation to the earlier legal status.

Firstly, the 1997 Constitution not only maintains the Constitutional Tribunal as a specialised, 'Kelsenian' constitutional court, but also extensively describes its constitutional position. Pursuant to art. 188(1) of the Constitution, the Constitutional Tribunal adjudicates on the compliance of statutes and international agreements with the Constitution, and pursuant to art. 188(2), it rules on the compliance of statutes with ratified international agreements whose ratification required prior consent expressed in a statute. Significantly, no parallel solutions can be found in the constitutional provisions relating to courts. Secondly, art. 195(1) of the basic law stipulates that judges of the Constitutional Tribunal are independent and subject 'only to the Constitution' in the exercise of their office, whereas art. 178(1) introduces a similar solution concerning judges (sitting in courts, not tribunals), with the important modification, however, that court judges are subject 'only to the Constitution and statutes'. Thirdly, the admissibility of undertaking constitutional review by the courts is affected by art. 193, in accordance with which any court may refer to the Constitutional Tribunal a question of law

14 In the years 1989–1992, the amended 'old' Constitution of the People's Republic of Poland of 1952 was in force. In turn, in the years 1992–1997, the constitutional system in Poland was shaped by the already mentioned 1992 Small Constitution, which regulated only a fragment of the typical constitutional matters (relations between bodies constituting the legislature, executive, judiciary and local government), selected provisions of the 'old' Constitution of the People's Republic of Poland of 1952 (particularly the list of freedoms and rights), as well as the Constitutional Act of 1992, which defined the procedure of drafting and enacting a new, comprehensive constitution.

15 K. Działocha, *Uwagi do art. 8*, (in:) L. Garlicki, M. Zubik (eds.), *Konstytucja Rzeczypospolitej Polskiej. Komentarz*, vol. 1, Warszawa 2016, p. 315.

concerning the conformity of a normative act to the Constitution, ratified international agreements, or a statute, if the outcome of a case pending before the court depends on the answer to the question of law. The institution of the 'question of law' introduced in this provision is one of the momentous systemic innovations of the 1997 Constitution. The fourth and final point is that the currently binding Constitution provided, for the first time in the history of Polish constitutionalism, for the principle of direct application of the constitution: pursuant to art. 8(2), the provisions of the Constitution are applied directly, unless the Constitution stipulates otherwise.

Although Polish constitutional legal scholars in the analysed period uniformly acknowledged (and still acknowledge) that all state bodies, including, of course, the courts, are obliged to apply the constitution, including to assess the constitutionality of statutory provisions, the majority of authors took the standpoint that only the Constitutional Tribunal could – in the event of declaring unconstitutionality – derogate the faulty provisions. However, they believe the courts were not competent to refuse the application of statutory provisions if it was the courts themselves that found such unconstitutionality (and thus the Constitutional Tribunal did not adjudicate the matter), and even less competent to derogate such provisions with an *erga omnes* effect. Instructive for this position are the comments of L. Garlicki, who argued that in the context of the principle of the separation of powers, it should be recognised that legislative competences have been reserved for the parliament, and that the encroachment of other constitutional bodies into this sphere is permissible only when a clear constitutional provision allows it. In this context, it is crucial to note that, as already mentioned, only the TK has been granted the competence to review the constitutionality of statutes under art. 188(1) of the Constitution. Moreover, the above-cited author noted that the intention of the authors of the Constitution had been to create a centralised model of constitutional review, i.e., a monopoly of the TK.[16]

The consequence of such a stance, shared among others by A. Mączyński,[17] P. Tuleja[18] or M. Safjan,[19] is the belief that in the event a court becomes convinced that a statutory provision relevant in a given case violates the Constitution, it may only make use of such competences as have been explicitly granted to the court by the provisions of law. In practice, this means referring a question of law to the Constitutional Tribunal pursuant to art. 193 of

16 K. Działocha, *Uwagi do art. 178*, (in:) L. Garlicki (ed.), *Konstytucja Rzeczypospolitej Polskiej. Komentarz*, vol. 4, Warszawa 2005, p. 14.

17 A. Mączyński, *Bezpośrednie stosowanie konstytucji przez sądy*, "Państwo i Prawo" 2000, vol. 5, p. 3.

18 P. Tuleja, *Stosowanie*..., pp. 376–378.

19 M. Safjan, *Uwagi wprowadzające*, (in:) M. Safjan, L. Bosek (eds.), *Konstytucja RP. Tom I, Komentarz. Art. 1–86*, Warszawa 2016, pp. 90, 91.

the Constitution. Importantly, it is the court's duty to take this step in the described circumstances, and not merely a possibility provided for by law.[20]

The remarks presented above have met with the full and consistently upheld approval of the Constitutional Tribunal itself. For example, in its judgment of 31 January 2001, file ref. P 4/99, the Tribunal firmly stated that:

> Article 188 of the Constitution grants the right to adjudicate the matters enumerated therein as the exclusive competence of the Constitutional Tribunal, irrespective of whether the ruling is to be of a universally binding nature or confined only to an individual case. The presumption of constitutionality of a statute may only be rebutted by a judgment of the Constitutional Tribunal, and the judge remains bound by the statute as long as the statute is in force.

In turn, in the further part of the argument, the TK added that:

> an important element of the model of constitutional review of laws adopted in the Polish constitution following the example of other European states is the institution of the question of law regulated under art. 193. The regulation based on art.188 and 193 of the Constitution, interpreted in the light of the principle of state ruled by law expressed in art. 2 of the Constitution, is not overridden by the subordination of judges to the Constitution and statutes provided for in art. 178(1) of the Constitution. This provision does not directly address the issue of resolving conflicts between the Constitution and the law, but it complements the regulation provided for in art. 193 of the Constitution by establishing the obligation to make use of the possibility granted in this provision whenever the adjudicating court comes to the conviction that the provision constituting the basis for adjudication is contrary to the Constitution. Furthermore, the courts cannot escape the principle expressed in art. 190(1) of the Constitution, according to which the judgments of the Constitutional Tribunal have universally binding force.

Advocates of the admissibility of dispersed constitutional review drew attention first of all to the imperative of direct application of the Constitution (art. 8(2)), which, in their view, affected the interpretation of the principle of the judge being subject to the provisions of the Constitution and statutes (art. 178(1)). The essence of this position was the belief that when the court finds a given statutory provision unconstitutional, the judge is obliged to apply the above-mentioned principle of direct application and to give precedence to the constitutional regulation, following the principle of *lex superior derogat legi*

20 K. Działocha, *Uwagi do art. 178...*, p. 13.

inferiori, and consequently to refuse to apply the statutory provision.[21] This position was complemented with the belief that it is not the duty of the court to refer a question of law to the Constitutional Tribunal if it becomes convinced that a given statutory provision violates the Constitution, and the argumentation in favour of such view is provided by the content of art. 193.[22] Thus, the proponents of the presented view virtually advocated a 'mixed' model of constitutional review, including both the admissibility of a dispersed review by the courts (which could refuse to apply an unconstitutional provision) and by the 'specialised' Constitutional Tribunal (with a derogatory, i.e., *erga omnes*, effect of declaring unconstitutionality). In Europe, this model would probably correspond to some extent only to the solutions employed in Portugal.[23]

An equivalent view was represented in some judgments of the Supreme Court, which however emphasised that said view did not prevail and that there were differences of opinion among the individual chambers of that court. For example, according to K. Gonera, the belief that a court may refuse to apply a statutory provision if it finds it unconstitutional independently (i.e., without resorting to the institution of a question of law referred to the Constitutional Tribunal) prevailed in the jurisprudence of the Labour, Social Insurance and Public Affairs Chamber of the Supreme Court.[24] In turn, in the opinion of L. Bosek, a sceptical position on this issue was expressed by the Court's Civil Chamber.[25] That said, it is worth noting that the other main judicial body in Poland, i.e., the Supreme Administrative Court, rather uniformly recognised the exclusive competence of the Constitutional Tribunal to declare the unconstitutionality of statutory regulations.[26]

4.4 Dispersed constitutional review of statutes in times of constitutional crisis (since 2015)

Although the crisis around the Polish Constitutional Tribunal, which broke out in December 2015, has already been extensively described by constitutional

21 View presented, e.g., in: W. Sanetra, *Sąd Najwyższy w systemie wymiaru sprawiedliwości*, "Przegląd Sądowy" 1998, vol. 7–8, p. 13, as well as B. Banaszak, *Porównawcze...*, pp. 116–121.

22 What is meant here is that the provision reads: 'any court may refer a question of law to the Constitutional Tribunal' (Polish: 'każdy sąd może przedstawić Trybunałowi Konstytucyjnemu pytanie prawne'), rather than 'must refer' ('musi przedstawić') or 'refers' ('przedstawia').

23 See P. Mikuli, *Zdekoncentrowana...*, pp. 33–35.

24 K. Gonera, *Rozproszona kontrola konstytucyjności w systemie kontroli scentralizowanej – według orzecznictwa Izby Pracy, Ubezpieczeń Społecznych i Spraw Publicznych Sądu Najwyższego*, (in:) M. Granat (ed.), *Sądownictwo konstytucyjne. Teoria i praktyka*, vol. II, Warszawa 2019, p. 152.

25 L. Bosek, *Bezpośrednie stosowanie Konstytucji RP w orzecznictwie Sądu Najwyższego – Izby Cywilnej*, (in:) M. Granat (ed.), *Sądownictwo konstytucyjne. Teoria i praktyka*, vol. II, Warszawa 2019, pp. 191–195.

26 K. Działocha, *Uwagi do art. 8*, p. 316.

scholars,[27] it is worth briefly recalling that it is related to the Tribunal's composition. In October 2015, the outgoing Sejm of the seventh term (politically dominated by today's opposition) elected five judges of the TK, while only three vacancies would need to be filled before that term ended. In November 2015, the Sejm of the next (eighth) term (dominated by the party in power today) declared by way of resolutions the election of the above-mentioned judges invalid and subsequently appointed five of its 'own' judges. In its judgment of 3 December 2015, file ref. K 34/15, the Tribunal found, *inter alia*, that art. 137 of the Act of 25 June 2015 on the Constitutional Tribunal (Journal of Laws, item 1064), i.e., the episodic provision that allowed the Sejm of the seventh term to fill the five vacancies, was unconstitutional only insofar as it applied to Tribunal judges whose term of office would expire after the beginning of the next, eighth term, i.e., to only two judges. Thus, it implicitly held that the 'adjustment' made by the new Sejm of the eighth term had been founded only in the case of these two judges, while the re-filling of the seats in the Constitutional Tribunal that had become vacant before the end of the previous, seventh term *de facto* proved unconstitutional. This ruling meant that the mandates of the three judges elected in November 2015 to seats that had been duly filled in October 2015 became almost universally contested in the subject literature. This state of affairs, which has persisted to the present day,[28] is one of the reasons for the fundamental decline in the authority of the TK, a clear expression of which has been the radical decrease in the number of applications and questions of law referred to this body.[29]

The above-outlined situation triggered a reaction in jurisprudence consisting in intensified attempts by the courts to carry out an independent (and therefore dispersed) review of the constitutionality of statutes, so to speak as a substitute

27 See, for instance, W. Sadurski, *Poland's Constitutional Breakdown*, Oxford 2019; M. Wiącek, *Constitutional Crisis in Poland 2015–2016 in the Light of the Rule of Law Principle*, (in:) A. von Bogdandy et al. (eds.), *Defending Checks and Balances in EU Member States Taking Stock of Europe's Actions*, Berlin 2021; M. Florczak-Wątor, *The Polish Constitutional Tribunal and its Transformation*, "European Review of Public Law" 2020, vol. 32, no. 1; O. Boryslavska, M. Granat, *Independence of Constitutional Justices: Stumbling Blocks in Ukraine and Poland*, "Access to Justice in Eastern Europe" 2021, vol. 2. Regarding the literature in Polish, see esp. P. Radziewicz, P. Tuleja (eds.), *Konstytucyjny spór o granice zmian organizacji i zasad działania Trybunału Konstytucyjnego czerwiec 2015 – marzec 2016*, Warszawa 2017.

28 For the sake of clarity, it should be added that currently only one of the three judges elected to the seats duly filled is still in office, while the other two died. Nevertheless, they have been replaced by new judges, which means that the opportunity to at least partially remedy the defect in the composition of the Tribunal by recognising the election of the two judges chosen by the Sejm of the seventh term, whose election was 'annulled' by the Sejm of the eighth term, has not been taken.

29 For example, while 80 questions of law were referred to the TK in 2014 and 135 in 2015, there were only 21 such questions in 2017 and only 15 in 2018, *Informacja o istotnych problemach wynikających z działalności i orzecznictwa Trybunału Konstytucyjnego w 2018 roku*, Warszawa 2019, p. 19. Interestingly, these statistical summaries were discontinued in later annual analyses.

for the partially defectively composed Constitutional Tribunal. An instructive example of this new trend in case law became the resolution of the Supreme Court of 23 March 2016, file ref. III CZP 102/15, in which it was stated that although 'the division of functions between the Constitutional Tribunal and the Supreme Court and ordinary courts is expressed in the fact that the review of the constitutionality of legal rules is carried out by the Constitutional Tribunal' and 'it is not carried out – in principle – by the Supreme Court or the courts', this 'principle is valid as long as the Constitutional Tribunal is competent – in the existing normative environment – to perform its constitutional functions'. It is also worth citing the decision of the Regional Court in Warsaw of 31 October 2019, file ref. XXIII Ga 797/18, in which, due to the fact that 'there are serious doubts as to the status, under the Constitution, of persons appointed as judges of the Constitutional Tribunal in 2016 or of persons elected to replace them', the court referred to the Supreme Court a legal issue 'whether, under Art. 8(2) of the Constitution of the Republic of Poland, it is permissible for an adjudicating court to refuse to apply a statutory rule due to its incompliance with a constitutional rule, without the court first referring a question of law to the Constitutional Tribunal (Article 193 of the Constitution)'. Interestingly, the Supreme Court refused to adopt a resolution in this case. The Regional Court in Warsaw then decided to refer the question to the Court of Justice of the European Union for a preliminary ruling, except that its content concerned the merits of the case and not doubts about the composition of the TK.[30]

The turmoil surrounding the composition of the TK has led to far-reaching revisions of views on the admissibility of dispersed constitutional review in the subject literature. P. Mikuli noted that 'two approaches to the permissibility of dispersed constitutional review in Poland can now be observed', the first 'being the claim that this type of judicial review has always been possible' and the second 'consisting in the claim that only extraordinary emergency circumstances justify the reviewing role of the courts'.[31] This position, however, apparently needs to be supplemented by the third approach, where some constitutionalists maintain their previously prevailing scepticism regarding the breaking of the monopoly of the TK in the constitutional review – even despite the ongoing constitutional crisis concerning this institution.[32]

The supporters of a broad admissibility of dispersed constitutional review refer to the argumentation presented in the previous part of the present text, i.e., they invoke the principle of direct application of the Constitution stated

30 Decision of the Regional Court in Warsaw of 9 July 2021, file ref. XXIII Ga 797/18, access via LEX legal database.

31 P. Mikuli, *Doktryna konieczności jako uzasadnienie dla rozproszonej kontroli konstytucyjności ustaw w Polsce*, "Gdańskie Studia Prawnicze" 2018, vol. 40, p. 641.

32 See esp. S. Wronkowska, *Kilka uwag porządkujących dyskusję o tzw. rozproszonej kontroli konstytucyjności*, (in:) M. Granat (ed.), *Sądownictwo konstytucyjne. Teoria i praktyka*, vol. II, Warszawa 2019.

expressis verbis in art. 8(2) of the Polish Constitution.[33] In recent years, an extensive theoretical concept referring to this principle as well as, among others, to the obligation of courts to apply the conflict rule of *lex superior derogat legi inferiori*, justifying the refusal to apply a statutory rule found unconstitutional by the court, was developed by M. Gutowski and P. Kardas. Interestingly, they published their position during the time of the ongoing constitutional crisis concerning the Constitutional Tribunal, yet without recognising said crisis as a relevant fact, but arguing that in the light of the Constitution, a mixed model of the constitutional review was appropriate.[34]

Authors who point to the exceptional permissibility of the model of dispersed constitutional review explicitly name the ongoing crisis concerning the Polish Constitutional Tribunal as the reason for this exceptional situation. For example, E. Łętowska stated that resorting to dispersed control was a 'subsidiary remedy in the face of the crisis of centralised constitutional review'.[35] Next, M. Małecki and M. Pach, referring to the institution of necessity known from criminal law, put forward the concept of 'constitutional necessity'. It should be noted for the sake of clarity that they did not refer it to the issue of dispersed constitutional review but treated it as a justification for the TK's refusal to apply the procedural rules that paralysed its activity and that had been introduced in the initial period of the constitutional crisis, i.e., in December 2015.[36] Although the concept was strongly criticised by P. Radziewicz shortly after it was put forward,[37] the above expression itself (or its alternative version: 'doctrine of necessity') was sometimes invoked in subject literature to justify the admissibility of dispersed constitutional review.[38] As it seems, the most coherent concept justifying the exceptional application of this model of judicial review was expressed by L. Garlicki, who outright admitted that he was revising his earlier view excluding dispersed review. He stated that courts may refuse to apply statutory provisions if the following conditions are met: '(1) firstly, the provision of the statute that would be the basis or premise of the decision cannot be reconciled (by means of the application of a pro-constitutional interpretation) with a particular constitutional rule or principle;

33 View argued especially in: W. Sanetra, *Bezpośrednie stosowanie Konstytucji RP przez Sąd Najwyższy*, "Przegląd Sądowy" 2017, vol. 2.

34 M. Gutowski, P. Kardas, *Wykładnia i stosowanie prawa w procesie opartym na Konstytucji*, Warszawa 2017, pp. 567–635, 700–705. See also another paper written by the above authors: *Sądowa kontrola konstytucyjności prawa. Kilka uwag o kompetencjach sądów powszechnych do bezpośredniego stosowania Konstytucji*, "Palestra" 2016, vol. 4.

35 E. Łętowska, *Aktualność sporu o zdekoncentrowaną kontrolę konstytucyjności w Polsce – uwagi na tle art. 10 Konstytucji*, (in:) M. Zubik (ed.), *Minikomentarz dla maksiprofesora. Księga jubileuszowa profesora Leszka Garlickiego*, Warszawa 2017, p. 799.

36 M. Małecki, M. Pach, *Stan wyższej konieczności konstytucyjnej*, "Państwo i Prawo" 2018, vol. 7.

37 P. Radziewicz, *O niedostatkach teorii stanu wyższej konieczności konstytucyjnej*, "Państwo i Prawo" 2018, vol. 11.

38 P. Mikuli, *Doktryna...*, p. 642.

(2) secondly, the TK has not yet ruled on the matter, and (3) thirdly, there is no possibility to obtain a ruling of the TK'.[39] The last-mentioned premise refers to the ongoing constitutional crisis, in particular to the objections as to the composition of the TK.

As a follow-up, it is worth adding that attempts by the courts to undertake dispersed constitutional review have not become common jurisprudential practice,[40] even despite the favour of a significant portion of Polish legal scholars. Nonetheless, they caused concern among representatives of the political camp that gained power in 2015. As a result, a Deputies' Bill to Amend the Act on the System of Ordinary Courts, the Act on the Supreme Court, and Certain Other Acts was submitted with the Sejm on 12 December 2019. It included a proposal to recognise the refusal to 'apply a provision of a statute if its incompatibility with the Constitution or an international agreement ratified with prior consent expressed in a statute has not been declared by the Constitutional Tribunal' as a manifest and gross offence of the law (as a disciplinary offence committed by the judge).[41] Ultimately, however, this solution was not enacted.

4.5 Summary – the future of dispersed constitutional review of statutes in Poland

It follows from the remarks contained in this text that the issue of dispersed constitutional review has for a long time remained only on the margins of theoretical considerations in contemporary Polish constitutionalism. This form of constitutional review was *de facto* 'blocked' by constitutional provisions (of the 1921 March Constitution or the 1935 April Constitution), and completely impossible in the times of the communist dictatorship in the period 1944–1989 due to the formally superior constitutional position of the Sejm. The legal subject literature, insofar as it demanded the introduction of mechanisms enabling extra-parliamentary review of laws, likewise primarily suggested the establishment of a 'Kelsenian' type of court (the Constitutional Tribunal). The positions of scholars admitting constitutional review by the courts were isolated and, in principle, expressed only during the period of the 1921 March Constitution. It was only in the 1990s that tentative attempts to

39 L. Garlicki, *Sądy a Konstytucja Rzeczypospolitej Polskiej*, "Przegląd Sądowy" 2016, vol. 7–9, p. 22.

40 For example, the Provincial Administrative Court in Warsaw in its judgment of 20 June 2018, file ref. V SA/Wa 459/18, stated that 'neither the Constitution of the Republic of Poland nor the provisions of the Act on administrative court proceedings, nor any other statute existing in the Polish legal system provide for the competence of an administrative court to rule on the legality of judgments of the Constitutional Tribunal', including in the case of doubts as to the due (lawful) composition of the Constitutional Tribunal in a given case.

41 The text of the bill in Polish is available at https://orka.sejm.gov.pl/Druki9ka.nsf/0/2B5623CD240138EBC12584CE006EBCDD/%24File/69.pdf (30.08.2022).

independently review the constitutionality of legislation appeared in the jurisprudence of the Supreme Court, but, as indicated, these were exceptional situations in the context of the entire case law. The situation began to change after the entry into force of the current 1997 Constitution, although the majority of legal scholars as well as of the judicial authorities continued to feel sceptical about this form of constitutional review.

A change of attitude towards dispersed review was only brought about by the outbreak of the still ongoing crisis concerning the Constitutional Tribunal, with the majority of legal theoreticians seeming to advocate only the exceptional permissibility of this model of constitutional review. Nevertheless, some authors argue that a return to the pre-2015 situation, i.e., the prevailing belief in the exclusivity of centralised review, is doubtful. For example, according to P. Radziewicz, the current benevolence in the subject literature towards dispersed review represents a kind of 'paradigmatic change in the Constitution', which in the future may be supported by a formal change in the provisions of the basic law aiming to provide for dispersed review.[42] In turn, M. Safjan found that it would be advisable to introduce in the future in Poland an 'eclectic model of constitutional review', combining the jurisprudential activity of the Constitutional Tribunal (once there are no more objections as to its composition) and a bolder than pre-2015 constitutional review performed by other judicial bodies.[43]

Considering these opinions, I also believe that it would be reasonable to introduce a mixed model in Poland in the future, which would combine both the classical 'Kelsenian' constitutional court with elements of dispersed review. It seems that such a model could hinder potential future attempts to paralyse constitutional review independent of political power, and thus undermine the rule of law – as merely incapacitating the Constitutional Tribunal would not be sufficient. However, as Professor Leonard Besselink pointed out in the text contained in this volume, courts can counteract political attempts to undermine the rule of law only to a limited extent, i.e., in principle only during the initial period of the erosion of democracy, when not all independent constitutional institutions have yet been 'politically appropriated'. This position seems to be confirmed by the situation evident in Poland in recent years, when, following the curbing of the Constitutional Tribunal, representatives of the political authorities turned their attention to limiting the independence of the ordinary judiciary and the Supreme Court, e.g., by amending the rules of appointing members of the National Council of the Judiciary (KRS), i.e., the body which has the exclusive competence to submit motions concerning the appointment of judges to the President of the Republic of Poland (art. 179 of

42 P. Radziewicz, *"Wyjątkowe okoliczności" jako podstawa zmiany wykładni konstytucji*, (in:) M. Granat (ed.), *Sądownictwo konstytucyjne. Teoria i praktyka*, vol. III, Warszawa 2020, p. 204.

43 M. Safjan, *Trybunał Konstytucyjny po trzydziestu latach, Doświadczenie i przyszłość*, "Przegląd Konstytucyjny" 2017, vol. 1, pp. 54, 55.

the Constitution). Consequently, the legitimacy of the judges appointed as a result of the recommendation of the 'new' KRS is currently questioned,[44] although it should be emphasised that the legal dimension of the problem is so complex that it would require a separate study. Nonetheless, in such a situation, the current scholarly benevolence towards dispersed constitutional review becomes debatable, when one can potentially doubt whether some judges of ordinary courts, administrative courts or the Supreme Court guarantee independent, impartial judicial proceedings.

Consequently, it seems that the future of constitutional review in Poland, including the development (or inhibition of the development) of dispersed review, will not be shaped by possible legal changes – based on in-depth theories – clarifying the scope of admissibility of this form of review. Instead, the future of constitutional review in practice will probably be determined by political settlements, i.e., the will of the parliamentary majority formed in the elections scheduled for the next year and its attitude to the post-2015 situation around the Constitutional Tribunal and other judicial bodies.

References

Boryslavska O., Granat M., *Independence of Constitutional Justices: Stumbling Blocks in Ukraine and Poland*, "Access to Justice in Eastern Europe" 2021, vol. 2, pp. 9–24.

Bosek L., *Bezpośrednie stosowanie Konstytucji RP w orzecznictwie Sądu Najwyższego – Izby Cywilnej*, (in:) M. Granat (ed.), *Sądownictwo konstytucyjne. Teoria i praktyka*, vol. II, Wydawnictwo Naukowe UKSW, Warszawa 2019.

Działocha K., *Uwagi do art. 8*, (in:) L. Garlicki, M. Zubik (eds.), *Konstytucja Rzeczypospolitej Polskiej. Komentarz*, vol. 1, Wydawnictwo Sejmowe, Warszawa 2016.

Działocha K., *Uwagi do art. 178*, (in:) L. Garlicki (ed.), *Konstytucja Rzeczypospolitej Polskiej. Komentarz*, vol. 4, Wydawnictwo Sejmowe, Warszawa 2005.

Florczak-Wątor M., *The Polish Constitutional Tribunal and its Transformation*, "European Review of Public Law" 2020, vol. 32(1).

Gajda-Roszczynialska K., Markiewicz K., *Disciplinary Proceedings as an Instrument for Breaking the Rule of Law in Poland*, "Hague Journal on the Rule of Law" 2020, vol. 12, pp. 451–483

Garlicki L., *Konstytucja a ustawy przedkonstytucyjne*, (in:) Z. Witkowski (ed.), Wejście w życie nowej Konstytucji Rzeczypospolitej Polskiej, Wydawnictwo TNOiK, Toruń 1998.

Garlicki L., *Sądy a Konstytucja Rzeczypospolitej Polskiej*, "Przegląd Sądowy" 2016, vol. 7–9, pp. 7–25.

Gonera K., *Rozproszona kontrola konstytucyjności w systemie kontroli scentralizowanej – Według orzecznictwa Izby Pracy, Ubezpieczeń Społecznych i Spraw Publicznych Sądu Najwyższego*, (in:) M. Granat (ed.), *Sądownictwo konstytucyjne. Teoria i praktyka*, vol. II, Wydawnictwo Naukowe UKSW, Warszawa 2019.

44 See, e.g., K. Gajda-Roszczynialska, K. Markiewicz, *Disciplinary Proceedings as an Instrument for Breaking the Rule of Law in Poland*, "Hague Journal on the Rule of Law" 2020, vol. 12.

Granat M., *Sądowa kontrola konstytucyjności prawa w państwach Europy Środkowej i Wschodniej*, Wydawnictwo Sejmowe, Warszawa 2003.
Gutowski M., Kardas P., *Sądowa kontrola konstytucyjności prawa. Kilka uwag o kompetencjach sądów powszechnych do bezpośredniego stosowania Konstytucji*, "Palestra" 2016, vol. 4, pp. 6–30.
Gutowski M., Kardas P., *Wykładnia i stosowanie prawa w procesie opartym na Konstytucji*, C.H. Beck, Warszawa 2017.
Jastrzębski R., *Konstytucyjność aktów ustawodawczych w judykaturze II Rzeczypospolitej*, "Przegląd Sejmowy" 2010, vol. 2, pp. 75–97.
Jastrzębski R., *Sądownictwo konstytucyjne w państwie polskim w XX wieku*, "Zeszyty Prawnicze Biura Analiz Sejmowych" 2021, vol. 2, pp. 50–81.
Komarnicki W., *Polskie prawo polityczne*, Wydawnictwo Sejmowe, Warszawa 2008 (reprinted issue of 1922).
Łętowska E., *Aktualność sporu o zdekoncentrowaną kontrolę konstytucyjności w Polsce – Uwagi na tle art. 10 Konstytucji*, (in:) M. Zubik (ed.), *Minikomentarz dla maksiprofesora. Księga jubileuszowa profesora Leszka Garlickiego*, Wydawnictwo Sejmowe, Warszawa 2017.
Małecki M., Pach M., *Stan wyższej konieczności konstytucyjnej*, "Państwo i Prawo" 2018, vol. 7, pp. 38–57.
Mączyński A., *Bezpośrednie stosowanie konstytucji przez sądy*, "Państwo i Prawo" 2000, vol. 5, pp. 3–14.
Mikuli P., *Doktryna konieczności jako uzasadnienie dla rozproszonej kontroli konstytucyjności ustaw w Polsce*, "Gdańskie Studia Prawnicze" 2018, vol. 40, pp. 635–648.
Mikuli P., *Zdekoncentrowana sądowa kontrola konstytucyjności prawa. Stany Zjednoczone i państwa europejskie*, Wydawnictwo Uniwersytetu Jagiellońskiego, Kraków 2007.
Radziewicz P., *Judicial Change to the Law-in-Action of Constitutional Review of Statutes in Poland*, "Utrecht Law Review" 2022, vol. 1 (18), pp. 29–44.
Radziewicz P., *O niedostatkach teorii stanu wyższej konieczności konstytucyjnej*, "Państwo i Prawo" 2018, vol. 11, pp. 114–126.
Radziewicz P., *"Wyjątkowe okoliczności" jako podstawa zmiany wykładni konstytucji*, (in:) M. Granat (ed.), *Sądownictwo konstytucyjne. Teoria i praktyka*, vol. III, Wydawnictwo Naukowe UKSW, Warszawa 2020.
Radziewicz P., Tuleja P. (eds.), *Konstytucyjny spór o granice zmian organizacji i zasad działania Trybunału Konstytucyjnego czerwiec 2015 – Marzec 2016*, Wolters Kluwer Polska, Warszawa 2017.
Rozmaryn S., *Kontrola konstytucyjności ustaw*, "Państwo i Prawo" 1948, vol. 12, pp. 3–21.
Rytel-Warzocha A., *Jak nie Trybunał Konstytucyjny to co? O rozproszonej kontroli konstytucyjności prawa w Polsce*, "Przegląd Prawa Konstytucyjnego" 2022, vol. 3, pp. 25–37.
Sadurski W., *Poland's Constitutional Breakdown*, Oxford University Press, Oxford 2019.
Safjan M., *Trybunał Konstytucyjny po trzydziestu latach, Doświadczenie i przyszłość*, "Przegląd Konstytucyjny" 2017, vol. 1.
Safjan M., *Uwagi wprowadzające*, (in:) M. Safjan, L. Bosek (eds.), *Konstytucja RP. Tom I, Komentarz. Art. 1-86*, C.H. Beck, Warszawa 2016.
Sanetra W., *Bezpośrednie stosowanie Konstytucji RP przez Sąd Najwyższy*, "Przegląd Sądowy" 2017, vol. 2, pp. 5–29.

Sanetra W., *Sąd Najwyższy w systemie wymiaru sprawiedliwości*, "Przegląd Sądowy" 1999, vol. 7–8, pp. 3–15.
Starzewski M., *Środki zabezpieczenia prawnego konstytucyjności ustaw*, Wydawnictwo Sejmowe, Warszawa 2009 (reprinted issue of 1928).
Tuleja P., *Stosowanie Konstytucji RP w świetle zasady jej nadrzędności (wybrane problemy)*, Zakamycze, Kraków 2003.
Wiącek M., *Constitutional Crisis in Poland 2015–2016 in the Light of the Rule of Law Principle*, (in:) A. von Bogdandy et al. (eds.), *Defending Checks and Balances in EU Member States Taking Stock of Europe's Actions*, Springer, Berlin 2021.
Witkowski Z., *Zagadnienie zgodności aktów Sejmu z Konstytucją PRL w świetle doktryny*, "Ruch Prawniczy, Ekonomiczny i Socjologiczny" 1981, vol. 1, pp. 37–49.
Wronkowska S., *Kilka uwag porządkujących dyskusję o tzw. rozproszonej kontroli konstytucyjności*, (in:) M. Granat (ed.), *Sądownictwo konstytucyjne. Teoria i praktyka*, vol. II, Warszawa 2019.

5 Admissibility of judicial review in states with a centralised model of constitutional review – in search of effective means of constitutional protection

Aleksandra Syryt

5.1 Introduction[1]

Law is an autonomous study subject. At the same time, it can be analysed in several planes, among which the normative, empirical, historical and axiological levels are of significant importance.[2] The starting point for studies on law, including those concerning dogmatic issues, is a reference to theoretical constructions. This is because they constitute a point of reference for the understanding of the adopted normative solutions, as well as the interpretations made and the decisions taken during the application of law. It is no different in the case of the analysis of the institutions in the field of constitutional law, including those relating to ensuring hierarchical compliance of the law as well as the legal and factual position of the constitutional courts. The above justifies getting to know the theoretical constructions and concepts that have been the reference point for creating system solutions. Research may facilitate the answer to whether the constitutional institutions applicable in each legal order may coexist with other institutions that result from other theoretical or doctrinal concepts. If so, what are the consequences thereof.

Political, social and economic changes, the internationalisation of the national law and the constitutionalisation of the international law mean that the tasks and competencies of the political institutions, as classically defined in constitutions, can adequately respond to the challenges of the present. This means that in order to effectively fulfil the roles entrusted to them, they have

1 This paper has been prepared as a result of the research project no. 2018/31/B/HS5/02667, financed by the National Science Centre (Poland) within the OPUS-15 funding scheme.

2 A. Kotowski, *Pojęcie zjawiska prawnego i płaszczyzny badania prawa*, (in:) A. Kotowski (ed.), *Wybrane zagadnienia teorii i filozofii prawa*, Warszawa 2021, pp. 33–34; see also J.A. Murley, *The Constitutionalism of George Anastaplo*, "The Political Science Reviewer" 1997, vol. 26, pp. 36–89.

DOI: 10.4324/9781003355793-6

to look for other formulas of action. This may result in a need to ask whether any changes in the manner of the state bodies' activities and the importance of the political institutions are consistent with the guiding principles.

Therefore, the subject of the study will be an attempt to answer the general question whether, in the states based on a centralised model of constitutional review, the judicial review by courts that formally do not have the status of constitutional courts is permissible. If the answer is yes, it is necessary to establish the legal grounds and consequences. The study will discuss whether the use of the judicial review may be justified in the case of the constitutional court malfunctioning. It is necessary to indicate the legal basis for this activity. The answer to the question requires an indication of the concepts of which the institution of constitutional review of law is a consequence. It is necessary to explain the possible models of control.

5.2 Constitutionalism and the concept of the constitutionality of law

Understanding the methods of verifying the hierarchical compatibility of law requires clarifying the concept of 'the constitutionality of law'. This issue is related both to the concept of law and to the principles determining the role of law to regulate human behaviour.

Legal positivism, which shaped contemporary thinking about law, closely combined the concept of law with written acts, primarily with normative acts. Although such an approach to the law is currently being abandoned in favour of non-positivist concepts, the constructions developed by legal positivism are and will be used in addition to the modern approach to the law, as long as sovereign public authorities will create the law.

When considering the issue of control over the constitutionality of law, it should be borne in mind that the term 'constitutionality of law' implies a specific relationship between legal norms. This relation takes a hierarchical form, which presupposes a specific place of particular norms in the system of sources of law. This relationship is the essence of the principle of constitutionalism.

There is no single definition of constitutionalism. However, it is undeniable that the idea of constitutionalism is connected with the 18th-century aspirations to limit absolute power and to subordinate political power to law, thus creating the rule of law. The rules related to this were to be formulated in written constitutions defining the ultimate framework for the operation of public authorities, including in the sphere of human affairs.[3] The principle of

3 M. Rosenfeld considered that constitutionalism appears in connection with a certain structure and social order, and it takes shape as a specific conception of the state system. At the same time, he stressed the relation of constitutionalism with the emergence of modern constitutions (M. Rosenfeld, *Constitutionalism, Identity, Difference and Legitimacy*, London 1994, pp. 3–5).

the separation and balance of power became the formula for providing such a framework.[4]

The idea of constitutionalism boils down to the postulate that the exercise of state power should be subject to the principles and rules determining the procedure of implementing legislative and executive acts and outlining their acceptable content.[5]

Constitutionalism relates to legality. Therefore it concerns public authorities' obligation to act on the basis and within the limits of the law. However, there is more to this idea than merely formally ensuring compliance with the law. Constitutionalism should also be combined with axiology. It should ensure that the law is compatible with the values on which the state is founded. In this way, the idea allows for formulating the principle that authorities should be controlled in order to create guarantees for the protection of the values for which they were established.[6]

The above indicates a close relationship between constitutionalism and the rule of law. This means that when considering the issue of constitutionality (constitutionality), which is an element of constitutionalism,[7] one should consider both legality and the implementation of the values on which the state is based.

In American constitutional law, constitutionalism is understood as a doctrine limiting government power, i.e., safeguards against arbitrariness. This limitation results from transparent and enforceable rules of political organisation and conduct expressed in the fundamental law.[8]

The indicated approach corresponds to the concept of constitutionalism as a principle of law, meaning that the constitution is the legal basis of the order in the state and has the highest binding force for all entities of state power.[9]

4 See more on the meaning and development of 'constitutionalism' (in:) Th.I. Cook, Ch.H. McIlwain, *Constitutionalism, Ancient and Modern*, Cornell University Press, Ithaca, NY 1947), p. 598.

5 S.A. de Smith, *The new Commonwealth and its Constitutions*, 1964, p. 106; W. Sokolewicz, *Demokracja, rządy prawa i konstytucyjność w postsocjalistycznym społeczeństwie Europy Wschodniej*, (in:) M. Domagała (ed.), *Zagadnienia prawa konstytucyjnego. Księga pamiątkowa ku czci Profesora Tadeusza Szymczaka*, Łódź 1994, pp. 32–33.

6 See more: M. La Torre, *Constitutionalism and Reasoning, A New Paradigm of Concept of Law*, Springer, Dordrecht 2007, p. 4.

7 A. Pułło noted that, from a lexical point of view, the term 'constitutionality' should remain reserved for a situation in which something is constitutional and therefore 'constitutional'. (A. Pułło, *Idea konstytucjonalizmu w systemie zasad prawa konstytucyjnego*, "Przegląd Sejmowy" 1996, no. 5, p. 15).

8 See: E.C. Smith, A.J.Zurcher, *Dictionary of American Politics*, New York 1968, p. 93; M. Richter, *The Political Theory of Montesquieu*, Cambridge 1977, p. 88; J. Sundberg, *Human Rights and the United States Constitution*, (in:) J. Justyński (ed.) *Konstytucja Stanów Zjednoczonych Ameryki w perspektywie nauk historycznych i prawnych*, Toruń 1988, p. 89.

9 M. Wyrzykowski, *Legislacja – demokratyczne państwo prawa – radykalne reformy polityczne i gospodarcze*, (in.) H. Suchocka (ed.), *Tworzenie prawa w demokratycznym państwie prawnym*, Warszawa 1992, p. 47; A. Jamróz, *Demokracja współczesna. Wprowadzenie*, Białystok 1993, pp. 84–85, 152.

Constitutional traditions do not agree on what should be understood by an arbitrary act and how to protect against arbitrariness (abuse of power). The classic neo-Republican tradition of political constitutionalism identifies arbitrariness with the dominance of those ruled by their rulers and tries to avoid it by establishing the condition of political equality. It is characterised by a balance of power between all relevant groups and parties within the system so that no one can rule without consulting the government. The liberal tradition equates arbitrariness with interference with individual rights and seeks to establish protection for them through the separation of powers and a judiciary that protects the constitution. Both traditions can be found in many constitutions. The first focuses on the design and functioning of democratic mechanisms, including those concerning electoral systems, the choice of the political system and the relationship between different segments of government. Although, here, too, procedural mechanisms are designed to create specific guarantees of protection against arbitrariness. The second tradition focuses primarily on the clarification and judicial protection of various competencies of the political system and constitutional rights by the constitutional court.[10] It is often necessary to ensure the integrity and fairness of procedures stemming from the Republican tradition.[11]

The assessment of the relationship between the traditions mentioned above is not uniform, which may be the reason for disputes when shaping the state system, as well as explaining the phenomena occurring in the existing political system.

Affirming the necessity of creating judicial protection of various powers of the political system and constitutional rights by the constitutional court also opens a discussion as to the importance of controlling the constitutionality of acts of public authority and the role of courts in this process. This is related to the question of whether entrusting to a given body – which, after all, belongs to the system of organs of public power and is obliged to obey the law – a control function (verifying fulfilling the requirements of constitutionalism) is not more prone to arbitrariness and the possibility of error in deciding on

10 The emergence of the first constitutions as a form of social contract led to the need to protect that contract and control its observance by public authorities. The formation of the liberal conception of the state and law, in which the written constitution occupied the supreme place, led to the emergence of institutions guaranteeing the supreme place of the constitution in the system of sources of law. This has become the starting point for examining the constitutionality of legal acts (M. Starzewski, *Środki zabezpieczenia prawnego konstytucyjności ustaw*, Kraków 1928).

11 R. Bellamy, *Constitutionalism*, (in:) B. Badie, D. Berg-Schlosser, L. Morlino (eds.), *International Encyclopedia of Political Science*, Rome 2012, IPSA/Sage: http://ssrn.com/abstract =1676321 (15.02.2022).

constitutionality than democratic procedures.[12] This is a question about the meaning of political constitutionalism, which has evolved from a mixed power model to representative democracy and legal constitutionalism initiated by the separation of powers and developed into legal protection and judicial review of public power activities. The constitution is meant to be a safeguard against the arbitrariness of power, and the constitution, in normative terms, is meant to correct the constitution in a political sense and therefore concerning the functioning of the state system and its bodies.

In the latter case, the principle of the supremacy of the constitution plays an important role, the consequence of which is the prohibition on issuing acts contrary to this act and the obligation to reconcile acts of the lower order with acts occupying a directly higher place and with constitutional norms. The supremacy of the constitution implies an order to implement constitutional provisions. It manifests itself in the issuing of normative acts developing general constitutional norms. Failure to comply with this order may involve the constitutional responsibility of state bodies.[13] Given such an approach, an essential element of contemporary constitutionalism has become the separation of the control system over the law's constitutionality of a jurisdictional nature.

The constitutionality of normative acts is primarily related to the structure of the legal system of a given state. Control of hierarchical compliance with the law refers to the shape of the system of sources of law. The issue of examining the constitutionality of legal acts covers various situations. First of all, this audit concerns the issue of compliance of norms within the entire hierarchy of legal sources.[14]

Compliance of law with the constitution (constitutionality of law) is a feature of the legal system. If the state order is based on a hierarchical structure of the system of normative acts, and the constitution is the normative act with the highest legal force, it means that mechanisms guaranteeing this order must be created.[15] One such mechanism is examining the constitutionality of law, understood in such a way that it is the activity of bodies organised on the principles of independence and organisational separateness from the legislative and executive power, conducted following a formalised procedure consisting of the examination and binding determination of disputes and other

12 See, e.g., R. *Bellamy, Political Constitutionalism: A Republican Defence of the Constitutionality of Democracy*, Cambridge 2007; R. Hirschl, *Towards Juristocracy: The Origins and Consequences of the New Constitutionalism*, Cambridge MA, Harvard University Press 2004.

13 See: M. Wyrzykowski, *Zasada demokratycznego państwa prawnego*, (in:) W. Sokolewicz (ed.), *Zasady podstawowe polskiej konstytucji*, Warszawa 1998, pp. 70–72.

14 See: E. Zwierzchowski, *Europejskie modele scentralizowanej kontroli konstytucyjności aktów prawnych*, (in:) E. Zwierzchowski (ed.), *Prawo i kontrola jego zgodności z konstytucją*, Warszawa 1997, p. 82.

15 See: K. Działocha, *Uwaga nr 6 do art. 33a*, (in:) L. Garlicki (ed.), *Komentarz do Konstytucji Rzeczypospolitej Polskiej*, Warszawa 1995.

matters related to the application of the constitution, in particular, assessing the compliance with the constitution of legal norms and other actions undertaken by state bodies or on behalf of these bodies.[16] This approach assumes that democratic governments are more susceptible to abuses of the law and restrictions of human rights and freedoms due to achieving specific political objectives. In this context, separated from pressures, the court can more impartially and independently assess the implementation of the principle of constitutionalism in various respects. However, there is also a risk of arbitrariness. For although the law binds judges, because of their ability to interpret the applicable law and – in the case of the constitution – very general law, they can change certain specific standards bypassing the democratic mechanisms inherent in the legislative and constitutional powers.

The above-mentioned different approaches to constitutionalism will also impact how to understand the mechanisms protecting the constitution and enable the verification of the law's constitutionality. It is not only a question of whether judicial control is to be exercised or whether other mechanisms in this respect are also permissible. The review exercised by the courts alone may involve different models and processes. For this reason, one speaks of constitutional justice, which consists of the judicial application of the constitution and includes both the constitutional judiciary and the ordinary courts belonging to the justice system.[17] And it is the various dimensions of constitutional justice that will be the subject of further argument.

It should be emphasised that regardless of whether we are dealing with judicial review or constitutional review, it is an element of constitutional justice that – according to liberal conceptions of constitutionalism – best ensures the protection of the constitution. The choice of a particular model in this regard is linked to constitutional traditions and the fact that the country in question belongs to a particular legal culture.

5.3 Some remarks on the models of judicial review of constitutionality of law

The review of the constitutionality of law results from the principle of constitutionalism. It is a derivative of the unique legal power of the constitution expressed in its supremacy over other sources of law. It is not the purpose of this paper to elaborate on detailed issues related to the models of implementing constitutional justice. For the sake of completeness, however, the general

16 See: L. Garlicki, *Sądownictwo konstytucyjne w Europie Zachodniej*, Warszawa 1987, p. 5; L. Garlicki, *Sądowa ochrona konstytucyjności prawa we współczesnym państwie kapitalistycznym Trybunał Konstytucyjny*, (in:) M. Granat, R. Mojak, J. Sobczak (eds.), *Kontrola konstytucyjności prawa*, Lublin 1987, p. 37.

17 See: E.A.G. Campillay, *Constitution and Judicial Review: Comparative Analysis*, (in:) R. Arnold, J.I. Martínez-Estay (eds.), *Rule of Law and Judicial Control of Power. Part I*, Springer 2017, p. 6.

assumptions of the basic models of judicial control of constitutionality of law should be recalled, which will make it easier to determine to what extent the solutions of these models may coexist in one system of government.

It is widely acknowledged that the basic models of control of the constitutionality of the law by bodies possessing the attribute of independence are the model of deconcentrated review and the model of concentrated review.[18] In addition, mixed or hybrid models are increasingly discussed in the literature, which is a consequence of the analysis of the systemic practice of various states, which combine elements inherent in both basic reviews' models of the constitutionality of law.[19]

As far as the distributed control model is concerned, the idea of such judicial control and constitutional review has been implemented in the United States (*American model, dispersed model, decentralised model, deconcentrated*).[20] This model is based on the supremacy of the constitution, which is a common element with the continental model. Since the constitution is the supreme law of the land, all other acts must conform to it. The essence of applying the law implies the obligation of a court to refuse to apply a lower-order norm if it opposes a higher-order norm.[21] It means that the provisions of the constitution limit legislative power.[22]

The examination of the constitutionality of a legal act in the American system takes place on the occasion of the resolution of a specific case before any court. It consists in assessing whether a given norm that is to form the basis of a judicial decision complies with a higher-order norm or a constitution. The courts may carry out this control in all instances based on its specific

18 See, e.g., M. Cappelletti, *Judicial Review in the Contemporary World*, Indianapolis: Bobbs-Merril 1971; L. Garlicki, W. Zakrzewski, *La protection juridictionnelle de la constitution dans le monde contemporain*, "Annuaire International de Justice Constitutionnelle" 1985, vol. I, pp. 17–37; L. Favoreu, *Modele American et modele Europeen de la justice constitutionnelle*, "Annuaire International de Justice Constitutionnelle" 1988, vol. IV, pp. 51–66. However, there are opponents of such a division. It is disputed that there are significant differences between American *judicial review* and European *constitutional review* (por. A. von Brünneck, *Verfassungsgerichtsbarkeit in den westlichen Demokratien*, Baden-Baden 1992, p. 30); A.H.Y. Chen, *The Global Expansion of Constitutional Judicial Review: Some Historical and Comparative Perspectives*, https://papers.ssrn.com/sol3/papers.cfm?abstract_id=2210340 (25.01.2022).

19 See more: S.G. Calabresi (ed.), *The History and Growth of Judicial Review, Volume 1: The G-20 Common Law Countries and Israel*, Oxford 2021; S.G. Calabresi (ed.), *The History and Growth of Judicial Review, Volume 2: The G-20 Civil Law Countries*, Oxford 2021.

20 See: L. Garlicki, *Sądownictwo konstytucyjne...*, pp. 15 et seq. On this institution see also: E. Zwierzchowski, *Sądownictwo konstytucyjne*, "Temida" 1994 no. 2, p. 281 et seq.; A. Pułło, *Badanie konstytucyjności aktów prawnych przez sądy powszechne*, (in:) E. Zwierzchowski (ed.), *Prawo i kontrola jego zgodności z Konstytucją*, Warszawa 1997, pp. 63–64; P. Mikuli, *Zdekoncentrowana sądowa kontrola konstytucyjności prawa*, Kraków 2007; A.R. Brewer-Carías, *Judicial Review in Comparative Law*, Cambridge1989, pp. 127–182, 263–324.

21 See: Case *Marbury v. Madison*, 5 U.S. (1 Cranch) 137 (1803).

22 See: P. Mikuli, *Zdekoncentrowana sądowa...*, p. 115.

application in the case at hand. Only exceptionally may the court find that all or part of a normative act violates the Constitution in isolation from its concrete application. However, it happens that in similar situations, similar decisions are applied. In practice, this extends the effectiveness of the court's review.[23] Decisions in which the court has found an act unconstitutional or illegal do not cause it to be removed from the legal system. However, the binding nature of such a decision is broader due to the importance of the precedent in United States law.

The essence of the *judicial review* is that a model of judicial control of normative acts has been created, which has the feature of universality. It is deconcentrated, concrete and relative. The court's position expressed in the justification of the decision on the unconstitutionality of the act does not result in its repeal.[24] However, under certain conditions of creating law through precedents, a given norm will not be applied in subsequent similar cases.

The model of concentrated control (*constitutional review, continental model, Kelsen model, centralised model*) is based on the tradition of subordinating a judge to the law. In this model, there is a special jurisdictional body, separate from other courts, which is appointed to deal with constitutional issues.[25]

From the H. Kelsen theory of the basic norm, the supremacy of the constitution was deducted.[26] According to H. Kelsen, the absence of an institution for the control of constitutionality means that there is no guarantee for the legal system's protection. The centralised system of norm control had more substantial legitimacy than the decentralised system of *judicial review*.[27] H. Kelsen considered the Constitutional Court as a body of legislative power. He included the control of the law's constitutionality in the legislative sphere of state action.[28] He also indicated the sphere of advantage of this institution over the parliament. A distinction was made between the creation and annulment of a law.[29]

Thus, the continental model is characterised by a state body being singled out within its framework, whose competence was to examine legislative acts

23 Ibidem, p. 63.

24 See: Z. Czeszejko-Sochacki, *Sądowa kontrola konstytucyjności w prawie szwajcarskim*, "Przegląd Sejmowy" 1995, no. 4, p. 74, A. Pułło, *Badanie konstytucyjności*..., p. 66.

25 The prototype of the institution of the Constitutional Court was regulated by art. 140 of the Constitution of the Republic of Austria of 1 October 1920. This regulation was created under the influence of H. Kelsen's ideas; Z. Czeszejko-Sochacki, *System konstytucyjny w systemie ustrojowym Austrii*, (in:) J. Trzciński (ed.), *Sądy konstytucyjne w Europie. Tom I: Austria, Francja, Niemcy, Włochy*, Warszawa 1996, p. 11 et seq.

26 See: H. Kelsen, *Pure Theory of Law*, California Library Reprint Series Edition 1978, pp. 198–201.

27 See: M Granat, *Legitymacja sądu konstytucyjnego na gruncie czystej teorii prawa H. Kelsena*, "Przegląd Sejmowy" 1999, no. 4, p. 17.

28 See: P. Mikuli, *Zdekoncentrowana sądowa*..., p. 117.

29 See: M. Granat, *Legitymacja sądu konstytucyjnego*..., p. 16.

and resolve constitutional disputes.[30] The initiative to institute proceedings before such a body belongs to a strictly defined circle of subjects. The Court is to exercise an abstract control of norms, separate from specific cases of law application. The decisions of that body were not subject to an appeal. It means that its decisions are to be final.

The development of the concept of control over the constitutionality of positive law required certain conditions to be met. It was necessary to introduce control of an objective nature so that the law-making institutions were not the only ones that could verify their activities. In this way, the arbitrariness of control was rejected. This approach was intended to ensure the implementation of the principle of the separation of powers. Institutions examining the hierarchical legality of the law required a precise basis for scrutiny. It could be found in the written constitution. In addition, the development of control instruments required the consolidation of the principle of constitutional supremacy over other elements of the legal system.[31]

When comparing the continental model of control over the constitutionality of law with the model of a deconcentrated one, it should be pointed out that in the judicial review model, the problem of the constitutionality of the law is considered based on the specific factual situation in which the norm is to be applied. In the Kelsen model, this is a separate legal issue decided by a body specially appointed for this purpose. In the dispersed model, the powers of constitutional review are held by all courts, and in the concentrated model, control can only be carried out by the constitutional court. The control is concrete in the judicial review system (initiated in a particular case). In the continental system, it is primarily an abstract control (undertaken in isolation from a particular case).

Specific public authorities initiate abstract control of standards in the Kelsen model or other entities indicated in the constitution. In a dispersed model, it can only be initiated by the court or parties to the proceedings in a specific case.

Differences between the above models also concern the effects of control. Decisions of the constitutional court are universally binding and lead to the elimination of norms deemed unconstitutional from the legal system. In the case of decentralised control, an unconstitutional decision is relevant only in a given case.[32]

Regarding the consequences of control in the centralised system, it is assumed that the law's unconstitutionality occurs *ex nunc*. The decision is usually prospective, establishes a new legal status or initiates the process of

30 See: L. Garlicki, *Sądownictwo konstytucyjne*..., p. 21 et seq.; L. Favoreu, *Modele American*..., pp. 51–66; E. Zwierzchowski, *Europejskie modele*..., p. 74.

31 A. Hamilton pointed out that no unconstitutional legislative acts can be considered binding (A. Hamilton, J. Madison, J. Jay, L. Goldman, *The Federalist Papers*, (reprint) 2008, p. 467).

32 See: E. Zwierzchowski, *Europejskie modele*..., pp. 74–75.

cancelling unconstitutional law by the body that issued it.[33] This means that a rule declared unconstitutional is eliminated from the legal order. In the model of judicial review, judgments concerning the constitutionality of standards can be challenged in the court proceedings relevant to the main proceedings. At the same time, a final decision is primarily applicable to the parties to proceedings (*inter partes*).

The review of legal solutions concerning constitutional justice in various states allows one to state that the legislator usually adopts a specific model of control over the law's constitutionality. Still, it sometimes modifies it so that it incorporates elements of another model into the system. This allows the conclusion that the states that create the system of control of constitutionality of law use both elements of the judicial review model and the Kelsen model.

However, while if a particular course of action is provided for in the constitutional acts of a given state, the problem arises when it is not fully known whether elements of another model of review of constitutionality of law can be applied. This is particularly relevant when the model of constitutional review is based on a constitutional court and a centralised system.

5.4 Use of dispersed review of the constitutionality of law in countries with a centralised model of constitutional review – general remarks

The admissibility of dispersed control of the constitutionality of law in a state having a constitutional court has become the subject of academic discourse and public debate in recent years and has been reflected in practice.[34]

The continental (*centralised*) model, in a specific context, shares the American concept of the constitution as an act of supreme legal force. This has led some authors to question the need to distinguish models of control systems of law's constitutionality. However, there is a fundamental difference between American law and the law of continental legal culture based on legal positivism. The constructs developed in the past concerning the sovereignty of law and the rule of law, as well as the principle of the separation of powers, which also bind courts and judges in adjudication, means that, in principle, these judges cannot refuse to apply the law. This is the case in Anglo-Saxon law, and this is how constitutional systems are built, with a model of centralised control of the constitutionality of law.

33 See: A. M. Ludwikowska, *Sądownictwo konstytucyjne w Europie środkowo-wschodniej*, Toruń 2002, pp. 14–15.

34 In Poland, this issue was related to changes in the law, including the Constitutional Tribunal legislation, since 2015 (see instead of many: P. Kardas, *Rozproszona kontrola konstytucyjności prawa w orzecznictwie Izby Karnej Sądu Najwyższego oraz sądów powszechnych jako wyraz konstytucyjnego posłuszeństwa*, "Czasopismo Prawa Karnego i Nauk Penalnych" 2019, no. 4 and the literature cited therein).

Currently, the literature indicates that this model can be divided into a traditional (Austrian, Kelsen) and a contemporary European model.[35] The first assumes the establishment of a particular constitutional court – not belonging to the judicial system – to protect against the legislature. The purpose of this court is to interpret and apply the constitution. The decision of such a court takes precedence over the law and is universally binding. For this reason, the constitutional court is sometimes assigned the role of a negative legislator. It should be noted that this model was modified in practice, and the constitutional court was given other competencies.

The contemporary European model of control of the constitutionality of law is concerned is based on the Kelsenian concept. Still, in each country, it adopts features characteristic of that state.[36] However, it is distinguished by the following common elements: (1) the existence of a special court with the exclusive right to adjudicate and derogate from the legal system of normative acts incompatible with the constitution; (2) ordinary judges and ordinary courts must apply the constitution, but may not refuse to apply a law contrary to the constitution unless the constitution itself allows such action;[37] (3) in some cases, the constitutional court has jurisdiction to adjudicate on constitutional complaints on violation of fundamental rights.[38]

In a classical approach, it is assumed that where a constitutional court exists in a state as part of a centralised model of control of the constitutionality of law, it has, in principle, the exclusive right to adjudicate the constitutionality of the law, unless the legislator considers otherwise.[39] At the same time, each state's case should be analysed separately, considering all legal solutions, including the principles and values on which the constitution is based. Actions may not be assumed that cause public authorities to act beyond their powers, thus in excess of the principle of legalism (i.e., illegally, against the rule

35 See, e.g., E.A.G. Campillay, *Constitution...*, p. 9.

36 See, e.g., the overview of solutions in selected European countries by E.A.G. Campillay, *Constitution...*, pp. 11–22.

37 E.g., art. 204 of the Portuguese Constitution of 1976 states 'In matters that are submitted for judgement the courts may not apply norms that contravene the provisions of the Constitution, or the principles enshrined therein'. In the Polish Constitution of 1997 art. 178(1) we can read 'Judges, within the exercise of their office, shall be independent and subject only to the Constitution and statutes'. It means that during the adjudication, they cannot refuse to apply the provisions of the Act (see on this subject review of the state of literature: P. Mikuli, *Doktryna konieczności jako uzasadnienie dla rozproszonej kontroli konstytucyjności ustaw w Polsce*, "Gdańskie Studia Prawnicze" 2018, vol. XL, p. 636 et seq. (text available at: http://www.tribunalconstitucional.pt/tc/conteudo/files/constituicaoingles.pdf; 15.01.2022)).

38 In this case, the approach to the constitutional complaint may also be narrow (as, e.g., in Polish law, art. 79 of the Polish Constitution) or broad (e.g., in Germany or Spain). In the latter case, the constitutional court exercises its power by deciding in individual cases, i.e., as an ordinary court does.

39 See, e.g., R. Hauser, J. Trzciński, *O formach kontroli konstytucyjności prawa przez sądy*, "Ruch Prawniczy, Ekonomiczny i Socjologiczny" 2008, no. 2 and the literature indicated therein.

of law). The reference point for the permissible limits of the operation of a public authority, and hence the use of dispersed control tools in a state with a centralised model of the constitutionality of the law, must always be the law, if constitutional justice itself is to ensure implementing of the rule of law.

If a given legal system is based on a particular system of organs of public authority to which the constitution has granted specific competencies, these competencies may not be granted by way of an expansive interpretation; in particular, particular organs may not consider themselves competent to perform actions that have not been entrusted to them by legal provisions.

In a given case, it is not possible to carry out a dispersed control of the constitutionality of the law. As rightly stated in the literature, the dispersed control of constitutionality of law (i.e., in simpler terms: control according to the American model) may not be identified with either direct application of the constitution or how the constitution is interpreted. It is a court decision, the element of which is the refusal to apply the applicable law as the basis for a judgment in a specific case. This refusal is the result of a self-assessment by the court of the hierarchical constitutionality of the act, regardless of whether the court applies directly the constitution or other legal norms in place of the omitted act and irrespective of the nature of the effect of this action on the legal system and participants in legal transactions. This action is carried out in jurisprudence and, therefore, on behalf of the state. It constitutes a refusal to apply an act established within the scope of specific competencies by the competent state authority.[40]

H. Kelsen has already pointed out that judicial review is not adapted to the realities of the legal systems of continental European countries, which are related to differences in legal culture, the design of sources of law and a different understanding of the constitutional principles, including the principle of the division and balance of powers.[41]

This approach is also confirmed by other authors, who point out that the court, refusing to apply the law and basing its decision directly on the constitution, usurps the competence reserved exclusively for the legislator.[42]

The question arises, therefore, whether the above-indicated state of affairs, i.e., relative separation of the centralised and dispersed control model, should be maintained in the situation of systemic crises when the actual significance of the body appointed to control the constitutionality of law changes. While there is a fundamental consensus that in everyday situations, public authorities should act within the scope of the competencies granted to them, in the

40 See: P. Radziewicz, *Kryzys konstytucyjny i paradygmatyczna zmiana konstytucji*, "Państwo i Prawo" 2020, no. 10, p. 9; S. Wronkowska, *Kilka uwag porządkujących dyskusję o tzw. rozproszonej kontroli konstytucyjności*, (in:) M. Granat (ed.), *Sądownictwo konstytucyjne. Teoria i praktyka, t. II*, Warszawa 2019, p. 238.

41 See: H. Kelsen, *Istota i rozwój sądownictwa konstytucyjnego*, trans. B. Banaszkiewicz, Warszawa 2009, p. 33 et seq.

42 See: P. Tuleja, *Stosowanie konstytucji w świetle jej nadrzędności*, Kraków 2003, pp. 382–383.

literature, concepts of changing the functioning of authorities in crises are proposed. Some state bodies, including courts, are recycling these concepts.[43] As justification for the use of dispersed control, even though it is not allowed in the given legal system, the arguments of constitutional obedience of judges,[44] the doctrine of necessity,[45] obvious unconstitutionality or exceptional circumstances are raised, among others.

In addition, attention is drawn to the possibility, and in some systems even the obligation, of directly applying the constitution, which is sometimes mistakenly identified with dispersed control. The Polish literature indicates that the provisions of the constitution:

1) may be applied on their own, insofar as the relevant norms of conduct can be extracted from them,
2) may be co-applied with other normative acts, especially in interpreting the law according to the Constitution, which is a consequence of the principle of constitutionalism. In this case, through systemic interpretation, it is possible to find such a meaning of the content of the sub-constitutional legal norms that will be best harmonised with the content of the Constitution,
3) may lead to the identification of a conflict with other norms, which is connected with the necessity to activate the procedures associated with the control of constitutionality of the law, depending on a given political system.[46]

However, it should be emphasised that the conditions for the direct application of the constitution have their limits set by law, including the constitution itself. Similarly, in the case of interpretation in compliance with the constitution, which should not lead to the situation that the norms interpreted as a result will be contrary not only to the legislator's intention; but, above all, they will violate constitutional principles and values, including those concerning the formation of public authorities in the state.

The above means that even in extraordinary situations, one should not deviate from the general rules of public administration unless such a deviation is expressly provided for by law, i.e., the constitution. Instead, the tools available should be used in this case, including those concerning the interpretation and application of the law. Otherwise, the state of uncertainty regarding the legal status and available instruments of action of public authorities may turn out to be as dangerous as the phenomena in connection with which the application of general rules is refused.

43 See, e.g., case law examples provided by P. Kardas, *Rozproszona kontrola...*, pp. 31–41.
44 Ibidem.
45 Ibidem.
46 L. Garlicki, *Bezpośrednie stosowanie Konstytucji*, (in:) *Konstytucja RP w praktyce*, Warszawa 1999, p. 21 et seq.

5.5 Conclusion

The control of constitutionality of law is a consequence of the requirement stemming from the principle of constitutionalism, which consists in the necessity to create in the state the mechanisms for protecting the constitution and ensuring the compliance of normative acts with the act of supreme legal force in the state. Currently, among the various traditions referring to constitutionalism, the predominant ones are those that refer to the liberal traditions and to the understanding of constitutionalism in the legal sense.

The consequence of this is to emphasise the importance of judicial mechanisms for reviewing the law's constitutionality, including, above all, the review carried out by constitutional courts. This type of control seems to be considered the best protection against the arbitrariness of public authorities' actions. This is to be guaranteed by impartial bodies independent of the executive and legislative powers. While appreciating this approach, it should be borne in mind that entrusting constitutional courts or ordinary courts with the competence to review the law's constitutionality does not always provide a guarantee that these bodies will adequately fulfil their tasks. Endowing courts with broad competencies, including the possibility to interpret the constitution (i.e., an act of great generality), may also lead to arbitrary rulings and construction of new standards bypassing the constitutional and legislative powers, and thus bypassing democratic mechanisms. This, in turn, can lead to an imbalance of power and be dangerous from the point of view of the rule of law. For this reason, a proper legal culture is essential, which must be shaped through appropriate legal education and the formation of the basis for respect for the law. In this way, cadres are raised who will know how to realise the common good by ensuring the law's constitutionality by balancing constitutional principles and values.

Despite the existence of various models of judicial review of the constitutionality of the law, one universal method of protecting the constitution is not apparent. Admittedly, through the establishment or absence of a separate constitutional court, individual constitutions indicate preferences and determine the manner of ensuring constitutionality. Often, however, states construct their system of constitutional review of the law using the solutions of the continental model and the American model. In such a situation, there is no doubt that they can adopt such constructions within the framework of their sovereignty.

This means that a dispersed review of the law's constitutionality under the Kelsen model would be permissible if the constitution provided for it.

However, it should be recognised that even in the face of crises, if the law does not provide for specific legal constructions and competencies for public authorities (e.g., to assess the constitutionality of the law), these competencies should not be created through an expansive interpretation or be presumed. Instead, one should make use of the available solutions and, at the same time, try to find solutions related to the crisis through dialogue and cooperation.

Suppose a country is in crisis, and this crisis has an additional systemic dimension and concerns the provision of guarantees of constitutionality. In that case, the crisis cannot be deepened by using solutions that are not based on the constitution. The use of given solutions outside the limits of the law or without a legal basis is also an arbitrary action and, therefore, infringing the principles for the assurance of which the institutions of constitutional review of the law were established. In the search for optimal means of ensuring the implementation of the principle of constitutionalism, measures that would constitute a negation of that principle may not be used. The framework concerning both the design and application of specific forms of constitutional protection must consider the constitutional principles and values specific to individual states and grounded precisely in the constitution.

References

Bellamy R., *Constitutionalism*, (in:) B. Badie, D. Berg-Schlosser, L. Morlino (eds.), International Encyclopedia of Political Science, Rome 2012, IPSA/Sage: http://ssrn.com/abstract=1676321; 15.02.2022.

Bellamy R., *Political Constitutionalism: A Republican Defence of the Constitutionality of Democracy*, Cambridge University Press, Cambridge 2007.

Brewer-Carías A.R., *Judicial Review in Comparative Law*, Cambridge University Press, Cambridge 1989, pp. 127–182, 263–324.

Calabresi S.G. (ed.), *The History and Growth of Judicial Review, Volume 1: The G-20 Common Law Countries and Israel*, Oxford University Press, Oxford 2021a.

Calabresi S.G. (ed.), *The History and Growth of Judicial Review, Volume 2: The G-20 Civil Law Countries*, Oxford University Press, Oxford2021b.

Campillay E.A.G., *Constitution and Judicial Review: Comparative Analysis*, (in:) R. Arnold, J.I. Martínez-Estay (eds.), *Rule of Law and Judicial Control of Power. Part I*, Springer, New York 2017, pp. 3–27.

Cappelletti M., *Judicial Review in the Contemporary World*, Bobbs-Merril, Indianapolis 1971.

Chen A.H.Y., *The Global Expansion of Constitutional Judicial Review: Some Historical and Comparative Perspectives*, https://papers.ssrn.com/sol3/papers.cfm?abstract_id=2210340; 25.01.2022.

Cook Th.I., McIlwain Ch.H., *Constitutionalism, Ancient and Modern*, Cornell University Press, Ithaca, NY 1947.

Czeszejko-Sochacki Z., *Sądowa kontrola konstytucyjności w prawie szwajcarskim*, "Przegląd Sejmowy" 1995, vol. 4, pp. 69–96

Czeszejko-Sochacki Z., *System konstytucyjny w systemie ustrojowym Austrii*, (in:) J. Trzciński (ed.), *Sądy konstytucyjne w Europie. Tom I: Austria, Francja, Niemcy,* Włochy, Wydawnictwo Sejmowe, Warszawa 1996.

De Smith S.A., *The New Commonwealth and its Constitutions*, Stevens & Sons, London 1964.

Smith E.C., Zurcher A.J., *Dictionary of American Politics*, Barnes & Noble, New York 1968.

Działocha K., *Uwaga nr 6 do art. 33a*, (in:) L. Garlicki (ed.), Komentarz do Konstytucji Rzeczypospolitej Polskiej, Wydawnictwo Sejmowe, Warszawa 1995.

Favoreu L., *Modele American et modele Europeen de la justice constitutionnelle*, “Annuaire International de Justice Constitutionnelle” 1988, pp. 51–66.
Garlicki L., *Bezpośrednie stosowanie Konstytucji*, (in:) *Konstytucja RP w praktyce*, Wydawnictwo Sejmowe, Warszawa 1999.
Garlicki L., *Sądowa ochrona konstytucyjności prawa we współczesnym państwie kapitalistycznym: Trybunał Konstytucyjny*, (in:) M. Granat, R. Mojak, J. Sobczak (eds.), *Kontrola konstytucyjności prawa*, UMCS, Lublin 1987.
Garlicki L., *Sądownictwo konstytucyjne w Europie Zachodniej*, Państwowe Wydawnictwo Naukowe, Warszawa 1987.
Garlicki L., Zakrzewski W., *La protection juridictionnelle de la constitution dans le monde contemporain*, “Annuaire International de Justice Constitutionnelle” 1985, vol. I, pp. 17–37
Granat M., *Legitymacja sądu konstytucyjnego na gruncie czystej teorii prawa H. Kelsena*, “Przegląd Sejmowy” 1999, vol. 4, pp. 9–20
Hamilton A., Madison J., Jay J., Goldman L., *The Federalist Papers*, (reprint), Oxford World’s Classics, Oxford 2008.
Hauser R., Trzciński J., *O formach kontroli konstytucyjności prawa przez sądy*, “Ruch Prawniczy, Ekonomiczny i Socjologiczny” 2008, vol. 2, pp. 9–21.
Hirschl R., *Towards Juristocracy: The Origins and Consequences of the New Constitutionalism*, Harvard University Press, Cambridge2004.
Jamróz A., *Demokracja współczesna. Wprowadzenie*, Temida 2, Białystok 1993.
Kardas P., *Rozproszona kontrola konstytucyjności prawa w orzecznictwie Izby Karnej Sądu Najwyższego oraz sądów powszechnych jako wyraz konstytucyjnego posłuszeństwa*, “Czasopismo Prawa Karnego i Nauk Penalnych” 2019, vol. 4, 1–45
Kelsen H., *Istota i rozwój sądownictwa konstytucyjnego*, trans. B. Banaszkiewicz, Wydawnictwo TK, Warszawa 2009.
Kelsen H., *Pure Theory of Law*, California Library Reprint Series Edition 1978.
Kotowski A., *Pojęcie zjawiska prawnego i płaszczyzny badania prawa*, (in:) A. Kotowski (ed.), *Wybrane zagadnienia teorii i filozofii prawa*, Difin, Warszawa 2021.
La Torre M., *Constitutionalism and Reasoning, A New Paradigm of Concept of Law*, Springer, Dordrecht 2007.
Ludwikowska A.M., *Sądownictwo konstytucyjne w Europie środkowo-wschodniej*, Towarzystwo Naukowe Organizacji i Kierownictwa “Dom Organizatora”, Toruń 2002.
Mikuli P., *Doktryna konieczności jako uzasadnienie dla rozproszonej kontroli konstytucyjności ustaw w Polsce*, “Gdańskie Studia Prawnicze” 2018, vol. XL, pp. 635–648
Mikuli P., *Zdekoncentrowana sądowa kontrola konstytucyjności prawa*, Wydawnictwo Uniwersytetu Jagiellońskiego, Kraków 2007.
Pułło A., *Badanie konstytucyjności aktów prawnych przez sądy powszechne*, (in:) E. Zwierzchowski (ed.), *Prawo i kontrola jego zgodności z Konstytucją*, Wydawnictwo Sejmowe, Warszawa 1997.
Pułło A., *Idea konstytucjonalizmu w systemie zasad prawa konstytucyjnego*, “Przegląd Sejmowy” 1996, vol. 5, pp. 9–20
Radziewicz P., *Kryzys konstytucyjny i paradygmatyczna zmiana konstytucji*, “Państwo i Prawo” 2020, vol. 10, pp. 3–24
Richter M., *The Political Theory of Montesquieu*, Cambridge University Press, Cambridge – London – New York, - Melbourne 1977.

Rosenfeld M., *Constitutionalism, Identity, Difference and Legitimacy: Theoretical Perspective*, Duke University Press, London 1994.
Sokolewicz W., *Demokracja, rządy prawa i konstytucyjność w postsocjalistycznym społeczeństwie Europy Wschodniej*, (in:) M. Domagała (ed.), *Zagadnienia prawa konstytucyjnego. Księga pamiątkowa ku czci Profesora Tadeusza Szymczaka*, Wydawnictwo Uniwersytetu Łódzkiego, Łódź 1994.
Starzewski M., *Środki zabezpieczenia prawnego konstytucyjności ustaw*, Kraków 1928.
Sundberg J., *Human Rights and the United States Constitution*, (in:) J. Justyński (ed.), *Konstytucja Stanów Zjednoczonych Ameryki w perspektywie nauk historycznych i prawnych*, Towarzystwo Naukowe w Toruniu, Toruń 1988.
Tuleja P., *Stosowanie konstytucji w świetle jej nadrzędności*, Zakamycze, Kraków 2003.
Von Brünneck A., *Verfassungsgerichtsbarkeit in den westlichen Demokratien*, Nomos, Baden-Baden 1992.
Murley, J. A.,, *Our Charakter is Our Fate: The Constitutionalism of George Anastaplo*, "The Political Science Reviewer" 1997, vol. 26, pp. 36–89.
Wronkowska S., *Kilka uwag porządkujących dyskusję o tzw. rozproszonej kontroli konstytucyjności*, (in:) M. Granat (ed.), *Sądownictwo konstytucyjne. Teoria i praktyka, t. II*, Wydawnitwo Naukowe UKSW, Warszawa 2019.
Wyrzykowski M., *Legislacja – Demokratyczne państwo prawa – Radykalne reformy polityczne i gospodarcze*, (in:) H. Suchocka (ed.), *Tworzenie prawa w demokratycznym państwie prawnym*, Wydawnictwo Sejmowe, Warszawa 1992.
Wyrzykowski M., *Zasada demokratycznego państwa prawnego*, (in:) W. Sokolewicz (ed.), *Zasady podstawowe polskiej konstytucji*, Wydawnictwo Sejmowe, Warszawa 1998.
Zwierzchowski E., *Europejskie modele scentralizowanej kontroli konstytucyjności aktów prawnych*, (in:) E. Zwierzchowski (ed.), *Prawo i kontrola jego zgodności z konstytucją*, Wydawnictwo Sejmowe, Warszawa 1997.
Zwierzchowski E., *Sądownictwo konstytucyjne*, Temida2, Warszawa 1994.

6 Contemporary issues of parliamentary constitutional review in Poland[1]

Ewelina Gierach

6.1 Introduction

The Constitutional Tribunal is a symbol of political transformation, the rule of law and democracy. It is a metaphorical bridge between the post-communist bloc and the other European countries.[2] Yet it holds no monopoly on reviewing the constitutionality of laws. Although parliamentary constitutional review has never been expressly stipulated in the constitution, this form of review is the oldest in Poland, dating back to the interwar period.

Parliamentary constitutional review is understood as constitutional review performed by the Sejm and Senate *in pleno* or alternatively by their internal bodies or by the members of the parliament, as well as review performed at the request of specified entities by special bodies of the Sejm's or Senate's Chancellery, which takes place in the course of a pending legislative process as well as outside of it. If the above bodies find a reviewed draft to be unconstitutional, they can take specific actions or request that such actions be taken in order to eliminate the unconstitutionality (e.g., introduce relevant changes to the draft at further stages of the legislative process).

After the establishment of the Constitutional Tribunal, the issue of parliamentary constitutional review was rarely taken up in the subject literature. It was deemed relatively less significant than judicial constitutional review, as it is affected by a strong political slant and lack of objectivity, and associated with the doctrine of the socialist state.

Ever since the outbreak of the crisis concerning the composition of the Constitutional Tribunal in November 2015, the question of the forms of constitutional review alternative to that performed by the constitutional court has been a permanent subject of consideration by constitutionalists. Yet the debate

1 This paper has been prepared as a result of the research project no. 2018/31/B/HS5/02667, financed by the National Science Centre (Poland) within the OPUS-15 funding scheme.

2 See M. Granat, *Sądowa kontrola konstytucyjności prawa w państwach Europy Środkowej i Wschodniej*, Warszawa 2003, p. 6; M. Smolak, *Uzasadnienie sądowe jako argumentacja z moralności politycznej. O legitymizacji władzy sędziowskiej*, Kraków 2003, p. 203; B. Szmulik, *Sądownictwo konstytucyjne. Ochrona konstytucyjności prawa w Polsce*, Lublin 2001, p. 7.

DOI: 10.4324/9781003355793-7

focuses on the admissibility of the so-called dispersed constitutional review performed by common courts in the course of adjudication under current constitutional provisions.[3] Parliamentary constitutional review of normative acts remains outside the scope of scholarly interest.

The subject of the analysis carried out in the present study is parliamentary constitutional review and the parliamentary practice of constitutional review performed by the Sejm and Senate as chambers of the parliament, by their bodies and by their individual members. In light of the ongoing crisis around the Constitutional Tribunal, it is worth considering whether the current situation has affected parliamentary constitutional review and whether this form of review could efficiently support the abstract and centralised constitutional review performed by the Constitutional Tribunal.

6.2 Origins of parliamentary constitutional review in Poland

Taking as a model the political solutions of the Third French Republic, where the parliament was tasked with reviewing the compliance of legislation with the constitution, the Polish Constitution of 21 March 1921[4] ruled out the possibility of judicial constitutional review. On the one hand, it included the reservation in art. 38 that no law could conflict with 'or violate this Constitution'. On the other hand, it provided for no institution that would declare such non-compliance, and even contained an express prohibition of judicial review of legislation: 'Courts shall have no right to examine the validity of duly promulgated laws' (art. 81). Then, the April Constitution[5] likewise stipulated in art. 64(5) that '[c]ourts shall not be authorised to examine the validity of duly promulgated legislative acts'. The rationale behind this solution was said to be concerns about the use of judicial review of constitutionality to 'defend the democratic institutions of the March Constitution" as well as "awareness of the need to protect the President, who was accountable to "God and history", from the restrictive actions of the reviewing body'.[6]

Similarly, judicial constitutional review of legislation was deemed inadmissible after World War II, albeit this time for different reasons. While the rationale behind the solution before the war was the intention to adopt the institutions present in the Third Republic and the views of the classic French doctrine, the post-war reason was the need to implement the principle of the people's supreme authority. It was believed that 'in a political system where power lies in the hands of the working classes, there is neither need nor possibility to

3 Extensively on this subject: P. Chybalski, *The Problem of the So-Called Dispersed Judicial Review of Parliamentary Acts in Poland – Traditions and Current Perspectives.*

4 Act of 17 March 1921 – Constitution of the Republic of Poland (*Journal of Laws of the Republic of Poland* No. 44, item 267).

5 Constitutional Act of 23 April 1935 (Journal of Laws No. 30, item 227).

6 J. Surowiec, *Ewolucja poglądów na instytucję sądowej kontroli konstytucyjności ustaw w Polsce Ludowej*, "Acta Universitatis Wratislaviensis" "Trybunał Konstytucyjny" 1987, no. 1037, p. 8.

establish institutions that would restrain the democratic, sovereign Assemblies, just as there is no room in such a system for monarchies or supreme chambers, which in their essence (albeit in other, less "legal" forms) serve parallel class functions to judicial constitutional review in capitalist countries'.[7] It was thought that in a socialist country, legislation was compliant with the constitution 'by nature' and the fact that the constitution was promulgated by way of a basic law of supreme legal force sufficed to ensure that all legislation was in fact constitutional.[8] Parliamentary review was said to be the fundamental form of constitutional review. 'The competences of the supreme representative body resulted from an express constitutional provision or from the entirety of the parliament's competences and its place in the structure of state bodies.'[9] It was pointed out that parliamentary review existed 'objectively', regardless of whether it was expressly stipulated in the constitution or whether a separate body authorised to review constitutionality existed.[10] Non-parliamentary review was believed to clash with the parliament's supreme position in the system of state authorities.[11] The only scholar who supported the introduction of judicial constitutional review in this period was J. Makowski.[12]

The Constitutional Act of 19 February 1947 on the system and scope of activity of the supreme bodies of the Republic of Poland (Journal of Laws No. 18, item 71, as amended) included the reservation in art. 24(3) that: 'Courts shall have no right to examine the validity of duly promulgated laws and decrees'. Moreover, the statute appointed no further non-parliamentary body that would be authorised to review the constitutionality of laws.

The 1952 Constitution did not regulate the matter of constitutional review of laws. While this silence of the constitution was regarded by S. Rozmaryn as tantamount to absolute inadmissibility of constitutional review, after October 1956, it was understood as at least allowing the review of laws. Indeed, after 1956, opinions emerged that admitted the possibility to appoint an institution that would review the constitutionality of laws by way of self-supervision, and that would be part of the supreme legislative body and be appointed by that body. Moreover, the establishment of such an institution as a body separate from the parliament was not ruled out during this period either.[13]

7 S. Rozmaryn, *Kontrola konstytucyjności ustaw*, "Państwo i Prawo" 1948, vol. 12, p. 13.

8 A. Gwiżdż, *Trybunał Konstytucyjny*, "Państwo i Prawo" 1983, vol. 12, p. 5; B. Szmulik, *Trybunał Konstytucyjny a transformacja ustrojowa Polski*, (in:) M. Żmigrodzki (ed.), *Kierunki ewolucji systemu politycznego Rzeczypospolitej Polskiej*, Lublin 1997, p. 43.

9 B. Szmulik, *Geneza kontroli konstytucyjności prawa*, (in:) M. Żmigrodzki, M. Chmaj (eds.), *Społeczeństwo, państwo, władza*, Lublin 1995, p. 146.

10 Cf. Z. Witkowski, *Rada Państwa jako organ czuwający nad zgodnością prawa z Konstytucją*, "Państwo i Prawo" 1977, vol. 7, p. 38.

11 Cf. ibidem.

12 See J. Makowski, *Materiały do projektu przyszłej konstytucji*, "Państwo i Prawo" 1947, vol. 11, p. 20.

13 M. Granat, *Droga do sądownictwa konstytucyjnego w państwach Europy Środkowej i Wschodniej*, "Państwo i Prawo" 2001, vol. 12, p. 16.

A symbolic beginning of a change in the approach to the issue of non-parliamentary constitutional review was the session of the Chairs of State Law in Kazimierz Dolny, which took place on 25 and 26 June 1961. After that session, voices began to emerge expressing the need for and desirability of a constitutional court. An event that was decisive in admitting the possibility of establishing a constitutional review body was the emergence of the concept of the rule of law. Characteristic of this notion was the belief that law is the supreme regulator of social relations and that the constitution is the basis of the system of law. By the same token, the rules of the constitution are the rules of a legal act, and not merely of a state act of political significance. Recognition of the rule of law entailed a tendency to strengthen the legal effectiveness of the constitution.[14] It was pointed out, however, that 'the institutional guarantees of the rule of law could not, under any circumstances, diminish the position of the supreme authority, or, worse still, conflict with that position'.[15]

The issue of constitutional review became the subject of further debate among scholars in the 1970s. They considered how to improve the system of guarantees of the rule of law and strengthen the review of the law's compliance with the constitution, while at the same time preserving the supreme position of the parliament. The desirability of creating a constitutional judiciary existing alongside and supporting the parliament's system of self-review was pointed out.[16] The first step towards strengthening self-review was the establishment of the Committee on Legislative Work by the Sejm on 29 March 1972.[17] This Committee was supposed to examine all bills considered by the Sejm from the point of view of their compliance with the principles of legislative drafting and with the system of law in force. Its establishment was seen as laying the formal foundations for a system of parliamentary review of the constitutionality of bills.[18] In 1976, supervision over the constitutionality of laws was entrusted to the Council of State.[19] This function was crystallised in the form of a resolution of the Council of State of 14 July 1979 on supervision over the compliance of laws with the constitution and the determination of the universally binding interpretation of laws (Official Journal of the Republic of Poland 'Monitor Polski' No. 19, item 113). As a result of the amendment, art. 30(1)(3) of the Constitution of the Polish People's Republic stipulated that the Council of State would ensure the compliance of the law with the

14 A. Gwiżdż, *Trybunał...*, p. 3; M. Granat, *Droga do sądownictwa...*, p. 17.

15 M. Granat, *Droga do sądownictwa...*, p. 18.

16 Cf. Z. Witkowski, *Rada Państwa...*, p. 39.

17 Art. 1(12) of the resolution of the Sejm of the Polish People's Republic of 29 March 1972 to amend the regulations of the Sejm of the Polish People's Republic (Official Journal of the Republic of Poland 'Monitor Polski' No. 21, item 127).

18 More in Z. Witkowski, *Rada Państwa...*, p. 40 and the publications cited therein.

19 Art. 1(12) of the Act of 10 February 1976 to amend the Constitution of the Polish People's Republic (Journal of Laws No. 5, item 29).

constitution.[20] Legal scholars emphasised the significance of this solution for the question of the admissibility of establishing institutional guarantees of the constitutionality of law in a socialist state. This form of the provision was thought to mean that the authors of the constitution rejected the thesis that the Sejm could not pass an unconstitutional act.[21] Taking into account the position of the Council of State in the political system and its subordination to the Sejm, some people maintained that acts of parliament were excluded from its supervision. It was argued that this body could only examine the drafts of such acts.[22] The majority, however, took the view that the constitutional term 'law' should be understood as the provisions of all binding normative acts.[23] Nonetheless, this stipulation was repealed in 1982, as it had proved to be dead in practice.[24]

The Constitutional Tribunal was established by the amendment to the Constitution of 26 March 1982.[25] Then, the Act of 29 April 1985 on the Constitutional Tribunal was passed.[26] The Tribunal began to operate on 1 January 1986. It was the result of a compromise, as political circles opposed the concept of a constitutional judiciary. The compromise resulted in the introduction of numerous restrictions on the Tribunal's competences and jurisdiction. In the first period of its operation, judgments declaring statutory provisions unconstitutional were not final but subject to examination by the Sejm, which was in a position to dismiss them with a two-thirds majority vote. By dismissing or approving the Tribunal's judgment, the Sejm acted as the 'supreme state authority', driven mainly by political rather than legal reasons. The need to keep the Tribunal, and even to further empower it, was evident after 1989. Still, it was agreed that its position in the legal and political system would be altered definitively with the entry into force of the new constitution.

20 Initially, the amendment concerned art. 25(1), which was supplemented with s. 2a. The change in the numbering of the provisions followed the promulgation of the uniform text of the 1952 Constitution in the form of an announcement of the Chair of the Council of State of 16 February 1976 promulgating the uniform text of the Constitution of the Polish People's Republic enacted by the Legislative Sejm on 22 July 1952 (Journal of Laws No. 7, item 36).

21 Cf. Z. Witkowski, *Rada Państwa*..., p. 41 and the publications cited therein.

22 Cf. K. Działocha, *Konstytucja PRL po nowelizacji z 10 II 1976 (Uwagi o zmianie koncepcji konstytucji)*, "Państwo i Prawo" 1977, vol. 2, p. 14; Z. Witkowski, *Rada Państwa*..., pp. 42–43.

23 See A. Burda, *Polskie prawo państwowe*, Warszawa 1978, p. 282; A.N. Wróblewski, *Kontrola konstytucyjności prawa w państwach socjalistycznych*, "Państwo i Prawo" 1978, vol. 10, p. 55; S. Gebert, *Czuwanie przez Radę Państwa nad zgodnością prawa z Konstytucją*, "Państwo i Prawo" 1980, vol. 1, pp. 28–29.

24 Art. 1(1) of the Act of 26 March 1982 to amend the Constitution of the Polish People's Republic (Journal of Laws No. 11, item 83).

25 Act of 26 March 1982 to amend the Constitution of the Polish People's Republic (Journal of Laws of the Polish People's Republic No. 11, item 83).

26 Act of 29 April 1985 on the Constitutional Tribunal (Journal of Laws of 1991, No. 109, item 470, as amended).

Even when the principle of the separation of powers was introduced under the Small Constitution of 1992, it did not result in introducing the finality and universally binding character of the Constitutional Tribunal's judgments regarding statutes. Moreover, the Sejm was not deprived of the competence to assess the constitutionality of bills and enacted laws. According to the Tribunal,

> The Sejm [...] has not only the right, but also the duty to assess whether the actions it takes as part of the law-making process conform to the Constitution. This duty results first and foremost from Article 3 of the Polish Constitution [the provision established the principle of the rule of law, now expressed in Article 7 of the Constitution – author's note]. The legislature abides by the Polish laws in its activity chiefly in that it abides by the Constitution and fulfils the fundamental duty following from its legal nature, which is the prohibition of enacting laws that are in conflict with the Constitution. The constitutional review of the Sejm's own actions in the law-making process prior to the final enactment of a law by the Sejm is one of the means that enable the fulfilment of this duty. [...] Establishing the institution of the Constitutional Tribunal – according to the general opinion of the jurisprudence – has not released the law-making bodies, and the Sejm in particular, from the duty to review the constitutionality of the law it makes. The existence of this duty of review on the part of the Sejm is further evidenced by the provisions of its own Standing Orders, under which the Presidium of the Sejm is obliged to refer draft laws or resolutions whose lawfulness is subject to doubt to the Legislation Committee for opinion (Article 31(6)). It ought to be added that currently, the review of 'lawfulness' should cover, besides the Constitution, also international treaties ratified upon prior consent granted by statute (cf. Article 91(2) of the Constitution), and in the future perhaps also – as pointed out by L. Garlicki – 'secondary' EU legislation (cf. Article 91(3) of the Constitution.[27]

6.3 Forms of parliamentary constitutional review

Based on the provisions of the 1997 Constitution, parliamentary constitutional review has no express legal basis. However, the principle of the supremacy of the constitution gives rise to the duty of state authorities with regard to all their competences to act in conformity with the constitution and to eliminate all unconstitutional acts from the legal regime.[28] Consequently, the chambers of the parliament are obliged to both comply with the rules enshrined

27 Judgment of the Constitutional Tribunal of 23 November 1993, ref. no. K 5/93, OTK ZU 1993, item. 39.

28 Cf. E. Zwierzchowski, *Sądownictwo konstytucyjne*, Białystok 1994, p. 20.

in the constitution and create conditions in which these rules can be fully implemented.

A characteristic feature of parliamentary constitutional review is its dispersion within the structure of the legislative process. An allegation of unconstitutionality does not, as a rule, trigger a special procedure to examine the compatibility of a draft with the Basic Law. Constitutional review is namely performed in the same mode in which the remaining reservations – both legal and political – about a draft are resolved. A draft is found unconstitutional by way of voting, usually after an in-depth discussion supported with legal expert opinions. More often than not, however, this decision does not take the form of an act declaring the unconstitutionality of a proposed regulation. It is rather a decision on the subject matter: it refers to the content of the draft in that specific legal solutions are approved or rejected. The sole exception is the proceedings of preliminary draft review before the Legislation Committee.[29]

Neither the Sejm nor the Senate includes any body or organisational unit that would be permanently and exclusively dedicated to analysing the constitutionality of all drafts under consideration by the chambers or of all passed acts. This does not mean, however, that the members of the parliament, as well as the chambers *in pleno* and their internal bodies, have no instruments to verify compliance with the constitution. Legal provisions specify that the Sejm's internal bodies particularly obliged to ensure the lawfulness, and thus constitutionality, of bills are the Speaker of the Sejm, the Presidium of the Sejm and the Legislation Committee. Another institution, apart from Sejm bodies, that can give its opinion on the constitutionality of draft laws is the Chancellery of the Sejm. It ought to be emphasised, however, that even if the provisions obligate certain institutions or bodies to review a bill's compatibility with the law, it does not mean that the remaining participants of the legislative process are free from the obligation to ensure the constitutionality of envisaged regulations. It is the duty of all entities involved in the process of enacting laws. That is why, when discussing constitutional guarantees, we cannot ignore the role of individual deputies, who can take action to perform an effective constitutional review of acts of the parliament both in the course of the law-making process and after the provisions have entered into force. The internal bodies of this type in the Senate, in turn, aside from the senators, are the Speaker of the Senate and the Legislation Committee.

An analysis of the provisions governing the legislative process leads to the conclusion that procedural guarantees of constitutionality can be divided into those provided for by law and those that have developed exclusively through

29 R. Piotrowski, *Parlamentarna kontrola konstytucyjności projektów aktów prawnych*, (in:) E. Zwierzchowski (ed.), *Prawo i kontrola jego zgodności z Konstytucją*, Warszawa 1997, p. 113; J. Ciemniewski, *Badanie zgodności ustaw z Konstytucją w procesie legislacyjnym*, "Przegląd Legislacyjny" 2004, no. 1, pp. 226–227; P. Radziewicz, *Pojęcie sejmowej kontroli legalności ustawy*, (in:) P. Radziewicz (ed.), *Kontrola legalności ustawy w Sejmie*, Warszawa 2015, p. 22.

parliamentary practice. Next, among the guarantees stipulated by the law, one can distinguish those that serve directly to protect constitutionality and those that, although they perform other functions in the legislative process, indirectly contribute to the reflection on the constitutionality of the proposed regulations. The latter procedural guarantees form the most numerous group.

Crucial for protecting the constitutionality of parliamentary bills is the initial stage of work in the Sejm, which takes place shortly after the draft is submitted for consideration by the Sejm. The significance of the review of bills at this stage of the procedure in the Sejm was emphasised by the Constitutional Tribunal itself, which found the phase essential from the perspective of verifying the lawfulness (constitutionality) of bills.[30] When a draft law is submitted for consideration by the Sejm, thus launching the legislative process, the Speaker of the Sejm is obliged to perform its preliminary review. The Speaker performs it even prior to assigning the bill a Sejm paper number and ordering it to be printed and delivered to the deputies. The review is performed with regard to two aspects – formal and substantive. The formal aspect concerns the duty to verify whether the bill meets the requirements set forth in the rules of procedure, especially in terms of the components of the explanatory memorandum (art. 34(7) of the Standing Orders of the Sejm). Then, the substantive analysis involves examining the content of the bill with regard to its substantive lawfulness.[31]

The analysis of the substantive aspect, based on art. 34(8) of the Standing Orders of the Sejm, is much more significant for the constitutional review of bills submitted for consideration by the Sejm. Pursuant to this provision, draft laws

> that are subject to concerns whether they are not in conflict with the law, including with EU law or fundamental rules of legal drafting, may be referred for opinion to the Legislation Committee by the Speaker of the Sejm after they have heard the opinion of the Presidium of the Sejm. The Committee may, by a majority of 3/5 of the votes in the presence of at least half the members of the Committee, declare the bill inadmissible. A bill that has been declared inadmissible may not be proceeded with by the Speaker of the Sejm.

It is emphasised here that 'conflict with the law' is a very broad concept and may refer to both unconstitutionality and systemic consistency, with the former being 'a review of constitutionality as a function of protecting the law from politics' and the latter being 'compliance with the principle of legality

30 Judgment of the Constitutional Tribunal of 23 March 2006, ref. no. K 4/06.

31 See K. Kubuj, *Marszałek Sejmu na straży jakości ustaw*, (in:) J. Wawrzyniak (ed.), *Tryb ustawodawczy a jakość prawa*, Warszawa 2005, p. 63.

and the principle of the rule of law'.[32] There are no legal grounds on which a draft law could be returned to its sponsor without complying with the procedure provided for in art. 34(8) of the Standing Orders of the Sejm if the Speaker perceives obvious unconstitutionality of the proposed solutions. In a situation where the Speaker of the Sejm has no doubts as to the lawfulness of the bill, i.e., where they are convinced that the bill is not contrary to the law, there is no need to initiate this procedure. There are divergent opinions in the subject literature regarding the constitutionality of art. 34(8) of the Standing Orders of the Sejm. However, it is not the Legislation Committee's competence to give an opinion on the constitutionality of bills itself, but the legal effect of the Committee's declaring the bill inadmissible that is controversial. This provision raises doubts as regards the extent to which it allows the Speaker of the Sejm not to proceed with a bill deemed inadmissible by the Legislation Committee.[33]

Apart from the aforementioned procedure of declaring a bill unconstitutional by the Legislation Committee as part of the preliminary review, the Standing Orders of the Sejm provide for no other specific procedures whose aim would be to assess the compliance of the submitted draft law with the Constitution. However, the problem of constitutionality of a bill is frequently raised in the course of further parliamentary work, both in debates in the forum of the Sejm and in the work of committees and subcommittees. The very fact of extending the legislative process and giving it a sequential character serves to secure a rational decision and the enactment of good law. The successive legislative steps taken by the various actors are staggered in time, which contributes to thinking through the proposed solutions.[34] One such guarantee is also the publicity of the Sejm's proceedings.[35] In this context, parliamentary services, i.e., the experts of the Legislative Bureau and the Bureau of Sejm Analyses, play an important role at the various stages of the law-making process.

The legislative process in the Sejm before the entire chamber provides for a range of legal solutions, and albeit their direct objective is not to review the constitutionality of a bill, these instruments indirectly contribute to ensuring the quality, including constitutionality, of new legislation. These instruments are, chiefly, the constitutional principle of three readings of a bill, and the institution of amendments to a bill.

32 Z. Czeszejko-Sochacki, *Prawo parlamentarne w Polsce*, Warszawa 1997, p. 228.

33 Extensively on this subject: A. Szmyt, *Badanie dopuszczalności projektu ustawy w trybie art. 34 ust. 8 regulaminu Sejmu*, "Przegląd Sejmowy" 2012, no. 5, pp. 9 et seq.

34 M. Kudej, *Proces ustawodawczy w Rzeczypospolitej* Polskiej, [in:] . Zwierzchowski (ed.), *Postępowanie ustawodawcze*, Warszawa 1993 p. 33.

35 Cf. M. Kudej, *Postępowanie ustawodawcze w Sejmie RP*, Warszawa 2002, p. 15.

A bill approved by the Sejm is then considered by the Senate, which decides to bring amendments or to reject it, and in this can 'strive to eliminate possible unconstitutionality' of the bill under consideration.[36]

It is not possible to regulate all activities that make up the law-making process without exception. 'The law-making process is namely a political process. It can be rationalised in so far as it is possible to rationalise political decision-making processes. The law-making process is affected by the legal rules that regulate it, but also by its entire political, cultural, and intellectual environment, especially the values, the political and legal culture of the decision-making elites, the moral standards in public life and the readiness to respect them, and the knowledge of the elites.'[37] Informal measures are intended to force certain changes or to impede the implementation of unconstitutional legislation. The informal mechanisms include the demonstrative leaving of the room for the time of voting or the refusal to participate in the vote despite being present in the room, both typical mainly of the opposition's activity. Another possibility is to sign up to speak during a debate in the Sejm or Senate and suggest in one's statement that the bill is unconstitutional.

6.4 Constitutional review in parliamentary practice

Due to the dispersion of parliamentary review within the structure of the legislative process, it is extremely difficult to estimate its practical dimension and effectiveness. An exception in this regard is the procedure before the Legislation Committee under art. 34(8) of the Standing Orders of the Sejm, which can be put down in numbers and which demonstrates the real extent of this form of review.[38]

Particularly important for the review of the constitutionality of bills is the preliminary stage of the procedure, which takes place after the bill is submitted for consideration by the Sejm and before it is assigned a Sejm paper number. It allows the defects of the bill to be detected before the Speaker of the Sejm assigns it a course of action, which in practice significantly reduces the risk of passing an unconstitutional bill. When inconsistency with the constitution is detected at such an early stage of the procedure, work on an unconstitutional

36 R. Piotrowski, *Parlamentarna kontrola*..., p. 109; see also: E. Popławka, *Lepsze prawo-wyzwanie dla Senatu*, (in:) J. Wawrzyniak (ed.), *Tryb ustawodawczy a jakość prawa*, Warszawa 2005, pp. 113 et seq.

37 S. Wronkowska, *Polski proces prawotwórczy – między autonomią a polityką*, "Ius et Lex" 2005, no. 1, p. 197.

38 The main source of information regarding the activity of the Sejm is the Sejm Information System (the Sejm's website), and regarding the activity of the Senate – the Senate's website. They are maintained in electronic form and their purpose is to collect, process and make available data related to the activity of the two chambers, their internal bodies and the supporting offices (art. 201a of the Standing Orders of the Sejm and art. 37(2) of the Standing Orders of the Senate). The purpose of the websites is for the Sejm and the Senate to provide public information.

bill is refused or attention is drawn to the need to make changes to its content, either by the sponsor, who brings an appropriate amendment, or by making relevant changes in the form of amendments at subsequent stages of the legislative process by entities entitled to present them.

The Speaker of the Sejm plays a special role at this stage. This is because they are obliged to carry out a preliminary review of the bill – with regard to both the formal and the substantive aspect. The analysis of parliamentary practice has shown that all bills submitted for consideration by the Sejm are subject to a preliminary opinion by the staff of the Legislative Bureau as to whether they meet formal requirements. Substantive doubts, on the other hand, may result in the commissioning of a substantive opinion on the bill also by experts of the Bureau of Sejm Analyses. The analysed statistics show that the activity of the Speakers of the Sejm consisting in seeking the legal opinion of the Bureau of Sejm Analyses on bills at the preliminary stage of the process has differed in intensity from one term of office to another.

According to the data in the Sejm's Information System, the procedure of referring a bill to the Legislation Committee for an opinion on its admissibility under art. 34(8) of the Standing Orders of the Sejm is in practice resorted to by way of exception. For 1,152 bills assigned a Sejm paper number during the third term of the Sejm (1997–2001), the Legislation Committee gave an opinion as part of the preliminary verification of a bill's constitutionality only three times and found one draft unacceptable. During the subsequent, fourth term of the Sejm (2001–2005), 1,265 bills were considered and the Legislation Committee gave 23 opinions (six bills were declared unacceptable). In the fifth term (2005–2007), the Legislation Committee gave opinions on 19 out of 708 bills. The Legislation Committee of the sixth term of the Sejm gave 46 opinions, and the Sejm considered 1,511 draft laws. During the seventh term of the Sejm (2011–2015), 115 bills were referred to the Legislation Committee (which gave 64 positive and 21 negative opinions, with the sponsors withdrawing the bills in the remaining 20 cases); 1,300 bills in total were submitted for consideration by the Sejm. In the course of the eighth term (2015–2019), the Committee gave 25 positive opinions while five bills were withdrawn. The Sejm debated on 1,342 bills in total in that period. Finally, during the current, ninth term of the Sejm, as of 30 September 2022, the Legislation Committee has analysed 12 draft laws out of 825 bills considered by the Sejm.

Analysis of individual proceedings leads to the conclusion that no objective grounds for referring a bill to the Legislation Committee by the Speaker of the Sejm can be found. The decisive factor in this respect was primarily their subjective need to consult a collegiate body. Significantly, almost all bills examined by the Legislation Committee under this procedure were deputies' bills. Undoubtedly, this is a consequence of the lack of legal regulation concerning the process of drafting deputies' bills. The conclusions of the Legislation Committee's resolutions concerning the admissibility of bills varied. More centrally, however, the content of the Committee sessions' records reveals that these opinions as a rule coincided with the views expressed in the conclusions of the opinions on the bills drafted by the legal services. In addition, the content of the legal opinion relatively often prompts the sponsor to make appropriate changes to the draft to eliminate the incompatibility with law.

The constitutional review of bills performed at the preliminary stage is continued in the course of successive phases of the legislative process. Practice proves that the special role of guarantor of constitutionality falls to the parliamentary committees considering the bill. Similarly important is the role of individual deputies. Furthermore, the Speaker of the Sejm remains responsible for ensuring that the proposed regulations conform with the basic law. While it is the Speaker of the Sejm who initiates review at the preliminary stage of the process, in the case of subsequent work on a bill, the review is launched by the members (most often the chairs) of the individual Sejm committees. The work of the parliamentary committees and subcommittees is handled by the staff of the Legislative Bureau. The Bureau's staff members take an active part in all sittings of these bodies, and their opinions, albeit only oral, play an important role in ensuring the constitutionality of the proposed regulations. When, during the committee's work, an issue requires a deeper legal analysis, both the committee chair and individual committee members may request a legal opinion from the Bureau of Sejm Analyses.

The study supports the conclusion that the law-making process is intrinsically political in nature. Political arguments often prevail over legal arguments. It happens in practice that politics is the main reason for the low efficiency of the parliamentary constitutional review of bills. However, there are also situations in the Sejm and in the Legislation Committee when political arguments lead to the recognition of a bill as unconstitutional or unlawful. Such situations most often occur when the bill is submitted by the opposition's deputies. For the ruling majority, arguments about the draft law's significant legal defects provide convenient justification not to support the initiative.

6.5 Conclusions

Parliamentary constitutional review of laws emerged in Poland earlier than judicial review; the origins of the concept can be traced back to the French doctrine of sovereignty and supremacy of the parliament and the belief in the infallibility of a body that is granted its mandate to make laws directly by the people. It played a fundamental role in the inter-war period as well as after World War II, up until the establishment of the Constitutional Tribunal in the 1980s.

A characteristic feature of parliamentary constitutional review is its dispersion within the structure of the legislative process. The constitutional review of the proposed legislation is performed as part of the preliminary review of the bill (by the Speaker of the Sejm and the Legislation Committee), at the stage of committee work and in the course of plenary work of the Sejm considering the bill (where it is supported by solutions such as the rule of three readings or the instrument of amendment). Moreover, the constitutionality of a bill approved by the Sejm is then verified by the Senate, which can eliminate unconstitutional provisions by bringing amendments or passing a resolution to reject the bill in its entirety.

Parliamentary constitutional review is very difficult to present in numbers due to its specific character. Most quantifiable is the initial stage of work on a bill, which includes a procedure to declare the bill inadmissible on the grounds of unlawfulness before the Legislation Committee. An analysis of the Sejm's and its bodies' records reveals that over the course of the successive terms of office, the review procedure under art. 34(8) of the Standing Orders of the Sejm has been rather exceptional in light of the overall number of bills considered by the chamber. The political influence on such review evidenced above leads to the conclusion that it cannot substitute for the review performed by the Constitutional Tribunal, and that it might at most be treated as a supporting (supplementary) form of constitutional review. Limiting the constitutional review of normative acts to parliamentary verification alone is found insufficient and incapable of guaranteeing effective verification. The parliament becomes a judge in its own cause; as a result, the review fails to be objective. A study of parliamentary practice in this regard confirms this thesis.

An effective parliamentary constitutional review of law free of the political element, or at least one which is only marginally affected by politics, undoubtedly could play a vital role in the preventive constitutional review of normative acts, along with the review performed by the Constitutional Tribunal. In practice, it can act as an essential guarantee of consistency and constitutionality of the provisions in force, because its effective implementation protects the legal system by precluding unconstitutional provisions from becoming part of the legislation. Thus, it can be an effective instrument for the protection of the constitution and, above all, a guarantee for the implementation of the principle of its superior position in the system of sources of applicable law and its supremacy over other acts.

References

Burda A., *Polskie prawo państwowe*, Polskie Wydawnictwo Naukowe, Warszawa 1978.

Ciemniewski J., *Badanie zgodności ustaw z Konstytucją w procesie legislacyjnym*, "Przegląd Legislacyjny" 2004, vol. 1, pp. 45–54.

Czeszejko-Sochacki Z., *Prawo parlamentarne w Polsce*, Wydawnictwo Sejmowe,Warszawa 1997.

Działocha K., *Konstytucja PRL po nowelizacji z 10 II 1976 (Uwagi o zmianie koncepcji konstytucji)*, "Państwo i Prawo" 1977, vol. 2, pp. 5–18.

Gebert S., *Czuwanie przez Radę Państwa nad zgodnością prawa z Konstytucją*, "Państwo i Prawo" 1980, vol. 1, pp. 26–41.

Granat M., *Droga do sądownictwa konstytucyjnego w państwach Europy Środkowej i Wschodniej*, "Państwo i Prawo" 2001, vol. 12, pp. 15–24.

Granat M., *Sądowa kontrola konstytucyjności prawa w państwach Europy Środkowej i Wschodniej*, Wydawnictwo Sejmowe, Warszawa 2003.

Gwiżdż A., *Trybunał Konstytucyjny*, "Państwo i Prawo" 1983, vol. 12, pp. 3–15.
Kubuj K., *Marszałek Sejmu na straży jakości ustaw*, (in:) J. Wawrzyniak (ed.), *Tryb ustawodawczy a jakość prawa*, Biuro Trybunału Konstytucyjnego, Warszawa 2005.
Kudej M., *Postępowanie ustawodawcze w Sejmie RP*, Wydawnictwo Sejmowe, Warszawa 2002.
Kudej M., *Proces ustawodawczy w Rzeczypospolitej Polskiej*, (in:) Zwierzchowski (ed.), *Postępowanie ustawodawcze*, Wydawnictwo Sejmowe, Warszawa 1993.
Makowski J., *Materiały do projektu przyszłej konstytucji*, "Państwo i Prawo" 1947, vol. 11, p. 32–44.
Piotrowski R., *Parlamentarna kontrola konstytucyjności projektów aktów prawnych*, (in:) E. Zwierzchowski (ed.), *Prawo i kontrola jego zgodności z Konstytucją*, Wydawnictwo Sejmowe, Warszawa 1997.
Popławka E., *Lepsze prawo-wyzwanie dla Senatu*, (in:) J. Wawrzyniak (ed.), *Tryb ustawodawczy a jakość prawa*, Biuro Trybunału Konstytucyjnego, Warszawa 2005.
Radziewicz P., *Pojęcie sejmowej kontroli legalności ustawy*, (in:) P. Radziewicz (ed.), *Kontrola legalności ustawy w Sejmie*, Wydawnictwo Sejmowe, Warszawa 2015.
Rozmaryn S., *Kontrola konstytucyjności ustaw*, "Państwo i Prawo", 1948, vol. 12, pp. 3–20.
Smolak M., *Uzasadnienie sądowe jako argumentacja z moralności politycznej. O legitymizacji władzy sędziowskiej*, Zakamycze, Kraków 2003.
Surowiec J., *Ewolucja poglądów na instytucję sądowej kontroli konstytucyjności ustaw w Polsce Ludowej*, "Acta Universitatis Wratislaviensis" "Trybunał Konstytucyjny" 1987, vol. 1037, pp. 7–30.
Szmulik B., *Geneza kontroli konstytucyjności prawa*, (in:) M. Żmigrodzki, M. Chmaj (eds.), *Społeczeństwo, państwo, władza*, Lubelskie Towarzystwo Naukowe, Lublin 1995.
Szmulik B., *Sądownictwo konstytucyjne*, *Ochrona konstytucyjności prawa w Polsce*, Wydawnictwo Uniwersytetu Marii Curie-Skłodowskiej, Lublin 2001.
Szmulik B., *Trybunał Konstytucyjny a transformacja ustrojowa Polski*, (in:) M. Żmigrodzki (ed.), *Kierunki ewolucji systemu politycznego Rzeczypospolitej Polskiej*, Wydawnictwo Uniwersytetu Marii Curie-Skłodowskiej, Lublin 1997.
Szmyt A., *Badanie dopuszczalności projektu ustawy w trybie art. 34 ust. 8 regulaminu Sejmu*, "Przegląd Sejmowy" 2012, vol. 5, pp. 9–29.
Witkowski Z., *Rada Państwa jako organ czuwający nad zgodnością prawa z Konstytucją*, "Państwo i Prawo" 1977, vol. 7, pp. 37–45.
Wronkowska S., *Polski proces prawotwórczy: Między autonomią a polityką*, "Ius et Lex" 2005, vol. 1, pp. 193–211.
Wróblewski A.N., *Kontrola konstytucyjności prawa w państwach socjalistycznych*, "Państwo i Prawo" 1978, vol. 10, pp. 47–60.
Zwierzchowski E., *Sądownictwo konstytucyjne*, Temida 2, Białystok 1994.

Part II

Problems of activity of constitutional courts in selected countries

7 From guarding the constitution to serving politics – the decline of the Hungarian Constitutional Court

Zoltán Szente

7.1 Introduction

As a matter of fact, the name of the Hungarian Constitutional Court (*Alkotmánybíróság*) is somewhat misleading; since 2012, the basic law has not been called the 'constitution', but the 'Fundamental Law'. Then, in contrast with its name, the Constitutional Court is not a real 'court', as it is not integrated into the judicial branch, and a number of the usual guarantees and principles of judicial independence and legal disputes are not respected in its functioning. However, that is not the biggest mystery about this body. The most puzzling is how this Court, which was one of Europe's most powerful and activist constitutional courts in the 1990s, has become a body that unscrupulously serves the will of the government majority. It is now widely accepted that the Court has been packed by the ruling parties that came to power in 2010 and has since served the interests of the government in a populist, semi-authoritarian regime.[1]

In this paper, on the one hand, I would like to describe this process, focusing in particular on the circumstances that have directly affected the composition, jurisdiction and functioning of the Court, which have been partly the cause and partly the consequence of the change in the role of the Constitutional Court in the system of separation of powers. On the other hand, I will examine

1 See, e.g., M. Bogaards, *De-democratization in Hungary: Diffusely Defective Democracy*, "Democratization" 2018, vol. 25, no. 8, p. 8; P. Castillo-Ortiz, *The Illiberal Abuse of Constitutional Courts in Europe*, "European Constitutional Law Review" 2019, vol. 15, no. 1, pp. 61–63; B. Bugarič, *Central Europe's Descent into Autocracy: A Constitutional Analysis of Authoritarian Populism*, "International Journal of Constitutional Law" 2019, vol. 17, no. 2, p. 605; T. Fournier, *From Rhetoric to Action, a Constitutional Analysis of Populism*, "German Law Journal" 2019, vol. 20, no. 3, pp. 370–372; G. Halmai, *Populism, Authoritarianism and Constitutionalism*, "German Law Journal" 2019, vol. 20, no. 3. p. 307; F. Gárdos-Orosz, *Challenges to Constitutional Adjudication in Hungary after 2010*, (in:) M. Belov (ed.), *The Role of Courts in Contemporary Legal Orders*, The Hague 2019, pp. 324, 336–339; N. Chronowski, Á. Kovács, Zs. Körtvélyesi, G. Mészáros, *The Hungarian Constitutional Court and the Abusive Constitutionalism*, "MTA Law Working Papers, 2022, no. 7, pp. 9, 19–22.

DOI: 10.4324/9781003355793-9

the impact of these changes on the functioning of the Constitutional Court, that is whether its jurisprudence has reflected these changes, or not.

For this purpose, Section 7.2 briefly describes the history of the Constitutional Court from its formative years until 2010, which marked a turning point in the existence of the Court. Section 7.3 illustrates the process by which the composition, powers and modus operandi of the Court have changed significantly. Section 7.4 analyses the practice of the Constitutional Court after 2010, exploring whether and how the Court's jurisprudence has changed as a result of these changes. The constitutional and legislative changes to the Constitutional Court were politically motivated; after that in 2010 the former right-wing opposition parties Fidesz and its satellite party, the Christian Democratic People's Party, won a two-thirds, constitution-making parliamentary majority and unilaterally reshaped the Court to suit their own interests. The question therefore rightly arises as to what impact this has had on the functioning and independence of the Constitutional Court.

7.2 The Court and the constitutional review before 2010

7.2.1 The formative years

Before 1990, constitutional review had no tradition in Hungary. Although in 1983, a special body was set up named the "Council of Constitutional Law", it could repeal only the unconstitutional decrees, but it had no power to annul parliamentary statutes. The Constitutional Court was one of the new institutions established by the revision of the 1949 Constitution in 1989.[2] During the system change, in which the communist state-party and opposition movements negotiated a process of democratic transition, both sides saw a strong constitutional court as a guarantee for democracy and against the other side's overreach. This political mistrust between the negotiating parties during the transition period led to the establishment of a powerful, independent constitutional court with wide-ranging responsibilities. Basically, the Court was established on the pattern of the German *Bundesverfassungsgericht*, installing a 'European' model of a centralised system of constitutional review.

The Constitutional Court began to work on 1 January 1990 with great ambition and elan. In its formative years, the Court, which is often called the Sólyom Court after its first President László Sólyom, handed down a number of decisions that not only had a decisive influence on the subsequent practice of the Constitutional Court but also had a major impact on the development of the constitutional system of the newly emerging democratic constitutional state. In the midst of the construction of a Western-style constitutional system and the dismantling of the legal system of the communist regime, the Court

2 Act XXXI of 1989 was a comprehensive revision of the 1949 Constitution. The detailed rules governing the Constitutional Court were laid down in Act XXXII of 1989 on the Constitutional Court.

inevitably had to deal with almost all the classic constitutional problems in its first years of operation.

In the 1990s, the Hungarian Constitutional Court was considered to be one of the most activist among the similar bodies in the world. This meant not only interpretative activism, but also attempts to extend its already extremely broad powers.[3]

As regards the Court's interpretative practice, it is often characterised by the so-called 'invisible constitution'. This was the term used by László Sólyom in his concurrent opinion on the decision abolishing the death penalty, explaining his own creed as constitutional judge, claiming that

> The Constitutional Court must continue its effort to explain the theoretical bases of the Constitution and the rights included in it and to form a coherent system with its decisions in order to provide a reliable standard of constitutionality – an 'invisible Constitution' – beyond the Constitution, which is often amended nowadays by current political interests; and because of this 'invisible Constitution' probably will not conflict with the new Constitution to be established or with future Constitutions.[4]

Although the doctrine of the invisible constitution was never explicitly accepted by the Court, it had a major impact on the functioning of the whole body. Thus, the Court invented several extraconstitutional concepts (mainly following the practice of the German Federal Constitutional Court), which were then used to annul laws. For example, the Court stated that human dignity is an expression of the 'general right of personality', which

> is a 'mother right', that is a subsidiary fundamental right which may be relied upon at any time by both the Constitutional Court and other courts for the protection of an individual's autonomy when none of the concrete, enumerated fundamental rights is applicable for a particular set of facts.[5]

At other times it established a hierarchy between certain constitutional provisions which did not follow from the constitutional text, when, for instance, it declared that the freedom of expression has a privileged position in the basic rights, and it is the 'mother right' of so-called 'communication rights', like the

3 G. Halmai, *The Hungarian Approach to Constitutional Review: The End of Activism? The First Decade of the Hungarian Constitutional Court*, (in:) W. Sadurski (ed.), *Constitutional Justice, East and West: Democratic Legitimacy and Constitutional Courts in Post-Communist Europe in a Comparative Perspective*, Berlin 2003, pp. 189–211.

4 Judgment of the Constitutional Court, 23/1990 (X. 31).

5 Judgment of the Constitutional Court, 8/1990 (IV. 23).

freedom of the press and speech, the liberty of religion or the right to assembly.[6] Or, while the constitutional text referred to the equality in basic rights, the Court extended the effect of the antidiscrimination principle to the entire legal system, after which the body began to use diverse tests for equality cases, depending on whether they affected basic rights, or other legal relationships.[7] Judicial activism can also be illustrated by the eclectic interpretative practice of the Constitutional Court, which shows that the Court generally chose among possible methods of interpretation in order to achieve the desired result.[8]

There are also several examples of 'jurisdictional activism'. This euphemistic term refers to attempts by the Court to overstep its constitutional competences or to exercise *ultra vires* powers. One of the most memorable cases of this was when the Court tried to invalidate a final judgment of the Supreme Court,[9] despite the fact that the legal rules in force at the time only granted such power when a judicial decision was based on unconstitutional legislation. While this attempt proved unsuccessful, the Constitutional Court successfully applied the doctrine of 'living law', which gave it indirect control over the application of law.[10] According to this rule, the Constitutional Court does not review the contested text of a legal rule, but its prevailing interpretation in practice. On the other hand, it also took on a guiding role by setting constitutional requirements for the implementation of certain provisions of the Constitution, following the German doctrine of *Verfassungskonforme Auslegung*.

It is worth noting that the Hungarian Constitutional Court gained considerable prestige and respect for itself in the 1990s. Besides that, its activism was hardly resisted because it was used to a significant extent for the protection of fundamental rights and to develop the content of the rule of law. Nevertheless, judicial activism of this period is paradoxical to some extent, because the Constitution was easily amendable: the Parliament, with the two-thirds majority votes of MPs, was itself the constitution-making power. Between the general revision of the 1949 constitution in 1989 and the general elections of 2010, the Constitution was modified more than 20 times.

The activity of the Constitutional Court was highly politicised even in its formative years. However, this meant at that time, above all, that it itself had become a power centre, which did not operate on the basis of purely legal considerations. Despite its essentially liberal approach to political rights, the Court supported conservative values in some morally difficult cases. Thus, such values were read into the constitutional text when the Court upheld

6 Judgment of the Constitutional Court, 30/1992 (V. 26).
7 Judgment of the Constitutional Court, 61/1992 (XI. 20).
8 See in details Z. Szente, *The Interpretive Practice of the Hungarian Constitutional Court: A Critical View*, "German Law Journal" 2013, vol. 14, no. 8, pp. 1591–1614. See also A. Jakab, J. Fröhlich, *The Constitutional Court of Hungary*, (in:) A. Jakab, A. Dyevre, G. Itzcovich (eds.), *Comparative Constitutional Reasoning*, Cambridge 2017, pp. 394–437.
9 Judgment of the Constitutional Court, 57/1991 (XI. 8).
10 Judgment of the Constitutional Court, 57/1991 (XI. 8).

the law prohibiting same-sex marriage,[11] as it always preferred the interests of the historic churches, for example, confirming the compensation law that allowed privatisation of the nationalised property during the Communist rule only for churches.[12] Beyond this, the Court sometimes supported the conservative political side. In the early 1990s, for example, in the conflict between the opposition, liberal President of the Republic and the conservative government of the day, it repeatedly supported the latter, even on the basis of arguments that did not follow from the Constitution at all.[13] In 2015, the Court repealed many elements of the left-wing government's economic stabilisation programme, attributing a level of protection to social and vested rights that it had previously rejected.[14]

7.2.2 The Court between 1998 and 2010 – moderated activism

After 1998 the general stance of the Court became more moderate and self-restrained, and in some areas, the Constitutional Court corrected the previous case law. For example, although the Court ruled in 1990 that freedom of expression could not be restricted on the basis of its content, it later upheld a number of such restrictions, such as the penalisation of the public wearing of authoritarian symbols[15] or Holocaust denial.[16]

Nevertheless, the Court's previous activism did not go away without remnants, nor did the case law become more predictable. The Constitutional Court sometimes continued to arbitrarily extend its own powers, such as in 2005, when it decided that it may review the constitutionality of the so-called uniformity resolutions of the Supreme Court[17] (decisions on the interpretation of the law binding on ordinary courts), although the Constitutional Court Act, which exhaustively listed the competences of the body, did not grant it such powers.

The mixed and inconsistent (in fact, tailored to the desired result) application of different interpretative methods continued to be a feature of the Court's jurisprudence. The doctrinal soundness of constitutional reasoning did not improve either, which may also have been due to the fact that the Constitutional Court often sought to adapt to political, professional or social

11 Judgment of the Constitutional Court, 14/1995 (III. 13).
12 Judgment of the Constitutional Court, 4/1993 (II. 12).
13 E.g., referring to the parliamentary form of government, the Court applied a restrictive interpretation to the powers of the Head of State to appoint the chairmen of the public media and to command the army. Judgment of the Constitutional Court, 8/1992 (I. 30), Judgment of the Constitutional Court, 36/1991 (VI. 10), Judgment of the Constitutional Court, 48/1991 (IX. 26).
14 See, e.g., Judgment of the Constitutional Court, 43/1995 (VI. 30).
15 Judgment of the Constitutional Court, 14/2000 (V. 12).
16 Judgment of the Constitutional Court, 13/2000 (V. 12).
17 Judgment of the Constitutional Court, 42/2005 (XI. 14).

expectations, and opted therefore often for pragmatic solutions. Some of the Constitutional Court's decisions, which unexpectedly went against previous practice, were seen by many as politically motivated. Thus, in particular, when, spectacularly breaking with its previous practice, it approved a national referendum initiated by the Fidesz and the Christian Democratic Party, then in opposition, to prevent the implementation of the government's economic programme.[18] In the euthanasia case, the Court ruled that passive euthanasia is part of the self-determination, but it also said that inducing death of an incurable patient through active medical help (i.e., active euthanasia) does not derive from this right, because it considered the health system not sufficiently developed to provide adequate guarantees to protect the right to life.[19]

The interpretative practice of the Court became more moderate in several respects. While the Constitutional Court still argued in its landmark decision on freedom of expression that

> [t]he right to free expression protects opinion irrespective of the value or veracity of its content (…) Every opinion, good and damaging, pleasant and offensive, has a place in this social process, especially because the classification of opinions is also the product of this process,[20]

it did not find unconstitutional the criminalisation of the defamation of national emblems[21] and the use of authoritarian symbols,[22] and the constitutional adjudication of hate speech tightened up as well.[23]

All in all, the Constitutional Court, which might have been thought to have gained sufficient respect among the political parties, was not prepared for the attack on its independence that came after 2010. Neither its composition, based on occasional political compromises, nor its weak dogmatic performance and professionalism made it capable of confronting a constitution-making parliamentary majority that was not afraid to use its power.

7.3 Subversion of the Constitutional Court

After the democratic transition of 1989/90, between 1990 and 2010, parliamentary elections were always won by former opposition parties, with one exception (in 2006). However, it was a milestone in the very recent constitutional and political development of Hungary, when the coalition of Fidesz and Christian Democrats came to power in 2010. This was made possible by

18 Judgment of the Constitutional Court, 16/2007 (III. 9).
19 Judgment of the Constitutional Court, 22/2003 (IV. 28).
20 Judgment of the Constitutional Court, 30/1992 (V. 26).
21 Judgment of the Constitutional Court, 13/2000 (V. 12).
22 Judgment of the Constitutional Court, 14/2000 (V. 12).
23 See Judgment of the Constitutional Court, 12/1999 (V. 21), Judgment of the Constitutional Court, 18/2004 (V. 25), Judgment of the Constitutional Court, 95/2008 (VII. 3).

the fact that the new right-wing government won a two-thirds, constitution-making parliamentary majority in the general election. The government led by Viktor Orbán saw this majority as a mandate that gave the government majority the right to completely overhaul the legal system without cooperating or having to reach an agreement with the opposition. This was significant because the new government majority immediately embarked on a substantial transformation of the whole constitutional system, amending the old constitutional text no less than 12 times before the adoption of a new constitution, the Fundamental Law, which it unilaterally voted for, and entered into force on 1 January 2012. The Constitutional Court quickly became a target for reforms, and the whole institution was restructured.

The new government, exploiting its overwhelming parliamentary majority, sought to neutralise all institutions whose role was to counterbalance and control the executive power. It was therefore important to put the once powerful Constitutional Court under political control. This was achieved as part of a process, in a variety of ways. Some of the changes were aimed at altering the composition of the Court, others at modifying its powers and procedures.[24]

7.3.1 Packing the Court: the change of the composition of the Constitutional Court

As to the composition of the Constitutional Court, one of the first steps was the transformation of the way of nominating the constitutional judges, practically introducing partisan selection of the members of the Court. Until the new regulation, the government majority and the opposition had been forced to compromise on the new members of the Court, as the composition of the parliamentary committee responsible for nominating them had been based on parity between the two sides, thus the election of each candidate needed a political compromise. This mechanism resulted in a more or less politically balanced composition, as both sides have generally nominated moderately committed lawyers to reach a compromise. However, this selection method changed rapidly after 2010, when the parliamentary committee that nominates constitutional judges was no longer based on parity and its composition reflected the balance of power in Parliament. Since this gave the governing parties a two-thirds majority, they were able to nominate their own loyal

24 For a general overview on the Hungarian Constitutional Court, see F. Gárdos-Orosz, K. Zakariás, *Organisational, Functional and Procedural Changes of the Hungarian Constitutional Court 1990–2020*, (in:) F. Gárdos-Orosz, K. Zakariás (eds.), *The Main Lines of the Jurisprudence of the Hungarian Constitutional Court. 30 Case Studies from the 30 Years of the Constitutional Court (1990 to 2020)*, Baden-Baden 2022, pp. 17–43. For an analysis of the government's toolkit for transforming the Constitutional Court after 2010 see A. Vincze, *Wrestling with Constitutionalism: the Supermajority and the Hungarian Constitutional Court*, "Vienna Journal on International Constitutional Law" 2014, vol. 8, no. 1, https://www.degruyter.com/document/doi/10.1515/icl-2014-0105/html (3.07.2022).

candidates without the opposition's approval, who were then elected by the whole Parliament. As a result of this, since 2016, there are only members of the Constitutional Court nominated by the governing parties.[25]

The occupation of the Court was also helped by the fact that the number of constitutional judges was increased from 11 to 15. Although the explanation of this measure was to help the Court tackle its workload, which was expected to grow in parallel with the Court's new function of handling constitutional complaints, the measure was really a 'court packing', as the government majority exploited the possibility to complete the Court with new judges without opposition input.

In 2011, the government majority hastily amended the old Constitution so that the Parliament could elect the president of the Court, preceding his or her election for a three-year term by the Court itself under the previous rules. This method has been institutionalised by the Fundamental Law.

7.3.2 Curbing the Court's powers

The government majority formed in 2010 was distrustful of the Constitutional Court from the very beginning. The ruling coalition parties probably felt that this body could be an effective obstacle to their ambitions for a comprehensive overhaul of the legal system. In retrospect, it is clear that these aspirations were also generally aimed at neutralising the institutions that constrained the executive and subordinating them to the political will of the government, and therefore could not leave the Constitutional Court, which had previously been so effective in counterbalancing the will of the political majority, untouched. This intention was obviously strengthened by some of the post-2010 decisions of the Court, which annulled several laws adopted by the new government majority.

Thus, when the Constitutional Court had declared unconstitutional and annulled a law that imposed with retroactive effect a 98 per cent tax on the exorbitant severance payments in the public sector,[26] the government majority immediately curtailed the Court's most important power of constitutional review. Since then the Court has only been able to review and annul budgetary laws and acts on taxes, duties, pensions, customs or any kind of financial contributions to the state if they violate the right to life and human dignity; the right to the protection of personal data; freedom of thought, conscience and religion; and the rights related to Hungarian citizenship. This restrictive rule was also put in the new Fundamental Law, which stipulated that this limitation

25 In 2016, three new members were elected, who had been nominated jointly by the governing parties and a small opposition party, LMP, after a secret political agreement. Since then, all those constitutional judges have been reliably loyal to the government.

26 Judgment of the Constitutional Court, 184/2010 (X. 28), Judgment of the Constitutional Court, 37/2011 (V. 10).

of the Court's power will last as long as state debt exceeds half of the GDP. In fact, even if this restriction was initially a form of revenge for a decision that was unfavourable to the government, and was supposed to be a temporary rule, it has become permanent: when it was adopted, the debt-to-GDP ratio was over 80 per cent, as it is today (in 2022).

The scope for action of the Constitutional Court has also been significantly reduced by the change that abolished the so-called *actio popularis*, that is, every citizen's right, even without any personal interest, to turn to the Court to review the constitutionality of a statutory act. As a result, only the government, at least one-quarter of the Members of Parliament, the President of the *Kúria* (the supreme court), the Prosecutor General and the Commissioner for Fundamental Rights may initiate ex-post review of the legislation at the Constitutional Court.

7.3.3 Reprogramming the Constitutional Court's activity

Among the changes affecting the jurisdiction of the Constitutional Court after 2010, the most important was probably the extension of the scope of individual constitutional complaints, which has significantly changed the nature of the Court's activities. This, together with the narrowing of the scope for initiating the constitutional review of parliamentary law-making, has had the consequence that the main focus of the Constitutional Court's activity has shifted from the review of the constitutionality of legislation to the constitutional control of the judicial branch.[27]

From the very beginning, the Constitutional Court had the power to hear constitutional complaints, but it was very limited; it could only annul final judgments if they were based on unconstitutional legislation. However, in 2011, following the German model, the possibility of lodging individual constitutional complaints was extended to cases where the final judgment itself was unconstitutional because it violated a constitutional right. As a result, the activity of the Court has changed significantly: more than 95 per cent of its decisions have been taken on constitutional complaints, while at the same time the abstract constitutional reviews have been reduced.

The government majority also sought to influence the work of the Constitutional Court by including several provisions on the methods of constitutional interpretation in the Fundamental Law.[28] Thus, art. N) of the new constitution declares that Hungary observes the 'principle of balanced, transparent and sustainable budget management' and, in performing its duties,

27 For more details see F. Gárdos-Orosz, *The Hungarian Constitutional Court in Transition: from Actio Popularis to Constitutional Complaint*, "Acta Juridica Hungarica, Hungarian Journal of Legal Studies" 2012, vol. 53, no. 4, pp. 302–315.

28 For details see F. Gárdos-Orosz, *Constitutional Interpretation under the new Fundamental Law of Hungary*, (in:) F. Gárdos-Orosz, Z. Szente (eds.), *Populist Challenges to Constitutional Interpretation in Europe and Beyond*, Abingdon-New York 2021, pp. 143–159.

among other public authorities, the Constitutional Court is obliged to respect this principle.[29] In addition, it states that the constitutional provisions must be interpreted 'in accordance with their purposes, the National Avowal contained therein and the achievements of our historical constitution'.[30] Beyond these, some general guidelines are also contained in the constitution al text, such as art. 28 which prescribes that '[w]hen interpreting the Fundamental Law or laws, it shall be presumed that they serve moral and economic purposes which are in accordance with common sense and the public good'. Even more abstract is the provision according to which '[t]he protection of the constitutional identity and Christian culture of Hungary shall be an obligation of every organ of the State'.[31]

Nevertheless, perhaps the most direct way of turning the functioning of the Constitutional Court in the government's favour was the provision of the Fourth Amendment to the Fundamental Law in 2013 which repealed all previous rulings of the Court made prior to the entry into force of the Fundamental Law on 1 January 2012. This measure was surely considered by the government majority to be of decisive importance, given that the Constitutional Court, despite the doctrinal inconsistency that has invariably been so characteristic of its jurisprudence, has always tried to refer to its previous case law and to decide cases brought before it frequently only on the basis of a previous decision.

All of these measures and processes alone could probably have weakened the position of the Constitutional Court. Nonetheless, it should be remembered that the reform of the organisational and operational rules took place in a political context in which the governing parties have had a constitution-making parliamentary majority and they have always been ready to make use of this exceptional opportunity. This can be best illustrated by the fact that the government majority has on several occasions overruled the decisions of the Court that were unfavourable to it, by writing the content of the law declared unconstitutional into the constitutional text, thereby removing it from constitutional review.[32]

29 Fundamental Law, art N) §§ (1) and (3).
30 Fundamental Law, art R) § (3).
31 Fundamental Law, art R) § (4).
32 For example, this was the primary aim of the Fourth Amendment to the Fundamental Law in March 2013, which inserted a number of provisions previously deemed unconstitutional into the constitutional text. See more details in I. Vörös, *The Constitutional Landscape After the Fourth and Fifth Amendments of Hungarian Fundamental Law*, "Acta Juridica Hungarica, Hungarian Journal of Legal Studies" 2014, vol. 55, no. 1, pp. 1–20.

7.4 Changes in interpretative practice after 2010

7.4.1 Assessing the political bias of the Constitutional Court

If a government majority has succeeded in packing a constitutional court, it is usually assumed for this reason alone that the court has become a subordinate of the government, a servant of its daily political interests. This is not an unfounded assumption, since the government probably occupied the court, by filling it with its own adherents, precisely to ensure its loyalty, i.e., to eliminate one of the most important veto players against the realisation of political will. It is conceivable, however, that in a position that provides its holder with such strong guarantees of independence as membership of the Constitutional Court, the members already elected could become autonomous and perhaps, in accordance with their oath, perform their constitutional functions impartially and independently of the interests of the government.

It is therefore worth examining whether there have been any changes in the jurisprudence of the Hungarian Constitutional Court since 2010 that can be attributed to the changes introduced by the government majority, as explained above. In other words, have the attempts to influence the Constitutional Court's activities been successful? The question is, of course, how this can be proven. As I explained earlier, the judicature of the Court has never been particularly consistent. Although the Constitutional Court has always sought to develop a stable case law, the possibility of further developing its interpretative practice can hardly be denied. In addition, adjudication under the new constitution, which entered into force in 2012, could naturally change, as often not the same text has had to be interpreted.

Although there are no generally accepted standards for assessing political bias, it does not mean that it cannot be tested. I believe that if

- governing parties abuse their constitutional majority to unilaterally change the composition of independent, controlling institutions appointing people politically loyal to them;
- the practice of these bodies is then substantially modified;
- in a way that cannot be justified by legal and technical arguments, and this
- coincides with the political interests of the governing parties or is unilaterally in their favour,

it is sufficient to prove the political bias of the institutions concerned.

If this test is applied, the first criterion has been met, because since 2016 all new members of the Court are those nominated or elected by the Fidesz majority, so since then the Court has been composed only of members loyal to the governing parties. But what about the other criteria?

7.4.2 Initial and moderate resistance, 2010–2012

As regards other criteria related to the jurisprudence of the Court, it is worth noting that in the first few years after the Fidesz-led coalition came to power, the Constitutional Court, which had several previous members elected on a consensual ground, annulled several laws passed by the new parliamentary majority that were blatantly unconstitutional on the basis of previous interpretative practice. Thus, in 2011 it invalidated a law that imposed a 98 per cent tax imposed on the extreme severance payment of public officials with retroactive effect, arguing that a legally acquired severance payment cannot be regarded as unfairly acquired income, as the contested law did, and retroactive taxation is contrary to the rule of law.[33] In 2012, it repealed the laws that empowered public authorities to sanction the use of public spaces for living accommodation (i.e., homelessness),[34] as well as the so-called 'Transitional Provisions' which contained a number of rules completing and detailing the new constitutional text.[35] In the same year, the Court struck down certain provisions of the Church Law of 2013 which deprived more than 300 religious denominations, with the exception of 32 churches, of their church status and made its granting conditional on parliamentary approval.[36] It is to be noted, however, that most of these unconstitutional provisions were incorporated into the text of the constitution by Parliament, with the votes of the governing party MPs, in the Fourth Amendment to the Fundamental Law in 2013.

Notwithstanding, the Court's initial resistance to the new parliamentary majority should not be overestimated. Thus, for example, the Constitutional Court tacitly acknowledged the exemption of public finance legislation from constitutional review, although the Fundamental Law allows it in certain narrowly defined cases (e.g., in case of the violation of the right to life and human dignity, the right to the protection of personal data, freedom of thought, conscience and religion and rights related to Hungarian citizenship). In spite of these exceptions, the Court has never made use of these possibilities, and therefore constitutional review has not been applied even in blatant cases such as the simple withdrawal by the state, without compensation, of savings held in private pension funds in 2011,[37] or the openly discriminatory and arbitrarily imposed so-called extra-profit taxes introduced in 2010 and 2022.

33 Judgment of the Constitutional Court, 184/2010 (X. 28.). The European Court of Human Rights declared the application of the law to be contrary to the European Convention on Human Rights. See Judgment of ECtHR of 14 May 2013 in the case of *N.K.M. v. Hungary*, application no. 66529/11, Judgment of ECtHR of 25 June 2013 in the case of *Gáll v. Hungary*, application no. 49570/11, Judgment of ECtHR of 2 July 2013 in the case of *R. Sz. v. Hungary*, application no. 41838/11.

Three years later, the Constitutional Court confirmed its earlier decision in Judgment of the Constitutional Court, 6/2014 (II. 26.). See also K. Kovács, G.A. Tóth, *Hungary's Constitutional Transformation*, "European Constitutional Law Review" 2011, vol. 7, no. 2, pp. 192–193.

34 Judgment of the Constitutional Court, 38/2012 (XI. 14).

35 Judgment of the Constitutional Court, 45/2012 (XII. 29).

36 Judgment of the Constitutional Court, 6/2013 (III. 1).

37 Z. Szente, *Breaking and Making Constitutional Rules: The Constitutional Effects of the Financial Crisis in Hungary*, (in:) C. Xenophon (ed.), *Constitutions in the Global Financial Crisis. A Comparative Analysis*, Farnham 2013, pp. 255–256.

7.4.3 Methods and techniques for serving government interests by the Constitutional Court

In its work, the Constitutional Court has used a variety of methods to serve the interests of the government. This is probably because the Constitutional Court is concerned to maintain the appearance of independence, and therefore takes care in some cases to balance the political expectations of the Orbán Government with professional requirements. For this purpose, the Court has developed various techniques, which, however, share the common characteristic of ensuring that the will of the government is to be ensured and legitimised in all politically highly important cases.

7.4.3.1 Changing the dominant interpretation of constitutional provisions

In some respects, the Court's interpretative practice has changed in parallel with the growing majority of those members who were selected out by the Fidesz-led government. These changes could easily be justified by the fact that a new constitution had entered into force in the meantime, but in many cases the constitutional text had not changed substantially, and the Constitutional Court itself stated that in such cases the earlier case law could be taken into account even if the Fourth Amendment repealed all decisions taken before the entry into force of the Fundamental Law.[38] Thus, while the Court in 2010, in its aforementioned decision, considered the retroactive imposition of the 98 per cent supertax unconstitutional, in 2011, the intimidated Court, after the curbing of its review power, held that retroactivity is not unconstitutional if it applies only to the beginning of the current tax year.[39]

The Court also struck a balance between different considerations when, in 2021, on the initiative of the Minister of Justice, it supported the government's position in a way by not following the example of the Polish Constitutional Tribunal[40] and refraining from declaring that it had the power to review the legal acts of the European Union. At the same time, the decision changed the previous practice on the relationship between domestic law and EU law, whereby it held that, if the exercise of shared competences is 'incomplete', Hungary is entitled, in accordance with the presumption of the preserved sovereignty, to act unilaterally until the EU institutions take the necessary measures to ensure the effective exercise of shared competences.[41]

38 Judgment of the Constitutional Court, 22/2012 (V. 11), Judgment of the Constitutional Court, 13/2013 (VI. 17).

39 Judgment of the Constitutional Court, 37/2011 (V. 10).

40 Judgment of the Polish Constitutional Tribunal of 7 October 2021 (K 3/21).

41 Judgment of the Constitutional Court, 32/2021 (XII. 20). The Minister of Justice wanted the Court to declare unconstitutional the judgment of the Court of Justice of the European Union in case C-808/18, according to which a foreign national illegally staying in Hungary cannot be expelled from the country, but must instead be subject to asylum or expulsion

In the same judgment, the Court spectacularly reinterpreted the right to human dignity. Whereas this concept, since 1990, had been of an individualistic nature, being the source of individual autonomy, this decision sought to redefine human dignity on a community basis, linking it to constitutional identity. According to the embarrassing reasoning of the decision, individual identity is part of human dignity, which cannot be separated from national identity, because 'the traditional social environment, which the individual occupies at birth and is independent of him, shapes his self-definition'. However, as the argumentation continues, this is threatened by the settlement in Hungary of persons or groups of persons who do not conform to the traditional social identity of the Hungarian population, against which the state must provide protection.[42]

7.4.3.2 Defining constitutional requirement instead of striking down the contested law

In support of the government's policy, another technique developed by the Court is to define a constitutional requirement of how a contested law should be implemented, instead of annulling it. However, since the subsequent implementation of such laws is no longer brought back to the Constitutional Court, the result of this method is the upholding of highly controversial laws.

This was the case, for example, with the law giving the Minister of Justice the power to authorise secret surveillance by the Counter-Terrorism Centre (a specialised police body) without providing basic guarantees.[43] Another example was the constitutional review of the 2011 judicial reform. After the Venice Commission's strong criticism of the laws on the organisation and administration of the courts and the status of judges, the Minister of Justice, on behalf of the government, initiated an ex-post review of these laws before the Constitutional Court. In this case, the Court only set out broad and general requirements as to what legal guarantees should be provided in the process of appointing judges.[44] However, this did not subsequently prevent the head of the National Office of Judiciary, who is close to the government, from negating the rights of the elected bodies of judges in the appointment process of judges and heads of courts.

---

proceedings. Although the Constitutional Court has refrained from doing so, its reasoning indirectly confirms the government's position.

42 Ibidem. For further examples of changing constitutional court practice, see N. Chronowski, *The Post-2010 'Democratic Rule of Law' Practice of the Hungarian Constitutional Court under a Rule by Law Governance*, "Acta Juridica Hungarica, Hungarian Journal of Legal Studies" 2020, vol. 61, no. 2, pp. 36–158.

43 Judgment of the Constitutional Court, 32/2013 (IX. 22).

44 Judgment of the Constitutional Court, 13/2013 (VI. 17).

7.4.3.3 Invalidating unconstitutional laws without effective judicial protection

In several times, the reviewed legislation was so clearly unconstitutional that the Constitutional Court could not escape from its annulment. In such cases, it used different methods, depending on the political significance of the subject of the law. Where a declaration of unconstitutionality was inevitable, the Court has on several occasions chosen to annul the law concerned, but not to remedy the infringement of rights it had caused, if this could have had serious practical consequences. It happened exactly when the Act CLXII on the Legal Status and Remuneration of Judges reduced the compulsory retirement age of judges from 70 to 62, as a result of which in 2012 altogether 274 judges – almost ten per cent of all serving judges – had to retire. The change affected court leaders even more, since most of them came from the older age group of judges.[45] The Constitutional Court in 2012 invalidated several provisions of the Act, holding that such age limits can only be determined by cardinal act.[46] The Court also defined a substantive requirement for such a regulation setting forth that the upper age limit for judicial service may be reduced only gradually, after a sufficient transitional period, without prejudice to the principle of a judge's irremovability. However, the Court's ruling failed to give any real remedy to the judges illegally removed, since it did not contain any provisions on how to reinstate or compensate them.

The Constitutional Court has also failed to ensure effective legal protection in a case in which more than 100,000 citizens[47] have suffered rights violations. True, it was only years later that the Court, under the pressure of necessity, ruled that the 2011 social security reform, which transformed former disability pensions into a significantly reduced allowance regardless of the medical condition of the persons concerned, had proved to be a violation of the European Convention on Human Rights.[48] In a 2013 decision, the Court still upheld the relevant legislation,[49] but later the European Court of Human Rights ruled that under this law, the Convention had been violated in several cases.[50] In 2018, the Constitutional Court did not annul the relevant part of the law either, but merely found an unconstitutional omission of Parliament and called on the National Assembly to bring the legislation into line with Hungary's international obligations, and, using a familiar technique, estab-

45 Z. Szente, *Constitutional Law in Hungary*, Alphen aan den Rijn 2021, p. 210.

46 Judgment of the Constitutional Court, 33/2012 (VII. 17).

47 According to the data of the Central Statistical Office, the number of people receiving disability pensions fell by around 180,000 between 2011 and 2016. Központi Statisztikai Hivatal, *Mikrocenzus 2016. A népesség gazdasági aktivitása*, https://www.ksh.hu/docs/hun/xftp/idoszaki/mikrocenzus2016/mikrocenzus_2016_5.pdf (3.07.2022).

48 Judgment of the Constitutional Court, 21/2018 (XI. 14).

49 Judgment of the Constitutional Court, 3027/2013 (II. 12).

50 Judgment of ECtHR of 13 December 2016 on the case of *Béláné Nagy v. Hungary*, application number 53080/13, and Judgment of ECtHR of 7 March 2017 on the case of *Baczúr v. Hungary*, application number 8263/15.

lished a constitutional requirement. However, by then, the reclassification of disability pensions had long been completed and the Court's decision did not provide any effective remedy for the concerned people.

7.4.3.4 The silence of the Court

On several occasions, the Constitutional Court has avoided uncomfortable decisions by simply not taking them.[51] In this respect, I call uncomfortable cases those that were constitutionally clear, but where the decision would have had some inconvenience for the government.

This happened with the review of the law that set impractical and unprecedented conditions for the foreign-funded universities with the obvious aim of making it impossible for the Central European University (CEU) to operate. This university was founded and sponsored by George Soros, outcried as a public enemy by the public and pro-government media. The law was clearly unconstitutional for several reasons.[52] The Constitutional Court first postponed the decision on the grounds that it had set up an ad hoc working group to study the case, although this working method had not been used before. Later, it suspended the proceeding saying that it had to wait for the outcome of the proceeding before the European Court of Justice on the same law, although it has never done so in other cases (as a matter of course, since the CJEU does not base its decisions on the Hungarian Fundamental Law). The Court thus postponed the issue for years until the CEU moved to Vienna. The CJEU subsequently ruled that the law was contrary to European Union law,[53] and the legislation was amended accordingly. Finally, in 2021, the Constitutional Court terminated its procedure for a formal reason, as the petitioners who had previously lodged a constitutional complaint in the case did not extend their petition to the new law.[54]

7.4.3.5 Directly serving the interests of the government

The Constitutional Court, especially after 2013, has often assisted the government, upholding a number of laws whose constitutionality was thoroughly disputed or which were later found to be contrary to EU law. The governing parties, with a constitution-making majority in Parliament, have used the

51 A. Jakab, *Informal Institutional Elements as Both Preconditions and Consequences of Effective Formal Legal Rules: The Failure of Constitutional Institution Building in Hungary*, "The American Journal of Comparative Law" 2020, vol. 68, no. 4, pp. 775–776.

52 See details in N. Chronowski, A. Vincze, *The Hungarian Constitutional Court and the Central European University Case: Justice Delayed is Justice Denied*, "European Constitutional Law Review" 2021, vol. 17, no. 4, pp. 688–706.

53 Judgment of CJEU of 6 October 2020 in the case of *Commission v. Hungary*, C-66/18.

54 Decision of the Constitutional Court 3318/2021 (VII. 23), Decision of the Constitutional Court, 3319/2021 (VII. 23).

Constitution as a tool to impose their political will, as illustrated by the ten amendments to the Fundamental Law that entered into force on 1 January 2012. The constitutional text has often been adapted to the political interests of the day, yet in many cases it has been necessary for the Constitutional Court to change the previously established constitutional standards, to support its decisions with extra-constitutional sources or even to depart from the constitutional text when necessary to achieve the desired result of interpretation.

There is a whole series of such decisions, some of which paved the way for the government's economic policy, while others legitimised decisions directly motivated by party politics.

This happened in the foreign currency loan case, when the Court upheld a law which retroactively changed thousands of loan agreements between banks and individuals.[55] The objective of this law was to help those who had previously borrowed in other currencies rather than forints because of low interest rates, but who found themselves in a difficult situation because of the deterioration of the forint exchange rate during the global economic crisis. The Court declared the law constitutional, despite the fact that it had to overrule its previous practice in some respects regarding the rule of law, legal certainty and the right to a fair trial.[56]

The Constitutional Court did not provide protection against market-restrictive measures of the state that transformed or decisively influenced the previous property and market structures. It was an important strategic tool in the hands of the government to build patronage and create a national capitalist class. For example, the re-regulation of the retail and wholesale distribution of tobacco products, which first withdrew retail licences by law and then redistributed them in the form of concession contracts, was considered constitutional.[57] The decision has significantly narrowed the scope of property protection against direct government intervention in the market compared to previous practice. By contrast, the ECtHR found the infringement of the previous licences without compensation to be a violation of property rights, contrary to art. 1 (protecting property rights) of the First Additional Protocol to the European Convention on Human Rights.[58]

55 Judgment of the Constitutional Court, 34/2014 (XI. 14).

56 N. Chronowski, F. Gárdos-Orosz, *The Hungarian Constitutional Court and the Financial Crisis*, "Acta Juridica Hungarica, Hungarian Journal of Legal Studies" 2017, vol. 58, no. 2, pp. 139–154; F. Gárdos-Orosz, *Constitutional Justice in Credit Crisis. The Hungarian Case*, "Südosteuropa: Journal of Politics and Society" 2018, vol. 66, no. 1, p. 94; F. Gárdos-Orosz, P. Gárdos, *Decision 34/2014 (XI. 14.) – Foreign Currency Loan*, (in:) F. Gárdos-Orosz, K. Zakariás (eds.), *The Main Lines of the Jurisprudence of the Hungarian Constitutional Court. 30 Case Studies from the 30 Years of the Constitutional Court (1990 to 2020)*, Baden-Baden 2022, pp. 393–411.

57 Judgment of the Constitutional Court, 3194/2014 (VII. 15).

58 Judgment of CJEU of 13 January 2015, on the case of *Vékony v. Hungary*, no. 65681/13.

Other decisions supported or legitimised the government's goals in party politics. In 2016, for example, the Court quickly came to the rescue of the government when it unsuccessfully attempted to include provisions on constitutional identity in the Fundamental Law (because it did not have a majority in Parliament at the time), and, on the petition of the Commissioner of Fundamental Rights, it stipulated its own powers to review the validity of EU law in the future in order to protect the sovereignty and constitutional identity of Hungary.[59] This was an innovation, as the notion of constitutional identity had been completely unknown in Hungarian constitutional law beforehand.[60] In fact, the Constitutional Court discovered this concept at the peak of the government's anti-migrant and anti-EU campaign, which sharply opposed the refugee policy of the European Union.

The political bias of the Constitutional Court was blatantly manifested in the case of the so-called letter-ballot. The Fidesz-led government ensured the possibility for Hungarians living outside the borders to acquire Hungarian citizenship, including the right to vote. Since every survey and the subsequent election results proved that the overwhelming majority of Hungarians living beyond the borders were Fidesz voters, the governing majority provided them with the opportunity to vote by post in order to promote their willingness to participate in the parliamentary elections. However, it refused to do so to Hungarian citizens who live in Hungary, but are abroad on election day, presumably because emigrant Hungarians are more likely to vote for opposition parties. They could only cast their votes in person at Hungary's diplomatic missions abroad, which often made it very difficult for them to exercise their right to vote. However, the partisan Court did not declare the apparent discrimination unconstitutional, saying that the protection afforded to the right to vote as a fundamental right does not extend to the way in which the fundamental right is exercised.[61]

The Constitutional Court also served the interests of the government when, in several decisions,[62] it allowed public authorities to lodge individual constitutional complaints with the Constitutional Court if a final judgment of an ordinary court had harmed their interests, even though this went against the internal logic of constitutional law and the previous practice of the Court. The constitutional complaint was from the beginning a means of individual legal protection in cases of violation of the rights guaranteed by the Fundamental Law, and according to the earlier jurisprudence of the Constitutional Court[63]

59 Judgment of the Constitutional Court, 22/2016 (XII. 5).

60 The concept of constitutional identity was introduced only by the Seventh Amendment to the Fundamental Law in May 2018.

61 Judgment of the Constitutional Court, 3086/2016 (IV. 26).

62 Judgment of the Constitutional Court, 3091/2016 (V. 12), Judgment of the Constitutional Court, 23/2018 (XII. 28).

63 The previous practice of the Constitutional Court did not recognise the right of public authorities to lodge a constitutional complaint, because, on the one hand, public authori-

and the prevailing scholarly approach, the state itself and the individual public authorities cannot be the subjects of fundamental rights. The basic mistake of this new practice is best demonstrated by the fact that it was only in 2019 that Parliament enacted the right of public authorities to lodge a constitutional complaint with the Constitutional Court when a final judicial decision allegedly breaches their powers.[64]

All this does not mean that the Constitutional Court does not occasionally engage in heated debates or act as an independent player in constitutional disputes. But this is strongly limited by the political interests of the government.[65]

7.5 Epilogue

In December 2021, Tamás Sulyok, President of the Constitutional Court, addressed an open letter to the President of the Republic, the Prime Minister and the Speaker of the National Assembly (all public figures are leading Fidesz politicians), asking them to take 'effective measures' to ensure the long-term viability of the Constitutional Court. He justified his unusual statement by saying that

> In recent months, there has been a growing number of ideas, now supported directly by political parties, to disrupt the functioning of the institution and ad absurdum to dissolve the Constitutional Court in the event of a change of government. Such manifestations constitute a direct and serious affront to the rule of law and democracy, and as such, are utterly unacceptable in a democratic State governed by the rule of law (...) With the support of some domestic political parties, a body of lawyers has been set up to devise a concept for overturning the constitutional order established by the Fundamental Law by disregarding the mandate of public officials who have been appointed on the basis of the Fundamental Law. This is an unprecedented attack on the Hungarian constitutional system, the continuity of law and the rule of law.[66]

The statement was issued a few months before the parliamentary elections in April 2022, and was a reaction to an open discussion among opposition parties on how to restore the rule of law and constitutional democracy if the

ties do not have fundamental constitutional rights, and on the other hand, the function of a constitutional complaint is precisely to protect the rights of individuals against the state. Judgment of the Constitutional Court, 65/1992 (XII. 17), Judgment of the Constitutional Court, 23/2009 (XI. 12).

64 Act CXXVII of 2019.

65 For a quantitative justification of the politically biased interpretative practice, see Z. Szente, *The Political Orientation of the Members of the Constitutional Court between 2010 and 2014*, "Constitutional Studies" 2016, vol. 1, no. 1, pp. 123–149.

66 See https://hunconcourt.hu/uploads/sites/3/2021/12/nyilt_level_en.pdf (3.07.2022).

opposition were to win a majority in the elections, but not enough to make constitutional changes. This was tantamount to a declaration of political loyalty, as he sided with the governing parties in a political debate.

There have been other explicit expressions of judicial deference since 2010. For example, in 2015, when the constitutional judges selected by Fidesz were already in a massive majority in the body, the then President of the Constitutional Court, Barnabás Lenkovics said in an interview that

> Nor is constitutional adjudication independent of time and space. It must keep pace with changing circumstances. The same standards that the Constitutional Court developed and applied to the legislator in stable or at least perceived circumstances cannot be applied unchanged in significantly changed historical circumstances. This would result in certain standards becoming dogma, paralysing the functioning of the legislature, governance and even the rule of law, making it impossible to tackle the crisis.[67]

As I have already mentioned, the Hungarian Constitutional Court has always operated in a highly politicised way. However, the fact that its composition is determined exclusively by the governing parties, which, moreover, have a constitution-making majority in Parliament, has fundamentally transformed the character of the Court: from being the supreme guardian of the Constitution, the counterweight of the legislative and executive powers, to a submissive servant and legitimiser of the government's will.

Apart from the erroneous individual decisions and the decline in the level of legal protection and constitutional standards, the most serious criticism of the Constitutional Court is that it has failed to prevent the systematic erosion of the rule of law after 2010. In fact, it has not been an obstacle to the authoritarian transition, but its promoter, and thus bears a heavy responsibility for the destruction of democracy, because it was precisely the defence of constitutional democracy that was to have been its basic function and raison d'être. Although it has failed in this role, the proposal to abolish this institution or to restructure it has not yet emerged in the domestic political and constitutional discourse. This would not be in the interests of the supporters of the Orbán regime anyway, as the Court reliably and effectively serves the interests of the government, while opposition-minded politicians and scholars may still look at the Court with nostalgia, and secretly hope that one day, in the distant future, the Constitutional Court with a different composition and approach may play a role in restoring constitutional democracy.

67 See https://www.jogiforum.hu/interju/2014/05/19/dr-lenkovics-barnabas/ (3.07.2022).

References

Bogaards M., *De-democratization in Hungary: Diffusely Defective Democracy*, "Democratization" 2018, vol. 25(8) 1481–1499.

Bugarič B., *Central Europe's Descent into Autocracy: A Constitutional Analysis of Authoritarian Populism*, "International Journal of Constitutional Law" 2019, vol. 17(2) 597–616.

Castillo-Ortiz P., *The Illiberal Abuse of Constitutional Courts in Europe*, "European Constitutional Law Review" 2019, vol. 15(1) 48–72.

Chronowski N., *The Post-2010 'Democratic Rule of Law' Practice of the Hungarian Constitutional Court Under a Rule by Law Governance*, "Acta Juridica Hungarica, Hungarian Journal of Legal Studies" 2020, vol. 61(2) 136–158.

Chronowski N., Gárdos-Orosz F., *The Hungarian Constitutional Court and the Financial Crisis*, "Acta Juridica Hungarica, Hungarian Journal of Legal Studies" 2017, vol. 58(2) 139–154.

Chronowski N., Kovács Á., Körtvélyesi Zs., Mészáros G., *The Hungarian Constitutional Court and the Abusive Constitutionalism*, "MTA Law Working Papers" 2022, vol. 71–41.

Chronowski N., Vincze A., *The Hungarian Constitutional Court and the Central European University Case: Justice Delayed is Justice Denied*, "European Constitutional Law Review" 2021, vol. 17(4)688–706.

Fournier T., *From Rhetoric to Action, a Constitutional Analysis of Populism*, "German Law Journal" 2019, vol. 20(3). 362–381.

Gárdos-Orosz F., *Challenges to Constitutional Adjudication in Hungary After 2010*, (in:) M. Belov (ed.), *The Role of Courts in Contemporary Legal Orders*, Eleven, The Hague 2019.

Gárdos-Orosz F., *Constitutional Interpretation Under the New Fundamental Law of Hungary*, (in:) F. Gárdos-Orosz, Z. Szente (eds.), *Populist Challenges to Constitutional Interpretation in Europe and Beyond*, Routledge, Abingdon-New York 2021.

Gárdos-Orosz F., *Constitutional Justice in Credit Crisis. The Hungarian Case*, "Südosteuropa: Journal of Politics and Society" 2018, vol. 66(1)94–118.

Gárdos-Orosz F., *The Hungarian Constitutional Court in Transition: From actio popularis to Constitutional Complaint*, "Acta Juridica Hungarica, Hungarian Journal of Legal Studies" 2012, vol. 53(4). 302–315.

Gárdos-Orosz F., Gárdos P., *Decision 34/2014 (XI. 14.): Foreign Currency Loan*, (in:) F. Gárdos-Orosz, K. Zakariás (eds.), *The Main Lines of the Jurisprudence of the Hungarian Constitutional Court. 30 Case Studies from the 30 Years of the Constitutional Court (1990 to 2020)*, Nomos,Baden-Baden 2022.

Gárdos-Orosz F., Zakariás K., *Organisational, Functional and Procedural Changes of the Hungarian Constitutional Court 1990–2020*, (in:) F. Gárdos-Orosz, K. Zakariás (eds.), *The Main Lines of the Jurisprudence of the Hungarian Constitutional Court. 30 Case Studies from the 30 Years of the Constitutional Court (1990 to 2020)*, Nomos, Baden-Baden 2022.

Halmai G., *Populism, Authoritarianism and Constitutionalism*, "German Law Journal" 2019, vol. 20(3). 296–313.

Halmai G., *The Hungarian Approach to Constitutional Review: The End of Activism? The First Decade of the Hungarian Constitutional Court*, (in:) W. Sadurski (ed.), *Constitutional Justice, East and West: Democratic Legitimacy and Constitutional*

Courts in Post-Communist Europe in a Comparative Perspective, Springer, Berlin 2003.
Jakab A., *Informal Institutional Elements as Both Preconditions and Consequences of Effective Formal Legal Rules: The Failure of Constitutional Institution Building in Hungary*, "The American Journal of Comparative Law" 2020, vol. 68(4) 760–800.
Jakab A., Fröhlich J., The Constitutional Court of Hungary, (in:), A. Jakab, A. Dyevre, G. Itzcovich (eds.), *Comparative Constitutional Reasoning*, Cambridge University Press, Cambridge 2017.
Kovács K., Tóth G.A., *Hungary's Constitutional Transformation*, "European Constitutional Law Review" 2011, vol. 7(2). 183–203.
Szente Z., *Breaking and Making Constitutional Rules: The Constitutional Effects of the Financial Crisis in Hungary*, (in:) C. Xenophon (ed.), *Constitutions in the Global Financial Crisis.* A Comparative Analysis, Farnham 2013.
Szente Z., *Constitutional Law in Hungary*, Kluwer, Alphen aan den Rijn 2021.
Szente Z., *The Interpretive Practice of the Hungarian Constitutional Court: A Critical View*, "German Law Journal" 2013, vol. 14(8)1591–1614.
Szente Z., *The Political Orientation of the Members of the Constitutional Court between 2010 and 2014*, "Constitutional Studies" 2016, vol. 1(1). 123–149.
Vincze A., *Wrestling With Constitutionalism: The Supermajority and the Hungarian Constitutional Court*, "Vienna Journal on International Constitutional Law" 2014, vol. 8(1) 86–97.
Vörös I., *The Constitutional Landscape After the Fourth and Fifth Amendments of Hungarian Fundamental Law*, "Acta Juridica Hungarica, Hungarian Journal of Legal Studies" 2014, vol. 55(1). 1–20.

8 *For now, we see in a mirror dimly* – a current perception of Hungarian constitutional justice from an international and comparative national perspective

Peter Kruzslicz

Instead of an introduction to this voluntarily incomplete analysis of the perception of Hungarian constitutional justice in institutionally or academically expressed international or comparative constitutional opinions, according to our professional conviction, it is more important to write a few words about constitutional culture. Behind all those discussions on the status and the efficiency of Hungarian constitutional justice, the question of the lack of a constitutional culture is raised. This question explains a lot about the actual situation and the answers that can be formulated to the question and can help us to better understand the problem which is not about the existence of a constitutional justice and the efficiency of the protection of constitutionalism, but a more abstract and deeper challenge about the formation of a constitutional culture.

While Hungarian constitutional justice can and must be the object of analysis: as much as the institutional framework, the appointment of judges then the access to constitutional justice or the case law of the Court can be described then commented on or criticised. However, we think that often those descriptions or critics are even more incomplete than our perception of them, without special attention that must be paid to constitutional culture. It is important, in order to give at least a methodological framework to the analysis, to mention, first, that constitutional culture exists. Second, there are many constitutional systems. Third, constitutional culture is changing, evolving. Fourth and finally, this evolution is influenced by political and legal factors, hence, it can be voluntarily directed. Those standpoints are especially relevant after constitutional transitions. They should serve as guidelines for constitutional analysis.

According to our hypothesis, in Hungary, and maybe in other Central European states, the constitutional culture could not, maybe not yet, be completely formed after the constitutional transition. Because of not always fortunate political and legal influences, a proper, organically developed and well-balanced constitutional culture is lacking in Hungary. The historic dynamic of the development of the constitutional framework was already interrupted after the First World War; this interruption became even more tangible

DOI: 10.4324/9781003355793-10

after the Second World War. The totalitarian regimes that occupied Hungary, first because of the German occupation at the end of the Second World War, then when the Red Army occupied Hungary, violently stopped a long lasting and more or less organic constitutional development. As mentioned before, the end of the historic monarchy that could find its way to renew even in the framework of the Habsburg Empire caused a first interruption. The historic constitution of Hungary survived after the war; however, it could not completely be maintained because of the change of situation.

It is after this tormented 20th century that Hungary, by the end of the century, once again after a radical change in the global situation, had the opportunity to reconstruct its constitutional structure in a more organic way. However, the fact that the constitutional development was historically interrupted had a great influence on the capacity of Hungary in that reconstruction. As will be demonstrated, the context of the constitutional transition was not always opportune for the consolidation of a renewed constitutional culture, but also a deeper problem of the loss of roots made the situation even worse. Without going into further details, one can easily realise that after such a tormented 20th century, it was not easy to find again the sources of a Hungarian constitutional framework. Going back in time is not possible; however, the particular constitutional characteristics of a lost but for a long time organically developed constitutional culture could not be ignored. It is in this context that the more concrete issues can also be discussed in the period of the constitutional transition and especially as regards constitutional justice.

First, after the constitutional transition, special importance was given to constitutional justice because of the mistrust between the old and the new political forces, in the absence of a political compromise allowing the adoption of a new constitution. Of course, the constitution was completely reformed, it became liberal, democratic and conformed to European standards. At the same time, it was incomplete, certainly legal, but not necessarily legitimate. A very rich case law followed the modified constitution; it was not always interpretating, as often, it also had to complete the constitutional provisions. From a sole professional point of view, certainly, the jurisprudence was extremely precise, and we would add, highly appreciated by international and academic opinions.[1] At the same time, it could be also criticised for perhaps too much evolutive interpretation, and for its role in replacing the democratic adoption of a completely new constitution.

Then, in a second period of Hungarian contemporary constitutional history, one political force obtained a huge and strong parliamentary majority, and, in our opinion, this fact turned everything upside down. Now, the democratic adoption of a legitimate constitution became more than possible.

1 J. Bóka, *Az összehasonlító módszertan alkalmazása az Alkotmánybíróság joggyakorlatában* (in:) L. Trócsányi (ed.), *Tanulmányok Kovács István emlékére*, Szeged: Dikaiosz Logosz 2012, pp. 11–26.

No compromises were made, as there was no need to do so, to adopt the Fundamental Law. Even though the political discourse was about changing everything, we can admit that the substance of the text, at least for its major part, has not been changed. In comparison with the reform by the time of the constitutional transition, here, the form is revolutionary and new, important symbolic changes are all over the text, but the content, for most of it, remains the same. Back then, by the time of the constitutional transition, the form remained the same, but the content was completely changed.

It is obvious that the function of constitutional justice could not be the same in such a new context. It was also the will of the authors of the new constitution to change the role, to limit the intervention of constitutional justice to the mere interpretation of the constitutional provisions. No need to remedy the shortcomings of the temporary constitution, the Fundamental Law can serve as the basis and should be enough for the constitutional interpretation. To put it that way, constitutional justice can only serve the text of the Fundamental Law, but cannot overcome it.[2] The international criticism coming from institutions and scholars because of that new constitutional reality was strong.[3] But what we try to highlight is that neither of those two periods and situations were fortunate enough to allow for the building up of a constitutional culture in Hungary which we are still waiting for.

Having said that, with another quote than that in the title, we would like to say, we came not to praise Hungarian constitutional culture but not to bury it either. The present analysis will offer a perception, not the whole perception, not a complete panorama, but a short overview of diverse opinions about Hungarian constitutional justice. As such, it will be voluntarily subjective; however, with the opinions chosen as examples, we hope a realistic but also nuanced image of Hungarian constitutional justice can be revealed. In the title of our presentation, we choose a well-known quote about seeing in a mirror dimly. For us, those opinions are mirrors. And those mirrors are very important. Both are mentioned in the title: the one that international organisations are holding before the Hungarian constitutional justice system, and the other that we can see thanks to the comparative method. They give us an interesting image of the situation in Hungary, and we can learn from them. However, as mirrors, they are not always reflecting the reality, to put it that way, with all three dimensions. That is why they should be analysed carefully.

8.1 Constitutional protection without constitutional judges?

To answer the question already at the very beginning of our development, we would state that Hungarian constitutional justice continues to function in the framework of the Hungarian Constitutional Court even after the

2 B. Ablonczy, *Sur les traces de la Constitution hongroise*, Budapest: Elektromedia 2012.
3 L. Trócsányi, *Constitutions nationales et intégration européenne*, Bruxelles: Larcier 2015.

constitutional reform engaged by the adoption of the Fundamental Law[4] and then by the adoption of the new Act on Constitutional Court,[5] and that there are no other bodies or processes, at least at a national level, to ensure the constitutional protection if the Constitutional Court failed in this function. To begin the demonstration of those two statements, we would like to go back to history in order to highlight two historical specificities and after those to make a theorical point.

First, it is important to remember that constitutionalism, constitutional protection, especially of the institutions, was always very important in Hungarian history. Political actors hoped that the protection of constitutional institutions could help to preserve the sovereignty of Hungary during the long period of Ottoman occupation, but also in the Habsburg Empire. The so-called historic constitution played a very important role in it. A first simple proof: by the end of the 19th century, so already in a modern and constitutional political regime, the political parties named themselves after the constitutional basis that they thought to be the right one and that they wanted to choose. And a second one: in the same period, even counties revendicated the capacity to control the constitutionality of executive acts and to not be obliged to apply those that they would judge as not conforming to the historic constitutions.

Second, if we look back to the political history of Hungary, we can conclude that, for the same historical reasons, occupation and foreign submission, a strong executive power was often demanded and established in Hungary. It is only during the period after the Compromise with the Habsburg Empire and the First World War, that a parliamentary regime with strong opposition and permanent political debates could be developed. This could be seen as contradictory to our first historical remark. But the two historical particularities of Hungary have not excluded each other. That is why, in our opinion, one must be very careful when using qualificatives such as authoritarian or even populist. A strong executive is not good for a parliamentary regime; however, it could be maintained if the constitution is effectively protected, in the limits of constitutional standards.

We would point out that in Hungarian constitutional history, as it has been mentioned before when describing the problem of the interruption of Hungarian constitutional development leading to a difficulty in re-establishing a constitutional culture, totalitarian regimes came from abroad by occupation. It was by resisting them that a strong executive was formed. At the same time, as it had no political or military force to resist them, Hungary was occupied militarily and politically by armies and by political ruse. Even though

4 The Fundamental Law of Hungary has been adopted by the National Assembly acting as the constituent power according to the former constitution on the 25 April 2011, it entered into force on the 1 January 2012.

5 Act number CLI of 2011 on the Constitutional Court of Hungary, adopted on the 21 November 2011, entered into force on the 1 January 2012.

Hungary has a long history of constitutional protection starting, according to the Hungarian historic constitution, with the so-called Golden Bull,[6] whose 800th anniversary is commemorated these days, long before the rise of modern constitutionalism, and the idea was reinforced, in the period of Ottoman Occupation, by the concept and the doctrine of the Holy Crown.[7] This protection could not help when Hungary was facing the totalitarian regimes of the 20th century that led to the above-mentioned interruption of constitutional development.

Finally, as for the theoretical element, we would highlight that there is a question, both important and delicate, about the borders that separate constitutionalism and its legal protection from political consideration and its influence on that. That border should exist and must be respected. But it is also obvious that constitutional interpretation, as much because of its object as because of its consequences, is always also a political matter. Even though, constitutional principles developed in theory and applied for centuries as much as the written provisions of national constitutions should serve as a strong basis to elaborate an objective and effective constitutional interpretation that respects the methodological and substantial standards of legal doctrine.

Concerning our first statement according to which constitutionalism is still protected in Hungary thanks to the Hungarian Constitutional Court, there are some international criticisms that we should mention. And we would not deny, but the opposite, we would like to highlight them in order to conclude that despite some facts, our statement can be maintained.

The most important criticisms are about the composition of the Constitutional Court. And it is true that as the parliamentary majority of one political force remained over the rate of the qualified majority for more than a decade, they could choose and elect the constitutional judges. So that for now, all 15 judges of the Court were nominated and elected by the same political majority. That is the reason why international academic opinion speaks about a captured court.[8] At the same time, it should be mentioned that they are elected for a period of 12 years and their mandate is not renewable.[9] Nobody knows what the political situation will be in 12 years in Hungary. Also, in such a long period, judges can change or evolve in their convictions on social or

6 The so-called Golden Bull was promulgated by King Andrew II in 1222; it is seen as the first document ensuring a protection of privileges, so some sort of constitutional rights. Its importance is reflected by the fact that it is the symbol of the Hungarian Constitutional Court.

7 The doctrine of the Holy Crown was legally explained and completely developed in the Tripartitum of István Werbőczy, published in 1517, confirmed as a source of law by the Diet in Hatvan, in 1525. The full Latin version with an English translation was published in 2005, J.M. Bak, P. Banyó, M. Rady (ed.), *The Customary Law of the Renowned Kingdom of Hungary: a Work in Three Parts, Tripartitum opus juris consuetudinarii inclyti regni Hungariae*, Budapest: Schlacks and CEU Press 2015.

8 See especially in the different essays published on the verfassungsblog.de.

9 Act number CLI of 2011 on the Constitutional Court of Hungary, art. 6 § 3.

even constitutional values. We would also ask the question: to which extent is the conviction of a judge important? Not all cases are about politically sensitive matters. On the contrary, most of them are politically neutral.

Anyway, cases should be decided according to the legal interpretation of the constitutional provisions which can be discussed by any professionals. Those discussions can also reinforce or weaken the legitimacy of the Court so that judges should pay attention to the professional quality of their jurisprudence.

A second criticism often also mentioned by European institutions, such as the Commission of Venice, brings into light the fact that some competences of the Hungarian Constitutional Court were abrogated. Especially, the authors of those opinions regret that the actio popularis has been abolished and some other restrictions were introduced.

A first restriction concerns budgetary matters, for those, only the protection of human dignity can be opposed. However, as this fundamental right can be and is interpretated by Hungarian constitutional judges in a very extended way, the protection of constitutional rights is ensured, also in the praxis, the jurisprudence shows no sign of constitutional weakness because of this first restriction.

A second is about the application of the former case law of the Court, adopted before the Fundamental Law entered into force. However, as it has been many times proven by the Court, the case law could be easily reintroduced, as the Court itself decided to use it for the provisions that remained the same or even as guidelines for more abstract or general principles.

The third and last often mentioned criticism about the new competencies concerns the constitutional control of amendment. As it has been decided that constitutional judges can only control their adoption from a sole formal analysis, this means that they only examine whether the procedure was respected.

This is a very interesting question that we will not discuss in its many details. We would simply mention that in European states, it is rather rare to have substantial control of constitutional amendments. Also, it is obvious that it concerns only a few cases before the Court even though, in Hungary, the Fundamental Law is often modified: 11 amendments were adopted in 11 years.

Facing those critics coming from international academic opinions or expressed by European institutions, we would like to show the complexity of the matter. A completely new system, a new economy of constitutional protection has been introduced in Hungary. It has a lot of consequences that should be carefully and objectively analysed also with regard to the constitutional praxis of the Court.

One could highlight that now the protection of the constitutionally guaranteed rights is based on real complaints which means that there is less room for the abstract interpretation of the constitutional provisions. Also, it could be mentioned that the interpretation as regulated by the Fundamental Law, itself, should be more based on the text of the constitution, so the so-called constitutional activism is repelled.

On another hand, a new flexible basis for constitutional interpretation also appeared such as the paragraphs of the constitutional preamble or the achievements of the historic constitutions.[10] When using those, the Constitutional Court can find new tools for strong protection of constitutional rights such as the freedom of the press, or even of institutional principles, such as parliamentarism. We would also mention that achievements of the historic constitutions were also applied when the Court decided on the non-conformity of the Fourth Amendment in its first and widely well-known decision.[11]

When reading the opinions of the Commission of Venice, we can acknowledge the serious concern expressed in a more and more accentuated way by the Commission. The first opinion about the reform of constitutional justice contained positive and negative remarks.[12] But the opinion about the Fourth Amendment, and one third of it dealt with issues related to the constitutional justice, expressed a great concern and could not find any positive signs.[13]

Despite those opinions, finally, we maintain our statement that the Hungarian Constitutional Court continues, certainly, in another constitutional economy, to ensure the protection of Hungarian constitutionalism. Also, we can see some positive evolution as well, due to the above-mentioned constitutional reform as the two judgments of the European Court of Human Rights, which will be presented in the next chapter, demonstrate.

8.2 A less known consequence of the last reform of constitutional justice in Hungary

An important evolution happened in 2018 and 2019, so a couple of years ago, in the perception of the Hungarian Constitutional Court by the European Court of Human Rights. In separate cases, the European Court decided, twice in less than one year, that the new procedures that individuals can initiate at the Hungarian Constitutional Court should be considered effective domestic remedies in the sense of art. 35 of the Convention and that, as such, they must be exhausted before asking for the protection of the European Court of Human Rights.[14]

10 Fundamental Law, art. R § 3.

11 Judgment of the Constitutional Court of Hungary number 12/2013 (V. 24).

12 Opinion number CDL-AD(2012)009 of the Commission of Venice, on the Act on the Constitutional Court of Hungary, adopted during the 91st plenary session in Venice, on 15 and 16 June 2012.

13 Opinion number CDL-AD(2013)013 of the Commission of Venice, on the Fourth Amendment of the Fundamental Law of Hungary, adopted during the 95th plenary session in Venice, on 14 and 15 June 2013.

14 Judgment of the European Court of Human Rights in the case *László Mendrei v. Hungary*, 5 July 2018, application number 54927/15; Judgment of the European Court of Human Rights in the case *Győző Szalontay v. Hungary*, 4 April 2019, application number 71327/13.

Those judgments are even more interesting in light of the precedent case law of the European Court of Human Rights about the Hungarian Constitutional Court. Before the reform in 2011, the European Court always refused to consider the Constitutional Court of Hungary as a tribunal that should be asked on a case before going to Strasbourg. On the contrary, Human Rights judges repeated several times that *actio popularis* before the Hungarian Constitutional Court cannot be considered a domestic judicial remedy in the sense of art. 35.

It is an important, and according to us a very positive consequence of the Hungarian reform, benefitting, also in the opinion of the European Court of Human Rights, any justiciable from a new and effective possibility to ask for the protection of fundamental rights. Thanks to the reform, we have the possibility to apply to the Constitutional Court for an effective remedy. As it is well-known, according to the case law of the European Court, in order to consider a domestic remedy as effective in the sense of art. 35, it should be accessible, be effective and offer a real chance for compensation.

Those are the conditions that *actio popularis* could not fulfil. Without going into the details, as we prefer to present a more complete description, the actual situation, the problem with the *actio popularis* was that although many of them arrived at the Court, some of them were never judged, so it could not be considered as an accessible remedy.[15] Also, in some cases of abstract interpretation, even though the non-conformity of the legislation to the constitution was declared, there were no possibilities for the Constitutional Court to redress the situation of the plaintiff, so it could not be seen as offering a real chance for compensation.[16]

To come closer to the actual situation and to be able to apply those three criteria to the new Hungarian constitutional claims, very briefly, we would like to summarise those three new possibilities for individuals to go before the constitutional judges in Hungary. It is obvious that there is no larger capacity offered for individuals to ask for constitutional protection than *actio popularis*; however, we would like to prove that the new, more judicial approach has even more benefits.

According to the Hungarian legislation on Constitutional Court, there are three possibilities to address the Court for individuals. First, the Court could be addressed when in a judicial procedure, one would deem that a fundamental right has been violated, and all other competent national tribunals have already heard the case.[17] Second, one can also address the Constitutional Court when the application of a national act would lead to the violation of a

15 Judgment of the European Court of Human Rights in the case *K.M.C. v. Hungary*, 10 July 2012, application number 19554/11.

16 Judgment of the European Court of Human Rights in the case *Csikós v. Hungary*, 5 December 2006, application number 37251/04; decision of the European Commission of Human Rights in the case *József Vén v. Hungary*, 30 June 1993, application number 21495/93.

17 Act number CLI of 2011 on the Constitutional Court of Hungary, art. 26 § 1.

fundamental right but there is no possibility to go before any other national judge.[18] Third, against any final judicial decision, an individual, in case of a breach of fundamental right, can go before the Constitutional Court.[19] The first is the so-called general, the second the so-called exceptional and the third the so-called integral remedy.

The basic idea behind the reform was not to exclude individuals from the possibility to ask the Constitutional Court for the protection of their constitutional rights, but to make it only available to those whose rights were violated by the application of national acts or by the action of national authorities, and to require them to first ask normal judges, if any action can be initiated before them, and to go before the Constitutional Court only after. Also, one can attack the decision of normal judges before the Constitutional Court if it is considered to violate constitutionally protected rights.

The fact that only those whose rights were violated and only after a judicial procedure can go before the Constitutional Court has the result that there are less cases and that the Constitutional Court can proceed to a judgment in time so it can be considered as accessible. Also, in those concrete cases, there is no difficulty in offering a real redress to the violation by abrogating the judicial decision that would be non-conforming to the Fundamental Law, or by declaring non-conforming any act causing a breach of fundamental rights that, consequently, won't be applied by the judges or could not be applied anymore to the person.

Of course, there can be some exceptions as the doctrine has already revealed, for example, for the decisions on the execution of criminal sanctions, there is a lack of procedure, even though many cases were introduced before the Constitutional Court on that matter. Also, it should be mentioned that according to the case law of the European Court of Human Rights, there must be an appreciation case by case with regard to the three above-mentioned criteria to apply art. 35 of the Convention.

The European Court needed some time to find the cases where such a new interpretation of the Hungarian individual constitutional remedies could be developed. Several cases introduced even after the reform could not lead to this conclusion. First, the new constitutional remedies were examined by the European Court in a case[20] where the constitutional claim of the plaintiff had been rejected, obviously, it could not be declared as an effective remedy in such a situation. In the next case,[21] the breach of rights was related to administrative measures that cannot be modified by the Constitutional Court even

18 Ibidem, § 2.

19 Act number CLI of 2011 on the Constitutional Court of Hungary, art. 27 § 1.

20 Judgment of the European Court of Human Rights in the case *Hálózati Gyógyszertárak Szövetsége and others v. Hungary*, 14 May 2013, application number 66925/12.

21 Judgment of the European Court of Human Rights (Grand Chamber), in the case *Karácsony and others v. Hungary*, 13 January 2015, application number 65681/13.

though a non-conformity is declared, so there was no real chance for redress or compensation.

Even, in the first case[22] where the new constitutional procedures were subject to a more detailed analysis, finally, the European Court could not yet conclude to consider those as a judicial tool for effective remedy. But, in that case, the problem was that the Constitutional Court has already abrogated the Act that causes the violation of rights but even though some financial claims of the plaintiff could not be satisfied.

So finally, first, the two normal, the so-called general and integral remedies, were interpretated as efficient remedies in the sense of art. 35. According to the European Court, they could be considered accessible, effective remedies offering a real chance to redress the violation of human rights. Their qualification as such remedies seems to be obvious as the individual action can be easily introduced before the Constitutional Court, that has to arrive at a final judgment in a relatively short period of time and by that judgment, in case of non-conformity, it can order the tribunal to not apply the act in question or, in the second hypothesis, it could abrogate the judicial decision in question and order a new proceeding.

But, interestingly, even the exceptional remedy was considered an effective one in the application of art. 35. This conclusion could be developed in a particular case where the fact that an existing piece of legislation was modified, resulted in a change in the status of the person without the possibility of going before a normal tribunal caused the breach of rights. As the European Court highlighted, according to the new Hungarian rules about constitutional justice, the person had 180 days, so about half a year, to ask the Constitutional Court for the protection of his rights. So the remedy was clearly accessible.

The effectiveness could be also easily declared in that case as the human rights which would have been violated are also protected by the Hungarian Fundamental Law. Also, the remedy, in case of success, could give a chance to come back to the previous situation before the modification of the national legislation causing the change in the legal status. Hence, the Constitutional Court could abrogate the modification if it were considered non-conforming to the Fundamental Law.

So not only the general and the integral individual constitutional remedy but also the exceptional one could be considered by the European Court of Human Rights as an effective remedy in case of the violation of human rights in the application of art. 35 of the European Convention on Human Rights. Once again, in our opinion, it is a very important evolution as the European Court recognised an important benefit of the Hungarian constitutional reform. Despite the concerns expressed by the Commission of Venice, also an organ

22 Judgment of the European Court of Human Rights in the case *Magyar Keresztény Mennonita Egyház and others v. Hungary*, 8 April 2014. application numbers 70945/11, 23611/12, 26998/12, 41150/12, 41155/12, 41463/12, 41553/12, 54977/12 et 56581/12

of the Council of Europe, finally, the reform resulted also in some advances as well. In those specific cases, the work of the Constitutional Court of Hungary is to be considered effective for the protection of fundamental rights. After the criticisms, such consideration is more than reassuring and shows that the protection of constitutional rights can be guaranteed by the Constitutional Court of Hungary. To put it that way, constitutional justice is maintained or even better ensured in the new system.

As final remarks, instead of a conclusion, we would like to bring to light the difficulty of the analysis of a constitutional justice system. It has always its specificities because of the historical context or the dominant theory about constitutionalism. Also, the fact that constitutional justice is always strongly related to politics can make the analysis complicated, sometimes delicate.

For Hungarian constitutional justice, those difficulties are especially relevant. First, because of the interruption of an organic constitutional development that was compensated by the direct implementation of other models not always fitting for the Hungarian constitutional and political background. Second, because of the absence of an opposition in a parliamentary regime, the constitutional structure becomes undoubtedly weak.

However, Hungary has a strong and well-known constitutional heritage for applying a strong protection of constitutionalism. Even the Hungarian theoretical framework, contrary to other dominant theories in other European states, such as France, suggests that constitutionalism should be legally protected. So, despite the fact that Hungarian constitutional justice was only established after the constitutional transition, there are strong roots making liveable such a judicial protection of constitutional rights.

Even though international academics and international organisations were concerned by the reform introduced ten years ago, in our opinion, the last decade demonstrated that Hungarian constitutional justice continues to work and to protect constitutionalism. This is also the opinion of the European Court of Human Rights that decided to consider the new constitutional remedies as accessible, efficient and able to redress the violation of human rights.

Opinions and declarations such as interpretations of the new Hungarian constitutional justice system are important. They can serve as mirrors, especially when using the comparative method, to see what the essential nature of the system is. However, to have an exact image, a detailed, case-by-case evaluation of the praxis in the new framework must be done. The situation is not always reassuring but some positive advances can also be detected after the reform, and according to our professional point of view, if there is a systemic constitutional problem, that is surely not about the functioning of the Hungarian constitutional justice, that is weaker than it was before, but at the same time, remains efficient, even more efficient under some specific aspects. We only wish that academic and institutional actors continue the scrutiny of the Hungarian constitutional justice system but in a detailed and nuanced analysis, as we are convinced that such an analysis is not only interesting but has also its role to play for the guarantee of Hungarian constitutionalism.

References

Ablonczy B., *Sur les traces de la Constitution hongroise*, Elektromedia, Budapest 2012.

Bak J.M., Banyó P., Rady M. (ed.), *The Customary Law of the Renowned Kingdom of Hungary: A Work in Three Parts, Tripartitum opus juris consuetudinarii inclyti regni Hungariae*, Schlacks and CEU Press, Budapest 2015.

Bóka J., *Az összehasonlító módszertan alkalmazása az Alkotmánybíróság joggyakorlatában* (in:) L. Trócsányi (ed.), *Tanulmányok Kovács István emlékére*, Dikaiosz Logosz, Szeged2012.

Trócsányi L., *Constitutions nationales et intégration européenne*, Larcier, Bruxelles 2015.

9 A missed dialogue: the European Court of Justice and the Romanian Constitutional Court

Elena-Simina Tănăsescu

9.1 General introduction

Democratic backsliding[1] and decay of the rule of law[2] seem to be gaining momentum all over the world and particularly in Europe. Within the European Union (EU) this trend, which appears manifest particularly in Central and Eastern Europe, came as a surprise for political actors and scholars alike, since most of them considered the successive enlargements, which started in 2004 and continued in 2007 and 2013, rather as a success story. Conditionalities imposed by the European Commission during pre-accession negotiations to all candidate countries have been considered helpful in the harmonisation and implementation of EU values across the entire Union. However, the external imposition of those conditionalities may have stimulated a corrosion of the quality of the internal political deliberation in those countries, as well as a deterioration of their leaders' discourse, where competing elites no longer acknowledge their opponents' legitimacy. The result of these evolutions may well be reflected in the substantive core of the democratic backsliding observed nowadays.[3] On the other hand, European integration relies heavily on courts and the necessary cooperation between the national and the supranational judiciaries. Given that the rule of law is a fundamental value of European construction and given

1 Among many other see S. Issacharoff, *Fragile Democracies*, Cambridge 2015; T. Ginsburg, H. Aziz, *How to Save a Constitutional Democracy*, "The University of Chicago Press" 2018; I.P. Karolewski, *Towards a Political Theory of Democratic Backsliding? Generalising the East Central European Experience*, (in:) A. Lorenz, L.H. Anders (eds.), *Illiberal Trends and Anti-EU Politics in East Central Europe*, "Palgrave Studies in European Union Politics" 2021, pp. 301–321; A. Gora, P. de Wilde, *The Essence of Democratic Backsliding in the European Union: Deliberation and Rule of Law*, "Journal of European Public Policy" 2022, vol. 29, iss. 3, pp. 342–362.

2 Among many other see D. Landau, *Abusive Constitutionalism*, "UC Davis Law Review" 2013, vol. 47, pp. 189–261; D.S. Law, M. Versteeg, *Sham Constitutions*, "California Law Review" 2013, vol. 101, no. 4, pp. 863–952; L. Pech, K. Lane Scheppele, *Illiberalism Within: Rule of Law Backsliding in the EU*, CYELS 2017, vol. 19, pp. 3–10; M. Smith, *Staring into the Abyss: A Crisis of the Rule of Law in the EU*, "European Law Journal" 2019, vol. 25, p. 563; T. Drinóczi, A. Bień-Kacała, *Rule of Law, Common Values, and Illiberal Constitutionalism: Poland and Hungary within the European Union*, Routledge & CRC Press 2020.

3 A. Gora, P. de Wilde, *The essence...*, p. 342.

DOI: 10.4324/9781003355793-11

the prominent role played by courts within any state governed by the rule of law, judicial independence became both the cornerstone of European integration and the target of illiberal or authoritarian executives. Hence, legal scholarship considered judicial independence as the key problem in countries where rule of law backsliding has been noticed.[4]

Against this background constitutional courts are among the institutions most frequently put under stress,[5] probably due to the fact that they represent one of the main limits on power. Understood equally as a constraint on power and as an instrument of protection of the normativity of the constitution,[6] constitutional courts naturally enjoy the attention of illiberal or authoritarian governments. At the same time and quite paradoxically, when they come into power, illiberal or authoritarian governments do not usually suppress constitutional courts, but rather carry out reforms meant to concentrate power in their hand and subordinate constitutional courts to their will.[7] However, constitutional courts may also surrender on their own to illiberal or authoritarian governments.[8] Legal and political culture, historical context and many other variables can impact the effectiveness of their resistance against democratic backsliding. And if that is the case, what role does a reformed or compliant constitutional court perform with regard to the protection of the constitution? Is there still room for proper constitutional review in the absence of a properly functioning constitutional court?

4 L. Pech, K.L. Scheppele, *Illiberalism…*, *passim*.

5 A number of studies have described the changes undertaken by constitutional courts under illiberal governments, as well as the reactions to those changes at the level of supranational institutions such as the EU. Among many other see C. Closa, D. Kochenov (eds.), *Reinforcing the Rule of Law Oversight in the European Union*, Cambridge University Press 2016; B. Bugarič, T. Ginsburg, *The Assault on Post-Communist Courts*, "The Journal of Democracy" 2016, vol. 27, p. 69; D. Kelemen, *Europe's Other Democratic Deficit: National Authoritarianism in Europe's Democratic Union*, "Government and Opposition" 2017, vol. 52, p. 211; M. Blauberger, R.D. Kelemen, *Can Courts Rescue National Democracy? Judicial Safeguards against Democratic Backsliding in the EU*, "Journal of European Public Policy" 2017, vol. 24, no. 3, pp. 321–336; D. Kochenov, P. Bard, *Rule of Law Crisis in the New Member States of the EU – The Pitfalls of Over-emphasizing Enforcement*, Working Paper no. 1, July 2018, available at: https://reconnect-europe.eu/wp-content/uploads/2018/07/RECONNECT-KochenovBard-WP_27072018b.pdf.

6 H. Kelsen, *Judicial Review of Legislation: A Comparative Study of the Austrian and the American Constitution*, "The Journal of Politics" 1942, vol. 4, no. 2, p. 183; A. Sweet Stone, *Governing with Judges*, Oxford University Press 2000.

7 For a recent overview of the situation across Europe see the "German Law Journal" special issue, vol. 22, no. 7 on *Judges Under Stress*, available at https://germanlawjournal.com/volume-22-issue-7/.

8 E.S. Tănăsescu, *Can Constitutional Courts Become Populist?*, (in:) M. Belov (ed.), *The Role of Courts in Contemporary Legal Orders*, The Hague 2019, pp. 305–319. The same may happen with ordinary courts who may seek to gain popularity amongst ordinary people in order to strengthen their institutional position in the field of politics. On this last subject see M. Bencze, *Everyday Judicial Populism in Hungary*, "Review of Central and East European Law" 2022, vol. 47, no. 1, pp. 37–59.

Bearing in mind this intellectual challenge, which represents the main narrative of the present collective publication, in my contribution I will endeavour to present the case of Romania, where the Constitutional Court has not been under visible pressure from authoritarian or populist executives but has proved compliant with those in power, particularly when they attempted to frustrate the rule of law and limit the independence of justice through a reform of the judicial system. The role played by the Romanian Constitutional Court (RCC) in this process cannot be underestimated.[9] And while its approach towards the reform of the judiciary might have been motivated also by considerations related to its own interaction with the judicial system,[10] the general outcome has proven rather detrimental to the independence of justice.

The jurisprudence of the RCC discussed here and the reactions triggered at the level of the ECJ refer to judicial reforms undertaken in Romania mainly between 2018 and 2019; therefore it is obvious that their interaction falls within the ambit of the general rule of law backsliding in the EU.[11] However, the same debate can also be envisaged from yet another perspective, namely the principle of primacy of EU law,[12] for two main reasons: first, because this seems to be the main challenge faced by the RCC, and second, because this has been an unique opportunity for the ECJ to assert the primacy of the post-accession conditionality imposed on Romania through Decision 2006/928/EC of 13 December 2006, namely the cooperation and verification mechanism (CVM), an original tool meant to ensure compliance of the new Member

9 B. Selejan-Guţan, *The Taming of the Court – When Politics Overcome Law in the Romanian Constitutional Court*, VerfBlog, 6.06.2018, https://verfassungsblog.de/the-taming-of-the-court-when-politics-overcome-law-in-the-romanian-constitutional-court/.

10 E.S. Tănăsescu, *Cour Constitutionnelle et système judiciaire: des rapports de force?*, "Analele Universităţii din Bucureşti – Drept" 2012, iss. 2, pp. 240–251; E.S. Tănăsescu, *The Romanian Constitutional Judge: Lost in Transition*, (in:) M. Jovanovic (ed.), *Constitutional Review and Democracy*, Eleven International Publishing, The Hague 2015, p. 223–252; V. Viţă, *The Romanian Constitutional Court and the Principle of Primacy: To Refer or Not to Refer?*, "German Law Journal" 2015, vol. 16, no. 6, p. 1627; M. Moraru and R. Bercea consider the current relationship between the RCC and ordinary courts to be an open 'rivalry'. See M. Moraru, R. Bercea, *The First Episode in the Romanian Rule of Law Saga: Joined Cases C-83/19, C-127/19, C-195/19, C-291/19, C-355/19 and C-397/19, Asociatia Forumul Judecatorilor din România, and their Follow-up at the National Level*, "European Constitutional Law Review" 2022, vol. 18, no. 1, p. 11.

11 E.S. Tănăsescu, *The Independence of Justice as Proxy for the Rule of Law in the EU. Case study – Romania*, "Nuovi Autoritarismi e Democrazie: Diritto, Istituzioni, Società" 2021, vol. 3, no. 1, pp. 103–123; M. Moraru, R. Bercea, *The First Episode…*, *passim*; A. Bobic, *The Jurisprudence of Constitutional Conflict in the European Union*, Oxford University Press 2022, p. 125.

12 E.S. Tănăsescu, B. Selejan-Guţan, *A Tale of Primacy: The ECJ Ruling on Judicial Independence in Romania*, VerfBlog, 2.06.2021, https://verfassungsblog.de/a-tale-of-primacy/; B. Selejan-Guţan, *A Tale of Primacy Part II: The Romanian Constitutional Court on a Slippery Slope*, VerfBlog, 18.06.2021, https://verfassungsblog.de/a-tale-of-primacy-part-ii/; B. Selejan-Guţan, *A Tale of Primacy, Part III: Game of Courts*, VerfBlog, 17.11.2021, https://verfassungsblog.de/a-tale-of-primacy-part-iii/.

State with the fundamental values of the EU and particularly with the rule of law. Ultimately, the entire issue revolves around the old topic of the judicial dialogue[13] between the ECJ and the constitutional courts of EU Member States, a theme that may remind to some the unsolved problem of geometry dealing with the quadrature of the circle.[14]

Considering that the approach taken deliberately in this paper emphasises the primacy of EU law against a more general background relating to the interaction between the ECJ and the RCC, this paper is structured as follows: after a brief presentation of the main characteristics of the rule of law backsliding in Romania, there follows an abstract of the three relevant decisions of the ECJ with regard to judicial reforms recently undertaken by Romania and of the corresponding case law of the RCC and an analysis of the parallel monologues of the two jurisdictions that still need to build up a dialogue. All these elements take us to the conclusion that the internalisation of the EU standard of the rule of law in Romania faces serious challenges as of lately, while the interaction between the RCC and the ECJ needs further corrections in order to become an active and effective judicial dialogue.

9.2 Rule of law backsliding in Romania

Romania joined the European Union (EU) on 1 January 2007. Decision 2006/928/EC 13 December 2006 put in place a mechanism for cooperation and verification (hereinafter CVM) in order to assess the progress made by the new Member State in the areas of judicial reform and the fight against corruption based on a set of specific benchmarks. Each year the European Commission (EC) issues a report assessing the situation and presenting recommendations meant to correct the course of the Member State in its endeavours

13 A number of articles and books have dealt with the topic of judicial dialogue, among which see A. Nollkaemper, *Conversations Among Courts: Domestic and International Adjudicators*, (in:) C. Romano, K. Alter, Y.Shany (eds.), *The Oxford Handbook of International Adjudication*, Oxford 2013; T. Tridimas, *The ECJ and the National Courts: Dialogue, Cooperation, and Instability*, Oxford 2015; E. Ferrer Mac-Gregor, *What Do We Mean When We Talk About Judicial Dialogue?: Reflections of a Judge of The Inter-American Court of Human Rights*, "Harvard Human Rights Journal" 2017, vol. 30, pp. 89–127.

14 A number of decisions issued by constitutional courts of Member States have challenged the jurisdiction of the European Court of Justice on matters related to the primacy of EU law. See particularly the Czech Constitutional Court Decision Pl. ÚS 5/12 following ECJ case C-399/09 *Landtova* (22 June 2011); the Danish Supreme Court Decision in case 15/2014 *Dansk Industri (DI)*, following ECJ case 441/14 *Dansk Industri v. Rasmussen* (19.04. April 2016); the German Bundesverfassungsgericht, Order of the Second Senate of 29 April 2021 – 2 BvR 1651/15 (the so-called *PSPP case*) following ECJ case C-493/17 *Weiss and Others* (11 December 2018). More recently, see the Polish Constitutional Tribunal Judgment of 7 October 2021 in case K 3/21 following the ECJ case law on judicial reforms in Poland, notably in case C-824/18 *A.B. and Others* (2 March 2021). Related to the judicial reforms in Poland and particularly referring to the composition of the Constitutional Tribunal, also see ECtHR (7 May 2021) *Xero Flor v. Poland*.

to comply with EU *acquis* in the relevant areas. Initially encompassing also Bulgaria,[15] since 2021 this original post-accession arrangement currently exists only with regard to Romania. The CVM itself has been assessed by the doctrine as lacking any preventive effect with regard to democratic backsliding since 15 yearly reports on the situation in Bulgaria and Romania have not managed to prevent or deter deliberate or systemic violations of the rule of law in these two countries.[16] It is interesting to note that, among the explanations provided for the establishment of this original post-accession arrangement, which – so far – has not been duplicated in subsequent enlargements, the first one refers to the fact that the 'European Union is founded on the rule of law' and that implies 'for all Member States the existence of an impartial, independent and effective judicial and administrative system properly equipped, inter alia, to fight corruption'.[17]

Democratic and rule of law backsliding started to manifest in Romania after the general elections of December 2016. At approximately the same time regular reports issued by the EC within the framework of the MCV started to mention 'possible systemic threats to the rule of law'. The short but concentrated backsliding culminated in 2018 with a general assault on judicial independence through legislative amendments to the laws pertaining to the judicial system and related institutional reforms. In a nutshell, judicial reforms in Romania focused, *inter alia*, on the creation of a special prosecutorial section meant to investigate crimes accomplished by magistrates coupled with the diminishing of powers of the prosecutorial section dealing with the fight against corruption, the personal liability of magistrates for judicial errors as well as the patrimonial liability of the state for miscarriages of justice. Also, the legal procedures for the appointment of the chief prosecutor of the newly created special section meant to investigate crimes accomplished by magistrates were revised by government immediately after their approval by Parliament in order to make possible the designation of a specific person.

I have discussed elsewhere[18] the political and constitutional context and consequences of that general assault on the Romanian judicial system. Here it suffices to say that even after the general elections of December 2020, which

15 See Decision 2006/929/EC for Bulgaria. See also the grim assessment made by the doctrine with regard to the impact of the CVM Decision 2006/929/EC on Bulgaria's progress towards a state governed by the rule of law at R. Vassileva, *Bulgaria's Failed Specialized Criminal Justice Experiment*, VerfBlog, 29.04.2022, https://verfassungsblog.de/bulgarias-failed-specialized-criminal-justice-experiment/.

16 L. Pech, P. Bard, *The Commission's Rule of Law Report and the EU Monitoring and Enforcement of Article 2 TEU Values*, document requested by the European Parliament's Committee on Civil Liberties, Justice and Home Affairs and the Committee on Constitutional Affairs, available at https://www.europarl.europa.eu/RegData/etudes/STUD/2022/727551/IPOL_STU(2022)727551_EN.pdf, p. 68.

17 See the first and the third recitals of Decision 2006/928/EC.

18 E.S. Tănăsescu, *Romania: From Constitutional Democracy to Constitutional Decay?*, (in:) V. Besirevic (ed.), *New Politics of Decisionism*, The Hague 2019, pp. 177–191.

produced rather ambiguous results, the tide has not been reversed. A shortly lived reformist government, made up of a coalition of three parties and which relied on a slim majority in Parliament, succumbed due to an internal clash on the specific manner in which it would undertake the reversing of judicial reforms performed in 2018–2019. It has been followed by a larger governmental coalition, which benefits from stronger support in Parliament due to the fact that it includes the political party which initiated those judicial reforms. The result is the fact that the bulk of the judicial reform undertaken is still in place, with only a tiny correction: the special prosecutorial section meant to investigate exclusively the crimes accomplished by magistrates was abolished in March 2022[19] and cosmetically replaced with a national network of prosecutors endowed with the same task.

Although the democratic backsliding and rule of law decay in Romania have been weaker and of a shorter duration than those observed in other EU Member States, as of 2019 Romanian courts capitalised on the experience gained by the ECJ with regard to the protection of the rule of law and started to address preliminary questions pertaining to the compliance of Romanian judicial reforms with EU *acquis* on judicial independence.[20] I have argued elsewhere[21] why the rule of law and independence of justice are core values of the EU and why they have an important position on the agenda of EU institutions. The fact remains that in recent years, in the absence of sustained and effective reactions at domestic or European level, the ECJ had to take an active stance in the judicial definition and protection of these legal standards.

9.3 The jurisprudence of the ECJ on rule of law referrals coming from Romania

As of recently the ECJ case law on the rule of law focused mainly on judicial independence, probably because such have been the cases and questions brought in front of it by the Commission and/or the Member States. Romania is no exception, as an impressive number of preliminary questions issued at an incredible pace[22] address precisely the impact that the judicial reforms of 2018–2019 had on the independence of justice. It is fair to say that Romanian

19 Through Law no. 49 of 11 March 2022 for the dismantling of the Section for the investigation of crimes in the judicial systems and for the modification of Law no. 135/2010 regarding the Criminal procedure code, published in the Official Journal of Romania no. 244 of 11 March 2022.

20 Particularly with the seminal case C-64/16 *Associação Sindical dos Juízes Portugueses* (2018).

21 E.S. Tănăsescu, *The independence...*

22 With more than 20 referrals already on the docket of the ECJ between, roughly, 2019 and 2021, Romania reaches an average of one referral every two months. 'The myriad preliminary references submitted by Polish and Romanian judges attempting to protect their independence in the face of political interventions' has also been noticed by the doctrine. See A. Bobic, *The Jurisprudence...*, p. 134.

judges used the mechanism of the preliminary question as a procedure of last resort, after all other political[23] and/or judicial tools proved inefficient[24] or insufficient.[25]

At a closer look, one may identify several types of broad queries that Romanian courts addressed to the ECJ: the legal nature and legal effects of the CVM Decision, the disciplinary regime of magistrates and the independence of ordinary judges in fulfilling their task as EU judges. While the ECJ decided to group referrals coming from Romania with regard to the rule of law in clusters and address them in – so far – three different rulings, this analysis will focus mainly on the first issue, namely the legal nature and legal effects of the CVM Decision, from the perspective of the primacy of EU law. Indeed, the primacy of EU law and particularly of the CVM Decision represents the common element of the three rulings delivered by the ECJ with regard to the rule of law in Romania, while the missed judicial dialogue between the RCC and the ECJ epitomises the 'collateral damage' induced by the originality of the legal instrument which is the CVM Decision.

9.3.1 Primacy of EU law and independence of justice

Thus, in what the doctrine has called a first 'wave of rule of law referrals',[26] Romanian courts addressed the ECJ preliminary questions in order to clarify (i) the legal regime of the CVM Decision and of the annual reports issued by the EC on this basis, (ii) the impact of the national judicial reforms on the independence of judges in their capacity as EU judges and (iii) the compatibility

23 Throughout 2018 various national and international actors have expressed their concerns with regard to the judicial reform in Romania, notably through a debate in the European Parliament on the threats to the rule of law in Romania in February 2018 (https://multimedia.europarl.europa.eu/en/threats-to-rule-of-law-by-romanian-justice-debate_I150531-V_v), the first Ad-hoc report on Romania (Rule 34) adopted by GRECO at its 79th Plenary Meeting on 19–23 March 2018 (http://www.just.ro/wp-content/uploads/2015/09/Greco-AdHocRep20182-Final-eng-Romania.pdf) and the Preliminary opinion n°924/2018 of the Venice Commission on the draft amendments to law n°303/2004 on the statute of judges and prosecutors, Law n°304/2004 on judicial organisation and law n°317/2004 on the Superior Council of Magistracy (https://www.venice.coe.int/webforms/documents/default.aspx?pdffile=CDL-PI(2018)007-e).

24 Throughout 2018 and up until 2022 the Constitutional Court has been notified with 28 cases referring to the judicial reform; it has constantly upheld it and defiantly refused the dialogue with the ECJ. Also see B Selejan Guțan and E.S. Tănăsescu, 'Romania' (in) R. Albert, D. Landau, P. Faraguna and S. Drugda (eds.), I·CONnect-Clough Center 2018 Global Review of Constitutional Law (18 October 2019), available at https://ssrn.com/abstract=3471638.

25 Romania has been condemned by the European Court of Human Rights for the removal of office of one prosecutor with the violation of the right of access to a court and of her freedom of expression (ECtHR 5 May 2020, *Kovesi v. Romania*), as well as for the removal of office of one judge with the violation of the right to a fair trial and of her freedom of expression (ECtHR 20 October 2020, *Camelia Bogdan v. Romania*).

26 M. Moraru, R. Bercea, *The First Episode*..., p. 3.

of the new disciplinary regime of Romanian judges with their mandate under EU law. All of these have been dealt with by the ECJ in the Judgment of the Grand Chamber of 18 May 2021 on the joined cases C-83/19, C-127/19, C-195/19, C-291/19, C-355/19 and C-397/19, *Asociaţia Forumul Judecătorilor din România*.

In a nutshell, in this first ruling the ECJ reached the obvious conclusion that the CVM Decision and the annual reports are EU legal acts which fall under its jurisdiction, but while the CVM Decision is legally binding, the annual reports are not enforceable although they enjoy legal effects through the requirement of sincere cooperation imposed by art. 4 § (2) TEU that obliges all authorities of all Member States to ensure consistent interpretation of national provisions with EU legal acts.

As for the impact of the judicial reform, and particularly of the disciplinary regime of magistrates, on the EU mandate of Romanian courts the ECJ stated that, although EU law does not require uniform judicial organisation or homogenous judicial accountability models, it does require that national courts are able to perform their functions as EU courts and, therefore, domestic disciplinary regimes must provide necessary guarantees in order to prevent any risk of them being used as tools of political control on the content of judicial decisions. Having said that, the ECJ has merely restated its previous case law pertaining to the competence of Member States with regard to their judicial organisation balanced with their obligation to comply with obligations deriving from EU law when exercising that competence,[27] as well as its previous case law referring to the disciplinary regime of magistrates.[28]

9.3.2 Primacy of EU law and disciplinary liability of judges

A second batch of referrals focused on (i) the binding legal effect of the CVM mechanism and relevant annual reports, (ii) the primacy of EU law over national legislation and institutional practice, including decisions of the RCC, in the area of the fight against corruption and protection of financial interests of the EU and (iii) the compatibility of the disciplinary regime of Romanian judges with their mandate under EU law in cases where they are bound to respect decisions of the RCC but where they also have to respect contrary rulings of the ECJ and therefore feel compelled to leave aside national legislation declared constitutional by the RCC but found in breach of EU law by the ECJ. All these issues have been dealt with by the ECJ in the Judgment of the Grand Chamber of 21 December 2021 in joined cases C-357/19, C379/19, C-547/19, C-811/19, C-840/19, *Euro Box Promotion*.

The nucleus of this ruling consists in the re-affirmation of the binding legal nature of the CVM Decision and the specific legal effects of annual reports

27 See case C-64/16 fn.20.
28 See cases C-558/18 *Miasto Lowicz* (2020) and C-896/19 *Repubblika* (2021).

through the obligation of sincere cooperation of Member States as provided by art. 4 § (2) TEU. As for the fight against corruption, apart from the fact that it is one of the reasons why the CVM was created in the first place, when it is in conjunction with the protection of 'the financial interests of the EU' it draws the priority of EU legislation also based on art. 325 TFEU. The ECJ convincingly uses both art. 325 TFEU on the EU's financial interests and the CVM Decision to emphasise the primacy of EU law in general, and the primacy of the EU legislation pertaining to the fight against corruption in particular, reaching the conclusion that domestic courts have to leave aside national provisions which prevent the sanction of fraud that affects the financial interests of the EU, including decisions of the RCC that go against this goal which Romania assumed in order to access the EU.

The ECJ found that the mandatory character of the RCC's decisions for domestic courts, and the subsequent disciplinary sanctions that might be incurred by judges in case they decide to leave aside such decisions which do not comply with the constant case law of the ECJ concerning the fight against corruption and the protection of the financial interests of the EU, is not contrary *per se* to EU law provided that the relevant national legislation also guarantees the full independence of the respective constitutional court from any interference, and particularly from the legislative and executive powers, otherwise such a constitutional court would not fulfil the requirements of an effective judicial protection as provided by art. 19 § (1) TEU. And the ECJ concluded by asserting that the principle of the primacy of EU law prevents national courts from leaving aside decisions of the RCC that are contrary to EU law if this is done under the constraint of disciplinary sanctions susceptible to be applied automatically and without any other condition.[29]

9.3.3 Primacy of EU law and the interplay between the ECJ and the RCC

Finally, the third ruling of the ECJ in the area of the rule of law with regard to Romania, case C-430/21 *RS*, deals directly with the relationship between the ECJ and the RCC, namely with the power of the RCC to limit the implementation of preliminary rulings by domestic courts.

In its judgment of the Grand Chamber of 22 February 2022 the ECJ reminded us that ordinary courts enjoy full jurisdiction to assess the compatibility of national law with EU law, without having to make a request to that end to the RCC. However, if national courts are deprived of that jurisdiction because the RCC declared national law consistent with a constitutional provision providing for the primacy of EU law, thus obliging them to merely execute that decision of the RCC instead of assessing themselves whether those national provisions are compatible with EU law, that would undermine the effectiveness of the cooperation between the ECJ and national courts by

29 Also see case C-791/19 *Commission v. Poland* (2021).

deterring ordinary courts from referring to the ECJ in order to comply with a decision of the RCC. This in itself would be a breach of EU law. Moreover, the mechanism of cooperation between national courts and the ECJ would be deeply affected if a constitutional court would forbid national courts to implement ECJ rulings and would itself refuse to give effect to a preliminary ruling, on the basis, *inter alia*, of the 'constitutional identity' and of the contention that the ECJ has exceeded its jurisdiction.

Again, referring to earlier case law,[30] the ECJ made clear that art. 2 combined with art. 19(1) of the TEU preclude national rules or practices under which national judges may incur disciplinary proceedings for any failure to comply with decisions of the RCC, in particular when such failures pertain to the RCC's decisions that refuse to implement a preliminary ruling delivered by the ECJ.

9.4 The jurisprudence of the RCC on the articulation of national law with EU law

Compared to the general case law of the ECJ on the issue of the rule of law and independence of justice, the one pertaining to Romania presents an element of novelty, which consists in the fact that it addresses head-on the original legal instruments which are the CVM Decision and its related reports. But, beyond this specificity, the three rulings of the ECJ expose the misunderstanding lingering on the side of the RCC with regard to the interaction between the national and the EU legal systems. This has not always been the case. Indeed, during pre-accession negotiations the RCC seemed open to the idea of cooperation rather than conflict with the ECJ, quoting ECJ case law and citing EU law in its decisions. However, following Romania's accession to the EU, the RCC gradually closed up and, save for a short moment when it welcomed the dialogue with the ECJ and the primacy of EU law, it refused to acknowledge EU law as a standard for the constitutionality review it performs. As of recently the RCC also refuses direct interactions with the ECJ,[31] despite the (unique) referral in case C-673/16 *Coman and Others*, Judgment of the Grand Chamber of 5 June 2018, which encountered a mitigated success.[32] Let us rewind.

30 Particularly to case C-791/19 *Commission v. Poland* (2021) and to joined cases C357/19, C-379/19, C-547/19, C-811/19 and C-840/19 *Euro Box Promotion and Others* (2021).

31 The RCC has previously declared itself outside the scope of art. 267 TFEU. See decisions no. 1249/2010, no. 137/2010 and no. 1596/2010.

32 Despite the ruling of the ECJ that allowed a third-country national of the same sex as a Union citizen, whose marriage to that citizen was concluded in a Member State in accordance with the law of that state, to reside in the territory of the Member State of which the Union citizen is a national for more than three months, Romanian authorities refused to comply. The couple has now addressed a case to the European Court of Human Rights.

Article 148 of the Romanian Constitution has been introduced in 2003, through a revision of the Fundamental law accomplished in order to allow Romania's accession to the EU. Entitled 'Integration into the European Union' it reads as follows:

(1) Romania's accession to the constituent treaties of the European Union, with a view to transferring certain powers to community institutions, as well as to exercising in common with the other member states the abilities stipulated in such treaties, shall be carried out by means of a law adopted in the joint sitting of the Chamber of Deputies and the Senate, with a majority of two thirds of the number of deputies and senators.
(2) As a result of the accession, the provisions of the constituent treaties of the European Union, as well as the other mandatory community regulations shall take precedence over the opposite provisions of the national laws, in compliance with the provisions of the accession act.
(3) The provisions of paragraphs (1) and (2) shall also apply accordingly for the accession to the acts revising the constituent treaties of the European Union.
(4) The Parliament, the President of Romania, the Government, and the judicial authority shall guarantee that the obligations resulting from the accession act and the provisions of paragraph (2) are implemented.
(5) The Government shall send to the two Chambers of the Parliament the draft mandatory acts before they are submitted to the European Union institutions for approval.

Article 148 establishes the primacy of EU law on domestic law and obliges all three powers of the state (legislative, executive and judicial) to guarantee the obligations arising from Romania's integration into the EU. Thus, art. 148 of the Constitution grants domestic constitutional value to the primacy of EU law as developed in the case law of the ECJ, although Romanian scholarship noticed that the constituent power referred to 'precedence over national laws' and not explicitly to 'precedence over the national Constitution'.[33]

In 2007, immediately after Romania's accession to the EU, the RCC attempted to distinguish between the constitutional review that it performs and the jurisdiction of the ECJ concerning the interpretation or the validity of EU legal acts, declaring, in decision no. 59/2007, that a domestic law may not be invalidated because it does not comply with EU law, and in decision

33 M. Andreescu, C. Andreescu, *Supremaţia Constituţiei în contextul principiului priorităţii dreptului Uniunii Europene* [The Supremacy of the Constitution in the Context of the Principle of Primacy of EU law], "Dreptul" 2017, iss. 8, pp. 48–60. For an acknowledgement of the primacy of EU law over the Constitution see A.-R. Lupu, *Suprematia Constitutiei – evolutia si limitele unui principiu fundamental al dreptului modern*, "Revista de drept public" 2017, iss. 3, pp. 124–149.

no. 311/2010 that the mere fact that EU law is more permissible or softer than domestic legislation does not make that domestic legislation *ipso facto* unconstitutional. Also, in decision no. 1596/2010 the RCC refused to check whether domestic law complies with EU law on the ground that, according to art. 148 § (4) of the Constitution, this is the exclusive jurisdiction of ordinary courts.

But then, in decisions no. 1519/2011 and no. 2/2012, the RCC acknowledged the CVM Decision and its benchmarks, and considered them relevant for the functioning of the Romanian judicial system, particularly for the fight against corruption, while at the same time declaring them legally binding and normative standards for the judicial review it performs based on the principle of primacy of EU law as captured in art. 148 § (4) of the Constitution. The RCC even emphasised the importance of the primacy of EU law as enshrined in art. 148 §§ (2) and (4) of the Constitution, stating that, by eliminating from a domestic procedural law the possibility to review final court decisions based on their breach of the primacy of EU law, the legislator disregards its obligations resulting from the accession act and … from the primacy of EU law itself, because 'even a final and irrevocable judgement cannot be considered legal as long as it is grounded on legal provisions which are contrary to EU law'.[34] This has been the golden era of the interaction between the Romanian and the EU legal systems and it is striking to see that it mostly concerned the original EU legal act which is the CVM Decision and the benchmarks it provides. After that grace-filled moment, a downward spiral started and the RCC complicated its jurisprudence up to the point where it got muddled in it.

Thus, in decision no. 668/2011 the RCC decided, without further explanations, not to apply art. 148 of the Constitution and simply accept the primacy of EU law, but to require two additional conditions in order to be able to consider EU law applicable in the review it performs: firstly, the EU norm must be sufficiently precise and clear or its normative content must have been clearly established by the ECJ and, secondly, the EU norm must be substantively relevant for the Constitution, i.e., its substantive matter must support and justify a breach of the Constitution by the domestic law because the Constitution remains the unique benchmark for the constitutional review. 'This reasoning is questionable in that it gives precedence, in defiance of the text, to a material perspective over the formal perspective. It is all the more so if one considers its consequences. It leads the RCC to set aside the EU law in the name of the conformity of the challenged law with the Constitution.'[35] Nevertheless, it is this second, subjective condition that allowed the RCC to

34 See decision no. 1039/2012.

35 A. Corre-Basset, *Cour constitutionnelle de Roumanie, décision 390/2021 du 8 juin 2021 (supériorité du droit constitutionnel interne sur le droit de l'Union)*, Titre VII, available at https://www.conseil-constitutionnel.fr/publications/titre-vii/chronique-de-droit-constitutionnel-compare-janvier-a-juin-2021.

refuse to interpolate EU norms in the constitutional review it performs on numerous other occasions.[36]

On the other hand, on those rare occasions when the RCC acknowledged the constitutional status of EU norms and actually used them in order to invalidate domestic laws,[37] it insisted that the mere finding of normative inconsistencies between domestic and EU norms cannot be a solution for the constitutional review it performs and, in order to declare a law unconstitutional, it has to find a breach of art. 148 of the Constitution because the Fundamental Law is the unique benchmark for the review the RCC performs.

Having said that, the RCC has not explained what is the difference between a breach of art. 148 of the Constitution and a breach of the principle of primacy of EU law, since art. 148 of the Constitution codifies with the normative value of Romanian constitutional law precisely the primacy of EU law as developed in the case law of the ECJ, making it compulsory and enforceable by all public authorities of the Romanian state, including the Constitutional Court. Legal scholarship has already remarked that art. 148 of the Constitution 'was not drafted to allow for elective but for imperative priority of EU law'.[38]

Nevertheless, the RCC went further down on the slippery slope. In decision no. 80/2014 it declared that 'EU law cannot be applied in the domestic legal system without the necessary distinction between the Constitution and the other laws' as this would mean that the Fundamental Law is placed in a secondary position in comparison to the Union's legal system.[39] Since the Constitution is 'the expression of the will of the people' it cannot lose its binding force due to the 'mere existence of a normative inconsistency between its provisions and European provisions'. Romania's accession to the EU 'cannot affect the supremacy of the Constitution over the entire national legal system (cf. the Judgment of 11 May 2005, K 18/04 of the Polish Constitutional Tribunal)'.[40]

Moreover, quoting the judgment of the German Constitutional Court on the Treaty of Lisbon (2 BvE 2/08), the RCC started – as early as 2012 – to refer to the concept of constitutional identity, without defining it, but simply stating that 'member states retain competences which are inherent in order to preserve their constitutional identity' and that it remains 'within the constitutional margin of appreciation of the Member States to cede competences and to rethink, emphasise or establish new guidelines within competences already ceded'.[41]

36 See decisions no. 802/2011, no. 750/2015, no. 64/2018 and no. 104/2018.
37 See particularly decision no. 64/2015.
38 M. Moraru, R. Bercea, *The First Episode…*
39 See § 455 of decision no. 80/2014.
40 See § 456 of decision no. 80/2014.
41 See § II.1 of decision no. 683/2012.

Therefore, it comes as no surprise that, later, the RCC repented from its polite case law pertaining to the CVM Decision[42] and even contradicted it. A twist of the argument allowed the RCC to rule in decisions no. 33/2018, no. 104/2018 and no. 682/2018 that 'since the meaning of Decision 2006/928/EC establishing a Cooperation and Verification Mechanism has not been clarified by the Court of Justice of the European Union as regards its content, character and temporal limit and whether all these are circumscribed to the provisions of the Treaty of accession [...], that Decision cannot be considered as a reference norm for the judicial review'. In addition, the RCC declared that the CVM Decision cannot be considered a normative standard for the constitutional review it performs because it had been adopted prior to Romania's accession to the EU, while after accession, as a Member State, Romania can no longer be subject to conditionalities. As for the yearly reports drafted by the EC and assessing the compliance of the situation in Romania with the benchmarks established in the CVM Decision, the RCC noticed they are mere recommendations, issued for political purposes, for the intention of the European Council and European Parliament, and are not addressed to Romanian authorities.

As a result, the RCC found the national legislator to be within its margin of appreciation, as provided by the 'constitutional identity' corroborated with national sovereignty, when legislating the substance matter of topics covered by the CVM. 'In this situation, similarly to Poland, the Constitutional Court becomes part of the problem as it endorses the legislative changes reducing judicial independence. In such a constellation, the Constitutional Court no longer participates in constructive constitutional conflict but forms part of the systemic, destructive nature of contesting the values in Article 2 TEU, namely the rule of law'.[43]

And the peak of the sovereigntist stance of the RCC has been reached in decision no. 390/2021, where it found that (i) the primacy of EU law only applies to ordinary legislation and not to the Constitution because primacy of EU law cannot be conceived or perceived as 'removing or disregarding the national constitutional identity, enshrined in Article 11(3) in conjunction with Article 152 of the Basic Law',[44] and that (ii) national courts do not have the power to examine the conformity with EU law of national provisions found constitutional in the light of art. 148 of the Romanian Constitution.

In order to justify the first assertion, the RCC explained that the 'constitutional relevance', i.e., the substantive constitutional character of the rule of law principle developed in EU law and clarified in the case law of the CJEU, cannot be confirmed because relevant EU law 'does not fill a gap in the Basic Law or establish a higher standard of protection than the constitutional standards

42 See decisions no. 1519/2011 and no. 2/2012 mentioned above.
43 A. Bobic, *The Jurisprudence...*, p. 125.
44 See § 81 of decision no. 390/2021.

in force'.[45] Therefore, the RCC used as a reference the equivalent provisions from the Romanian Constitution and, without further explanation, it stated that it will perform a constitutional review only 'with regard to the principle of the rule of law as expressly protected in domestic law, in Article 1 (3) of the Romanian Constitution'.[46]

> Such a reduction in the operation of EU law in the Romanian legal order grants virtually free rein to the government under whose control the Constitutional Court currently operates. Any and all legislation that undermines the rule of law simply needs to be confirmed as constitutional and is no longer subject to art. 2 TEU nor to art. 19 (1) TEU under the control by the Court of Justice, in direct contradiction of the judicial independence findings of the Court of Justice in *Juizes Portugueses* and most recently in *A B and Others*.[47]

As for the limitation to the jurisdiction of ordinary courts in their capacity as EU courts, the RCC followed an equally domestically twisted argument. The patent of constitutionality mentioned above is able to rule out any possibility of reviewing the conformity with EU law of domestic legislation found in conformity with art. 148 of the Romanian Constitution. That is why such legislation can potentially be examined only in the light of domestic law: since the Romanian legal order is based on the primacy of the Constitution and the principle of legality, since the separation of powers and the constitutionality review guarantee democratic legislation, then a law that passes the constitutionality test is necessarily irreproachable, including from the perspective of EU law. Consequently, an ordinary court is not allowed to set aside, on the basis of EU law, domestic legislation that has been declared constitutional on the basis of art. 148 of the Romanian Constitution. That such a conclusion might limit the general jurisdiction of ordinary courts and, by the same token, blatantly contradict established case law of the ECJ[48] has not bothered the majority of Romanian constitutional judges who adopted that decision. Rather to the contrary, concerned about its position within the institutional architecture of the Romanian judicial system, the RCC joined the cluster of constitutional courts who decided to resort to 'splendid isolation'[49] and retort to the ECJ for the fact that it empowered ordinary courts to apply EU law against any contrary domestic law, even of a constitutional nature.

45 See § 49 of decision no. 390/2021.

46 Ibidem.

47 A. Bobic, *The Jurisprudence*..., p. 125.

48 See Judgment of the Court (Grand Chamber) of 22 June 2010 in joined cases C-188/10 *Aziz Melki* and C-189/10 *Sélim Abdeli*.

49 M. Bobek, *The Impact of the European Mandate of Ordinary Courts on the Position of Constitutional Courts*, (in:) M. Claes, M. de Visser, P. Popelier, C. Van de Heyning (eds.), *Constitutional Conversations in Europe*, "Intersentia" 2012, p. 287.

9.5 Parallel monologues

As already mentioned, all three rulings of the ECJ dealing with the rule of law in Romania have in common the primacy of EU law in the specific context of Romania's accession to the EU. They have provided the ECJ with the unique opportunity to analyse the primacy of the original legal act which is the CVM Decision and the characteristics of the annual reports delivered yearly by the EC on the basis of the CVM Decision.

Unlike the classic case law on the primacy of EU law,[50] where the ECJ had based its reasoning on grand principles related to the original nature of EU law, in these three cases the ECJ had the possibility to ground the principle of primacy in legal texts, thus making the potential *ultra vires* criticism harder to substantiate. Indeed, for all the originality of its normative substance, which imposes to a specific EU Member State conditionalities under the disguise of benchmarks, the CVM Decision remains a legal act provided by art. 288 TFEU and amenable to interpretation under art. 267 TFEU. The CVM Decision enjoys a well-established legal regime: it is binding in its entirety on Romania from its accession and it obliges the Member State to address the benchmarks set out in its annex, benchmarks which are also binding.

Initially, attempting not to overtly antagonise the RCC, in the judgment delivered in *Asociația Forumul Judecătorilor din România* (2021) the ECJ has *de facto* succeeded in considerably reducing the margin of appreciation of Romanian authorities and obliging them to comply with the substance matter of the CVM. Later, when the RCC displayed a strict sovereigntist stance, in the judgments delivered in *Euro Box Promotion* (2021) and in *RS* (2022), the ECJ resolved to explain in detail the interaction between the national and the European legal systems and the necessary relationship which needs to be established between the RCC and the European jurisdiction.

Thus, the primacy of EU law makes it impossible for a Member State to rely on national law, be it of constitutional nature, in order to undermine the unity and effectiveness of EU law. And if the national law does not guarantee the independence of the relevant constitutional court from the legislature and the executive as required by 'Article 2 TEU, the second subparagraph of Article 19(1) TEU and Decision 2006/928',[51] EU law precludes national rules or national practices under which decisions of that constitutional court are binding on the ordinary courts because such a constitutional court is not in a position to ensure the effective judicial protection required by the second subparagraph of art. 19(1) TEU.

This may sound like a harsh reminder of the fact that the primacy of EU law concerns the entire legal system of a Member State and is binding on all bodies of that Member State, as it has been clarified by the ECJ already in *Simmenthal*

50 See cases C-6/64 *Costa v. E.N.E.L.* (1964) and C-106/77 *Simmenthal* (1978).
51 See case C-430/21 RS (2022), point 44.

(1978). On the other hand, this is also the normative substance of art. 148 of the Romanian Constitution that the RCC decided not to apply as such but, instead, made it conditional upon its own requirements. The Romanian legal system is unique also in this respect: it contains a constitutional provision imposing the primacy of EU law upon domestic law to all national authorities. Under these circumstances, the posture taken by the RCC in decision no. 390/2021 seems a bit sardonic.

Against this background, and given the statement of the RCC that the annual reports drawn up by the EC on the basis of the CVM Decision are 'mere recommendations issued for political purposes' which are addressed to the European Council and European Parliament and not to Romanian public authorities, it is worth mentioning that those reports have been differently approached by the Advocate General of the Court and by the ECJ itself. Thus, the Advocate General[52] found that the reports, and the recommendations therein, do not enjoy binding value although they 'amount to much more than a "traditional" recommendation' (point 160) and 'they are to be duly taken into consideration by that Member State' (point 164). But given their specificity, national judges cannot be expected to rely on the recommendations contained in MCV reports in order to set aside the application of national legislation that they deem contrary to such recommendations (point 168).

On the contrary, the ECJ considered that those reports formulate requirements with regard to Romania and address 'recommendations' to it with a view to the benchmarks set in the CVM Decision being met. In accordance with the principle of sincere cooperation, Romania must take due account of those requirements and recommendations, and must refrain from adopting or maintaining measures in the areas covered by the benchmarks which could jeopardise the result prescribed by those requirements and recommendations.

This is not the only occasion nor the only issue on which the ECJ has not followed the advice of AG Bobek.[53] Indeed, unlike its Advocate General, the ECJ considered not only that CVM reports and the recommendations therein should be respected and may be invoked by ordinary courts when assessing the compatibility of domestic law with the principle of primacy of EU law, but also that the reasoning of the Court should not be grounded on art. 47 of the Charter, but on art. 19(1) TEU.

Thus, the ECJ has expanded the scope of art. 19 (1) TEU and differentiated it from the right to an effective remedy in art. 47 of the Charter: for art. 47 of the Charter to be applied the condition of 'implementation of EU law'

52 See Opinion of Advocate General Bobek delivered on 23 September 2020 in joined cases C-83/19, C-127/19 and C-195/19.

53 Also see L. Pech, S. Platon, *How Not to Deal with Poland's Fake Judges' Requests for a Preliminary Ruling: A critical Analysis of AG Bobek's Proposal in Case C-132/20*, VerfBlog, 28.07.2021, https://verfassungsblog.de/how-not-to-deal-with-polands-fake-judges-requests-for-a-preliminary-ruling/.

in art. 51(1) of the Charter must be met, while, on the other hand, the right to an effective legal protection in art. 19(1) TEU only refers to 'fields covered by EU law'[54] and therefore it has a broader scope. This condition has become crucial for judicial independence to acquire a central position in the normative core of the EU's constitution.[55] The idea is that, if courts of Member States are liable to rule on the application and interpretation of EU law, they also have to meet the requirements of effective judicial protection provided by art. 19(1) TEU, without specifically needing the case to deal with EU law. This approach may decrease the risk of destructive conflicts within EU as courts have to apply both national and EU law and, therefore, have to be compliant with both functional requirements. Therefore, the fact that the ECJ has consistently applied this approach also with regard to Romania comes as no surprise and should not be considered as a mere antagonism of the RCC.

Also, it is worth mentioning that, although in their parallel discourses both the RCC and the ECJ mentioned the concept of constitutional identity,[56] they did not extensively elaborate on the ***kompetenz-kompetenz*** theory. The ECJ simply referred to the solution it had provided for this issue in previous cases,[57] probably in reaction to the ambiguity of the RCC's own jurisprudence on this matter.[58] According to a commentator, 'by misrepresenting the efforts made, with varying degrees of vigour and continuity, by the other European supreme courts, it seems to us that the Romanian Constitutional Court fails to recognise the richness, even in mere terms of legal technique, that the confrontation with the Union's legal order brings to the Member States'.[59]

54 Case C-64/16 Associação Sindical dos Juízes Portugueses (2018), point 29.

55 See also C-619/*18 Commission v. Poland* (2019), point 55; C-192/18 *Commission v. Poland* (2019), point 103; joined cases C-585/18, C-624/18 and C-625/18 *AK and Others* (2019), point 83; C-824/18 *AB and Others* (2021), point 112.

56 Among many other see L. Tribe, *American Constitutional Law*, Foundation Press 2000, p. 70 et seq. and p. 110 et seq.; G.G. Jacobsohn, *Constitutional Identity*, "The Review of Politics" 2006, vol. 68, p. 361; G.G. Jacobsohn, *The Formation of Constitutional Identities*, (in:) T. Ginsburg, R. Dixon (eds.), *Comparative Constitutional Law*, Edward Elgar 2014, p. 131; C. Calliess, G. van der Schyff (eds.), *Constitutional Identity in a Eu- rope of Multilevel Constitutionalism*, Cambridge University Press 2020; D. Fromage, B. de Witte, *National Constitutional Identity Ten Years on: State of Play and Future Perspectives*, "European Public Law" 2021, vol. 27, no. 3, p. 412. For an up-to-date synthesis of the practice and scholarship on the concept of constitutional identity see J. Scholtes, *Abusing Constitutional Identity*, "German Law Journal" 2021, vol. 22, no. 4, pp. 534–556.

57 See cases C-58/13 and C-59/13 *Torresi* (2014), point 58; case C-673/16 *Coman and Others* (2018), point 46.

58 M. Guțan, *Este Curtea Constituțională a României un port-drapel al identității constituționale naționale ? [Is the Romanian Constitutional Court a Flagship of national constitutional identity?]*, "Revista română de drept european" 2022, iss. 1, pp. 28–45.

59 A. Corre-Basset, *Cour constitutionnelle...*

9.6 Conclusion

In conclusion, it seems fair to assert that the RCC endorsed the reform of the judicial system taking as referential exclusively the national constitutional framework. At no point has it sought to take into account the relevant EU legal framework, and even less the jurisprudence of the European Court of Justice (ECJ), despite the fact that parties raised such issues and inquired whether it would not be suitable to send preliminary questions.[60] From this perspective, it is clear that the RCC has chosen not to navigate in chartered waters and decided not to follow the path of the judicial dialogue, unlike, for instance, the Italian Constitutional Court.[61] When confronted with a ruling of the ECJ[62] requiring national judges to disregard any national legislation, including decisions of the Constitutional Court, that would prevent full compliance with EU principles on financial frauds, specifically with art. 325 TFEU as it was the case in the joined cases *Euro Box Promotion* (2021), the Italian Constitutional Court decided to repeatedly address preliminary questions to the ECJ. Although *Tarrico* (2015) was simply repeating the *Simmenthal* (1978) doctrine, just like the ECJ has done in the joined cases *Euro Box Promotion* (2021), it was the first ECJ ruling referring to the statutes of limitation in criminal matters, an area where the principle of legality has to be strictly observed, among others, as a matter of constitutional guarantees for the right to a fair trial and for the rights of the defence. In the end, the ECJ understood what was at stake and, in C-42/17, *M.A.S. and M.B (Tarrico bis)* (2017), it found a compromise which allowed for the statute of limitations in criminal matters to be observed as regulated at the national level. The key to the successful dialogue between the Italian Constitutional Court and the ECJ is to be found in those parts of the preliminary question where the Italian Court gave evidence of the fact that the national constitutional requirements at stake are not foreign or opposed to the European ones, but – on the contrary – are part of the very same constitutional discourse.[63] The RCC has not attempted such an endeavour, but rather decided to narrow its norms of reference only to the Romanian Constitution claiming that the concept of the rule of law there enshrined is identical with the one referred to in the EU treaties.

It is therefore interesting to note that, despite the contrary will of the RCC, a dialogue of sorts did start with the ECJ, albeit not a constructive one. But

60 The Constitutional Court had explicitly refused a direct dialogue with the ECJ in decision no. 137/2019, which has been considered by Romanian scholarship 'a missed opportunity'. See C. Pintilie, *Curtea Constituţională a României la o răscruce de drumuri (The Constitutional Court at a Crossroads)*, available at https://www.juridice.ro/732329/curtea-constitutionala-a-romaniei-la-o-rascruce-de-drumuri.html.

61 A. di Gregorio, *Constitutional Law and European Integration: the Italian Case*, "Analele Universităţii din Bucureşti – Drept" 2013, iss. 1, pp. 1–15.

62 C 105/14, *Tarrico* (2015).

63 M. Cartabia, *Europe Today: Bridges and Walls*, "International Constitutional Law Review" 2018, vol. 16, iss. 3, p. 750.

because none of the actors involved acted as if a dialogue was on-going, it might be appropriate not to analyse their interaction as a mutually fruitful exchange of ideas and use instead the image of parallel monologues.

On one hand, the RCC did not and cannot act in a vacuum. Irrespective of its will, it performs constitutional review in a Member State of the European Union and it takes part in a network of constitutional courts that, often times, emulate and stimulate each other.[64] It would have been a surprise if the RCC acted in perfect autarchy and would not have been 'contaminated' by the surrounding democratic backsliding and decay of the rule of law. Let us be clear: this does not mean that the RCC necessarily had to be involved in a specific democratic backsliding, nor that it should have been targeted by a populist government or that it should have resisted the temptation to side (by its own will) with such a government, although this last option seems rather self-evident to this author.[65] But it is a fact that democratic backsliding and decay of the rule of law did happen, at various degrees,[66] in several Member States of the EU[67] and, more often than not, it impacted judicial systems,[68] afflicting particularly the independence of justice. Constitutional courts have been either targeted by executives who wanted to subordinate the entire national judiciary or they have contributed, together with such executives, to the undermining of the judiciary in their respective countries. However, having constantly endorsed the judicial reform undertaken during 2018–2019, the RCC could not escape from the attention of the ECJ and its jurisprudence on judicial independence. Although not intended, a sort of dialogue between the RCC and the ECJ was unavoidable, but instead of a constructive discussion their interaction resembled more a dialogue between deaf persons.

On the other hand, the judicial dialogue between the ECJ and constitutional courts is not necessarily a horizontal one. More often than not, the ECJ attempts to take advantage of the surrounding constitutional pluralism. Starting with the jurisprudence of the Italian (*controlimitti*) and German (*Solange*) constitutional courts in the beginning of the '70s and continuing with the jurisprudence of the French, German or Belgian constitutional courts in the beginning of the '90s pertaining to the Treaty of Maastricht the issue of

64 T. Groppi, M.-C. Ponthoreau, *The Use of Foreign Precedents by Constitutional Judges*, Oxford: Hart Publishing 2013.

65 Cf. E.S. Tănăsescu, *Can Constitutional Courts...*

66 States can satisfy the principle of the rule of law 'to greater or lesser extent'. See P. Gowder, *The Rule of Law in the Real World*, Cambridge University Press 2016, p. 26.

67 Most often cited are Hungary and Poland, but Romania as well. See A. von Bogdandy, P. Sonnevend (eds.), *Constitutional Crisis in the European Constitutional Area: Theory, Law and Politics in Hungary and Romania*, Oxford: Hart Publishing 2015; W. Sadurski, *Poland's Constitutional Breakdown*, Oxford University Press 2019.

68 A. Arato, *Populism and the Courts*, VerfBlog, 25.04.2017, https://verfassungsblog.de/populism-and-the-courts/; B. Petkova, *Populism and Judicial Backlash in the United States and Europe*, VerfBlog, 30.04.2017, https://verfassungsblog.de/populism-and-judicial-backlash-in-the-united-states-and-europe/.

the interplay between state powers and EU powers has been a constant source of debates. The Treaty of Lisbon intended to put an end to these disputes by codifying the principle of conferral and providing a list of EU powers grouped into three categories (exclusive, shared and supporting) but even this solution proved incomplete. The issue of the final arbiter on disputes pertaining to EU powers and their limits, namely the ECJ or constitutional courts, remains open and is probably better dispensed within the terms of constitutional pluralism, i.e., never solved and continuously nourishing judicial dialogue no matter how difficult this may seem at times.[69] In its interaction with the RCC the ECJ simply performed its role, strengthening ordinary courts as privileged partners in the effective joint implementation of EU law[70] and imposing the primacy of EU law on all national authorities, constitutional court included. That, by the same token, this also diminished the RCC's hold on domestic courts looks like a collateral damage necessary for the accomplishment of the European integration. In answering preliminary questions raised by ordinary courts with regard to the fate of decisions issued by the RCC the ECJ inevitably generates a dialogue of sorts, albeit not a direct or consensual one.

Given these premises, for the interaction between the RCC and the ECJ to become a fruitful judicial dialogue further iterations and corrections are needed.

References

Andreescu M., Andreescu C., *Supremația Constituției în contextul principiului priorității dreptului Uniunii Europene [The Supremacy of the Constitution in the Context of the Principle of Primacy of EU law]*, "Dreptul" 2017, (8), pp.48–60.

Arato A., *Populism and the Courts*, VerfBlog, https://verfassungsblog.de/populism-and-the-courts/; 25.04.2017.

Bencze M., *Everyday Judicial Populism in Hungary*, "Review of Central and East European Law" 2022, vol. 47(1), pp.37–59.

Blauberger M., Kelemen R.D., *Can Courts Rescue National Democracy? Judicial Safeguards against Democratic Backsliding in the EU*, "Journal of European Public Policy" 2017, vol. 24(3), pp.321–336.

Bobek M., *The Impact of the European Mandate of Ordinary Courts on the Position of Constitutional Courts*, (in:) M. Claes, M. de Visser, P. Popelier, C. Van de Heyning (eds.), *Constitutional Conversations in Europe*, Intersentia, Antwerp, 2012.

Bobic A., *The Jurisprudence of Constitutional Conflict in the European Union*, Oxford University Press, Oxford 2022.

von Bogdandy A., Sonnevend P. (eds.), *Constitutional Crisis in the European Constitutional Area: Theory, Law and Politics in Hungary and Romania*, Hart Publishing, Oxford 2015.

69 A. Bobic, *The Jurisprudence...*, p. 76.

70 A.M. Burley, W. Mattli, *Europe before the Court: A Political Theory of Legal Integration*, "International Organisation" 1993, vol. 47, p. 41; W. Mattli, A.M. Slaughter, *Revisiting the European Court of Justice*, "International Organisation" 1998, vol. 52, p. 177.

Bugarič B., Ginsburg T., *The Assault on Post-Communist Courts*, "The Journal of Democracy" 2016, vol. 27, pp.69–82.

Burley A.M., Mattli W., *Europe Before the Court: A Political Theory of Legal Integration*, "International Organisation" 1993, vol. 47, pp.41–76.

Calliess C., van der Schyff G. (eds.), *Constitutional Identity in a Europe of Multilevel Constitutionalism*, Cambridge University Press, Cambridge 2020.

Cartabia M., *Europe Today: Bridges and Walls*, "International Constitutional Law Review" 2018, vol. 16(3), pp.741–752.

Closa C., Kochenov D. (eds.), *Reinforcing the Rule of Law Oversight in the European Union*, Cambridge University Press, Cambridge 2016.

Corre-Basset A., *Cour constitutionnelle de Roumanie, décision 390/2021 du 8 juin 2021 (supériorité du droit constitutionnel interne sur le droit de l'Union)*, Titre VII, https://www.conseil-constitutionnel.fr/publications/titre-vii/chronique-de-droit-constitutionnel-compare-janvier-a-juin-2021.

Drinóczi T., Bień-Kacała A., *Rule of Law, Common Values, and Illiberal Constitutionalism: Poland and Hungary within the European Union*, Routledge & CRC Press, London 2020.

Ferrer Mac-Gregor E., *What Do We Mean When We Talk About Judicial Dialogue?: Reflections of a Judge of The Inter-American Court of Human Rights*, "Harvard Human Rights Journal" 2017, vol.30, pp.89–127.

Fromage D., de Witte B., *National Constitutional Identity Ten Years on: State of Play and Future Perspectives*, "European Public Law" 2021, vol. 27(3), pp.411–426.

Ginsburg T., Aziz H., *How to Save a Constitutional Democracy*, "The University of Chicago Press", Chicago and London 2018.

Gora A., de Wilde P., *The Essence of Democratic Backsliding in the European Union: Deliberation and Rule of Law*, "Journal of European Public Policy" 2022, vol. 29(3), pp.342–362.

Gowder P., *The Rule of Law in the Real World*, Cambridge University Press, Cambridge 2016.

di Gregorio A., Constitutional Law and European Integration: The Italian Case, "Analele Universității din București – Seria Drept" 2013 (1), pp.1–15.

Groppi T., Ponthoreau M.-C., *The Use of Foreign Precedents by Constitutional Judges*, Hart Publishing, Oxford 2013.

Guțan M., *Este Curtea Constituțională a României un port-drapel al identității constituționale naționale ? [Is the Romanian Constitutional Court a Flagship of National Constitutional Identity?]*, "Revista română de drept european" 2022 (1), pp.28–45.

Issacharoff S., *Fragile Democracies*, Cambridge 2015.

Jacobsohn G.G., *Constitutional Identity*, "The Review of Politics" 2006, vol. 68(3), pp.361–397.

Jacobsohn G.G., *The Formation of Constitutional Identities*, (in T. Ginsburg, R. Dixon (eds.), *Comparative Constitutional Law*, Edward Elgar, Cheltenham & Northampton 2011.

Karolewski I.P., *Towards a Political Theory of Democratic Backsliding? Generalising the East Central European Experience*, (in:) A. Lorenz, L.H. Anders (eds.), *Illiberal Trends and Anti-EU Politics in East Central Europe, Palgrave Studies in European Union Politics,* "Palgrave Macmillan", Cham 2021.

Kelemen D., *Europe's Other Democratic Deficit: National Authoritarianism in Europe's Democratic Union*, "Government and Opposition" 2017, vol. 52 ,(2), pp.211–238.

Kelsen H., *Judicial Review of Legislation: A Comparative Study of the Austrian and the American Constitution*, "The Journal of Politics" 1942, vol. 4(2), pp.183–223.

Kochenov D., Bard P., *Rule of Law Crisis in the New Member States of the EU: The Pitfalls of Over-emphasizing Enforcement*, Working Paper no. 1, July 2018, https://reconnect-europe.eu/wp-content/uploads/2018/07/RECONNECT-KochenovBard-WP_27072018b.pdf.

Landau D., *Abusive Constitutionalism*, "UC Davis Law Review" 2013, vol. 47, pp.189–260.

Law D.S., Versteeg M., *Sham Constitutions*, "California Law Review" 2013, vol. 101, no. 4, pp. 863–952.

Lupu A.-R., *Suprematia Constitutiei – Evolutia si limitele unui principiu fundamental al dreptului modern*, "Revista de drept public" 2017 (3), pp. 124–149.

Mattli W., Slaughter A.M., *Revisiting the European Court of Justice*, "International Organisation" 1998, vol. 52, pp.177–209.

Moraru M., Bercea R., *The First Episode in the Romanian Rule of Law Saga: Joined Cases C-83/19, C-127/19, C-195/19, C-291/19, C-355/19 and C-397/19, Asociatia Forumul Judecatorilor din România, and Their Follow-up at the National Level*, "European Constitutional Law Review" 2022, vol. 18(1), pp.82–113.

Nollkaemper A., *Conversations Among Courts: Domestic and International Adjudicators*, (in:) C. Romano, K. Alter, Y.Shany (eds.), *The Oxford Handbook of International Adjudication*, Oxford 2013.

Pech L., Bard P., *The Commission's Rule of Law Report and the EU Monitoring and Enforcement of Article 2 TEU Values*, document requested by the European Parliament's Committee on Civil Liberties, Justice and Home Affairs and the Committee on Constitutional Affairs, https://www.europarl.europa.eu/RegData/etudes/STUD/2022/727551/IPOL_STU(2022)727551_EN.pdf.

Pech L., Lane Scheppele K., *Illiberalism Within: Rule of Law Backsliding in the EU*, CYELS 2017, vol. 19, pp.3–47.

Pech L., Platon S., *How Not to Deal with Poland's Fake Judges' Requests for a Preliminary Ruling: A critical Analysis of AG Bobek's Proposal in* Case C-132/20, VerfBlog, https://verfassungsblog.de/how-not-to-deal-with-polands-fake-judges-requests-for-a-preliminary-ruling/; 28.07.2021.

Petkova B., *Populism and Judicial Backlash in the United States and Europe*, VerfBlog, https://verfassungsblog.de/populism-and-judicial-backlash-in-the-united-states-and-europe/; 30.04.2017.

Pintilie C., *Curtea Constituțională a României la o răscruce de drumuri (The Constitutional Court at a Crossroads)*, https://www.juridice.ro/732329/curtea-constitutionala-a-romaniei-la-o-rascruce-de-drumuri.html.

Sadurski W., *Poland's Constitutional Breakdown*, Oxford University Press, Oxford 2019.

Scholtes J., *Abusing Constitutional Identity*, "German Law Journal" 2021, vol. 22(4), pp. 534–556.

Selejan-Guțan B., *A Tale of Primacy Part. II: The Romanian Constitutional Court on a Slippery Slope*, VerfBlog, https://verfassungsblog.de/a-tale-of-primacy-part-ii/; 18.06.2021.

Selejan-Guțan B., *A Tale of Primacy, Part III: Game of Courts*, VerfBlog, https://verfassungsblog.de/a-tale-of-primacy-part-iii/; 17.11.2021.

Selejan-Guțan B., *The Taming of the Court: When Politics Overcome Law in the Romanian Constitutional Court*, VerfBlog, https://verfassungsblog.de/the

-taming-of-the-court-when-politics-overcome-law-in-the-romanian-constitutional-court/; 6.06.2018.

Smith M., *Staring into the Abyss: A Crisis of the Rule of Law in the EU*, "European Law Journal" 2019, vol. 25(6), pp. 561–576.

Sweet Stone A., *Governing with Judges*, Oxford University Press, Oxford 2000.

Tănăsescu E.S., *Can Constitutional Courts Become Populist?*, (in:) M. Belov (ed.), *The Role of Courts in Contemporary Legal Orders*, Eleven International Publishing, The Hague 2019.

Tănăsescu E.S., *Cour Constitutionnelle et système judiciaire: Des rapports de force?*, "Analele Universității din București –Drept" 2012 (2), pp. 240–251.

Tănăsescu E.S., Romania: From Constitutional Democracy to Constitutional Decay?, (in:) V. Besirevic (ed.), *New Politics of Decisionism*, Eleven International Publishing, The Hague 2019b.

Tănăsescu E.S., *The Independence of Justice as Proxy for the Rule of Law in the EU. Case Study: Romania*, "Nuovi Autoritarismi e Democrazie: Diritto, Istituzioni, Società" 2021, vol. 3(1), pp. 103–123.

Tănăsescu E.S., *The Romanian Constitutional Judge: Lost in Transition*, (in:) M. Jovanovic (ed.), *Constitutional Review and Democracy*, Eleven International Publishing, The Hague 2015.

Tănăsescu E.S., Selejan-Guțan B., *A Tale of Primacy: The ECJ Ruling on Judicial Independence in Romania*, VerfBlog, https://verfassungsblog.de/a-tale-of-primacy/; 2.06.2021.

Tribe L., *American Constitutional Law*, Foundation Press, New York 2000.

Tridimas T., *The ECJ and the National Courts: Dialogue, Cooperation, and Instability*, (in:) D.Chalmers, A.Arnull (eds.), Oxford Handbook of European Union Law, Oxford University Press, Oxford 2015.

Vassileva R., *Bulgaria's Failed Specialized Criminal Justice Experiment*, VerfBlog, https://verfassungsblog.de/bulgarias-failed-specialized-criminal-justice-experiment/; 29.04.2022.

Viță V., *The Romanian Constitutional Court and the Principle of Primacy: To Refer or Not to Refer?*, "German Law Journal" 2015, vol. 16(6), p. 1623–1662.

10 The Turkish Constitutional Court and emergency regimes in the age of democratic backsliding

Selin Esen

10.1 Introduction

In democratic regimes, constitutional courts are the bulwark of the rights and freedoms. The Constitutional Court was introduced to the Turkish legal system to accomplish the same purpose. Indeed, the foundation of the Constitutional Court under the 1961 Constitution was the fruit of a reaction to the authoritarian tendencies of the government during the 1950s and the belief that the Court would be an effective instrument to implement the supremacy of the Constitution and to furnish a democratic state and rule of law by checking the arbitrary power of parliamentary majorities.[1]

Since the 2000s, the deterioration of democratic rule has been a global phenomenon. Turkey is considered one of the earliest cases of this trend and it has had a significant impact on the Turkish Constitutional Court (TCC). Since its introduction in the 1961 Constitution, until the democratic backsliding was established, the TCC was considered a veto power in Turkish politics, especially in high-profile cases.[2] Democratic backsliding in Turkey has altered the Constitutional Court's general attitude on the protection of the rights and freedoms and limitation of political power. In this chapter first, it will be explained briefly how democracy gradually declined in Turkey. Second, the TCC's composition and powers will be explained with the relevant constitutional alterations in the 1982 Constitution that enabled the court-packing and centralisation of political power. Third, the approach of the Constitutional Court to the protection of the rights and freedoms during the authoritarianisation of the country will be revealed, exemplifying its most significant judgments during the state of emergency.

1 Y. Aliefendioğlu, *Anayasa Yargısı*, Yetkin 1997, p. 71.

2 B.E. Oder, *Populism and the Turkish Constitutional Court: the Game Broker, the Populist and the Popular*, VerfBlog, 2017, https://verfassungsblog.de/populism-and-the-turkish-constitutional-court-the-game-broker-the-populist-and-the-popular.

DOI: 10.4324/9781003355793-12

10.2 Democratic breakdown

Starting from the mid-1970s, the transition of authoritarian regimes toward democracies started in Southern Europe and spread to different parts of the world. As from 1989, a wave of democratisation came to East and Central Europe, the former Soviet Union and parts of Africa and Asia.[3] During the era of democratisation, recognition and implementation of international standards on human rights have shown a growing tendency. It began to influence Turkey in the second part of the 1980s. The 1982 Constitution, which abolished the 1961 Constitution, was a product of the military coup that was staged in 1980. While the 1961 Constitution gave special importance to freedoms and limited government, the 1982 Constitution's aim was strengthening the state's authority by empowering the executive branch and restricting freedoms. Hence, it placed more emphasis on the limits of freedoms rather than their exercise.

Meanwhile, Turkey has always been part of the international system. It became a member of the Council of Europe in 1948. It signed an Association Agreement with the then European Community in 1963. The democratisation wave revived Turkey's European Union (EU) membership aspirations. It submitted its application for full membership in 1987 and was accepted by the EU as an official candidate for accession in 1999. In this regard, starting from the 1980s two matters for Turkey are noteworthy. First, Turkey accessed many international human rights treaties, e.g., the Convention on the Elimination of the All Forms of Discrimination against Women in 1985, the European Convention for the Prevention of Torture and Inhuman or Degrading Treatment or Punishment in 1988, the United Nations Convention against Torture and Other Cruel, Inhuman or Degrading Treatment or Punishment in 1988 and the European Social Charter in 1989. Turkey has become a party to the International Covenant on Civil and Political Rights, the International Covenant on Economic, Social, and Cultural Rights, the Convention on the Elimination of All Forms of Racial Discrimination, the Convention on the Rights of the Child and Protocol Six of the European Convention on Human Rights concerning the death penalty. In order to protect human rights following international standards, Turkey recognised the right of individual application to the European Commission of Human Rights in 1987 and the mandatory jurisdiction of the European Court of Human Rights (ECtHR) in 1990. In addition, Turkey recognised the jurisdiction of some of the quasi-judicial supervisory bodies established by the United Nations human rights treaties, such as the Human Rights Committee, the Committee on Economic, Social and Cultural Rights, the Committee on Elimination of Racial Discrimination,

3 S.P. Huntington, *The Third Wave. Democratization in the Late Twentieth Century*, Norman: University of Oklahoma Press 1993.

the Committee on the Elimination of Discrimination against Women, the Committee against Torture and Committee on the Rights of the Child.

Second, amendments to the 1982 Constitution made in 1987, 1993, 1995, 1999, 2001 and 2004 strengthened human rights in general. Some of the alterations in 2006 and 2010 also reinforced the fundamental rights and freedoms. Turkey's integration into international human rights systems, e.g., the ECHR system, instigated the adoption of some rules in the country. For this purpose, in 2004 the Parliament reestablished the place of international treaties concerning human rights in the Constitution. According to the original version of art. 90(5) of the 1982 Constitution, 'International agreements duly put into effect bear the force of law. No appeal to the Constitutional Court shall be made regard to these agreements, on the grounds that they are unconstitutional'. In 2004, the sentence in art. 90(5) was added stipulating 'In case of contradiction between international agreements regarding basic rights and freedoms approved through proper procedure and domestic laws, due to different provisions on the same issue, the provision of international agreements shall be considered'. Hence, the amendment made it clear that international human rights agreements have priority over domestic laws.[4]

Beginning with the mid-2000s not only has the democratisation trend been decelerating, but also autocratic states have become more prominent actors on the global stage. Rather than abrupt changes of the regime via the classic coup d'état, regression from democratic rule took place through a process that has come to be known as 'backsliding'[5] that results from the actions of duly elected governments, typically driven by an autocratic leader. Democratic erosion has been witnessed in many countries from the consolidated democratic regimes, such as the US to the third wave or unconsolidated democracies such as Hungary, Poland, Ecuador, Serbia and Brazil. Starting from 2010, Turkey is considered one of the early examples of this global trend.[6]

Since 2002, Turkey has been ruled by the pro-Islamist Justice and Development Party (Adalet ve Kalkınma Partisi-AKP). Initially, the AKP's priority was economic stability, European Union membership and an overall emphasis on democracy and human rights.[7] As of 2010, these aspects of the

4 L. Gönenç, S. Esen, *The Problem of Less Protective International Agreements in Domestic Legal Systems: Article 90 of the Turkish Constitution*, "European Journal of Law Reform" 2006, no. 8(4), pp. 490–497.

5 N. Bermeo, *On Democratic Backsliding*, "Journal of Democracy" 2016, vol. 27, pp. 5–19.

6 S. Haggard, R. Kaufman, *Backsliding Democratic Regress in the Contemporary World*. Cambridge: Cambridge University Press 2021, p. 58.

7 A. Insel, *The AKP and Normalizing Democracy in Turkey*, "The South Atlantic Quarterly" 2003, vol. 102, pp. 293–308; A. Rabasa, F.S. Larrabee, *The Rise of Political Islam in Turkey*, Santa Monica: RAND Corporation 2008, p. 51 et seq.; Z. Öniş, *Monopolizing the Center: The AKP and the Uncertain Path of Turkish Democracy*, "The International Spectator" 2015, vol. 50, iss. 2; S. Belmek, *The Rise of Hybrid Political Islam in Turkey. Origins and Consolidation of the JDP*, Palgrave Macmillan 2019, p. 107.

AKP rule began to drift toward centralisation, weakening democratic institutions that resulted in a lack of an adequate system of checks and balances and authoritarianism.[8]

The AKP used the constitutional amendments as a method to influence and change the democratic institutions to some extent for the first time in 2007, but mainly in 2010 and 2017. The underlying reason for some of the constitutional alterations was the tension between the TCC and the AKP. In other words, the growing dissatisfaction of the ruling party over a number of TCC decisions prompted the AKP to introduce constitutional amendments to overcome these judgments. The TCC prevented the AKP, which had a majority in the Parliament, to elect its candidate in 2007. At the end of President Ahmet Necdet Sezer's term of office, the governing AKP seemed to have enough votes in the parliament to elect its own candidate. According to the 1982 Constitution, the president of the Republic is elected by the GNAT by two-thirds of the full membership of the Assembly on the first two rounds, and the absolute majority of the full membership on the third and fourth rounds. The Constitution contains no special quorum rule for the meeting of the Assembly, in which case the general rule in art. 96 should apply, that is, the quorum should be one-third of the full membership. The parliamentary arithmetic then gave the AKP the power to elect the president alone on the third or fourth rounds, but not on the first two rounds. After the first round in which the two-thirds quorum was not obtained because of the boycott by the opposition deputies, the main opposition party carried the case to the TCC and the Court ruled that two-thirds majority is not only the decisional quorum, but also the necessary quorum for the opening of the session.[9] The TCC's decision put an end to the election process since the required quorum was not obtained on the first round and the AKP's candidate failed to get elected. As a result of the deadlock over the presidency, the Assembly decided unanimously to call new elections. The parliamentary elections of 22 July gave the AKP a strong mandate with 46.7 per cent of the vote and 340 out of 550 seats. Thanks to some of the opposition deputies' attendance at the parliamentary sessions for the election of the president the necessary quorum was provided for the opening of the session following the TCC's judgment. Abdullah Gül was elected by the votes of the MPs of the AKP. Subsequently, the parliamentary majority led by AKP and the right-wing extremist Nationalist Movement Party (MHP) altered the form of government from the parliamentary to a semi-presidential system that enabled the president of the Republic to be elected by the popular vote for a maximum of two five-year terms.[10] Thus, the constitutional

8 Z. Öniş, *Monopolizing...*; E. Özbudun, *Otoriter Rejimler, Seçimsel Demokrasiler ve Türkiye*, Ankara: Yetkin 2021, p. 172 et seq.

9 TCC, E. 2007/45. K. 2007/54, 1 May 2007, Official Gazette, 27 June 2007: 26565.

10 E. Özbudun, Ö.F. Gençkaya, *Democratization and Politics of Constitution-Making in Turkey*, Central European University Press 2009, pp. 97–102.

amendment overcame the TCC's controversial judgment. It was approved by the referendum with a turnout rate of 67.5 per cent. This change was not related to the judiciary, but it was a departure from the parliamentary system and popular elections increased the political weight of the president already endowed with broad constitutional powers.

Also, the TCC annulled the constitutional amendments made in art. 10 (equality) and 42 (right to education) to provide a constitutional basis to lift the headscarf ban on women university students.[11] The tension between the TCC and the AKP was further aggravated by the closure case against the ruling party. A majority of the judges voted in favour of banning the party, but the qualified majority (three-fifths) required by the Constitution was not obtained. Therefore, the party was not banned, but ten members out of 11 of the TCC concluded that the AKP had become a focus of anti-secular activities.[12]

The AKP government with the support of the MHP made the main changes in the Constitution in 2010 by amending its 24 articles. This package contained some improvements in civil rights, including children's rights, the protection of personal data and freedom to travel. However, the most important provisions of the amendment package were those related to the composition of the TCC and the High Council of Judges and Public Prosecutors (HSYK). The HSYK is a body competent to decide on all personnel matters of judges and public prosecutors, such as appointment, dismissal, promotion and transfers. The package changed the structure of the Supreme Council of Judges and Prosecutors by allowing all senior judges and prosecutors to select a part of the Council's members. These amendments were of a nature to weaken its independence.[13] The TCC's annulment of some parts of the constitutional amendments regarding the HSYK engendered executive control over the judiciary. Indeed, the Court deemed unconstitutional on a controversial basis the 'one judge/prosecutor one vote' principle for the Council's elections. This preference of the Court engendered the election of candidate lists prepared by the government which dominated discussions in the Council. Thereby, the 2010 constitutional amendments reorganised the TCC by changing its composition. Besides, it made some changes regarding the powers of the Court, such as introducing the 'constitutional complaint', namely an individual application into the Turkish legal system, and raising the quorum of the Court in political party prohibition cases and the review of the constitutionality of constitutional amendments.

11 E.2008/16, K.2008/116, 5 June 2008, Official Gazette 22 October 2008: 27032. M. Öden, S. Esen, *Fundamental Rights and Freedoms in Turkey and the Turkish Constitutional Court*, (in:) R. Arnold (ed.), *The Convergence of the Fundamental Rights Protection in Europe*, Springer 2013, p. 146.

12 E.2008/1, K.2008/2, 30 July 2008, Official Gazette 24 October 2008: 26923.

13 S. Esen, *The Constitutional Court of Turkey*, (in:) *Max Planck Encyclopedia of Comparative Constitutional Law*, 2018; Ş. Gümüşçü, *The Emerging Predominant Party System in Turkey*, "Government and Opposition" 2013, vol. 48, p. 228.

The final step regarding amendments to the Constitution was initiated by the AKP in 2016. The GNAT enacted Law No. 6771 on Amendments to the Constitution on 21 January 2017 that changed about 40 per cent of the Constitution. The referendum concerning this package was held under the state of emergency on 16 April 2017 and approved by 51.4 per cent of the total valid votes. The 2017 constitutional 'reforms' largely aimed to turn the form of government from a premier-presidential to a super-presidential system, the so-called 'Turkish style presidency' or a form of government peculiar to Turkey by its advocates. This package made a small change to the composition of the Court by reducing the number of its judges, but significant alterations to the structure of the Council of Judges and Prosecutors.[14] Ultimately, the AKP government has solidified its advantage in the constitution by distorting the strength of its temporary majorities to create an entirely new constitution in the form of ordinary amendments.[15]

Note that, as for other illiberal rulers,[16] the national crisis allowed the AKP government to consolidate its power. Hence, the coup attempt in 2016 and the COVID-19 outbreak in 2020 accelerated the authoritarianism of the regime and the weakening of the fundamental rights and freedoms in Turkey. As stated above, the 2017 constitutional amendments made under the state of emergency altered the form of government from semi-presidential to presidential with a weakened legislature and judiciary and a very powerful president with broad powers and very limited accountability.[17] In other words, the AKP government used the constitutional revisions in 2017 to transform the country into a competitive authoritarian regime.[18] The government also exploited the extraordinary circumstances resulting from the COVID-19 pandemic as an opportunity for its supporters and for suppressing the opposition.

As a result, starting from the 2010s democracy began to decay in Turkey. The decline of critical elements of democracy gradually has transformed Turkey into a 'competitive authoritarianism'.[19]

14 According to the recent changes, the Council of Judges and Prosecutors (HSK) is composed of 13 members. As previously, the Minister of Justice is its chair, and the Deputy Minister of Justice is its natural member. Six members are directly appointed by the President of the Republic. The remaining seven members are elected by the Grand National Assembly as follows: 'In the first voting the two-thirds majority of the full membership, if this is not obtained in the second voting three-fifth majority of the full membership is required. If a member is not elected in the second voting, there will be a lot-taking between the two highest vote-getters'. Thus, the process ends up in the decision of the simple majority. This arrangement enabled court-packing the Council with loyal names.

15 S. Esen, *The 2017 Constitutional Reforms in Turkey: Removal of Parliamentarism or Democracy?*, IACL-IADC Blog, 2017, blog-iacl-aidc.org.

16 S. Haggard, R. Kaufman, *Backsliding*..., p. 79.

17 S. Esen, *The 2017*...

18 E. Özbudun, *Otoriter*..., p. 182.

19 E. Özbudun, *Anayasalcılık ve Demokrasi*, Yetkin, Ankara 2019, pp. 140–146. According to V-Dem's Electoral Democracy Score, which grades countries on a 0-1 scale, Turkey dropped

10.3 Composition and structure of the TCC

According to the original text of the 1982 Constitution, the TCC was composed of 11 regular and four substitute judges. The Constitution adopted an appointment-based system in that the President of the Republic would exclusively appoint all members, seven regular members from among candidates nominated by high courts, namely the Court of Cassation, the Council of State, the Military Court of Cassation, the Military High Court of Administration and the Court of Accounts, and one by the Council of Higher Education, and the remaining three directly from among senior administrative officers and lawyers, and the Council of Higher Education. Note that the original text of the Constitution had designed the presidency as impartial with symbolic powers.

As stated above, the 2010 constitutional amendments made significant changes to the TCC. The number of its judges was raised from 11 to 17. The appointment system was converted into a mixed system. Accordingly, three judges are selected by the GNAT, from among candidates nominated by the Court of Accounts (two) and the presidents of the bar associations (one). Four members are directly appointed by the President of the Republic from among all judges and public prosecutors, rapporteur judges of the Constitutional Court, practising lawyers and high-level public administrators. The president also chooses three members from among three candidates nominated for each seat by the Council of Higher Education, three members nominated by the Court of Cassation, two nominated by the Council of State (the supreme administrative court), one nominated by the Military Court of Cassation and one nominated by the High Military Administrative Court, again from among three nominees from each vacant seat. As a result, the president continued to have a significant influence on the composition of the Court. Observe that the president of the Republic was then elected by popular vote, which prevents him from being impartial.

In 2017 the last changes to the composition of the Court were made. The 2017 constitutional alterations reduced the number of judges to 15 with the elimination of the High Military Administrative Court and the Military Court of Cassation. The source of judges and the appointment system remain the same. Still, only three judges are elected by the GNAT. The vast majority of the judges are appointed by the President. The President appoints seven judges from among a list of candidates nominated by high courts for each vacant position by their respective plenaries. Specifically, three members are appointed from the candidates proposed by the Court of Cassation, and two members by the Council of State. Additionally, the President appoints three members from among three candidates for each vacant seat put forward by

from 0.55 to 0.28 in the last decade (dr_2021.pdf (v-dem.net)). The World Justice Project's Rule of Law Index ranked Turkey 117 out of 139 countries in 2021.

the Council of Higher Education from among the university professors of law, economy and political science. At least two of these three members must be appointed from among the candidates who serve in the field of law. The President directly appoints four of the TCC judges from among the senior administrative officers, self-employed lawyers, first category judges and prosecutors or rapporteurs of the TCC.

Since three of the TCC members are elected by the Parliament, one may claim that the election of the Parliament strengthened the democratic legitimacy of the Court. Indeed, before 2010, it was claimed by the ruling party that the TCC was suffering from a relative lack of democratic input. However, the role of the legislative body in the composition of the Court is designed to be very limited. First, the ratio of the number the judges elected by the Parliament is very low. Second, the GNAT is not entirely free in its choice. Indeed, the Parliament elects two judges from the members of the Court of Accounts. However, the Parliament elects from among a list of three candidates nominated for each vacant seat by the Court of Accounts and it elects one judge from a list of three candidates nominated by heads of the bar associations from among self-employed lawyers.

Additionally, the election procedure contradicts the principle of independence of the judiciary. Indeed, to elect a TCC judge, a two-thirds majority of the total number of the GNAT members is required on the first ballot and an absolute majority of the total number of the GNAT members on the second ballot. If an absolute majority is not obtained on the second ballot a third ballot shall be held between the two candidates who have received the greatest number of votes on the second ballot. The candidate who receives the highest number of the votes on the third ballot shall be deemed elected. In many cases of countries using such a system, the elected judges are chosen, in practice, after negotiations and reconciliation between the main political parties in the parliament. However, in the Turkish case under the 2010 amendment the ruling party that obtained the absolute majority in the GNAT and obtained the presidency as well, did not negotiate the nominees with opposition parties or provide public discussion regarding candidates.

The TCC judges sit on the Court for 12 years and cannot be re-elected. Several qualification requirements are imposed upon the election of a TCC judge. The minimum age to be appointed to the TCC is 45. Candidates from the higher education institutions must have the position of full professor or associate professor; lawyers must have working experience of at least 20 years; senior administrative officers must have completed a higher education degree and have worked for at least 20 years and first category judges and prosecutors must have a working experience, of at least 20 years, including their candidacy periods. The retirement age is 65. The Chief Justice position and two Deputy Chief Justices are elected by the members of the Court for a term of four years from among the Court's members by secret ballot. The Court is comprised of a Plenary and two Chambers. The Plenary is composed of 15 members and it convenes with the participation of at least 10 members headed by the Chief

Justice or a Deputy Chief Justice designated by the President. Each Chamber of the TCC convenes with the participation of at least five judges, including a Deputy Chief Justice who acts as chairperson. Plenary and the Chambers shall rule by an absolute majority of judges present. Cases regarding constitutional amendments and dissolution of political parties are ruled by two-thirds of the judges present. Except for the constitutional complaints, all functions of the TCC are exercised by the Plenary. The Plenary is also empowered to maintain case law coherence between judgments of the chambers.

The structural reforms have amounted to court-packing. The 2010 constitutional amendments retained the incumbent judges at the TCC, but increased the seats on the bench by adding new judges. All members currently serving on the TCC have been appointed either under Abdullah Gül's or Recep Tayyip Erdogan's presidency. Erdoğan has packed the court by appointing people directly from his close circle. A judge, appointed by Erdogan in 2016, was a member of the now-defunct 'Wise People' – an AKP-organised group of intellectuals tasked with aiding the government's former policy of resolving what was then termed 'the Kurdish problem'[20] and one of two advisors of the AKP in the *ad hoc* Reconciliation Committee that was established in the GNAT to draft a new constitution between 2011 and 2013. He appointed two other judges in 2019. One of them was a former MP from the AKP and deputy justice minister, and the other one also had served as a deputy justice minister and the chief advisor for Erdoğan. The judge who was appointed in 2020 had been previously deemed 'unqualified' to be a judge at the ECtHR by the Parliamentary Assembly of the Council of Europe (PACE). Finally, in 2021, Erdoğan appointed another controversial name who had also close ties to him and was the prosecutor of many high-profile political cases.

In addition, the GNAT's selections to the TCC have become part and parcel of court-packing. For example, in 2022, the GNAT selected among three contenders named by the presidents of bar associations for the seat on the Constitutional Court with the support of the AKP and its ally, the MHP, one who was a senior member of the AKP and was a former nominee for a seat in parliament on the AKP ticket.[21]

10.4 The TCC's approach in times of authoritarianism

Since 2010, the TCC has increasingly supported the legislative preferences of the government in controversial cases. This new approach is considered not a judicial restraint, but rather explicit judicial advocacy for the government on contentious issues. This ideological deviation has required major

20 C. Tecimer, *Recognizing Court-Packing: Perception and Reality in the Case of the Turkish Constitutional Court*, VerfBlog, 2019, https://verfassungsblog.de/recognizing-court-packing.

21 Official Gazette 22 January 2022: 31727. *Sozcu Daily* 22 January 2022.

shifts in the Court's case-law and established doctrines.[22] The failed coup in July 2016 framed the Court's new position on critical matters. The TCC's departure from its case law on decree-laws issued during the state of emergency, its ruling on dismissal of its judges under the state of emergency and its judgments on matters related to the COVID-19 pandemic are noteworthy examples.

10.4.1 Emergency legislation

The 1982 Constitution provides for the executive branch to issue emergency decree-laws during the emergency regime. Article 119.6 of the Constitution empowers the President to issue presidential decrees during a state of emergency on matters necessitated by the emergency. Emergency decrees have the force of law. These decree-laws do not require a prior enabling act of the Parliament. Also, exercise of the fundamental rights and freedoms can be partially or entirely suspended by these decree-laws (Cons. art. 15). However, the discretionary power of the executive in this matter is not unlimited. It can interfere with fundamental rights and freedoms only on the condition of complying with the limitations in art. 15 of the Constitution.[23] After emergency decree-laws are published in the Official Gazette they must be submitted for approval to the GNAT on the same day. The Constitution prohibits the constitutional review of these decree-laws (Cons. art 148.1). Note that the original text of the Constitution had granted the power to issue emergency decree-laws to the Council of Ministers and had also banned their constitutional review. Hence, in regard to the emergency regime, the prohibition of judicial review of emergency decree-laws is the most problematic part of the Constitution. Guarantees of the Constitution under art. 15 serve no useful purpose because of the constitutional ban on judicial review of emergency decree-laws. Given the fact that for some 43 years of its 99 years Turkey has been under extraordinary regime, such limitation on judicial review gains even greater significance. Meanwhile, once they are ratified by the Parliament emergency, decree-laws become ordinary laws and then may be subject to judicial review. However, observe that the Constitution does not place a time limit

22 B.E. Oder, *Populism*...

23 Article 15 – in times of war, mobilisation or a state of emergency, the exercise of fundamental rights and freedoms may be partially or entirely suspended or measures derogating the guarantees embodied in the Constitution may be taken to the extent required by the exigencies of the situation, as long as obligations under international law are not violated.

Even under the circumstances indicated in the first paragraph, the individual's right to life, the integrity of his/her corporeal and spiritual existence shall be inviolable except where death occurs through acts in conformity with the law of war; no one shall be compelled to reveal his/her religion, conscience, thought or opinion, nor be accused on account of them; offences and penalties shall not be made retroactive; nor shall anyone be held guilty until so proven by a court ruling.

for the approval of emergency decree-laws in the parliament. For that matter, there had been decrees that were not ratified for years by the parliament.

Since the 1982 Constitution came into force, a state of emergency was imposed during the 1990s and between 2016 and 2018 in Turkey. Until 2002, a state of emergency was declared and implemented in the southeast provinces of the country because of Kurdish separatist terrorism, namely the PKK terrorist organization. Between 2016 and 2018, differently from the 1990s, the Turkish government proclaimed the nationwide state of emergency because of the failed coup.

In both periods of the state of emergency, the executive took various measures by issuing a series of emergency decree-laws. However, differently from the previous period of the state of emergency, the measures taken after the proclamation of the state of emergency on 21 July 2016 were extreme and unprecedented. These decree-laws stipulated fundamental and permanent changes to some of the state and private institutions, such as immediate and permanent closure of hundreds of schools, hospitals, foundations, associations, unions, confederations, newspapers, television and radio stations. They also contained immediate dismissal of tens of thousands of public employees including academics, teachers, police and military officers, judges and prosecutors on grounds of their linkage to US-based cleric Fethullah Gülen, who the government holds responsible for the coup attempt, and confiscation of their assets and a prohibition on claiming damages. They provided authorisation of detention without access to a judge for up to 30 days, and automatic cancellation of passports of persons being investigated or prosecuted without a court order. Decree-laws also envisaged complete legal, administrative, criminal and financial impunity for administrative authorities acting within its framework and the fact that administrative courts would not have the power to stay the execution of any of these measures. Emergency decree-laws also contained provisions unrelated to the state of emergency, e.g., changing the procedure for the nomination of the university rectors, establishing new institutions, such as the Turkish Sovereign Wealth Fund, and implementing mandatory winter tire.[24] In short, the emergency measures undertaken by the Turkish authorities during the 24 months suggest that they reached an unprecedented level, targeting economic, social, cultural, civil and political rights, through excessive detentions, massive dismissals, broad institutional closures and confiscation measures.

As stated above, the ban in art. 148.1 of the Constitution on constitutional review of emergency decree-laws has been criticised since some of the worst violations of human rights take place during the periods of emergency regimes. Indeed, such prohibition enables the arbitrary and unlimited exercise

24 S. Esen, *The Right of Derogation from the ECHR and the Case of Turkey*, (in:) J. Gacia Roca, R. Bustos Gisbertm (eds.), *Identidades Europeas, Subsidieridad e Integracion*, Thomson Reuters Aranzadi 2022, pp. 263–264.

of executive power. But the TCC had partly eliminated adverse consequences of this restriction with three judgments in 1991 and 2003.[25] In these cases, the Court pointed out that emergency regimes are limited 'legal regimes' deriving from the Constitution within the understanding of 'democratic state governed by the rule of law'. The TCC noted that it will not depend on the title of a legal document designated by the Parliament or the executive in order to decide whether it is within the scope of the constitutional review. While deciding the legal status of a rule, the TCC takes account of the content of the relevant rule. Whilst the Constitution recognises the authority of the government to issue decree-laws under a state of emergency, it also limits this power in various ways. That is to say, according to art. 120 and 121 of the original text of the Constitution emergency decree-laws can be issued only during a time of emergency and on matters necessitated by emergencies. The power to issue emergency decree-laws is also limited geographically to the regions for which the state of emergency is declared. Thereby, the Court concluded that art. 148.1 of the Constitution only excludes constitutional review of decree-laws issued within the foregoing limits. To put it another way, the Court accepted that it could review the constitutionality of emergency decree-laws and judge whether they exceed the limits provided in the Constitution.[26] Accordingly, the TCC deemed an 'emergency decree-law' an 'ordinary decree-law' should the former exceed the limits drawn by the Constitution and reviewed its constitutionality. Thereby, the TCC did not allow an emergency regime to either become an 'extra-legal regime', or to change its extraordinary character and turn into an 'ordinary regime'. This precedent of the Court made a significant contribution protecting fundamental rights and freedoms and ensuring that the executive operate within the constitutional limits in times of emergency.

However, the TCC departed from its precedent after the proclamation of the state of emergency in 2016. The Court unanimously rejected applications claiming unconstitutionality of emergency decree-laws.[27] In these judgments, following its previous decisions, the Court observed that emergency regimes in democratic countries are not arbitrary governments that exclude law. The objective of an emergency regime must be guarding and defending the constitutional order. The TCC also remarked that all acts and actions of the administration to be under the control of the judiciary is part of the principle of the rule of law. The TCC applied the literalist interpretation method while assess-

25 E.1990/25, K.1991/1, 10 January 1991, Official Gazette 5 May 1992: 21162; E.1991/6, K.1991/20, 3 July 1991, Official Gazette 8 March 1992: 21165; E.2003/28, K.2003/42, 22 May 2003, Official Gazette 16 March 2004:25404.

26 S. Esen, *State of Emergency in Comparative Law and Turkey*, (Turkish), Adalet Publications, Ankara 2008, pp. 277–286.

27 E.2016/166, K. 2016/159, 12 October 2016, Official Gazette 4 November 2016: 29878; E. 2016/167, K.2016/160, 12 October 2016, Official Gazette 4 November 2016: 29898; E. 2016/171 K. 2016/164, 2 November 2016, Official Gazette 8 November 2016: 29882; E. 2016/172 K. 2016/165, 2 November 2016, Official Gazette 8 November 2016: 29882.

ing art. 148.1 of the Constitution and also studied the original intention of the framers of the Constitution. The Court stated that art. 148.1 explicitly prohibits actions to be brought before the TCC alleging the unconstitutionality as to the form or substance of decree-laws issued during the state of emergency. The Court also concluded that the framers of the Constitution aimed at only parliamentary control for emergency decree-laws.

The rationale of the TCC in these decisions seems self-contradictory. On the one hand, the Court still recognises its discretionary power to designate the nature of a legal document whether it is within the scope of the constitutional review. On the other hand, the Court claims that such designation regarding the nature of a rule should not result in the constitutional review of an emergency decree-law. But such designation requires review of the content of the decree-law and that will render art. 148.1 of the Constitution meaningless. However, the TCC disregards that its counterview is equally valid. In other words, the Court's rationale will provide the executive with an absolute discretionary power to issue anything with an emergency decree-law, such as suspending all constitutional rights and freedoms without consideration of the constitutional limitations or abolishing all democratic institutions including the TCC.

According to the Court, reviewing the constitutionality of emergency decree-laws would infringe upon art. 11 of the Constitution that stipulates the superiority and binding effect of the Constitution, art. 6 that prohibits persons and organs to exercise state authority that does not emanate from the Constitution, the wording of art. 148.1 and the intention of the framers of the Constitution. It seems like the Court disregards one of the fundamental functions of the constitutional courts which is to maintain the superiority and binding effect of the Constitution by reviewing the constitutionality of laws or other norms having force of law. Still, a constitutional court must interpret the constitution as a whole and embrace a rights-based approach. This requires the Court to read constitutional limitations regarding the rights and freedoms as narrowly as possible. In this respect, the TCC's judgments are unfortunate for democratic constitutionalism wherein the primary aim is to limit the government and to safeguard rights and freedoms.[28]

As mentioned above, the TCC reviews the constitutionality of the emergency decree-laws passed by the GNAT into law. Some of the emergency decree-laws issued between 2016 and 2018 became law by the Parliament's approval and the Court has reviewed their constitutionality. It is noteworthy that the Court applies a method of limitation on the constitutional review of such laws. According to the TCC, for such law to be subject to constitutional

28 S. Esen, *Judicial Control of Decree-laws in Emergency Regimes – A Self destruction Attempt by the Turkish Constitutional Court?*, IACL Blog, 2016, https://blog-iacl-aidc.org/2016-posts/2018/5/18/analysis-judicial- control-of-decree-laws-in-emergency-regimes-a-self-destruction-attempt-by-the-tur- kish-constitutional-court.

review the rule should be aimed at eliminating the threats or dangers that engendered the proclamation of the state of emergency and should be applicable only within the period of the state of emergency. The 1982 Constitution provides separate regimes for the limitation of fundamental rights and freedoms in times of normalcy and emergency. Article 13 of the Constitution provides principles for the limitation of fundamental rights and freedoms during normal times.[29] Accordingly, they may be limited only by law without infringing upon their essence. The limitations of the law should be in conformity with the letter and spirit of the Constitution. Namely, limitations should comply with the constitutional guaranties and prohibitions. In addition, the Parliament should consider the whole of the Constitution while restricting rights and freedoms. Restrictions on freedoms must be in conformity with the reasons mentioned in the relevant articles of the Constitution. Limitations cannot conflict with the requirements of the democratic social order, the secular Republic and the principle of proportionality. Accordingly, the Parliament should proceed under the principle that 'freedom is the rule, restriction is the exception'. This is the principle upon which democratic regimes are based.[30]

On the other hand, limitations on the rights and freedoms during times of emergency are provided for in art. 15 of the Constitution. According to art. 15, in times of war, mobilisation or a state of emergency, the exercise of fundamental rights and freedoms can be partially or entirely suspended, and even measures that derogate the guarantees stipulated in the Constitution can be taken. Namely, in states of exception, fundamental rights and freedoms may be restricted in broader terms than in usual times, and their exercise may be partially or entirely suspended.[31] Article 15 stipulates three principles to protect the fundamental rights and freedoms under states of exception. First, measures taken under states of exception will not violate Turkey's obligations under international law. This principle refers to international treaties and agreements duly put into effect in the area of the fundamental rights and freedoms and general principles of international law. Second, measures must be taken to the extent required by the exigencies of the situation, i.e., conform with the principle of proportionality. Third, the rights and freedoms named in the second paragraph may not be violated even under an emergency regime. Accordingly, a right to life, and the integrity of his or her material and spiritual entity shall be inviolable except where death occurs through a lawful act of warfare; no one may be compelled to reveal his or her religion, conscience, thought or opinion, nor be accused on account of them; offences and penalties may not

29 Article 13 as amended in 2001, 'Fundamental rights and freedoms may be restricted only by law and in conformity with the reasons mentioned in the relevant articles of the Constitution without infringing upon their essence. These restrictions shall not be in conflict with the letter and spirit of the Constitution and the requirements of the democratic order of the society, the secular Republic and the principle of proportionality'.

30 Y. Sabuncu, *Anayasaya Giriş*, İmaj 2006, p. 63.

31 F. Sağlam, *Temel Hakların Sınırlanması ve Özü*, AÜSBF Yayını, Ankara 1982, pp. 180–181.

be made retroactive, nor may anyone be held guilty until so proven by a court judgment. In other words, the Constitution draws up an untouchable core area composed of a few rights and freedoms.

According to the TCC, an emergency decree rule approved by the GNAT in the form of law, in some cases, is subject to emergency regime stipulated in art. 15 of the Constitution. The TCC notes that in order for a statutory rule to be subject to art. 15 of the Constitution, it must be aimed at eliminating the threats or dangers that induced the declaration of the state of emergency and must be applied during the period of the state of emergency. In cases where a statutory rule does not meet these conditions, its constitutional review is carried out under art. 13 of the Constitution. The constitutionality of a statutory provision that responds to these conditions first is reviewed within the scope of art. 13 of the Constitution. If it is deemed that the provision is contrary to the guarantees outlined in art. 13, then it will be reviewed as to whether it complies with art. 15 of the Constitution.[32] As a result, the Court's reading creates two types of law, one based on the principles and rules in art. 15 and the other in art. 13 of the Constitution. However, the TCC's understanding is problematic given that the Constitution does not stipulate such a distinction. Indeed, the Constitution provides for emergency decree-laws, not emergency laws, to meet the needs of the emergency regime. Since the Constitution does not differentiate emergency laws from ordinary laws, art. 15 of the Constitution can only set a limit for emergency decree-laws. As a state of emergency decree-law is approved by the GNAT in the form of 'law', it shall not be subject to the state of emergency procedures. Even if the content of the statute is the approval of an emergency decree-law and enacted during the state of emergency, it is still an ordinary law and is subject to judicial review stipulated by the Constitution for all laws. Because, unlike the emergency decree-laws, laws do not cease to be effected with the end of the state of emergency. The TCC's approach makes it possible to interfere with the fundamental rights by law beyond the limits stipulated by art. 13. As a result of this approach, the Court found several statutory provisions that violate art. 13 constitutional by reviewing them within the scope of art. 15.

10.4.2 COVID-19 pandemic

Unlike many countries, the AKP government imposed very stringent measures aimed at controlling the spread of COVID-19 and its economic effects without declaring a state of emergency. However, many measures imposed

32 Among others *see* E.2017/18, K.2019/66, 25 July 2019, Official Gazette 1 November 2019:30935; E. 2018/92, K.2019/67, 25 July 2019, Official Gazette 31 October 2019:30934; E.2017/21, K.2020/77, 24 December 2020, Official Gazette 8 April 2021:31448; E.2021/104, K.2021/87, 11 November 2021, Official Gazette 25 March 2022:31789.

by the government were unconstitutional.[33] The AKP government used the extraordinary circumstances resulting from the pandemic as an opportunity for its supporters and for suppressing the opposition. The government severely restricted the rights of peaceful assembly, association, travel, speech, etc., of those who oppose the government's actions on the grounds of the pandemic.[34] Law No. 7242 amending the Law on the Enforcement of Judgments and Security Measures adopted on 14 April 2020 may be cited as a clear example of abuse of the pandemic.

Law No. 7242 provides for the reduction of the general service requirement for some of the convicts to lower the prison population both of a general nature and as a particular measure of the COVID-19 pandemic.[35] It reduces the general service requirement for parole eligibility from two-thirds to half of the sentence and grants temporary release provision for inmates who were sentenced to imprisonment for three years or less. The statute provides for the immediate release of prisoners over the age of 60 with chronic illnesses and disabilities and women with children younger than three to serve the rest of their term under house arrest. At the same time, it excludes various categories of crimes and prisoners, namely persons on remand and convicted prisoners serving a sentence for crimes against state intelligence services; violation of the National Intelligence Agency Act; Anti-Terrorism Act; espionage; deliberate manslaughter; intentional injury; injury to a child, an elderly person or a spouse; sexual violence crimes; drug production and trade. Note that anti-terrorism legislation in Turkey has been heavily criticised, as the concepts of terrorism and terrorist act are defined broadly and vaguely.[36] Observe that a considerable portion of the imprisoned journalists, lawyers and political and human rights activists are prosecuted for violating anti-terrorism legislation.

MPs of the Republican People's Party (Cumhuriyet Halk Partisi-CHP), the main opposition party in the Parliament, filed for an annulment of Law No. 7242 to the TCC claiming its unconstitutionality with two applications. The first application based its assertion of the unconstitutionality of the law on formal grounds, the second one on substantial grounds. In the first application, the applicants claimed that art. 87 of the Constitution stipulates the majority of three-fifths of the GNAT to adopt amnesty and pardon. Despite the nature of the provisions of Law No. 7242 being an amnesty, it was enacted with a simple majority. Accordingly, it is unconstitutional. However, ignoring

33 S. Esen, *Impacts of the Covid 19 Pandemic on the Constitutional Rights in Turkey*, (in:) J.M. Serna de la Garza (coor.), *Covid 19 and Constitutional Law*, UNAM 2020 (https://biblio.juridicas.unam.mx/bjv/detalle-libro/6310-covid-19-and-constitutional-law-covid-19-et-droit-constitutionnel), pp. 211–220.

34 S. Esen, *Impacts...*

35 Law No.7242 adopted in 14 April 2020, Official Gazette 15 April 2020: 31100.

36 S. Esen, *Constitutional Perspective on Fighting Terrorism in Ordinary Times in Turkey and the Turkish Constitutional Court*, (in:) O. Depenheuer, A. Scherzberg (eds.), *Der Rectstaat in Zeiten von Notstand un Terrorabwehr*, Lit Verlag, Münster 2019, pp. 29–44.

its previous case law, the majority of the judges of the TCC deemed that the statute regulates proceedings of execution of penalties, it is not related to the scope of the penalty imposed. Hence, the provisions do not propose an amnesty, but rather a change in execution policy which could be adopted by the Parliament through normal procedures.[37] As the TCC defines in its previous rulings, amnesty is an official pardon granted by the Parliament that removes, mitigates or changes a final sentence, drops the criminal proceedings or lifts a conviction with all its consequences.[38] Contrary to what the majority of the members of the Court stated, Law No. 7242 clearly reduces the length of time of the prisoners or commutes the sentence. In this respect, the statute provides a special amnesty. As stated in some of the dissenting votes, the Court's interpretation renders art. 87 of the Constitution useless and hollow and is contrary to the Constitution.

In the second application,[39] the applicants, among others, alleged that the provision that excludes the high number of prisoners sentenced under anti-terrorism laws contradicts art. 10 of the Constitution that guarantees the principle of equality, and prohibits discrimination on the ground that the difference between categories of offenses made by the statute does not rest on a legitimate aim. As in the previous decision, the TCC also found these claims meritless. The Court noted that Law No. 7242 indeed makes a difference in treatment on the basis of categories of offences and inmates. However, according to the Court, the legislation has a reasonable and objective basis, because it aims to serve as a deterrence for certain crimes, such as terrorism offences. Law No. 7242 represents a new criminal justice and execution policy, an area that falls completely within the discretion of the Parliament. Accordingly, the Court deemed that the different treatment of Law No. 7242 did not exceed the reasonable permissible limitations and found the statute constitutional.[40]

10.4.3 Dismissal of the TCC judges

Two judges of the TCC were arrested and detained in the aftermath of the coup attempt in 2016 on suspicion of belonging to the terrorist organisation led by an Islamic clergy allegedly that was behind the attempt. The TCC dismissed the judges shortly after their arrest pursuant to Emergency Decree-law No. 667. According to the emergency decree-law, judges and prosecutors assessed to be members of terrorist organisations or assessed to be connected or in contact with them will be permanently dismissed from their posts and banned

37 E.2020/44, K.2020/41, 17 July 2020, Official Gazette 7 October 2020: 31267.

38 E.2001/4, K.2001/332, 18 July 2001, Official Gazette 27 October 2001:24566; E. 2004/92, K.2008/119, 12 June 2008, Official Gazette 5 November 2008:27045.

39 E. 2020/53, K. 2021/55, 14 July 2021, Official Gazette 20 October 2021: 31634.

40 For a detailed study of these two cases see E. Turkut, *Emergency Powers, Constitutional (Self-Restraint) and Judicial Politics: the Turkish Constitutional Court During the COVID-19 Pandemic*, "Jus Cogens" 2022, https://doi.org/10.1007/s42439-022-00064-7.

permanently from practising as a judge or prosecutor. They will not be directly or indirectly assigned to public service. Dismissal of the TCC judges from their post shall be decided by the simple majority of the Plenary of the TCC.

The Court ruled that the emergency decree-law does not require the link between the members and the organisations or groups in question to be conclusively established and deemed sufficient the Plenary of the TCC's 'assessment' regarding the existence of such link. The Court observed that the relevant decree-law prescribes no requirements to rely on a certain kind of evidence in order to reach this conviction. Hence, the Court concluded to dismiss its two judges based upon 'the social network information' that they are connected with the organisation in question and the 'common impression' of the members of the TCC that two members had links with the terrorist organisation. Note that the Court gave the judgment unanimously.

The decision of the Court raises criticism. The emergency decree-law that provides for the TCC to dismiss its judges without being convicted of an offence is clearly incongruous with the Constitution. Indeed, the Constitution specifically provides dismissal of the membership of the TCC only in two circumstances. First, the membership of the TCC will terminate automatically those who are convicted of an offence requiring their dismissal from the judicial profession. Second, the TCC shall dismiss its judge with an absolute majority of the total number of its members if it is definitely established that he/she is unable to perform his/her duties on account of ill-health (cons. art 147.2).

Yet, the reasoning of the TCC to justify the dismissal is general, abstract and subjective considering 'information from the social circle' and the 'common conviction'. The judgment neither mentions any personal wrongdoing for the dismissed judges nor rests upon any evidence in support of the decision. Clearly, the justification of the Court falls short of meeting the principle of the rule of law.

One of the dismissed judges also lodged an individual application with the TCC complaining about the unlawfulness of his detention and his dismissal, the Court held in 2018 that he had failed to bring an appropriate compensation claim under art. 141(1) of the Turkish Code of Criminal Procedure (CCP) and had therefore not exhausted all remedies. All remaining complaints were held to be manifestly ill-founded. The ECtHR ruled that the TCC in this judgment had referred to items of evidence such as statements by anonymous witnesses accusing the applicant of belonging to the terrorist organisation behind the failed coup, and messages exchanged via the ByLock messaging service. The ECtHR concluded that the TCC and the Turkish government had failed to address the absence of any concrete evidence justifying the applicant's pre-trial detention and that the TCC's judgment was both in breach of the principle of legal certainty and manifestly unreasonable.[41] Moreover, the

41 *Alparslan Altan v. Turkey*, appl. no. 12778/17, 16 April 2019, at 134–138; The ECtHR also reached the same conclusion in the case of Erdal Tercan, also a judge of the Constitutional

Court held that this extensive interpretation of *flacrante delicto* could not be regarded as an appropriate response to a state of emergency. Such an approach was found not only to be problematic in terms of legal certainty, but also to negate procedural safeguards affording judges independence from the executive, and has 'legal consequences reaching far beyond the legal framework of the state of emergency'. The Court went on to find that '[t]he detention order was based on a mere suspicion of membership of a criminal organisation. Such a degree of suspicion cannot be sufficient to justify an order for a person's detention.' Regardless of the circumstances, states cannot have a blank cheque under art. 5 to order the detention of an individual during a state of emergency without any verifiable evidence or information or without a sufficient factual basis satisfying the minimum requirements of art. 5.1(c).[42]

10.5 Conclusion

Democratic recession is a global phenomenon. Starting from the 2010s, Turkey has been considered one of the early examples of this global trend. Indeed, the executive branch has been gradually strengthened through constitutional amendments. Some of these alterations, especially the 2010 changes, specifically targeted the judiciary. Owing to the constitutional amendments and the same political party, i.e., the AKP in power since 2002, the TCC has been court-packed with ideologically friendly and loyal lawyers to the president. The decline of democracy also led to a visible change in the TCC's judicial attitudes. The TCC has increasingly supported the legislative preferences of the government in controversial issues that resulted in major shifts in the Court's case law. The failed coup in July 2016 and the COVID-19 pandemic have displayed the Court's new position on critical matters. The Court's approach to critical issues produced a constitutional moment, one where the AKP government used the devices of constitutional democracy to access unrestricted powers and served to normalise the extraordinary situations. The TCC fails both to act as a barrier against attempts to establish authoritarianism through law and slow down its grow in the country. The Court plays a limited role to ensure both the legislative and executive branches operate within the constitutional boundaries, thereby protecting the fundamental rights.

References

Aliefendioğlu Y., *Anayasa Yargısı*, Yetkin, Ankara, 1997.

Belmek S., *The Rise of Hybrid Political Islam in Turkey. Origins and Consolidation of the JDP*, Palgrave Macmillan London 2019.

Court, who was arrested and dismissed. *Erdal Tercan v. Turkey* appl no.61158/18, 29 June 2021.

42 *Alparslan Altan v. Turkey* at 147.

Bermeo N., *On Democratic Backsliding*, "Journal of Democracy" 2016, vol. 27, pp. 5–19.
Esen S., *Constitutional Perspective on Fighting Terrorism in Ordinary Times in Turkey and the Turkish Constitutional Court*, (in:) O. Depenheuer, A. Scherzberg (eds.), *Der Rectstaat in Zeiten von Notstand un Terrorabwehr*, Lit Verlag, Münster 2019.
Esen S., *Impacts of the Covid 19 Pandemic on the Constitutional Rights in Turkey*, (in:) J.M. Serna de la Garza (coor.), *Covid 19 and Constitutional Law*, UNAM 2020, https://biblio.juridicas.unam.mx/bjv/detalle-libro/6310-covid-19-and -constitutional-law-covid-19-et-droit-constitutionnel.
Esen S., *Judicial Control of Decree-laws in Emergency Regimes: A Self Destruction Attempt by the Turkish Constitutional Court?*, IACL Blog, 2016, https://blog-iacl-aidc.org /2016-posts/2018/5/18/analysis-judicial- control-of-decree-laws-in-emergency -regimes-a-self-destruction-attempt-by-the-tur- kish-constitutional-court.
Esen S., *State of Emergency in Comparative Law and Turkey*, (Turkish), Adalet Publications, Ankara 2008.
Esen S., *The 2017 Constitutional Reforms in Turkey: Removal of Parliamentarism or Democracy?*, IACL-IADC Blog, 2017, blog-iacl-aidc.org.
Esen S., *The Constitutional Court of Turkey*, (in:) *Max Planck Encyclopedia of Comparative Constitutional Law*, 2018.
Esen S., *The Right of Derogation from the ECHR and the Case of Turkey*, (in:) J.G. Roca, R. Bustos Gisbertm (eds.), *Identidades Europeas, Subsidieridad e Integracion*, Thomson Reuters Aranzadi 2022.
Gönenç L., Esen S., *The Problem of Less Protective International Agreements in Domestic Legal Systems: Article 90 of the Turkish Constitution*, "European Journal of Law Reform" 2006, vol. 8(4): 485–500.
Haggard S., Kaufman R., *Backsliding Democratic Regress in the Contemporary World*, Cambridge University Press, Cambridge 2021.
Huntington S.P., *The Third Wave. Democratization in the Late Twentieth Century*, University of Oklahoma Press, Norman 1993.
Insel A., *The AKP and Normalizing Democracy in Turkey*, "The South Atlantic Quarterly" 2003, vol. 102, https://birikimdergisi.com/articles/7399/the-akp -and-normalizing-democracy-in-turkey
Oder B.E., *Populism and the Turkish Constitutional Court: The Game Broker, the Populist and the Popular*, VerfBlog, 2017, https://verfassungsblog.de/populism-and-the -turkish-constitutional-court-the-game-broker-the-populist-and-the-popular.
Öden M., Esen S., *Fundamental Rights and Freedoms in Turkey and the Turkish Constitutional Court*, (in:) R. Arnold (ed.), *The Convergence of the Fundamental Rights Protection in Europe*, Springer, Cham 2013.
Öniş Z., *Monopolizing the Center: The AKP and the Uncertain Path of Turkish Democracy*, "The International Spectator" 2015, vol. 50(2): 22–41.
Özbudun E., *Anayasalcılık ve Demokrasi*, Yetkin, Ankara 2019.
Özbudun E., *Otoriter Rejimler, Seçimsel Demokrasiler ve Türkiye*, Yetkin, Ankara 2021.
Özbudun E., Gençkaya Ö.F., *Democratization and Politics of Constitution-Making in Turkey*, Central European University Press, Budapest, 2009.
Rabasa A., Larrabee F.S., *The Rise of Political Islam in Turkey*, RAND Corporation, Santa Monica 2008.
Sabuncu Y., *Anayasaya Giriş*, "İmaj, Ankara, 2006.
Sağlam F., *Temel Hakların Sınırlanması ve Özü*, AÜSBF Yayını, Ankara 1982.

Tecimer C., *Recognizing Court-Packing: Perception and Reality in the Case of the Turkish Constitutional Court*, VerfBlog, 2019, https://verfassungsblog.de/recognizing-court-packing.
Turkut E., *Emergency Powers, Constitutional (Self-Restraint and Judicial Politics: The Turkish Constitutional Court During the COVID-19 Pandemic*, "Jus Cogens" 2022, https://doi.org/10.1007/s42439-022-00064-7.

TCC judgments

E.1990/25, K.1991/1, 10 January 1991, Official Gazette 5 May 1992: 21162.
E.1991/6, K.1991/20, 3 July 1991, Official Gazette 8 March 1992: 21165.
E.2003/28, K.2003/42, 22 May 2003, Official Gazette 16 March 2004:25404.
E.2001/4, K.2001/332, 18 July 2001, Official Gazette 27 October 2001:24566.
E. 2007/45. K. 2007/54, 1 May 2007, Official Gazette, 27 June 2007: 26565.
E.2008/1, K.2008/2, 30 July 2008, Official Gazette 24 October 2008: 26923.
E.2008/16, K.2008/116, 5 June 2008, Official Gazette 22 October 2008: 27032.
E. 2004/92, K.2008/119, 12 June 2008, Official Gazette 5 November 2008:27045.
E.2016/166, K. 2016/159, 12 October 2016, Official Gazette 4 November 2016: 29878.
E. 2016/167, K.2016/160, 12 October 2016, Official Gazette 4 November 2016: 29898.
E. 2016/171 K. 2016/164, 2 November 2016, Official Gazette 8 November 2016: 29882.
E. 2016/172 K. 2016/165, 2 November 2016, Official Gazette 8 November 2016: 29882.
E.2017/18, K.2019/66, 25 July 2019, Official Gazette 1 November 2019:30935.
E. 2018/92, K.2019/67, 25 July 2019, Official Gazette 31 October 2019:30934.
E.2020/44, K.2020/41, 17 July 2020, Official Gazette 7 October 2020: 31267.
E.2017/21, K.2020/77, 24 December 2020, Official Gazette 8 April 2021:31448.
E.2020/53, K.2021/55, 14 July 2021, Official Gazette 20 October 2021: 31634.
E.2021/104, K.2021/87, 11 November 2021, Official Gazette 25 March 2022:31789.

ECtHR judgments

Alparslan Altan v. Turkey, appl. no. 12778/17, 16 April 2019,
Erdal Tercan v. Turkey appl no.61158/18, 29 June 2021.

11 Constitutional review in the abusive constitutionalism (continuation, corruption or disappearance?)

Lech Garlicki and Marta Derlatka

11.1 Introduction

Constitutional review is regarded today as one of the necessary components of the rule of law and, therefore, of any constitutional democracy. In Europe, the doctrinal (as well as institutional) model of constitutional review remains linked to concepts elaborated by the Kelsenian school. It was assumed that – for the traditional civil law systems – it is better to vest the power of constitutional review into a single judicial body separated from the system of the 'regular' courts and operating next to the regular Supreme Court(s). The concentrated (centralised) model of constitutional review has been gradually adopted in almost all countries of Western (continental) Europe. Later, it was also adopted – in an almost automatic manner – in the post-authoritarian constitutions of the 'new democracies' in Central and Eastern Europe.[1]

It is, of course, true that constitutional review can operate, in an equally efficient manner, without a separate constitutional court. The experience of the American system of judicial review, as well as of several younger courts (such as, in the first place, the Supreme Court of Israel) are quite instructive in this respect. In some other countries (such as the UK, Australia, New Zealand and Canada), constitutional review emerged in a 'softer' form, reserving more room for the legislative decisions.[2] And, finally, some – undisputedly democratic – countries decided not to have any formally established system of constitutional review (the two prominent examples, the Netherlands and Finland, are separately presented in this volume). It would be risky to suggest any uniformly imposing receipt – each country must determine what system

1 See, for the formative period: O. Luchterhandt, Ch. Starck, A. Weber (ed.), *Verfassungsgerichtsbarkeit in Mittel- und Osteuropa*, Heidelberg 2007; H. Schwartz, *The Struggle for Constitutional Justice in Post-Communist Europe*, Chicago 2000; M. Brzezinski, L. Garlicki, *Judicial Review in Post-Communist Poland. The emergence of a "Rechtsstaat"?*, "Stanford Journal of Int. Law" 1995, vol. 31.

2 See: S. Gardbaum, *The New Commonwealth Model of Constitutionalism*, CUP 2013; *Symposium: Weak-form Review in Comparative Perspective*, "International Journal of Constitutional Law" 2019, vol. 17, no. 3.

DOI: 10.4324/9781003355793-13

of constitutional protection corresponds with its history, tradition and legal culture.

At the same time, however, it seems that 'soft' or non-judicial systems of constitutional review can genuinely operate only within the framework of the entrenched respect for laws, constitutions and human rights. Transition to democracy is better ensured where the 'last word' in constitutional controversies belongs to the court and not to the political branches of government. That was why almost all 'new democracies' opted for the centralised system of constitutional review and vested their constitutional courts with powers typically exercised by the West-European homologues. Within the next 20 years, several (albeit, clearly, not all) of the 'new courts' managed to establish an independent position and to elaborate a solid body of jurisprudence. The Courts of Hungary, Poland and the Czech Republic were often regarded as a 'success story', gradually joining the global family of constitutional jurisdictions.

The success became, however, tantamount to a death warrant once the populist governments emerged in our region. Strong and independent courts are hardly compatible with the so-called 'abusive constitutionalism'.

This presentation[3] begins with a few general observations on the nature of the abusive constitutionalism (section 11.2). Then it considers the past, the present and the future of constitutional review in the affected countries.[4] As concerns the past, we recapitulate the techniques of political capture of constitutional courts (section 11.3). Next, we discuss the present record of the 'new' constitutional courts. We conclude that it shows more change than continuation (section 11.4.1), more decay (corruption) than 'regular' change (section 11.4.2) and we analyse the role and nature of the corruptive trend (section 11.4.3). Finally, we raise some questions concerning the future of constitutional review once the political context would change (section 11.5).

11.2 The 'abusive constitutionalism'

The concept of 'abusive constitutionalism', used along several similar terms,[5] provides a valid description of the backsliding process infecting several coun-

3 It is based, at least as concerns its two opening sections, on our paper: L. Garlicki, M. Derlatka, Constitutional courts in the abusive constitutionalism [in:] *Le constitutionnalisme abusif en Europe, sous la dir.* de P.-A. Collot, Editions Mare et Martin 2022 (Paris), pp. 311–315.

4 The most instructive in this respect are there experiences of Hungary and Poland, albeit they remain far from being identical (see T. Drinoczy, A. Bien-Kacala, *Illiberal Constitutionalism: The Case of Hungary and Poland*, "German Law Journal" 2019, vol. 20, pp. 1142–1145) K. Scheppele noted that Poland 'used the map drawn by Orban' (*Autocratic Legalism*, "The University of Chicago Law Review" 2018, vol. 85, p. 553); see also T. Daly, *Diagnosing Democratic Decay, Comparative Constitutional Law Roundtable*, Sydney 2017 (Academia 34052302), p. 11; A. Sajo, J. Tuovinen, *The Rule of Law and Legitimacy in Emerging Illiberal Democracies*, "Ost-Europa Recht" 2018, no. 4, p. 512.

5 We subscribe to David Landau's observation: 'Abusive constitutionalism involves the use of the mechanisms of constitutional change [...] to undermine democracy. While traditional methods

tries in the modern world. This is a mid-way process, its nature being no longer democratic, but not yet purely authoritarian. It develops within the formal structure of laws and constitutions and attempts to maintain the pretense of legal legitimacy.

In a brief recapitulation,[6] the abusive constitutionalism:

- constitutes a process of the systemic dimension: it affects – albeit in a differentiated manner – all branches of government. It begins with the electoral success of the populist parties, but soon it departs from its original legitimacy by degrading the operations of parliament and marginalising the role of the opposition. It leads to a political capture of the entire executive branch, including segments (such as the public broadcasting, auditing chamber or the National Bank) which should remain separated from the actual political constellation. Finally, it extends the political absorption to the judicial branch, including the constitutional court;
- remains legalistic in its external appearances. The abusive constitutionalism unfolds within the existing legal framework, slowly replaced by new statutes, constitutional amendments and judicial decisions.[7] The latter are of a particular attractiveness since confirmations rendered by supreme or/and constitutional courts are presented as the final proof of respect and continuation of the rule of law. This creates an appearance of a 'regular' constitutionalism;[8] and – unlike in purely authoritarian systems – the political controllers are genuinely interested in maintaining this appearance;
- is abusive in its technique and substance. It constantly refers to terms and concepts established in the traditional constitutionalism and consecrated by the local doctrine and jurisprudence. At the same time, it gives them a new, often twisted meaning which severs any link to their original substance. The

of democratic overthrow such as the military coup have been on the decline for decades, the use of constitutional tools to create authoritarian and semi-authoritarian regimes is increasingly prevalent. [...]. The resulting constitutions still look democratic from a distance and contain many elements that are no different from those found in liberal democratic constitutions. But from close up they have been substantially reworked to undermine the democratic order'. Other scholars refer to 'illiberal democracy' (Fareed Zakaria), 'illiberal constitutionalism' (Mark Tushnet), 'constitutional retrogression' (Aziz Huq and Tom Ginsburg), 'autocratic legalism' (Kim Lane Scheppele), 'democratic decay (Tom Daly) and 'constitutional dismemberment' (Richard Albert). Finally, Wojciech Sadurski (*Poland's Constitutional Breakdown*, OUP 2019, p. 242) concludes his presentation by the question: 'illiberal democracy or populist authoritarianism?'.

6 See M. Derlatka, L. Garlicki, *Constitutional Courts...*, p. 312.

7 This approach is – to a considerable extent – based on the legalistic formalism, well established in the historic practice of the 'socialist constitutionalism', equating 'the rule of law' with due observation of the existing legal rules (see, e.g., M.A. Glendon, M.W. Gordon, Ch. Osakwe, *Comparative Legal Traditions*, Minneapolis-St, Paul 1994, pp. 401–403). A. Sajo, J. Tuovinen (*The Rule of Law...*, pp. 521–522) noted, in this respect, that 'the rule of law is often replaced by rule by law'.

8 T.G. Daly, *Diagnosing...*, p. 5, referring to R. Dixon.

new techniques of interpretation contain components of manipulation and bad faith,[9] and are used to apply pretenses of constitutionalism and legalism to measures which are inherently foreign to these concepts;

- is dynamic in both the intensity of departures from the past, and the forms and techniques employed in the consolidation of the new regime. Its development is – generally – determined by the history, tradition and political culture of the specific countries, the quality and durability of the democratic governments in the pre-capture period, the range of electoral success of the populist parties,[10] the solidity of supranational limitations resulting – in our region – from participation in such regional arrangements as the EU and the ECHR. The practice of abusive constitutionalism is far from creation of coherent structures. It rather provides a spectrum dominated by hybrids and mixtures which cannot be organised into any definable concept;
- cannot be – doctrinally – regarded as one of the democratic forms of government.[11] The legitimacy of electoral success cannot balance the de facto departure from such basic concepts as the rule of law and the independence of the judicial branch. The abusive constitutionalism is a vehicle serving the principal goal which is the concentration of the controlling powers over the State and society.[12]

11.3 The past

The abusive constitutionalism needs the law to consolidate the legalistic pretenses of the new regime and, therefore, ***needs courts*** to confirm and consecrate that consolidation. In our region, the populistic reformers encountered the already existing judicial systems. In nearly all of them, constitutional disputes were entrusted to separate constitutional courts, and – in some of them – those courts were already able to create their own power and identity. It was rather obvious that, if allowed to continue in a non-modified form, the judicial branch would not be ready to support the anti-constitutional nature of the new policies.

9 See, in general: D.E. Pozen, *Constitutional Bad Faith*, "Harvard Law Review" 2016, vol. 126, p. 885.

10 Whereas, in Hungary, the Fides Party immediately managed to achieve the 'constitutional majority' (and – already in 2011 – was able to adopt a new constitution), constitutional amendments have always remained outside the reach of the PiS Party in Poland. This triggered more anti-constitutional practices in Poland than in Hungary.

11 In particular, it cannot be assimilated to the concept of 'political constitutionalism' and with its resistance to the constitutional emancipation of the judicial branch (see, e.g., G. Halmai, *Dismantling Constitutional Review in Hungary*, "Rivista di Diritti Comparati" 2019, no. 1, p. 45).

12 See, e.g., T.T. Koncewicz, *The "Emergency Constitutional Review" and Polish Constitutional Crisis*, "Polish Law Review" 2016, no. 1, p. 73.

That was why *constitutional courts became 'central targets'* of the new government.[13] Although the other segments of the judicial branch also were regarded as potentially harmful, the constitutional court was perceived as not only the principal danger but also the most attractive booty.[14] In other words, the control on the constitutional court was critical for the entire program of capture of the state machinery and dismantlement of the constitutional system of checks and balances.

Two basic techniques, neutralisation and absorption, have been used in this respect.[15] Both were applied to constitutional courts as well as to other segments of the judicial branch.

The technique of 'absorption' (capture) relies on the sequence on measures mostly affected the personal composition of the Court. In the end, the court reappears in almost identical 'legal shell' as its predecessor, but with a new team of judges sympathetic to the governmental policies.

The technique of 'neutralisation' (disablement) is used where 'absorption' has not yet been completed due to the existing constitutional or European constraints. It is focused on measures attacking operational capacities of the Court, establishing limitations on jurisdiction and access, restricting enforcement of the rulings. In brief, the goal of 'neutralisation' is to paralyse the Court's operational ability and to eliminate it (at least – temporarily) from the political scene.

In practice, both techniques have been used in a parallel manner, at least until the successful conclusion of the Court's capture. A lot, however, depended on the context. Mere political persuasion could sometimes occur quite effective. Weaker courts have always tended towards loyalty to the actual holders of the political power; such tradition did not encourage dissent and led to a voluntary subordination.[16] Stronger courts might be able to resist political pressure but may not be ready to resist the authority of constitutional amendments or the 'brand-new' constitutions.[17] If, however, the populist government had neither

13 B. Bugaric, T. Ginsburg, *The Assault on Postcommunist Courts*, "Journal of Democracy" 2016, vol. 27, no. 3, p. 69; O.W. Lembcke, Ch. Boulanger, *Between Revolution and Constitution*, (in:) G.A. Toth (ed.), *Constitution for a Disunited Nation*, Budapest 2012, p. 280.

14 L. Garlicki, *Constitutional*..., pp. 160–161; A. Sajo, J. Tuovinen, *The Rule of Law*..., p. 513.

15 L. Garlicki, *Constitutional*..., p. 159 (with references to the historical terms of Gleichschaltung and Ausschaltung).

16 A. Sajo, J. Tuovinen, *The Rule of Law*..., p. 512, indicating that 'this was the scenario in most post-Soviet Republics'. Also, about the Russian Court, A. di Gregorio, *Constitutional Courts in the Context of Constitutional Regression*, (in:) M. Belov (ed.) *Courts, Politics and Constitutional Law*, London-New York 2021, p. 216.

17 P. Castillo Ortiz (*The Illiberal Abuse of Constitutional Courts in Europe*, "European Constitutional Law Review" 2019, vol. 15, p. 57) talks about 'a smooth takeover of the Constitutional Court in Hungary'. G. Halmai (*Unconstitutional Constitutional Amendments*, "Constellations" 2012, vol. 19, no. 2, p. 19) observed that 'the process of personal renewal took more discreet form since the new government could use constitutional amendments to neutralize decisions of the "old" court'.

control over constitutional amendments nor the political leverage over the Court and its judges,[18] it may be tempted, as in the case of Poland, to resort to 'quasi-constitutional' (or – sometimes – blatantly unconstitutional) measures of neutralisation or/and absorption of the constitutional court.

The abusive constitutionalism is based on the pretense of legalism and, therefore, it cannot simply get rid of a constitutional court. Dissolution or suspension of the court albeit typical for 'regular' authoritarianism,[19] would be dysfunctional in the setting of 'illiberal democracies'.

There are *four principal areas* covered by the neutralisation and/or absorption measures:[20]

1. *The control over the personal composition of constitutional courts* is the most efficient tool of absorption. The process of appointment of constitutional judges is politicised even in the most respected democracies.[21] The problem, however, is with its intensity and style. Only then, is it possible to distinguish between legitimate appointment policies and the illicit court-packing practices.

The abusive constitutionalism inevitably gravitates toward the latter. The modalities of the process, however, are far from uniform.

In a more 'civilized' version, the new government may wait for the arrival of regular openings and – only then – fill the court with former (or actual) politicians or with other sympathisers. Such scenario (typical for Hungary)[22] offers no general indications to nature of the process. Court-packing aberrations are identifiably only on the case-to-case basis.[23] The external perception of the fairness in the appointment policy and of the impartiality and independence of

---

It should, however, be noted that the Hungarian Court, in 2011–2012, has attempted some countermeasures, and that the process of its absorption was more complicated.

18 P. Castillo Ortiz, *The Illiberal Abuse...*, p. 56.

19 In Yeltsin's Russia, the 'first' Constitutional Court was suspended in 1993 and revived (in the modified setting) in 1995 (see, e.g., A. Blankenagel, *Detstvo, otročestvo i junost' rossijskogo konstitucionnogo suda*, Moskva 1996).

In Belarus, the beginning of Lukashenka's rule was marked by the dissolution of the Court and the appointment of new judges in 1997 (see, Human Rights Committee, Communication no. 814/1998, *Pastukhov v. Belarus*, U.N. Doc. CCPR/C/78/D/814/1998, 2003).

20 See L. Garlicki, M. Derlatka, *Constitutional Courts in Abusive...*, p. 315.

21 As it was observed in the opinion of Advocate General Bobek of 4 March 2021 (C-357/19 and C-547/19, pkt 215): 'The fact that "political" institutions participate in the appointment of a body such as the Constitutional Court does not per se transform it into a political body being part of or subordinated to the executive'.

22 Additionally assisted by the changes of the number of judges and – in respect of 'regular' courts – the change of the retirement age.

23 See, e.g., K. Keleman, *Appointment of Constitutional Judges in a Comparative Perspective – with a Proposal for a New Model for Hungary*, "Acta Juridica Hungarica" 2013, vol. 54, no. 1, p. 5ff.; T. Daly, *"Good" Court-Packing. The Paradoxes of Democratic Restauration in Contexts of Democratic Decay*, "DEM-DEC Repairing Decayed Democracies Working Paper Series" 2022, no. 1.

new judges may constitute one of the important indicators in the assessment process.

On the other hand, the populist government may decide that the immediate capture of the court is critical for the success of the entire process of transformation. It may give rise to extraordinary measures disregarding the established procedures[24] and terms of office. The Polish controversy around the 'double' appointments of judges in the end of 2015 could be regarded as a clinical example of such practices.[25] On top of it, the 'old' judges may be 'persuaded' or encouraged to resign before the end of their tenure. Finally, they may be marginalised by an extensive practice of disqualifications and of manipulation in the composition of the judicial panels.[26] Although, the level of legal sophistication of the adopted measures may vary, they have the common aim: to pack the court with such new judges who would ensure the 'correct' directions of the case law.

The politics of judicial appointments, combined with the limited tenure of constitutional judges, ensures – in the very end – the full absorption of the Court. This is, however, a long-lasting process: in Poland, the 'new' judges were able to build a solid majority only in 2018 (and the last 'lone dissenter' left the Court in 2021), in Hungary the capture of the Court was completed in 2014, four years after the beginnings of the Orban government.[27] In the meantime, the continuing absorption has been accompanied by different neutralisation measures aimed at the disablement of the court.

2. *The control over the appointment of the Court president.* This is a crucial matter because the Court's ability to resist depends – largely – on the personality and resolution of its president.

In Hungary, the problem was solved almost immediately since the 2011 Constitution terminated the tenure of the sitting president and vested the parliament with the power to appoint the new one.

In Poland, where constitutional amendment remained beyond the reach of the new government, the sitting president managed to complete his term. It was only in the end of 2016 when the new president of the Constitutional Court was appointed by the President of the Republic, not – however – without

24 Such as elimination of rules ensuring the formal participation of the opposition in the nomination process (K. Kovacs, G.A. Toth, *Hungary's Constitutional Transformation*, "European Constitutional Law Review" 2011, vol. 7, p. 93).

25 L. Garlicki, *Pologne*, "Annuaire International de Justice Constitutionnelle" 2016, vol. XXXI, pp. 847–850; T.T. Koncewicz, *On Institutions, Democracy, Constitutional Self-defense, and the Rule of Law*, CMLR 2016, vol. 53, p. 1753 ff.; M. Derlatka, *Constitutional Court and the Constitutional Crisis in Poland*, "Torunskie Studia Polsko-Wloskie" 2019, vol. XV, pp. 9–11; W. Sadurski, *Poland's…*, pp. 61–70.

26 L. Garlicki, *Pologne*, AIJC 2017, vol. XXXII, pp. 896–897; W. Sadurski, *Poland's…*, pp. 67–70.

27 K.L. Scheppele, *Autocratic…*, p. 550.

some assistance of the legislature who revised the procedure within the Constitutional Court.[28]

3. *Regulation of jurisdiction of and access to the court* belongs, in both countries, to constitutional matters. Thus, significant modifications were possible only in Hungary. The new government decided to eliminate procedures offering the biggest potential for confrontation. A limited version of a 'regular' constitutional complaint replaced the so-called *action popularis*. The Court's jurisdiction was limited in respect to the financial laws. The Court's jurisdiction over constitutional amendments was limited to the procedural review, whereas any review of the substantive constitutionality was expressly excluded.[29] Finally, the so-called Fourth Amendment annulled the authority of the entire case law of the Court preceding the 2011 Constitution.[30] All the above-mentioned changes were of mostly instrumental origin and were adopted to neutralise the actual or anticipated reactions of the Court to the policies of the new government.

No fundamental changes in the access arrangements were adopted in Poland; this area is regulated on the constitutional level. The political change affected, however, the attractiveness and openness of constitutional review. As concerns the 'abstract review', the capture of the state apparatus left but a limited space for cases that could collide with the governmental interests. Although the parliamentary opposition is still able to launch such procedures, it largely abstains from doing so.[31] The political identity of the 'new' Court offers very limited chance of success. Similar reasons discourage potential litigants in procedures of the 'concrete review' and constitutional complaint.

4. *The procedure of judicial review* is mostly regulated on the legislative level and, therefore, remains within political control of every parliamentary majority. In Poland, procedural provisions have been constantly rewriting during

28 Under the Polish Constitution the President of the Court is appointed, from among the judges, by the President of the Republic acting upon the proposal of the Court. The modalities are regulated in the Constitutional Court Act. The modification of the CC Act in the Fall of 2016 neutralised the role of the Court by allowing the President to appoint a candidate submitted by a minority of its judges (see: L. Garlicki, *Pologne*, 2017, pp. 896–897; W. Sadurski, *Poland's…*, pp. 65–66). Six years later, the government paid toll for the irregularities of the 2016 arrangements. An internal crisis erupted within the Polish Court. Six of the judges claimed that the term of office of the president expired in December 2022 and refused to participate in the Court's sessions. It blocked a considerable part of the Court's activities, and was quite detrimental for political needs of the government.

29 See T. Drinoczy, F. Gardos-Orosz, Z. Pozsar-Szentmiklosy, *Formal and Informal Constitutional Amendment in Hungary*, "MTA Law Working Papers" 2019, no. 18, particularly in Part IV.

30 G. Halmai (*Dismantling…*, p. 36) observed that this 'annulled primarily the cases that defined and protected constitutional rights and harmonized domestic protection […] with European human rights law'.

31 A similar "policy of rejection" was adopted by the Polish Ombudsman who withdrew several cases previously lodged before the (old) Constitutional Court.

the first phase of the take-over. The general idea was to disable the Court by establishing complicated and tiresome framework of its operation. Practically, the Court was confronted with a dilemma: either to observe new regulations (which would destroy its capacity to decide constitutional cases) or to reject them as unconstitutional. In effect, the Court – refusing to follow new procedural provisions – ruled that those provisions were unconstitutional.[32] The government responded by refusing the official publication of the Court's rulings under the pretense that they had not been adopted in a correct procedure, and – therefore – were invalid.[33] Although the governmental action was devoid of any constitutional basis, it created legal doubts as to the validity of the Court's judgments. Thus, the government was successful at least in part. It managed to corner the Court into a self-defensive action, to paralyse its capacity to decide on constitutionality of other legislative regulations and to weaken the binding authority of all the Court's decisions.

The neutralisation measures were of a purely instrumental nature. Therefore, they remained useful only as long as the process of Court's absorption has not been completed. Once the leadership of the Court has been installed, the parliament abolished most of the 'paralysing' provisions and restored most of the procedural arrangements existing prior to the crisis. There was no need to neutralise the 'new' Court; on the contrary – the Court was regarded as a valuable ally in the transformation process. Nevertheless, some 'special' arrangements remained in place and the internal operations were far from continuation and affected by highly controversial practices.[34]

11.4 The present

11.4.1 Continuation or change?

The abusive constitutionalism cannot function without the courts, nor can it erase a constitutional court without losing the pretense of legitimacy. The principal strategy is 'to make [the court] docile [...] relying on the personal loyalty of the new appointees'[35] or – in a plain language – to capture the

32 See, e.g., L. Garlicki, *Pologne*, 2017, pp. 892–896; M. Derlatka, *Constitutional...*, pp. 11–14.

33 The refusal of publication constituted a breach of relevant constitutional provisions (e.g., L. Garlicki, *Constitutional...*, p. 149; W. Sadurski, *Poland's...*, pp. 74–77) and was only in part rectified in 2017, where the 'new' Court began to operate. Ironically, also the 'new' Court fell victim of the similar measure when, in 2020, its decision in the abortion case was so cumbersome that the government delayed publication for several months. See also – about Romania: V. Perju, *The Romanian Double Executive and the 2012 Constitutional Crisis*, I-CON 2015, vol. 13, p. 257.

34 As regards, in the first place, the discretionary selection of the 'rapporteurs' and frequent changes in composition of adjudicating panels of the Court (M. Pyziak-Szafnicka, *Trybunał Konstytucyjny a rebours*, "Państwo i Prawo" 2020, no. 5, pp. 40–42).

35 A. Sajo, J. Tuovinen, *The Rule of Law...*, p. 513.

court. Only then can the new system 'behave as if it were a constitutional democracy'.[36]

In this perspective, constitutional courts remain on the safe side of the equation. Does it mean that, once the stormy period of neutralisation has been completed, the courts simply continue their existence? This is not the case, at least in the countries where the backsliding process has reached an advanced stage. Institutional continuity cannot hide the political reality. 'New' constitutional courts cannot be regarded as a simple continuation of the 'old' ones. Even leaving aside the dubious legitimacy and distorted lawfulness of the backsliding process, the most dramatic break with the past affects the substance of the jurisprudence and of the functions of the 'new courts'.[37]

Hungary and Poland may serve as illustrations of this rupture.

In Poland, the jurisprudential practice of the new Constitutional Court coincides, to a very considerable degree, with the needs of the political majority. Since 2017, the legal position of the government has not been rejected in any serious case. The rulings of the 'new' Court are playing an instrumental role in the on-going process of absorption of non-constitutional courts. In particular, the Court confirmed the constitutionality of modifications of the National Council of Judiciary, of the 'reforms' of Supreme Court and of the procedure of judicial appointments.[38] At the same time, it adopted interpretations restricting the jurisdictional autonomy of the Supreme Court and limiting its role in the implementation of EU law. A similar approach is visible in other areas of judicial review, particularly in the rulings on same-sex partnerships,[39] access of sexual minorities to the commercial services,[40] 'Sunday blue laws'[41] and – last, but clearly not least – abortion.[42]

The Hungarian Court also follows a deferential standpoint. It was demonstrated already in the initial controversies about the constitutionality of constitutional amendments.[43] In later years, 'when exercising either competence in human rights cases, the Court had displayed the primacy of the "interest of the community" over the individual'.[44]

Particularly significant is the role of both Constitutional Courts in the controversies between the populist governments and the European institutions.

36 Toth, *Breaking*..., p. 322.

37 T.T. Koncewicz (*Polish Counter-Revolution 2015–2019 and Beyond*, JöR 2020, vol. 68, p. 664) discusses 'five lasting scars [that] transformed the institutional identity of the Court'.

38 Judgments of: 25.03.2019 (K 12/18); 20.04.2020 (U 2/20); 21.04.2020 (Kpt 1/20); 2.06.2020 (P 13/19).

39 E.g., decisions of 1.07.2021 (SK 4/19) and of 15.12.2021 (SK 13/17).

40 Judgment of 26.06.2019 (K 16/17). See L. Mirocha, *Religion-Based Refusal to Perform Services for Homosexuals in Poland*, "Italian Journal of Public Law" 2020, vol. 12, no. 2, p. 372ff.

41 Judgment of 27.07.2021 (K 10/18).

42 Judgment of 22.10.2020 (K 1/20).

43 See, e.g., G. Halmai, *Unconstitutional*..., p. 194ff.

44 K. Kelemen, M. Steuer, op. cit., note 26.

In Hungary, the anti-European stance was confirmed by the Court already in 2016.[45] The Court, referring to the language of art. 4(2) TUE, elaborated the concept of the 'Hungarian constitutional identity'. As observed by Gabor Halmai:

> The Court held that the constitutional (self-)identity of Hungary was a fundamental value that had not been created, but only recognized, by the Fundamental Law and, therefore, it could not be renounced by an international treaty. The defense of the constitutional (self-)identity of Hungary will be the task of the Constitutional Court [...] The controls of sovereignty and identity need to be employed considering one another. [...] Based on the above, the Hungarian justices ruled that the Court itself can examine whether the EU's exercise of power violates (a) human dignity or any other fundamental right, (b) Hungary's sovereignty, or (c) Hungary's constitutional identity rooted in its historical constitution, and based on this examination, had the power to override EU law in the name of constitutional identity.[46]

Although the 2016 ruling had only interpretative authority, it provided a useful basis for future disputes about the limits of primacy of EU law. It goes without saying that the position of the Court corresponded with the political needs of the Fidesz Party.

A similar approach is present in other cases involving EU law, such as the decision on the Higher Education Act (2018) or the decision on the asylum procedures in Hungary (2019).[47] Nevertheless, the Hungarian Court has been cunning enough to avoid 'frontal collisions' with the European Courts.

In case of Poland, the instrumentalisation of the Constitutional Court went beyond pronunciation of the general concepts of potential importance. The Polish Court is taking an active part in the government policy to challenge the authority of the European Convention on Human Rights as well as of the law of the European Union. It should be noted that both European Courts, the CJEU and the ECtHR, expressed a clear and open criticism of the Polish judicial 'reforms'. The Luxembourg Court, already in 2019, ruled that the new status of the National Council of Judiciary is not compatible with the EU standards and put in doubts the independence of newly nominated judges.[48]

45 Judgment no. 22/2016 (XII.5).

46 G. Halmai, *National(ist) Constitutional Identity? Hungary's Road to Abuse Constitutional Pluralism*, "EUI Working Papers, LAW" 2017, no. 8, pp. 13–14. See also K. Kelemen, *The Hungarian Constitutional Court and the Concept of National Constitutional Identity*, "Ianus Diritto e Finanza" 2017, no. 15–16, p. 23.

47 K. Kelemen, M. Steuer, op. cit., note 29.

48 Judgment of 19.11.2019, *A. K. v. Krajowa Rada Sądownictwa* (C-585/18), and *CP* (C-624/18) and *DO* (C-625/18) *v. Sąd Najwyższy*. A similar position was taken by the ECtHR in *Grzeda v. Poland* (judgment of 15.03.2022).

This ruling was supported and reinforced by the Polish Supreme Court which questioned – albeit indirectly – the legitimacy of judicial decisions taken with the participation of the 'new' judges.[49] The Constitutional Court's reaction was, initially, focused on negation of the position taken by the Supreme Court: the resolution of 23 January 2020 was declared unconstitutional[50] and the Supreme Court was denied the power to assess the validity of judicial appointments.[51] In several companion cases, some legislative provisions were upheld and some struck down, always, however, in concordance with the government's briefs.[52]

The CJEU confirmed and elaborated its position in several further judgments.[53] In 2021, the ECtHR entered the field. It ruled that the presence of 'irregular' judges in the Constitutional Court violated the fair trial requirements entrenched in art. 6(1) of the Convention.[54] The same approach was adopted to decisions taken by 'new' judges of the Supreme Court.[55] In response, the Constitutional Court declared partial unconstitutionality of some TEU provisions[56] as well as of art. 6(1) of the ECHR.[57]

The latter rulings were of an unprecedented nature. Whereas, the 2016 Hungarian case was drafted in a declaratory manner and was not applied to any actual case or controversy, the Polish Court decided to openly negate the applicability of European instruments to some aspects of the national judicial process.

49 The Supreme Court of Poland. Resolution of the formation of the combined Civil Chamber, Criminal Chamber, and Labour Law and Social Security Chamber of 23 January 2020 (BSA I-4110-1/20).

50 Judgment of 20.04.2020, U 2/20 – it is not clear, however, whether the jurisdiction of the Constitutional Court extends to the review of the Supreme Court's resolutions.

51 Decision of 21.04.2020 (Kpt 1/20) adopted in the procedure of dispute between constitutional organs of the State.

52 Judgments: of 4.03.2020, P 9/19; of 2.06.2020, P 13/19; of 23.02.2022, P 10/19. See also decisions: of 2.12.2020, K 5/20; of 27.04.2021, P 17/19.

53 See L. Pech, D. Kochenov, *Respect for the Rule of Law in the Case Law of the European Court of Justice. A Casebook Overview of Key Judgments since the Portuguese Judges Case*, SIEPS [Swedish Institute for European Policy Studies], no. 3/21, Stockholm, October 2021.

54 Judgment of 7.05.2021, *Xero Flor w Polsce v. Poland* (no. 4907/18) – see note by M. Szwed ("European Constitutional Law Review" 2022).

55 Judgments: of 22.07.2021, *Reczkowicz v. Poland* (no. 43447/19), of 8.11.2021, *Dolinska-Filcek and Ozimek v. Poland* (nos. 49868/19 and 57511/19), and of 3.02.2022, *Advance Pharma v. Poland* (no. 1469/20). See also the judgment of 15.03.2022, *Grzeda v Poland* (no. 43572/18) in which the Grand Chamber of the Court endorsed the jurisprudential line adopted in earlier cases.

56 Judgment of 7.10.2021, K 3/21.

57 Judgments: of 24.11.2021, K 6/21 and of 10.03.2022, K 7/21.

11.4.2 Change or corruption?

There is but a limited degree of continuation in the case law of the 'new' Courts. It may be more visible in routine cases of no political importance. In such cases, the Polish Court regularly refers to precedents established by the 'old' Court. In Hungary, although the legal authority of pre-2011 rulings was abolished in 2010 (see, supra), the 'new' Court established 'the interpretative principle that earlier references are legitimate with respect to those constitutional provisions which were copied to the Fundamental Law from the 1989 constitution'.[58] This may have some beneficial effect on protection of (non-political) fundamental rights. However, in the politically sensitive matters, particularly in cases addressing the constitutional system of checks and balances, the 'new' Courts are developing new, sometimes quite original, interpretations of constitutional provisions.

Such an approach corresponds with the general trend of abusive constitutionalism, namely the disappearance of the political distance between the constitutional court and the centre of political power. This is not so much the problem of the substance of 'new' case law; it is obvious that constitutional interpretations cannot be immune to a legitimate change.[59] The real problem lies in the continuing proximity of the case law and the political interests of the populist government. The substance, the language and the timing of Court's decisions display blatant coincidences with governmental policies and tactical needs. This creates the appearance of instrumentalisation of constitutional courts.

In effect, the absorption process corrupts the principle of the separation of powers. The initial form of the process is mainly 'negative': the Court's independence is curtailed to remove the risk that it would block the core reforms of the state and society.[60] The stabilisation of the new regime activates a new, 'positive' function of the court: to protect the transformation process by providing legalistic justification for the reform measures and by shielding those measures from attacks of the hostile forces. The 'new' courts are developing a deformed (corrupt) version of the 'insurance function' that, generally, belongs to the nature of every constitutional jurisdiction.[61]

In other words, the deformation consists of the 'inverted' role of the court.[62] Instead of protecting the Constitution against the political govern-

58 K. Kelemen, M. Steuer, op. cit., note 16.

59 As it was rightly observed by the ECtHR: 'a failure by the Court to maintain a dynamic and evolutive approach would indeed risk rendering it a bar to reform or improvement' (*Christine Goodwin v. the U.K.*, para. 74).

60 B. Bugaric, T. Ginsburg, *The Assault…*, p. 72.

61 T. Ginsburg, *Judicial Review in New Democracies: Constitutional Courts in Asian Cases*, Cambridge 2003, p. 22ff. See also M. Derlatka, *Constitutional…*, pp. 24–25.

62 See A. di Gregorio's observation that 'in some respects, the "degeneration" and "transition" paradigms seem to overlap' (*Constitutional courts in the context…*, p. 211) of constitutional regression.

ment, the Court protects the government against the Constitution. The role of the Court 'is now understood *a rebours*, where its decisions serve to confirm the constitutionality of laws enacted by the majority and to provide them with additional legitimacy'.[63] In politically important cases, the rulings of court follow the expectations of the political leadership and – if necessary – provide fresh interpretations of constitutional provisions and the earlier case law. Since in several countries, such as Poland, the transformation is taking place within the 'old' constitutional framework, the 'new' courts are expected to be overcreative. It may lead to de-normativisation of constitutional texts[64] and – in the final effect – to the destruction of the legal role of the constitution as the supreme law of the land.[65] Eventually, it may lead to situations where the 'constitutional decay' dominates the element of a legitimate change.

11.4.3 Corruption: the nature of the 'new' Courts

The 'new' Courts are new not only in their personal composition but – first of all – in the content and style of their jurisprudence. They operate in a new context of the abusive constitutionalism, in which instrumentalisation of Courts prevails over their independence.

Constitutional courts, in their 'new' version, are not endangered species. But, just like the abusive constitutionalism has no place in the spectrum of constitutional systems of government, also the 'new' constitutional courts may easily lose their institutional identity.[66]

Illiberal trends are present in many constitutional democracies. The real problem arises only in extreme situations, where isolated symptoms of infection have transformed in a permanent deformation of the system of government. It may, then, give rise to questions about the very nature of the 'new' Courts.

What, exactly, makes a 'constitutional court'? The doctrine does not provide any – uniformly accepted – list of necessary features. Nevertheless, there are some points which might merit consideration.

63 M. Pyziak-Szafnicka, *Trybunał…*, pp. 42–43.

64 P. Castillo Ortiz, *The Illiberal Abuse…*, p. 51. The same author distinguishes four illicit features in the constitutional interpretations developed by the 'new courts': opportunistic instrumentalism, transformation of a constitutional constraint into a legitimising tool, tool of constitutional mutation and creation of perverse constitutional incentive (ibid., p. 67).

65 As put by M. Krieger: 'the government sends petitions to the [Court] so that it can lend legal legitimacy to purely political inroads on the system of justice and the Constitution' (quoted after W. Sadurski, *Poland's…*, p. 77).

66 This identity is based upon separation and independence. As recently reminded by the CJEU in one of the Polish cases: independence requires arrangements 'that are such as to dispel any reasonable doubt in the minds of individuals as to the imperviousness of that body to external factors and its neutrality with respect to the interests before it' (judgment of 2.03.2021, *A.B. and Others v. National Council of Judiciary*, C-824/18, no. 117).

1. *The term 'constitutional'* refers, in the first place, to the jurisdiction. It suggests that a constitutional court must have a power to decide on cases and controversies involving application and protection of the national constitution. The list of powers and procedures of constitutional review may vary to a considerable degree. Nevertheless, under the 'classic' approach, a 'constitutional court' must be – in any case – vested with the power to review constitutionality of the parliamentary legislation, and with the power to render final and binding decisions in this area.[67] It is true that this approach does not give justice to – newly emerging – systems of 'soft' judicial review.[68] This, however, is not directly relevant for our conclusions. All 'new Courts' in Europe retained extensive powers of judicial review, including the power to render binding and final decisions. In this sense, they have a potential to act as 'constitutional courts'.

2. *The term 'court'* refers, in the first place, to the independence and impartiality of the adjudication procedure. A body which does not meet the requirements of independence and impartiality cannot be recognised as a 'court'. In principle, independence and impartiality cannot be ensured without placing the courts within a separate branch of government. This gives rise to the specificity of the appointment procedures as well as of the status of the sitting (and retired) judges. The requirement of political neutrality constitutes an important corollary of independence and impartiality.

The same requirements apply to a 'constitutional court'; however, the special nature of these courts generates additional challenges. The appointment procedure of constitutional judges is often less separated from politics, particularly where decisions are taken by the parliaments. This may give rise to both the temptations to pack the court and the suspicions that the court has already been packed.[69] Furthermore, constitutional courts decide cases of paramount political importance. It leaves often a very fine line between the political context and impact of judicial decisions, and the preservation of impartiality and political neutrality of the court and its judges. In consequence, the assumption of independence and impartiality of constitutional judges may not always be as strong and convincing as in respect of 'ordinary' judges. Therefore, the assessment of independence and impartiality of constitutional judges must go beyond analysing the legal framework of their appointment and status. Although the 'classic' statement that 'justice should not only be done but must also be seen to be done'[70] applies to any court, the threshold of proof may be higher in respect to a constitutional court. The political connotation

67 L. Favoreu, Les cours constitutionnelles, Paris 1986, p. 24.

68 See, note 2, supra.

69 See, recently, D. Kasar, K. Sipulova, *How to Fight Court-Packing*, "Constitutional Studies" 2020, vol. 6, p. 133.

70 See, the famous *dictum* of Lord Hewart in *Rex v. Sussex Justices, Ex parte McCarthy* [1924] K.B. 256, 259.

of constitutional disputes connects impartiality not only with the judge's personal interest in the outcome of the case. Such interest may also be generated by value-oriented considerations where a judge supports the same 'cause' as one party to a dispute.[71] This put more weight on the external perceptions of the composition and operation of constitutional courts. Appointment of active (and, often, controversial) politicians to the bench, lack of logic in the manner and timing of the court's decisions and lack of transparency of procedural arrangements may corrupt the external perception of impartiality and – in consequence – the legitimacy of the court. Furthermore, the self-perception of a constitutional court may be of some relevance. An open denial of its judicial nature may appear counter-productive for the general image of a constitutional court.[72]

In brief, the question whether a particular constitutional court is still retaining its nature of 'a court' is whether – in its practical operation – it confirms or dispels doubts as to its independence and impartiality.

3. The term *'constitutional court'* goes beyond a simple combination of two technical notions. It contains an added value generated by the general mission of the constitutional review and by its nature as one of the safeguards of the primacy of the constitution. Accordingly, the 'insurance function' of constitutional courts[73] enhances two interconnected areas: the protection of fundamental rights and the protection of the institutional architecture of the state. The latter is organised, in all democratic states, upon the separation of powers principle. The specific arrangements take many different forms, but their common feature is to ensure a pluralistic nature of the state machinery, and to prevent a 'unicolour' political absorption of all its branches and segments. A total capture of the state machinery by a single political group eliminates the primacy of the Constitution over the will of the political government.

The separation of powers is critically important in regard to the position of the judicial branch. The basic mission of the judiciary is to protect individuals against the state, particularly by enforcing fundamental rights enshrined in

71 In the so-called '*Pinochet case*', the House of Lords decided to set aside its initial order against Pinochet because Lord Hoffmann was on the bench and his wife had worked with Amnesty International which had pursued the case against Pinochet. As observed by Lord Browne-Wilkinson: 'The rationale of the whole rule is that a man cannot be a judge in his own cause. In civil litigation the matters in issue will normally have an economic impact; therefore a judge is automatically disqualified if he stands to make a financial gain as a consequence of his own decision of the case. But if, as in the present case, the matter at issue does not relate to money or economic advantage but is concerned with the promotion of the cause, the rationale disqualifying a judge applies just as much if the judge's decision will lead to the promotion of a cause in which the judge is involved together with one of the parties' (*In re Pinochet*, 17.12.1998, [1999] UKHL 1).

72 As the Polish Constitutional Court observed in the judgment K 6/21 of 24.11.2021 (III.6.3): 'The Constitutional Court is not a "court" ["tribunal"] in the meaning of art. 6.1 of the European Convention on Human Rights'.

73 See, albeit in a slightly different meaning, T. Ginsburg, *Judicial Review...*, p. 22.

the national constitution and in the international human rights instruments. Political capture of the judicial branch (or any other attempt to restrict its independence and autonomy) affects not only the separation of powers principle, but also the protection of individual rights. Thus, attacks on the judicial branch engage both aspects of the 'insurance function' of the constitutional court.

A 'constitutional court' is more than a body equipped with sufficient powers to protect the primacy of the Constitution. The legal framework must be accompanied by a genuine will of the court (and its judges) to use these powers in an impartial and independent manner. Judicial self-restraint cannot degenerate into an unlimited deference to the political branches of government. A court that concentrates on instrumental legitimisation of decisions taken or expected by the political authorities, abandons its constitutional mission. This may lead to an ultimate corruption of the 'insurance function' of the court: the protection of the Constitution against governmental action transforms into assistance of the political government in evading constitutional restraints.

4. *What is the identity of the 'new' constitutional courts?* Should they be seen as defective courts, infected by the corruption process, but – nevertheless – offering a good chance of recovery? Or, should they be regarded as bodies acting under the false flag and lacking the substantive features of a genuine 'constitutional court'?

The latter situation is typical for all complete systems of authoritarianism. The concept of the 'semantic (apparent) constitution', elaborated by Karl Loewenstein,[74] could easily be applied to all bodies and institutions of an authoritarian state. Also in the present times, there are several countries where 'constitutional courts' are purely decorative or ornamental bodies. The nature of the 'abusive constitutionalism' is, however, different.

On the one hand, the abusive constitutionalism creates a hostile environment for the independence and autonomy of the judicial branch. Constitutional courts are both targets and victims of the transformation process. This cannot but affect their nature and status. A decay of the judicial branch constitutes an inevitable feature of the populistic government. On the other hand, the abusive constitutionalism needs constitutional courts to ensure the legalistic pretense of the regime. As correctly observed by Ortiz, 'these institutions are functional to the illiberal system of governance and fulfil a central role in the illiberal form of constitutionalism'.[75]

74 K. Loewenstein, Verfassungslehre… *(It is a clear means by which dictatorial governments pretend to disguise their authoritarianism or even totalitarianism. In fact, instead of limiting the government's power in favor of the individual rights, those so-called 'constitutions' do exactly the opposite: they are meant to reinforce or strengthen an already oppressive previous political system).*

75 P. Castillo Ortiz, *The Illiberal Abuse…*, p. 70.

The intensity of decay may vary from country to country and is determined by numerous factors. There are different stages of the abusive constitutionalism and, accordingly, the evolution of constitutional courts represents a wide spectrum of diversity. The question about the nature of the 'new' constitutional courts cannot be answered but on a country-to-country base. Consideration of the legal framework, although important, can hardly be conclusive: after the initial stage of 'neutralisation', new courts regained – in principle – powers and competences of constitutional review. The abusive constitutionalism is, to a considerable extent, built on appearances and false labels. Therefore, the assessment of 'new' courts requires researching their record in the real time and place.

The principal question is whether a 'new' court is capable and willing to meet *two substantive characteristics of the constitutional justice.*

First, whether it is *capable and willing to preserve its independence and impartiality.* This question must be assessed not only in respect of the internal operation of the court and attitudes of its justices, but also in the external perspective. The latter requires that a court is capable and willing to deliver the appearance that constitutional justice has been duly done.

Second, whether the jurisprudential record of a court demonstrates, in a convincing manner, that it is *capable and willing to protect the primacy of the constitution.*

The assessment of these two factors cannot be complete without consideration of the external perception of the court and its jurisprudence. A court which is not able to dispel doubts as to independence and impartiality may easily lose its identity and legitimacy.

It is true that 'new' constitutional courts are not endangered species. The preservation of constitutional courts under the abusive constitutionalism may be, however, tantamount to their corruption. It cannot, therefore, be excluded that, in some situations, the intensity of decay may transform a court into an apparent body deprived of the substantive characteristics of a 'constitutional court'.

The question whether a 'constitutional court' can still be regarded as a genuine constitutional court is not of a merely academic nature. It may gain a crucial importance once the change of political context allows the return to democratic system of government.

11.5 The future: what to do and what better not to do

The abusive constitutionalism is developing in the dynamic and diversified manner. It is too early to predict the future events. Surely, the duration of the crisis as well as the intensity of damage would vary in different countries. Some judicial systems might be targeted and corrupted in more intensive manner than the others. Some constitutional courts might have better chances of survival than the others. Consideration of future options and priorities must not be detached from the experiences accumulated under the abusive constitutionalism. Doctrinal perfection of the new arrangements should always be assessed in the pragmatic perspective, i.e., in the perspective of their capability to prevent the return to the illiberal practices.

Four suggestions could be submitted to the further discussions.

First, as concerns *the immediate future*, it seems that some 'new' constitutional courts are losing their identity and may be very close to the final stage of corruption. This is a regrettable situation which may, ultimately, prompt a general departure from the Kelsenian model of constitutional justice. Already today, it seems worth to consider to what extent constitutional review might be implemented within the other segments of the judicial branch. Although 'non-constitutional courts' cannot claim the power to annul unconstitutional statutes, there are other ways to ensure constitutional protection outside the constitutional court. It is not necessary to elaborate on arguments supporting the activisation of non-constitutional courts.[76] The decay of the constitutional court cannot result in a disappearance of constitutional protection of individual rights. In other words, the shift of review powers to the other courts may be warranted by 'a doctrine of necessity': the development of an incidental (decentralised) judicial review may be regarded as the only way of ensuring comprehensive protection of fundamental rights.[77]

Second, a debate on the *institutional model of constitutional review* would reemerge, in a more distant future, when changes of political context allow restauration of a regular system of democratic government. A continuation of the Kelsenian model might not be seen as the only alternative. It will depend on the record of a particular constitutional court and its role in legitimisation of illiberal practices. A conclusion that such court had entirely degenerated into an obedient instrument of abusive interpretations, may trigger a departure from the centralised concept of judicial review. A revitalisation of a court which no longer has features of a genuine constitutional court, may appear as too complicated[78] and less promising for the future. Accordingly, *a radical shift towards the decentralized model of judicial review might be seen as a more attractive arrangement.*

Such option may also be supported by practical considerations. On the one hand, the experience of several 'illiberal democracies' demonstrated that constitutional courts are less resistant to capture and corruption than the other

76 See, e.g., L. Garlicki, *The Limits of Independence. A Judges' Compliance with the Constitution and "the Law*, (in:) G. Borkowski (ed.), *The Limits of Judicial Independence?*, Warszawa 2016, pp. 108–111; L. Garlicki, M. Derlatka, *Constitutional Court...*, pp. 166–169.

77 See P. Mikuli, *Doktryna konieczności jak uzasadnienie dla rozproszonej kontroli konstytucyjności ustaw w Polace*, „Gdańskie Studia Prawnicze" 2018, vol. XL.

78 A proposal of a democratic 'de-packing' of the 'new' courts (see, T. Daly, *"Good" Court-Packing...*, p. 23), although quite seducing, seems quite risky in practical implementation (see R. Dixon, *Court-Packing in Comparative Perspective*, IACL-AIDC Blog, 22.03.2022 (https://blog-iacl-aidc.org/can-good-courtpacking-repair-democracy/2022/3/22/).

segments of the judicial branch. On the other hand, in the European context, the non-constitutional courts are well-acquainted with the concept of the judicial review. They are equipped with the power to impose the primacy of EU law upon the national legislation. Similarly, they are able to protect the primacy of the European Convention on Human Rights and other international human rights instruments. The (incidental) review of constitutionality should, therefore, be seen as an extension of the existing powers rather than as a venture into an uncharted territory. In brief, an evolution towards the judicial review of constitutionality without a constitutional court could be regarded as a valid alternative.

Third, irrespective of the choice of the model of constitutional review, its final shape should be based on the ***final and binding authority of the judicial decisions***. The 'last word' in cases and controversies on the constitutionality of the laws of Parliament should belong to the judicial branch and not to the political branches of government. In other words, no serious consideration should be given to the concepts of the 'soft' judicial review, where a decision on unconstitutionality requires validation or tacit consent of the legislature. Any 'soft' model would be foreign to the established constitutional traditions of the region and would suggest the return of authoritarianism.[79] Furthermore, any such model would be impracticable if ever again confronted with legislatures dominated by the populistic parties.

Finally, the same considerations militate again any ***departures from the judicial nature of the procedures of constitutional review***. Any system which would reserve the 'final word' to the discretion of the legislature would endanger the operation of the separation of power principle. A satisfactory operation of the 'political review' requires a very high level of political culture, in the first place – an embedded respect for the Constitution as the supreme law of the land. This is not the case in most countries of our region, where parliaments (as well as the entire political class) were severely damaged by the illiberal infection. In the global perspective, there are only a few democracies that can afford the "political model" of constitutional review. And, even in those countries, the courts enter the field through the back door since they have

79 In the Central European perspective, such model is rather associated with authoritarian regimes striving to exercise full control over 'their' countries. The development of constitutional review in Poland provides a good illustration. The Constitutional Court was created in 1986, still under the communist regime. Its powers were, however, limited: all rulings on unconstitutionality of parliamentary statutes were submitted to the examination of the parliament and could be overridden by its decision taken by the two-thirds majority. The parliamentary override was abolished only in the 1997 Constitution, but some transitory limitations remained in place until 1999 (L. Garlicki, *Das Verfassungsgericht und das Parlament (die Zurückweisung von Entscheidungen des polnischen VfGH durch den Sejm)*, (in) *Kontinuität und Neubeginn. Staat und Recht in Europa zu Beginn des 21. Jahrhunderts (Festschrift für Georg Brunner)*, Baden-Baden 2001).

jurisdiction to assess compatibility of national laws with international human rights instruments and/or with other sources of supranational law.

Whereas a judicial review without a constitutional court may be regarded as a valid (and – perhaps – seducing) alternative to the resurrection of the constitutional court, the concept of a political review seems very risky for countries emerging from the abusive constitutionalism.

References

Blankenagel A., *Detstvo, otročestvo i junost' rossijskogo konstitucionnogo suda*, Moskva 1996.

Brzezinski M., Garlicki L., *Judicial Review in Post-Communist Poland. The Emergence of a "Rechtsstaat"?*, "Stanford Journal of International Law" 1995, vol. 31, pp 13–59.

Bugaric B., Ginsburg B., *The Assault on Postcommunist Courts*, "Journal of Democracy" 2016, vol. 27(3), 69–82.

Castillo Ortiz P., *The Illiberal Abuse of Constitutional Courts in Europe*, "European Constitutional Law Review" 2019, vol. 15, 48–72.

Daly T., *Diagnosing Democratic Decay, Comparative Constitutional Law Round-table*, Gilbert and Tobin Centre for Public Law, UNSW Law School, Sydney 2017.

Daly T., *"Good" Court-Packing. The Paradoxes of Democratic Restauration in Contexts of Democratic Decay*, "DEM-DEC Repairing Decayed Democracies Working Paper Series" 2022, vol. 23, no. 8, pp 1071–1103.

Derlatka M., *Constitutional Court and the Constitutional Crisis in Poland*, "Torunskie Studia Polsko-Wloskie" 2019, vol. XV, 7–26.

Dixon R., *Court-Packing in Comparative Perspective*, IACL-AIDC Blog. https://blog-iacl-aidc.org/can-good-courtpacking-repair-democracy/2022/3/22/; 22.03.2022.

Drinoczy T., Bien-Kacala A., *Illiberal Constitutionalism: The Case of Hungary and Poland*, "German Law Journal" 2019, vol. 20, 1140–1066.

Drinoczy T., Gardos-Orosz F., Pozsar-Szentmiklosy Z., *Formal and Informal Constitutional Amendment in Hungary*, "MTA Law Working Papers" 2019, vol. 18.

Favoreu L., Les cours constitutionnelles, Presses Universitaires de France, Paris 1986

Gardbaum S., *The New Commonwealth Model of Constitutionalism*, Cambridge University Press, Cambridge 2013.

Garlicki L., *Constitutional Court and Politics. The Polish Crisis*, (in:) Ch. Landfried (ed.), *Judicial Power*, Cambridge University Press, Cambridge 2019.

Garlicki L., *Das Verfassungsgericht und das Parlament (die Zurückweisung von Entscheidungen des polnischen VfGH durch den Sejm)*, (in:) *Kontinuität und Neubeginn. Staat und Recht in Europa zu Beginn des 21. Jahrhunderts (Festschrift für Georg Brunner)*, Nomos, Baden-Baden, 2001.

Garlicki L., *Pologne*, "Annuaire International de Justice Constitutionnelle" 2016, vol. XXXI, 847–860.

Garlicki L., *Pologne*, "AIJC" 2017, vol. XXXII, 891–899.

Garlicki L., *The Limits of Independence. A Judges' Compliance with the Constitution and "the Law*, (in:) G. Borkowski (ed.), *The Limits of Judicial Independence?*, Warszawa 2016.

Ginsburg T., *Judicial Review in New Democracies: Constitutional Courts in Asian Cases*, Cambridge University Press, Cambridge 2003.
Glendon M.A., Gordon M.W., Osakwe Ch., *Comparative Legal Traditions*, West Publishing Co., Minneapolis-St, Paul 1994.
di Gregorio A., *Constitutional Courts in the Context of Constitutional Regression*, (in:) M. Belov (ed.) *Courts, Politics and Constitutional Law*, Routledge. Tylor and Francis Group, London-New York 2021.
Halmai G., *Dismantling Constitutional Review in Hungary*, "Rivista di Diritti Comparati" 2019, vol. 1, 31–47.
Halmai G., *National(ist) constitutional identity? Hungary's road to abuse constitutional pluralism*, "EUI Working Papers, LAW" 2017, no. 8, 1–17.
Halmai G., *Unconstitutional Constitutional Amendments*, "Constellations" 2012, vol. 19, no. 2, 182–203.
Kasar D., Sipulova K., *How to Fight Court-Packing*, "Constitutional Studies" 2020, vol. 6, 133–164.
Keleman K., *Appointment of Constitutional Judges in a Comparative Perspective: With a Proposal for a New Model for Hungary*, "Acta Juridica Hungarica" 2013, vol. 54(1), 5–23.
Koncewicz T.T., *On Institutions, Democracy, Constitutional Self-defense, and the Rule of Law*, "CMLR" 2016, vol. 53, 1753–1792.
Koncewicz T.T., *Polish Counter-Revolution 2015–2019 and Beyond*, "JöR" 2020, vol. 68, 641–704.
Koncewicz T.T., *The "Emergency Constitutional Review" and Polish Constitutional Crisis*, "Polish Law Review" 2016, vol. 1.
Kovacs K., Toth G.A., *Hungary's Constitutional Transformation*, "European Constitutional Law Review" 2011, vol. 7, 183–203.
Lembcke O.W., Boulanger Ch., *Between Revolution and Constitution*, (in:) G.A. Toth (ed.), *Constitution for a Disunited Nation*, CEU Press Budapest, Budapest 2012.
Luchterhandt O., Starck Ch., Weber A. (ed.), *Verfassungsgerichtsbarkeit in Mittel- und Osteuropa*, Nomos, Heidelberg 2007.
Mikuli P., *Doktryna konieczności jak uzasadnienie dla rozproszonej kontroli konstytucyjności ustaw w Polace*, "Gdańskie Studia Prawnicze" 2018, vol. XL, 635–648.
Mirocha L., *Religion-Based Refusal to Perform Services for Homosexuals in Poland*, "Italian Journal of Public Law" 2020, vol. 12(2), 372–399.
Pech L., Kochenov D., *Respect for the Rule of Law in the Case Law of the European Court of Justice. A Casebook Overview of Key Judgments since the Portuguese Judges Case*, (in:) *SIEPS [Swedish Institute for European Policy Studies], 3/21*, Swedish Institute, Stockholm, October 2021, 246–278.
Perju V., *The Romanian Double Executive and the 2012 Constitutional Crisis*, "I-CON" 2015, vol. 13.
Pozen D.E., *Constitutional Bad Faith*, "Harvard Law Review" 2016.
Pyziak-Szafnicka M., *Trybunał Konstytucyjny a rebours*, "Państwo i Prawo" 2020, vol. 5.
Sadurski W., *Poland's Constitutional Breakdown*, Oxford University Press, Oxford 2019.
Sajo A., Tuovinen J., *The Rule of Law and Legitimacy in Emerging Illiberal Democracies*, "Ost-Europa Recht" 2018, vol. 4, 506–529.

Scheppele K., *Autocratic Legalism*, "The University of Chicago Law Review" 2018, vol. 85, 545–583.
Schwartz H., *The Struggle for Constitutional Justice in Post-Communist Europe*, University of Chicago Press, Chicago 2000.
M. Tushnet, S. Jhaveri, P. Jen Yap, F. Chung, K. roach, S. Stephenson, R. Dixon, S. Gardbaum, *Symposium: Weak-form Review in Comparative Perspective*, "International Journal of Constitutional Law" 2019, vol. 17(3), pp 807–942.

Part III

The variety of forms of guaranteeing constitutionality of law

12 The curious case of the Netherlands – reflections on the question whether the dismantling of democracy and the rule of law can be stopped by courts of law

Leonard F.M. Besselink

The Netherlands Constitution [*Grondwet*] prohibits courts from reviewing the compatibility of provisions of acts of parliament with provisions of the Constitution. Article 120 of the Netherlands Constitution provides:

> No court shall assess the compatibility of acts of Parliament and treaties with the *Grondwet* [Dutch: *grondwettigheid*].

Does this prohibition limit the possibilities to stop the dismantling of democracy and the rule of law as we see it happen across the world, and might it very well also occur in the Netherlands, although this is not yet imminent?

Answering this question requires, firstly, a recapitulation of the possibilities of courts to engage in constitutional adjudication, and secondly it requires a reflection on the possibilities of courts to intervene in favour of democracy under the rule of law. I do this under two headings: can Dutch courts, in the absence of a constitutional court in the traditional European sense, stop a dismantling of democracy and the rule of law? Could any constitutional court stop a dismantling of democracy and the rule of law?[1]

1 My views on judicial review of constitutionality of parliamentary legislation have always leaned towards the preservation of art. 120 Dutch Constitution since I began writing about the topic in 1991; see, e.g., L.F.M. Besselink, *Constitutionele toetsing in internationaal perspectief*, (in:) "Ars Aequi" 2003, vol. 52, no. 2, pp.89–95, https://dspace.library.uu.nl/bitstream/handle/1874/19327/besselink_03_constitutionele_toetsing.pdf;sequence=1, where I critically discussed the arguments adduced in the then pending proposal for constitutional amendment to abolish the prohibition of judicial review of acts of parliament as far as review against classic fundamental rights provisions of the Constitution are concerned. These views have subsequently been deepened by the reading of relevant works by M. Tushnet, *Richard Bellamy's Political Constitutionalism* (although he has somewhat moderated some of his views on judicial review in recent work), and of course J. Waldron's *The Core of the Case against Judicial Review*, that originally appeared in "Yale Law Journal" 2005–2006, vol. 115, p. 1346, as will be apparent from what follows. I limit myself here to saying that, although I agree on the main thrift of their arguments on judicial review, I do not share them necessarily in all respects.

DOI: 10.4324/9781003355793-15

12.1 Prohibition of review of constitutionality in the narrow sense; full powers of review against human rights treaties

It is a common misperception that in the Netherlands there is no constitutional adjudication by courts. Far from it, all and any court can engage in constitutional adjudication, with one exception: they are not allowed to set aside acts of parliament that allegedly infringe the provisions of the constitutional document called the *Grondwet* (hereinafter: Constitution). This prohibition of review of acts of parliament against provisions of the Constitution, I call the prohibition of 'constitutionality review in the narrow sense'. But in the Dutch legal order there are many more constitutional norms than those of the Constitution only; the *bloc de constitutionnalité* is considerably larger than the Constitution only.

The multi-document constitution of the Netherlands comprises, in hierarchical order:

- directly effective provisions of treaties and decisions of international organisations that are binding on the Kingdom (or within the Kingdom: the Netherlands), particularly those of constitutional substance like the human rights, or regulating the powers of legislature, executive and courts;
- the Charter for the Kingdom (*Statuut voor het Koninkrijk*; it essentially determines the relations between the Netherlands and the other autonomous countries of the Kingdom in the Caribbean);[2]
- the Constitution (or better: Basic Law, *Grondwet*);
- legislation and other regulations and measures implementing the Constitution.[3]

Moreover, there are important unwritten constitutional rules. One of them is the rule of no-confidence which is the core of the parliamentary system, and another the rule that public international law that is binding on the Kingdom is automatically part of the Netherlands legal order (monism). Note that the

2 That the Charter for the Kingdom is hierarchically subordinate to directly effective international law has been submitted several times by the government, but is disputed by some scholars. This is relevant for the topic of this paper, in as much as art. 43 of the Charter stipulates 'the realization of fundamental human rights and freedoms, legal certainty and good governance' as a constitutional duty of each of the countries to observe; if this to be assumed to be a higher norm than international law, this would act as an absolute requirement of constitutionalism that overrides international obligations within the legal order of the Kingdom. This has so far only been a theoretical debate.

2. The safeguarding of such rights and freedoms, legal certainty and good governance shall be a Kingdom affair.

3 Arguably the latter category is of the same or similar rank as the *Grondwet*, but both the doctrine and the case law are underdeveloped and inconclusive. This author holds to the view that this type of constitutional implementing legislation cannot be considered part of the *Grondwet* and is therefore not within the scope of the prohibition of constitutional review in the narrow sense.

rule which grants *primacy* of directly effective provisions of international law over law of national origin and intends courts to enforce this primacy is contained in a provision of the Constitution (art. 94).

When art. 120 of the Constitution prohibits the review of acts of parliament against the provisions of the *Grondwet*, then this also delineates the scope of the restriction of courts' powers of review.[4] There is only one extension of the prohibition to review under the standing case law of the Supreme Court (*Hoge Raad*), which holds that courts are not allowed to review acts of parliament against *unwritten general principles* of law either. All other governmental rules, regulations and decisions can be reviewed against the provisions of the Constitution. Moreover, already since the second half of the 19th century, the Supreme Court has engaged in the judicial technique of interpreting acts of parliament consistent with provisions of the *Grondwet* (*Verfassungskonforme Auslegug*). In principle, there would seem to be the possibility of a mere judicial declaration of incompatibility of an act of parliament's provisions with a provision of the Constitution, short of disapplying the relevant legislative provisions for reason of such incompatibility – although in practice this has occurred only once during the 20th century.[5]

Most importantly, all courts can review acts of parliament against directly effective international provisions (art. 94 Constitution),[6] and they have done so regularly since the 1980s. Very often treaty provisions are invoked in court. To give an impression: a search in the database of the Netherlands judiciary

4 For a full treatment of the matter, see L.F.M. Besselink, *Constitutional Adjudication in the Netherlands*, (in:) A. von Bogdandy, P. Huber, Ch. Grabenwarter (eds.), *The Max Planck Handbooks in European Public Law*, vol. III, *Constitutional Adjudication: Institutions*, Oxford University Press, https://oxford.universitypressscholarship.com/view/10.1093/oso/9780198726418.001.0001/oso-9780198726418-chapter-11; DOI:10.1093/oso/9780198726418.003.0011; this is an updated version of 48.Verfassungsgerichtsbarkeit in den Niederlanden. In: Handbuch Ius Publicum Europaeum, von Bogdandy/ Grabenwarter/ Huber (Hg.), Bd VI Verfassungsgerichtsbarkeit in Europa: Institutionen [C.F. Müller] pp. 357-411. ISBN 978-3-8114-6006-5, Open Access at: https://pure.uva.nl/ws/files/2743962/172593_Verfassungsgerichtsbarkeit_in_den_Niederlanden_Handbuch_Ius_Publicum_Europaeum_VI.pdf.

5 Hoge Raad (burgerlijke kamer) 14 April 1989, *Nederlandse Jurisprudentie* 1989/469 (*Harmonsatiewet*). Unlike the prohibition for courts to review against the provisions of the Constitution, which is very controversial and has been subject to regular attempts to abolish it, the prohibition to review acts of parliament against unwritten general principles is far less controversial. As a justification for this prohibition mostly legal uncertainty as to what a general principle of law should entail is adduced as a justification. The *Hoge Raad* in the judgment referred to gave as other major arguments the intention of the makers of the 1983 Constitution not to change the broad scope of 'inviolability of acts of parliament', as the prohibition was formulated prior to 1983, as well as the 'constitutional tradition' of 'non-review' of parliamentary legislation.

6 'No legislative provision in force within the Kingdom shall be applicable if such application is in conflict with provisions of treaties or of decisions by international organizations under public international law that are binding on everyone.'

on the acronym <EVRM>, which is the Dutch acronym for the European Convention of Human Rights, leads to no less than 43,495 judgments which include this acronym in the period from the year 2000 to 2021 (included), on a total of 584,025 judgments in the data base for those years.[7] On this counting, the ECHR is invoked in 7.5 per cent of all the judgments registered. Nevertheless, the judicial disapplication of acts of parliament is quite rare and occurs merely in a handful of cases: numerical counts – although these might be incomplete – have not reached beyond 20 judgments.[8] As in most other jurisdictions, in the majority of cases of constitutional adjudication courts conclude compatibility with constitutional provisions.

Directly effective treaties of constitutional substance, in particular human rights treaties, are indeed part of the *national*, Dutch constitution. Let us not forget that general public international law is neutral on the question whether treaties to which a state is a party, is or is not to be incorporated automatically or through an act of parliament (or the executive), and if so on what conditions and with what consequence for their enforceability through whichever national organs of the state. The Dutch option for monism is an autonomous Dutch constitutional decision to give priority to directly effective international provisions over law of national origin and have courts enforce this (curiously and different from the situation in most European countries, customary international law is inferior vis-à-vis national legislation). Dutch courts reviewing any act of public authority against directly effective human rights treaties – human rights being classically a constitutional matter – is therefore an authentic form of constitutional adjudication.

Although international human rights treaties are part of the national constitutional law of the Netherlands, on the basis of the purely national choice of granting them judicially enforceable primacy (if they are directly effective in nature), the fact that those treaty rights are of international origin remains a difference for the justification of granting them the status of a benchmark of judicial review that extends to acts of parliament. However strong their constitutional nature may be from a national point of view, the major argument for distinguishing review against human rights treaties, from judicial review of constitutionality in the narrow sense (review against provisions of the Constitution) lies in the commitment undertaken towards other states to respect directly effective treaty provisions, *a fortiori* when it concerns international commitment to observe human rights. It is this element of international

7 www.rechtspraak.nl. Search key <EVRM>, selected for the date of the judgment in the years 2000 to 2021 (2021 included); only judgments selected (not advocate-general opinions); search repeated several times in August 2022.

8 M. Claes, A.W. Heringa, M. van der Sluis, M. Stremler, *Rechtsvergelijkend onderzoek constitutionele toetsing*, University of Maastricht, Maastricht 2021, p. 65, footnote 73, mentions 11 cases, but only looked at the highest courts. If we also look at lower courts' judgments the number is somewhat higher.

accountability and responsibility that is totally absent as regards constitutional review in the narrow sense.

This differentiation between the justification of judicial review against human rights treaties and against the Constitution is often overlooked, because in practice the rights provisions of the Constitution mostly have an equivalent in the many human rights treaties to which the Netherlands is a party.[9] This leads to the common misunderstanding that review against treaties and against the Constitution makes little difference. That said, human rights treaties, not least the European Convention on Human Rights, fill many of the gaps that the prohibition of art. 120 of the Constitution may otherwise create.

Why then this exception? What is the constitutional significance of the prohibition to review acts of parliament against the provisions of the Constitution?[10]

12.2 Constitutional adjudication and the separation of powers

12.2.1 The legislature as guarantor of the Constitution

The specific prohibition for *courts* to engage in establishing the constitutionality of acts of parliaments, and more precisely the prohibition to set aside provisions of acts of parliament for an alleged incompatibility with provisions of the Constitution, entails that the guarantor of the constitutionality of acts of parliament is the legislature itself. This highlights the separation of powers framework in which we have to understand constitutional adjudication: the prohibition of art. 120 of the Dutch Constitution is directed at courts and clearly indicates that it is not the courts but the legislature itself that has to be the guarantor of the constitutionality of the laws it makes.

Of course, one may wonder whether in the Netherlands parliament takes up its role in scrutinising the compatibility of bills with the Constitution. This is an empirical question on which little empirical research has been done. What we can say about this, is that both the Lower House, but more particularly the Upper House tend to have a look at the issue of the constitutionality of bills. In this respect they look as much to international treaties, the ECHR and EU law, as to the Constitution. But there is not the systematic scrutiny comparable to the work of the Finnish *Perustuslakivaliokunta*. This is to be lamented, and much improvement is possible. But it would go too far to say that parliament and government totally disregard their role as guarantors of the constitutionality of laws. And certainly it would be wrong to say that they would take their task more seriously if there had been a constitutional court

9 There are some differences between human rights treaties and the Constitutional rights. The most important is that the Constitution requires a basis in an *act of parliament* before constitutional rights can be restricted. This formal requirement, which guarantees the democratic legitimacy of restricting rights, is generally absent in human rights treaties.

10 As we mentioned, this prohibition extends also to unwritten general principles of law, see text at footnote 6.

of the German, Italian or French type, or a semi-decentralised system like the Portuguese. It might just as well be that parliament may take its task (even) less seriously if there is a court to act as a back up. For the Netherlands this, however, is entirely hypothetical only.

12.2.2 The variety of solutions to the separation and balancing of powers issue

The separation and balance of powers is premised on the 18th century idea that power should never end up being absolute and that the exercise of public power should therefore never be concentrated in one person, institution or public office.[11] This requires a separation between the various powers, that is to say, an amount of independence from each other in the exercise of their respective tasks. The actual amount of independence determines the relationship between those powers. Judicial review of the constitutionality of acts of parliament would seem to place the judiciary over the legislature, thus upsetting the intuition not only that the judiciary must necessarily be subject to the law which – to a large extent – is set by the legislature, but also the intuition that within the always delicate balance between the powers of the *trias politica* in a well-functioning democratic state under the rule of law the legislature in principle should enjoy primacy. In the context of judicial review, in Europe the solution was found by placing the court to adjudicate issues on the exercise of power by the various branches of government, which of course includes the judiciary, *outside* the *trias politica* and should be located in a separate constitutional court, the issue of separation of powers being itself a matter of interpretation of the constitutional rules and principles. This solution of type of constitutional adjudication is associated with the name of Kelsen, and hence has been called the *Kelsenian* type of constitutional court.

Although in many European countries this solution was accepted in the course of the 20th century, it has by no means been generally accepted in Europe either. We find mixed types in for instance Estonia, and somewhat differently in the non-exclusive power of the Portuguese *Tribunal Constitucional*, and the diffuse system of court review in Greece and the Nordic countries. In

11 In the country of which students were told that the separation of powers is most strictly institutionalised in the Constitution, the 45th President of the United States famously claimed 'I have an Article II [of the Constitution] where I have the right to do whatever I want as a President'; for a compilation these assertions in the context of investigative powers of the Justice Department and the public prosecution see https://youtu.be/sl_gO3uOds8. In the context of his powers over state governors, the claim is that '[w]hen somebody is president of the United States, the authority is total', (13 April 2020), see https://www.youtube.com/watch?v=r3QXrQDTDYo. For a general discussion of the more nuanced constitutional doctrine of a strongly unitary executive, as an ongoing issue of American constitutional law to this day, see e.g., L. Lessig, C.R. Sunstein, *The President and the Administration*, "Columbia Law Review" 1994, vol. 94, pp. 1–123.

the Netherlands the adjudication of the compatibility with human rights treaties, which are a major source of Dutch constitutional law, is decentralised and to that extent constitutional adjudication is like in Greece and the Nordic countries.

The choice to leave the ultimate authority to assess the compatibility with the provisions of the Constitution ('constitutionality in the narrow sense') to the legislature in the Netherlands, the UK and Switzerland, must be viewed as a national choice in balancing powers and is in principle legitimate, and has in these countries never been considered to conflict with the idea of a democratic state under the rule of law. Quite to the contrary, these states have overall been considered to be states with reasonably well functioning democratic systems of government with equally well-functioning judicial systems.

Saying this is of course not to say that these systems are flawless either from the perspective of democracy, nor of that of the rule of law. As regards democracy in the UK, with England traditionally viewed as the mother of all parliaments and hence as parenting parliamentary systems of government that have become dominant in Europe, the examples may be the British Prime Minister's advice the Queen to shut down ('prorogue') Parliament in order to avoid it discussing the terms on which the UK was to leave the European Union. At the same time, this very case proves the possibility of courts, though it is extremely rare, to intervene in favour of democracy[12] – courts are mostly considered to be 'counter-majoritarian', about which I make a remark below. The UK and its 'winner takes all' principle of representative democracy (the 'power hoarding arch type' of government as Anthony King called it[13]) has in recent years also proven to be exposed to rampant corruption as became obvious under prime minister Boris Johnson.[14] These cases of political corruption have eroded public trust in democratic government, and in the absence of hard law, courts have not been able to play a significant role in countering it.

As to the rule of law, we mention the Netherlands highest administrative court, the Administrative Jurisdiction Division of the Council of State (*Afdeling bestuursrechtspraak Raad van State*), which legitimated in its case law from before October 2019[15] allowed the quasi-punitive recovery from over 24,000 families of child day care support that was administered in the form of

12 The UK Supreme Court had to intervene against this excess of power in *R (on the application of Miller) (Appellant) v The Prime Minister (Respondent) Cherry and others (Respondents) v Advocate General for Scotland (Appellant)* (Scotland), 24 September 2019 (Miller-II).

13 A. King, *Does the United Kingdom Still Have a Constitution?*, The Hamlyn Lectures, 52nd Series, Sweet & Maxwell, London 2001.

14 See for a summing up of cases https://www.theguardian.com/politics/2022/jul/08/boris-johnson-no-confidence-vote-partygate and https://www.theguardian.com/politics/2022/jul/09/scandalous-legacy-as-johnson-heads-for-the-exit-many-issues-remain-unresolved.

15 In two judgments of 23 October 2019, ECLI:NL:RVS:2019:3536 and ECLI:NL:RVS:2019:3536, the *Afdeling bestuursrechtspraak*, on in part different grounds, reverted its earlier case law.

fiscal bonuses. This practice of quasi-punitive recovery meant that persons who made even minor administrative mistakes like missing signatures, or failed to pay their own yearly contribution of sometimes no more than a few hundred Euros or less, or did not do so in time, had to refund tens of thousands of Euros for the actual full cost of day care that had been provided on the basis of the imperfect or incomplete file – the full cost being a sum of money which they could not pay in the first place, which is why they received the fiscal bonus. The group of citizens included hundreds of cases based on ethnic profiling.[16] The statistics show that the benefits affair particularly affected many single-parent families, many families with a migrant background, many families with a low income, many families on social assistance and many families with low or negative assets.[17] In many cases (figures vary between 1115[18] and 1675[19] cases), parents subsequently lost parental authority over their children due to their being registered as fraudsters, impoverishment and similar problems they ended up in. The parliamentary investigation committee concluded in its report that in this whole affair

> the fundamental principles of the rule of law have been infringed. This reproach does not only regard the executive, more specifically the Tax Administration, but also the legislature and the judiciary ... Without wishing to express an opinion on individual court rulings, the Committee observes that for years also the administrative courts have made an essential contribution to maintaining a rock hard implementation of the regulations on childcare benefits that do not follow from the law. In doing so, the administrative courts have neglected their important function of (legal) protection of individual citizens.[20]

An important *caveat* is therefore in place. But I suppose we may still conclude that also countries where legislatures, and not constitutional or ordinary courts, are the ultimate guarantor of the constitution, like Switzerland, the

16 See letter of the State Secretary of Fiscal Affairs 30 May 2022, Parliamentary Documents (*Kamerstukken*), Tweede Kamer (*Lower House*), 31 066, nr 2030.

17 Central Office for Statistics (*Centraal Bureau voor de Statistiek*), 28 June 2022, https://www.cbs.nl/nl-nl/maatwerk/2022/26/kenmerken-van-gedupeerde-gezinnen-toeslagenaffaire; see also Ministry of Justice https://www.inspectie-jenv.nl/actueel/nieuws/2022/06/28/toeslagenaffaire-trof-vooral-eenoudergezinnen.

18 Central Office for Statistics (*Centraal Bureau voor de Statistiek*) October 2021, see https://www.cbs.nl/-/media/_excel/2021/47/samenloop_jeugdbescherming_jeugdhulp_kinderopvangtoeslagenaffaire_nieuw.xlsx.

19 Central Office for Statistics (*Centraal Bureau voor de Statistiek*), 11 May 2022, https://www.cbs.nl/nl-nl/maatwerk/2022/19/actualisatie-uithuisplaatsingen-toeslagenaffaire-2015-t-m-2021.

20 Parliamentary hearing committee, Final Report, *Ongehoord onrecht*, p. 7–8, http://www.tweedekamer.nl/sites/default/files/atoms/files/20201217_eindverslag_parlementaire_ondervragingscommissie_kinderopvangtoeslag.pdf.

United Kingdom and the Netherlands, can be reasonably well-functioning democratic states under the rule of law. The three examples I just presented from the UK and the Netherlands have also exposed that these systems are still in principle able to correct what has gone terribly wrong within these countries. If I am right in this, this implies that democracy under the rule of law is not dependent on the existence of a constitutional court.

12.3 Democracy and the rule of law

The diversity of arrangements in constitutional adjudication in Europe and elsewhere reveals the delicacy of distinguishing, separating and balancing powers – its relation to the tension within the concept of democracy under the rule of law (*demokratische Rechtsstaat, demokratyczne państwo prawa*): who determines the law, with what democratic legitimacy and in which cases?

The tension between democracy and the rule of law is tangible in particular when the parliamentary legislature is taken as the institutional embodiment of democracy and the courts the embodiment of the rule of law, two branches of government that are essentially independent from one another.

This way of viewing the separation of powers is a bit of a caricature. There is always some truth in caricatures. But the details of the picture may give a distorted view of reality. There are at least three elements we have to bear in mind to keep a clear view concerning courts and democracy.

Firstly, it is incorrect to say that courts have no democratic legitimacy. The interpretation of the meaning of the law itself is to a large extent as democratic as that law itself is democratic. Precisely in democracies under the rule of law, the law is to a large extent – though certainly not exclusively – determined by parliamentary legislation. Moreover, the courts' mandate to interpret and apply the law is at any rate as democratic as the laws that give them that mandate. So when courts carry out their constitutional duty to review act of parliament or other acts of public authorities against constitutional norms, this task is as democratically legitimate as those who have established those constitutional norms are democratically legitimate.[21] It is precisely this type of democratic legitimacy of adjudication, derived from the democracy of law, which can justify that courts are indeed separate, independent, from legislatures.

Secondly, this acknowledgment of the democratic legitimacy of courts can yet not detract from the fact that the democratic legitimacy of duly elected and representative parliaments,[22] at least in a democratic system that overall

21 For reasons of space, I here leave aside what is referred to as the 'Jeffersonian objection' that long-dead generations cannot govern us today, and that no generation has a right to bind another. This point is made anew by, e.g., J. Colon-Rios, *Weak constitutionalism: Democratic Legitimacy and the Question of Constituent Power*, London-New York-Routledge 2012.

22 With duly elected parliaments, I mean parliaments in free and fair elections with a secret ballot after a fair, open and lawful campaign on the basis of an as level as possible playing field. In the US it is quite clear that the role of money – legitimated by the Supreme Court – has

functions reasonably well, is both different from and stronger than that of courts. This explains why the very country that is the cradle of judicial review, the United States, is also the country where this very power of constitutional review has remained the object of much controversy among constitutional lawyers, and not only them. The United States has become one of the few countries where citizens make an intensive use the democratic right to demonstrate not only before the White House and Congress but also virtually permanently and prominently before the building of the Supreme Court. To demonstrate is of course making use of a right that is exquisitely democratic. And yet, a situation in which a court's case law leads to permanent demonstrations, is not a situation that chimes with European understandings of the separation of powers and the role of courts in it.

This brings me to a third point to keep in mind. It is true that ordinarily courts decide by a majority on the bench or jury (although ordinary courts in many countries in Europe – and some constitutional courts – generally decide by consensus, and so is the first aim of most cases of trial by jury). But this is not the essence of the idea that impartiality of court judgments and judicial independence. Judicial independence and impartiality require courts to establish the meaning of the law by different principles from those of democratic majoritarian decision-making in the other branches of government. Hence, in the American debates on judicial review, with the typically American tendency to exaggerate, the emphasis has been on the 'counter-majoritarian' nature of constitutional adjudication; this may be a caricature if we were to apply it to all forms of constitutional adjudication by courts in Europe (and even for all the case law over time in the US).

These considerations form part of the groundwork for considering the general question of whether courts can stop the dismantling of democracy and the rule of law. But before we enter into a further reflection on this general question, I first make some more practical remarks about whether in a situation like the Dutch, where courts cannot review the compatibility of parliamentary acts with the provisions of the Constitution.

played a disproportionate role in elections to the point of making the open democratic nature of elections highly doubtful. The attempts at corruption of the electoral process at presidential elections by the 45th President of the US, as well as the changes in state electoral law brought about by one of the two major parties in a significant number of states, make it difficult to think of the USA as a democracy any longer. The criteria of 'representative parliaments' in my view exclude situations in which large sections of society are factually excluded from representation. Indeed, there are very many borderline cases, and the more specific criteria can legitimately differ from country to country, but gerrymandered districts can make parliaments unrepresentative if they are used to exclude forms of opposition from representation in parliament and infringe the very idea of the equal vote.

12.4 Can courts stop a dismantling of democracy and the rule of law? The Dutch case

As we mentioned, in many cases where Dutch courts cannot review acts of parliaments against provisions of the Constitution, they can do so against directly effective treaty provisions, like those contained in the European Convention of Human Rights and other classic human rights treaties. So the aspect of the protection of human rights as a barrier to dismantling democracy under the rule of law can be effective even in the Netherlands. This extends also to democracy itself in as much as art. 3 of the first Protocol to the ECHR (the right to free elections at reasonable intervals by secret ballot, under conditions which will ensure the free expression of the opinion of the people in the choice of the legislature) is involved, as well as the attendant provisions on free speech, freedom of demonstration, of association, of religion, protection against inhuman and degrading treatment, the right to life, privacy and other democracy related rights and freedoms – the 'thicker' rule of law rights. As to the rights and freedoms that are more associated with the rule of law in a thinner sense, a very important right is that of access to justice as protected by art. 6 ECHR (and its equivalents in other human rights treaties). In particular, Dutch courts take precedents in the case law of the European Court of Human rights in particular cases as a quite strict ground for judgment. They do this so much so that also in cases that do not involve acts of parliament but administrative decisions and regulations – i.e., when the prohibition of art. 120 of the Constitution is not in play – these function as the major constitutional benchmark.

The other 'external' source of protection derives from EU law. Democracy, as such, in particular electoral rights are limited mainly to European citizenship contexts, although arguably they are better protected in the case law of the European Court of Justice than in the European Court of Human Rights.[23] There is also, of course, the ever further developing rule of law case law on (mainly) judicial independence under art. 19 TEU, in sync with the European Court of Human Rights. This focus on judicial independence is

23 A good example of this are the *Eman and Sevinger* preliminary rulings in which Dutch citizens living in the Caribbean parts of the Kingdom won the right to vote in European Parliament elections, as the ECJ found that although these territories do not fall under EU law (see art. 355 and Annex II TFEU) their exclusion was unjustified discrimination in as much as Dutch citizens living in any other territory were not excluded from this right to vote, see ECJ, Case C-300/04, 12 September 2006. For an analysis of the larger set of judgments on electoral rights, including a brief comparison with the ECtHR case law, see L.F.M. Besselink, *Colonial Voting Rights*, [Case Note to] *Case C-145/04, Spain v. United Kingdom, judgment of the Grand Chamber of 12 September 2006; Case C-300/04, Eman and Sevinger, judgment of the Grand Chamber of 12 September 2006; ECtHR (Third Section), 6 September 2007, Applications Nos. 17173/07 and 17180/07, Oslin Benito Sevinger and Michiel Godfried Eman (Sevinger and Eman)*, "Common Market Law Review" 2008, vol. 45, pp. 787–813, Open Access https://dspace.library.uu.nl/handle/1874/27001.

to be associated with a 'thinner', more lawyerly understanding of the rule of law concept. It does not extend into the broader issues of political rights and freedoms or other aspects of the separation and balancing of powers in the member states, issues and aspects that must be associated with a 'thick' rule of law understanding that also encompasses political democracy.[24]

Notwithstanding the fact that the case law of the Court of Justice relates judicial independence under art. 19 TEU to the founding values that are common to the member states and the Union specified in art. 2 TEU, the Court has not been able to go beyond this particular legal and lawyerly issue of judicial independence. This is notwithstanding the consensus in the literature that art. 2 TEU is not limited to the 'scope of EU law' in the ordinary sense of powers on substantive matters conferred on the Union, but, as the enforcement mechanism of art. 7 TEU makes clear, any action of member states that relates to – more specifically action that threatens or infringes – the foundational values which the Union and the member states hold in common. I understand very well why the Court of Justice has not gone so far as to base itself on art. 2 TEU itself, at any rate so far. Firstly, 'values' are not 'rules' and not even 'principles', let alone 'legal rules' or 'legal principles'. The predecessor to the present version of art. 2 TEU spoke of 'principles', but in the Lisbon version of the TEU this has been changed to 'values'. And the actual summing up of the values mentioned in art. 2 is such that they easily clash in concrete cases, supposing that we know their exact meaning in such concrete cases. More importantly, the enforcement of art. 2 is explicitly regulated through the specific mechanism of art. 7 TEU, which seems to rule out their enforcement in the cases covered by this political mechanism through the ordinary proceedings at the Court of Justice. Regretfully, the political mechanism has so far failed to deliver, precisely through political manoeuvring of member states, not least the member states that are the object of grave doubts – to put it quite mildly – as to their compliance with the values of art. 2 TEU.

In sum, one may say that the rule of law in the thinner sense, comprising judicial independence and access to justice, is indeed protected through the sources of Dutch constitutional law that derive from international and European treaties. 'Thicker' understandings of the rule of law comprising democracy, separation of powers, and social rights which essentially hinge on considerations of distributive justice, are not strongly and prominently protected by courts. In cases in which democracy under the rule of law in a thicker sense are being systematically undermined by the powers that be, may not be stopped by courts of law in the Netherlands, simply because courts have less to say when it comes to the political elements of the state, which are traditionally left to politics. My sense is that this is not only true of the Netherlands,

24 For the distinction between 'thinner' and 'thicker' understandings of the rule of law see B.Z. Tamanaha, *On the Rule of Law: History, Politics, Theory*, Cambridge 2004, chapter 7; see also Lord T. Bingham, *The Rule of Law*, London 2011, p. 61.

but more universally in democracies under the rule of law, precisely because they are democracies under the rule of law the preconditions of which are not within the powers of courts to maintain. In the next section I provide some further reflections on this.

12.5 Could *any* constitutional court stop a dismantling of democracy and the rule of law?

No doubt the role of constitutional courts in upholding the rule of law is in democracies, which have taken their particular form in and through constitutional law, of utmost importance. This is not the same as saying that courts with constitutional jurisdiction are actually capable of stopping the dismantling of democracy and the rule of law. This has various explanations, some of which go beyond the specifically legal questions of the jurisdiction of courts and institutional arrangements within democratic states under the rule of law.

One reason of those more structural explanations is that law is an inherently political phenomenon. Parliament and the executive determine to a large extent the law, thus making it a product of politics. Also the constitution itself is a political product. When political agendas aim to change the constitution and its arrangements, both the constitution's and the law's subordination to politics are conspicuous. This is so under ordinary political circumstances, that is to say, when more or less fundamental changes do not place the relevant political order outside the category of democracies under the rule of law. For instance, in case a strictly parliamentary system is changed into a semi-presidential system of government (or the other way round), or an electoral system of proportional representation changes to a majoritarian system, these are changes which have profound consequences for the political system, but they do not in themselves imply it is no longer a democracy under the rule of law. Constitutional law and parliamentary legislation as major sources of the law are equally subordinate to politics under circumstances that are revolutionary, that is to say, aimed at changing the very foundations of democracy and the rule of law. Revolutions that lead to constitutional change usually do not bring about those changes in full accordance with the ordinary rules for constitutional amendment; or even if they are followed, it often occurs after the rules of constitutional amendment themselves are changed with the ultimate aim to enable the radical transformation of the constitutional order.

When, as a consequence of political agendas to dismantle democracy under the rule of law, the institutions of political democracy and the rule of law can no longer be said to be reasonably well functioning, it may also be the case that the judicial institutions can no longer be said to be reasonably well functioning. If the political system is backsliding, courts will sooner or later also be backsliding, and this is precisely what we see happening, and not by accident, in European countries like Hungary and Poland.

This implies that constitutional backsliding cannot be reversed by the courts and the law once the dismantling is becoming successful. Only in the borderland of not yet having been achieved could the law and the courts play some role in reversing the course towards a system that can no longer be considered a democracy under the rule of law as it has been understood in late 20th century European countries.

12.6 Implications

The arguments presented in the previous section have the important implication that constitutional 'backsliding' is firstly a political problem. What we lawyers think of as a 'rule of law' problem, is – if we rightly distinguish between 'rule of law' and democracy – in reality a problem of political democracy. Courts have proven to be better at protecting the specifically legal aspects of the rule of law, such as judicial independence and certain forms of access to justice, than in protecting democracy. Courts are also relatively good in protecting the rights of individuals, including and classic political rights if called upon to do so, but they are, for quite obvious reasons, reticent in adjudicating social rights and generally quite impotent in the face of issues of distributive justice which are typically drivers of popular and populistic resentment. Even in a country like South Africa, with a strong constitutional court that is also prepared to adjudicate social rights, this has in no way stopped the further steep growth of the abyss between the poor and the rich.

The conclusion I draw from this is that the dismantling of democracy and the rule of law can best be addressed not as a legal problem but as a political problem. It can better be addressed by political institutions rather than courts. Saying that the threat to democracy under the rule of law which we can perceive in all EU member states can only effectively be addressed by politics, is not to deny the deep roots of the problem and difficulty in addressing these. In many ways, democracy can only function on the basis of an ethical commitment to values that are necessary for its orderly operation. Among these are openness, the willingness to engage and resign and commit to the outcome of public decision-making (whether in elections or in court judgments) also if one disagrees with it, and the preparedness to concede to the better argument and to compromise for the sake of the public interest. Clearly the *ethos* of narcissism of a whole league of leaders in Western states – and beyond – threatens to derail into corruption in the literal sense of the breakdown of the general good into self-seeking self-interest in the accumulation and maintenance of power.[25]

25 I described some aspects of this in L.F.M. Besselink, *On Some of the Pre-Conditions for Democracy under the Rule of Law*, (in:) J. Urbanik, A. Bodnar (eds.), Περιμένοντας τους Βαρβάρους. *Law in a Time of Constitutional Crisis: Studies Offered to Mirosław Wyrzykowski*, Warszawa: C.H. Beck 2021, pp. 83–92, https://hdl.handle.net/11245.1/210bfcab-0c1c-4de5-830b-fbefd34fe1a2; and on democracy and representational claims *Talking about European Democracy*, "European Constitutional Law Review" 2017, vol. 13, iss. 2, pp. 207–220. doi:10.1017/S1574019617000128; https://www.cambridge.org/core/journals/european-constitutional-law-review/article/talking-about-european-democracy/C1B1E92CE91F11EFC0B0765A264B5AF0#, pp. 210 ff.

Courts do not exist to adjudicate the democratic ethos of those in office, they are essential in the situation of what I described above as the 'borderland' between an authentic democracy under the rule of law and being in a state of illiberal authoritarianism and corrupted constitutional institutions. We have to look not only to court powers to review parliamentary legislation against constitutional norms of national, European and international origin, but also to a more appropriately intensive review of administrative action against such constitutional norms to avoid a derailing of democracy. This is particularly urgent given the highly increased executive dominance also in parliamentary systems of government in Europe, an increase that is at least in part also fostered by processes of Europeanisation. Once the judiciary, not only that part of the judiciary with the jurisdiction to assess the constitutionality of laws, has become itself infected and undermined, it is too late to stop the dismantling of democracy and the rule of law. In such a situation it may require a democratic revolution to turn back to a situation of democracy and rule of law.

References

Besselink L.F.M., *Colonial Voting Rights, [Case Note to] Case C-145/04, Spain v. United Kingdom, judgment of the Grand Chamber of 12 September 2006; Case C-300/04, Eman and Sevinger, judgment of the Grand Chamber of 12 September 2006; ECtHR (Third Section), 6 September 2007, Applications Nos. 17173/07 and 17180/07, Oslin Benito Sevinger and Michiel Godfried Eman (Sevinger and Eman)*, "Common Market Law Review" 2008, vol. 45, 787–813.

Besselink L.F.M., *Constitutional Adjudication in the Netherlands*, (in:) A. von Bogdandy, P. Huber, Ch. Grabenwarter (eds.), *The Max Planck Handbooks in European Public Law, vol. III, Constitutional Adjudication: Institutions*, Oxford University Press, https://oxford.universitypressscholarship.com/view/10.1093/oso/9780198726418.001.0001/oso-9780198726418-chapter-11.

Besselink L.F.M., *Constitutionele toetsing in internationaal perspectief*, "Ars Aequi" 2003, vol. 52(2).

Besselink L.F.M., *On Some of the Pre-Conditions for Democracy under the Rule of Law*, (in:) J. Urbanik, A. Bodnar (eds.), Περιμένοντας τους *Βαρβάρους. Law in a Time of Constitutional Crisis: Studies Offered to Mirosław Wyrzykowski*, C.H. Beck, Warszawa 2021.

Bingham T., *The Rule of Law*, Penguin Books, London 2011.

Claes M., Heringa A.W., van der Sluis M., Stremler M., *Rechtsvergelijkend onderzoek constitutionele toetsing*, University of Maastricht, Maastricht 2021.

Colon-Rios J., *Weak Constitutionalism: Democratic Legitimacy and the Question of Constituent Power*, Routledge, London-New York 2012.

King A., *Does the United Kingdom Still Have a Constitution?, The Hamlyn Lectures, 52nd Series*, Sweet & Maxwell, London 2001.

Lessig L., Sunstein C.R., *The President and the Administration*, "Columbia Law Review" 1994, vol. 94.

Talking about European Democracy, "European Constitutional Law Review" 2017, vol. 13(2).

Tamanaha B.Z., *On the Rule of Law: History, Politics, Theory*, Cambridge University Press, Cambridge 2004.
Waldron J., *The Core of the Case against Judicial Review*, "Yale Law Journal" 2005–2006, vol. 115, 1346ff.

13 Finnish constitutional exceptionalism: the pluralist system of constitutional review combining *ex ante* and *ex post* functions of review

Tuomas Ojanen

13.1 Introduction

As with other Nordic countries, Finland has no centralised system of constitutional review[1] by a constitutional court. Instead, the Finnish review system constitutes a combination of abstract *ex ante* and concrete *ex post* mechanisms of review in which various organs from legislative, executive and judicial branches of the state are charged with the review of the constitutionality of ordinary legislation. Hence, the Finnish system is essentially decentralised and pluralist by nature.[2]

Moreover, the contemporary system of constitutional review is openly political since *ex ante* review by the Constitutional Law Committee of the Parliament still assumes a principal role in this review system. By contrast, *ex post* judicial review by courts is restrained and features as a weak form of judicial review even if the Europeanisation of Finnish law has brought about

1 By constitutional review is here meant review of legislation for its compatibility with the Constitution. It is worth emphasising that constitutional review can be practised by a wide range of other institutions and that it does not necessarily entail judicial review, although constitutional review can also be exercised by courts. In this article, the notion of judicial review is occasionally used to denote constitutional review conducted by courts.

2 For the Finnish system of constitutional review see J. Lavapuro, T. Ojanen, M. Scheinin, *Rights-Based Constitutionalism in Finland and the Development of Pluralist Constitutional Review*, "International Journal of Constitutional Law" 2011, vol. 9, p. 505. See also J. Lavapuro, T. Ojanen, M. Scheinin, *Intermediate Constitutional Review in Finland: Promising in Theory, Problematic in Practice*, (in:) J. Bell, Marie-Luce Paris (eds.), *Rights-Based Constitutional Review: Constitutional Courts in a Changing Landscape*, Edward Elgar Publishing 2016, p. 218. See also T. Ojanen, *From Constitutional Periphery toward the Center – Transformations of Judicial Review in Finland*, "Nordic Journal of Human Rights / Nordisk Tidsskrift for Menneskerettigheter" 2009, vo. 27, no. 2, p. 194. This article takes advantage of these previous academic writings on the characteristics of the Finnish system of constitutional review, including their assessments of the benefits and tensions involved within the Finnish pluralist form of constitutional review while also taking into account more recent constitutional developments in the 2010s and early 2020s in Finland.

DOI: 10.4324/9781003355793-16

judicial empowerment and the rise of judicial review of domestic law for its compatibility with EU law and the ECHR since the 1990s onwards.[3]

Overall, the Finnish system of constitutional review clearly stands out as quite extraordinary among systems of constitutional review in Europe, let alone in other regions of the world. To be sure, outside observers often consider Nordic constitutionalism as *terra incognita*, and the Finnish system of constitutional review may very well be yet another vivid example of Nordic constitutional exceptionalism.[4]

At the same time, Finland is renowned for democracy, the rule of law and the protection of fundamental and human rights. Aside from enshrining the rule of law, democracy and fundamental rights in its Constitution and through its international human rights treaties, Finland also *de facto* upholds these core principles of the Finnish Constitution on which the Council of Europe and the European Union are also founded. Together with other Nordic countries, Finland regularly tops rankings in various surveys on the observance of the rule of law, democracy and human rights. In 2021, for instance, Finland ranked third out of 139 countries and jurisdictions worldwide on the rule of law.[5] Of course, this is not to imply that Finland would have no problems insofar as fundamental and human rights,[6] the rule of law and democracy are concerned, but the extent to which Finland falls short of these core constitutional

3 For the impact of Europeanisation on judicial review, see Tuomas Ojanen, *From Constitutional Periphery Toward the Center – Transformations of Judicial Review in Finland*. Nordic Journal of Human Rights/ Nordisk Tidsskrift for Menneskerettigheter Vol. 27 Nr. 2:2009, 194–207. On the impact of EU membership on Finnish constitutional law, see also Tuomas Ojanen, *The Europeanization of Finnish Law*, in Luif, P. (Hrsg.), Österreich, Schweden, Finnland – Zehn Jahre Mitgliedschaft in der Europäischen Union, Böhlau Verlag, Wien, 2007, 145–178.

4 On Nordic constitutional exceptionalism see, e.g., R. Hirschl, *The Nordic Counternarrative: Democracy, Human Development, and Judicial Review*, "International Journal of Constitutional Law" 2011, vol. 9, no. 2, pp. 449–469. See also A. Follesdal, M. Wind, *Introduction – Nordic Reluctance towards Judicial Review under Siege*, "Nordic Journal of Human Rights" 2009, vol. 27, p. 137, and J.E. Rytter, M. Wind, *In Need of Juristocracy? The Silence of Denmark in the Development of European legal norms*, "International Journal of Constitutional Law" 2011, vol. 9, no. 2, pp. 470–504.

5 See World Justice Project, WJP Rule of Law Index, https://worldjusticeproject.org/rule-of-law-index/country/Finland, https://worldjusticeproject.org/rule-of-law-index/country/Finland (20.09.2022).

6 The terms 'constitutional rights', 'fundamental rights' and 'basic rights' are often used interchangeably in European and Nordic constitutional discourse to refer to rights enshrined in domestic constitutions. The term 'human rights', in turn, is typically used to denote rights guaranteed by international human rights treaties such as the European Convention on Human Rights (ECHR) or the International Covenant on Civil and Political Rights (ICCPR). In this chapter, the concept of 'fundamental rights' denotes rights enshrined in the Finnish Constitution, whereas the notion of 'human rights' refers to rights enshrined in international human rights treaties binding upon Finland.

principles and values is nonetheless quite small in European and international comparisons.[7]

Given the peculiarities of the Finnish system of constitutional review and its excellent track record in the field of the rule of law, democracy and fundamental and human rights, Finland also provides an interesting case study for assessing some widely held assumptions about constitutionalism, such as the assumption of the existence of a centralised and fully-fledged *a posteriori* judicial review typical of continental constitutional courts as a *conditio sine qua non* for constitutional compliance with such fundamentals of modern constitutionalism as the rule of law, democracy and fundamental and human rights. But can such a decentralised and pluralist system of constitutional review as the Finnish one provide an alternative way of effectively guaranteeing fundamental and human rights, the rule of law and democracy?

This chapter seeks to provide an overview of the Finnish system of constitutional review of legislation. It will also take stock of the strengths and weaknesses or pitfalls of this very peculiar model, including assessing the possibility of transplanting the elements of this model to other constitutional systems. The chapter is structured as follows. Section 13.2 will outline the historical context of the contemporary system of constitutional review, while Section 13.3 will take a closer look at the characteristics of the contemporary system of constitutional review. Section 13.4 will explore the composition and function of the Constitutional Law Committee of Parliament, whereas Section 13.5 will be devoted to a discussion of the strengths and weaknesses or pitfalls of the Finnish system of constitutional review, including pondering the question of to what extent, if any, the structural or functional elements of the Finnish review system can be exported to other European countries. Section 13.6 will briefly wrap up the main findings and considerations.

13.2 Historical background: tradition of legalism, legislative sovereignty, majoritarian democracy and the prohibition of judicial review

The Constitution, as a legal and a political instrument, has traditionally been highly esteemed in Finland. Respect for the Constitution originates in the legal-positivist resistance by the Finnish legal and political elite to the campaigns of so-called 'Russification' between 1899 and 1905. While Finland was an autonomous Grand Duchy within the Russian Empire for over a century, from 1809 to 1917, Finland maintained its own legal system, including constitutional enactments inherited from the era of the Swedish rule (from the late

7 For an overview of international human rights treaties in Finland and Nordics in general see T. Ojanen, *Human Rights in Nordic Constitutions and the Impact of International Obligations*, (in:) H. Krunke, B. Thorarensen (eds.), *The Nordic Constitutions: A Comparative and Contextual Study*, Hart Publishing 2018, p. 133.

13th century onwards until 1809). During the years of 'Russification', however, the Finns fought against arbitrary Russian interferences with Finland's domestic legal and political affairs by advancing a constitutional challenge, essentially founded on a simple yet firm claim that all authorities, including those of the Russian Empire, had to strictly observe Finland's constitutional enactments and Finnish law in general in the exercise of their powers. As this constitutional challenge proved quite successful, a strong tradition of legalism, including respect for the rule of law, has characterized Finnish constitutional and political culture from those years onwards.[8]

The other major legacy of Finnish constitutionalism is the conception of law as an expression of the democratic will of the people. As with Nordic constitutionalism in general, Finnish constitutionalism has traditionally been premised on the conception of the law as a supreme expression of the people's will, as well such ideas about democracy as majority rule and the idea of parliament as elevated above other branches of government.[9] The current Constitution of Finland is also founded on the primacy of Parliament, which is reinforced by a statutory legal system and presumptions of positivist notions of law.[10]

These traditional idiosyncrasies of Nordic constitutionalism, including the Finnish one, have resulted in weak courts and weak judicial powers. As with other Nordic countries except Norway, Finland has no strong tradition of judicial review. When Finland separated from the Russian Empire and declared independence on 6 December 1917, there was debate over the form of government, including some discussion on the adoption of a centralized system of judicial review concerning the constitutionality of legislation. Soon, however, the Finns decided on a republican constitution in which political power in Finland was vested in the people who were represented by Parliament, and at the same time popular sovereignty was counterbalanced by strong presidential powers. These basic premises of the Constitution Act of 1919 were complemented by an equally rigid doctrine prohibiting judicial review of the constitutionality of laws enacted by Parliament. The prohibition of judicial review was formally based on *e contrario* interpretation of the wording of s. 92.2 of the Finnish Constitution Act, providing that courts and authorities have a

8 See in more detail T. Ojanen, *The Europeanization*..., pp. 146–148.

9 See J. Nergelius, *The Nordic States and Continental Europe: A Two-Fold Story*, (in:) J. Nergelius (ed.), *Nordic and other European Constitutional Traditions*, Martinus Nijhoff 2006. See also J.E. Rytter, M. Wind, *In Need*...

10 A difference can be detected between the Nordic countries to the extent that Finland has maintained a more traditional Kantian-Kelsenian normativist perspective of legal positivism than other Nordic countries in which so-called Scandinavian realism has been the mainstream philosophy. As a historical background to this, reference can be made to the successful legal positivist resistance by the Finnish legal and political elite to campaigns of Russification in the late 19th and early 20th centuries when Finland still was an autonomous grand duchy within the Russian Empire until 1917. See M. Scheinin, *Constitutionalism and Approaches to Rights in the Nordic Countries*, (in:) J. Nergelius (ed.), *Constitutionalism: New Challenges – European Law from a Nordic Perspective*, Martinus Nijhoff 2008, pp. 135–138.

duty to disapply government decrees that conflict with the Constitution or any Act of Parliament. Since this constitutional provision remained silent on judicial review of the constitutionality of Acts of Parliament, the provision was interpreted as a prohibition of such a review. This interpretation was based on the Nordic understanding of government, which essentially subordinated the judiciary to the legislature.[11]

In addition, the prohibition of judicial review and a distrust of courts originated in the class tensions and socio-political tendencies that prevailed in the late 1910s and the 1920s in Finland. At the time, the political and economic elite had confidence in the capability of the parliament-centred constitutional review mechanism to effectively safeguard vital property rights and vested rights from majority rule.[12] Hence, there was no pressing need for judicial review in the first place. To top it all, the Nordic doctrine of judicial self-restraint also existed. As courts were in the habit of exercising their limited judicial powers against the backdrop of self-restraint, there was no risk whatsoever that courts would start challenging the prevailing interpretation prohibiting judicial review of the constitutionality of laws enacted by Parliament.

The constitutional doctrine emphasising the role of Parliament and prohibiting the courts from reviewing the constitutionality of ordinary legislation remained stable until the late 1980s. Its effects also transcended the constitutional landscape to include the Finnish legal culture in general. For instance, constitutional provisions on fundamental rights lacked practically all legal significance in Finnish court and administrative practices. Before 1990, even cursory references to constitutional rights provisions of the Constitution remained rare and sporadic, and the same was true regarding the application of international human rights treaties by courts even though such treaties were almost invariably formally incorporated into the domestic legal order by Acts of Parliament. Hence, international human rights treaties enjoyed the status of ordinary laws within the Finnish legal order.[13] Moreover, the protection of fundamental and human rights proceeded from the constitutional doctrine that the legislature has the competence to define and concretise what the protection of fundamental and human rights is all about. Hence, courts were expected to exercise their limited judicial powers in this pre-legislated framework against the backdrop of judicial self-restraint. There was no room

11 A proposal to authorise the Supreme Court to conduct judicial review over laws passed by Parliament was explicitly rejected when adopting the 1919 Constitution Act, as well as again in 1931. See, for instance, A. Jyränki, *Lakien laki [Law of the Laws]*, Lakimiesliiton kustannus 1989, pp. 515–519; A.M. Scheinin, *Ihmisoikeudet Suomen oikeudessa [Human Rights in Finnish Law]*, Suomalainen Lakimiesyhdistys 1991, p. 340.

12 See J. Lavapuro, T. Ojanen, M. Scheinin, *Rights-Based Constitutionalism*... See, in more detail, A. Jyränki, *Lakie*..., supra note 18, pp. 465–468, and P. Länsineva, *Perusoikeudet ja varallisuussuhteet [System of Basic Rights and Property]*, Suomalainen lakimiesyhdistys 2002, pp. 43–44.

13 A.M. Scheinin, *Ihmisoikeudet*..., pp. 158–169 and 358–360.

for 'judicial activism' and judicial 'law-making' in this Nordic constitutional architecture.

13.3 The tendency towards rights-based review and the major characteristics of the contemporary system of constitutional review

Over the last few decades, the traditional patterns and premises of Nordic constitutionalism have been challenged due to the impact of international human rights treaties, EU membership or European Economic Area membership (in the case of Iceland and Norway) and reforms of domestic systems for the protection of fundamental and human rights. Basically, the constitutional tendency has been increasingly towards rights-based constitutionalism, which has entailed a marked shift from the traditional legislative sovereignty paradigm to one in which legislative acts are increasingly subordinated to rights-based constitutional review, including judicial review by courts.

Finland provides a vivid illustration of this constitutional turbulence and the decline of long-standing patterns of Nordic constitutionalism. Finland joined the Council of Europe and its human rights treaty system in 1990 and the European Union in 1995. The crucial change made by this Europeanisation of Finnish law in relation to the traditional premises of Finnish constitutionalism was judicial empowerment of Finnish courts to review national law to assess its compatibility with the ECHR and EU law. This new judicial competence was all the more striking because Finnish courts were not allowed to examine the constitutionality of Acts of Parliament in the 1990s.[14]

In addition, Finland made a comprehensive reform of its domestic system for the protection of fundamental and human rights.[15] This reform entered into force on 1 August 1995. Human rights treaties binding on Finland with the ECHR at their apex featured as the main source of inspiration and stimulus for this reform. As a result of the reform, the catalogue of fundamental rights in the Finnish Constitution is fairly broad. It sets out a range of economic, social and cultural rights, in addition to traditional civil and political rights. Moreover, there are specific provisions on everyone's responsibility for the environment and on environmental rights (s 20) as well as on the right to good administration (s 21(2)). Almost all of these rights are granted to everyone, an exception being made only with regard to freedom of movement (s 9)

14 J. Lavapuro, T. Ojanen, M. Scheinin, *Rights-Based Constitutionalism...*, pp. 510–518. See also T. Ojanen, *From Constitutional...*, pp. 197–198.

15 For the Finnish constitutional system for the protection of fundamental and human rights see T. Ojanen, *Finland*, (in:) L. Burgorgue-Larsen (ed.), *La Chartre des droits fondamentaux de l'Union européenne saisie par les juges en Europe/The EU Charter of Fundamental Rights as Apprehended by National Judges*, Paris: Pedone 2017.

and certain electoral rights (s 14).[16] Moreover, the domestic standard of rights protection is intended to ascend to a high level as the constitutional doctrine is that international human rights obligations binding upon Finland only feature as a minimum standard of protection.

It is important to emphasise the combined effect of international human rights treaties, EU membership and domestic reform of the system of rights protection as the main source of constitutional transformations since the early 1990s. Indeed, the most bewildering constitutional dynamics challenging the traditional patterns of Finnish constitutionalism can ultimately be traced back to the ways in which interaction between international human rights treaties, EU law and the domestic system of rights protection have stimulated and reinforced the changes regarding constitutional review, the protection of fundamental and human rights and other constitutional fundamentals in Finland.

As a result of rights-based constitutionalism from the turn of the 1990s onwards, the prohibition of judicial review was abolished in 2000, when the new Constitution of Finland entered into force. Section 106 of the Constitution, entitled 'the Primacy of the Constitution', obliges courts to give primacy to the Constitution by providing as follows:

> If in a matter being tried by a court, the application of an Act of Parliament would be in evident conflict with the Constitution, the court of law shall give primacy to the provision in the Constitution.[17]

As displayed by the wording of this constitutional provision, judicial review of the constitutionality of legislation enacted by Parliament under s 106 is not only decentralised to all courts and intended to be exercised in *concreto* at the level of a particular case in light of its specific circumstances. The power of judicial review is also very restricted, for courts are only supposed to apply s 106 and to give primacy to the Constitution very rarely and in situations in which the 'constitution-oriented interpretation approach' in which a court tries to construe an Act of Parliament in accordance with the Constitution, does not dissolve a *prima facie* tension between the Constitution and the application of an Act. In particular, the criterion of an 'evident conflict' is designed to curtail the scope of judicial review by setting the bar of application very high so that the provision can be triggered only in very exceptional

16 See, e.g., M. Scheinin, *Finland* (in:) M. Scheinin (ed.), *International Human Rights Norms in the Nordic and Baltic Countries*, The Hague-London-Boston, Martinus Nijhoff Publishers 1996, pp. 257–280. On economic, social and cultural rights under the Finnish Constitution, see M. Scheinin, *Protection of Economic, Social and Cultural Rights in Finland – A Rights-Based Variant of the Welfare State?*, (in:) M. Scheinin (ed.), *Constitutionalism and the Welfare State*, København: Nordic Perspectives 2001, pp. 245–285. A thorough Finnish Constitutional Rights Commentary is provided by P. Hallberg et al., *Perusoikeudet [Fundamental Rights]*, Helsinki: Werner Söderström Lakitieto Oy 1999.

17 For s 106, see T. Ojanen, *From Constitutional...*, pp. 202–206.

cases. Moreover, the criterion of an 'evident conflict' is deliberately designed to guarantee the main authority of the Constitutional Law Committee in constitutional interpretation and constitutional review. The *travaux préparatoires* of s 106 also explicitly state that, as a rule, a court cannot regard the conflict as evident within the meaning of s 106 if the Constitutional Law Committee, in its *ex ante* constitutional preview, has already reviewed the constitutionality of the Act at issue and concluded that this Act is compatible with the Constitution.[18]

Overall, s 106 of the Constitution amounts to a weak judicial review and it is not intended to shake the principal role of *ex ante* constitutional review by the Constitutional Law Committee in the system of constitutional review. At least so far, court practice has also been carried out in the spirit of s 106. While there are over 10 cases involving the application by s 106, the overall court practice displays that judicial review under s 106 has *de facto* most likely functioned to plug loopholes left in the abstract *ex ante* review of the constitutionality of legislative proposals, rather than courts actively searching for conflicts between the Constitution and Acts of Parliament and making full use of s 106. What is also noteworthy is that several judgments involving the application of s 106 and giving primacy to the Constitution include dissenting opinions by judges. Thus, there are often differences of views between judges about the existence of 'evident conflict' of the application of an Act of Parliament with the Constitution within the meaning of s 106.[19]

Therefore, even if the Europeanisation of Finnish law and the tendency towards rights-based constitutionalism have challenged the traditional patterns of Nordic constitutionalism founded on legislative supremacy and reluctance *vis-à-vis* judicial review, including judicial activism and law-making, this constitutional dynamics has not pushed aside the presence and functioning of those structures of constitutional review that continue to centre around *ex ante* preview by the Constitutional Law Committee of Parliament.

The structural and functional framework of the Finnish model of constitutional review of legislation is even today firmly founded on the supremacy of *ex ante* review by the Constitutional Law Committee which, as a matter of both constitutional doctrine and practice, still occupies centre stage on the Finnish scene of constitutional review. While there have been calls for strengthening

18 See Government Bill for the Constitution HE 1/1998, p. 164. See also the Report by the Constitutional Law Committee on government proposal HE 1/1998, PeVM 10/1998, p. 31.

19 See, e.g., the first two landmark cases by the two highest courts (Supreme Court KKO 2004:26 and Supreme Administrative Court KHO 2008:25), in which justices disagreed as to whether there was a conflict at all, or an 'evident conflict' between the Constitution and an ordinary Act of Parliament. Both cases also illustrate that the identification of an evident conflict between the Constitution and the application of an Act of Parliament in a given case is by no means the only way by which courts can try to guarantee the observance of the Constitution.

the role of courts in the system of constitutional review by abolishing the criterion of 'evident' conflict from s 106 of the Constitution, these calls have so far been in vain.[20] Occasionally, too, there have also been some odd efforts to launch discussion of the need to establish a centralised system of constitutional review by establishing a constitutional court, but these calls have immediately died out.

13.4 The composition and function of the Constitutional Law Committee of Parliament

The Finnish system of constitutional review represents something extraordinary and original in the landscape of European constitutionalism especially insofar as the central organ of constitutional review, the Constitutional Law Committee of Parliament, is concerned. Therefore, it is necessary to shed light on what the Constitutional Law Committee of Parliament is concerned with and how it performs its *ex ante* preview of the constitutionality of legislative proposals.

The constitutional mandate of the Constitutional Law Committee is provided in s 74 of the Constitution, entitled 'Supervision of constitutionality', and is as follows:

> The Constitutional Law Committee shall issue statements on the constitutionality of legislative proposals and other matters brought for its consideration, as well as on their relation to international human rights treaties.

Accordingly, the constitutional mandate of the Committee transcends the review of the constitutionality of legislative proposals to include the review of legislative proposals for their harmony with international human rights treaties. Hence, s 74 of the Constitution is one of those several constitutional provisions that give rise to as 'semi-constitutional' status of international human rights norms, thereby rendering them constitutionally 'special' among international treaty obligations. Moreover, s 74 of the Constitution is one of those provisions that effectively impels the harmonisation of the domestic and international protection of fundamental and human rights. This harmonisation is

20 In 2010, a governmental commission with a parliamentary composition considered the need for a reform of the Constitution of Finland. Among various questions on the agenda was the issue whether the criterion of evident conflict should be removed from s 106. A clear majority of constitutional law scholars were in favour of eliminating the criterion for the purpose of giving the courts a stronger constitutional mandate to guarantee the observance of the Constitution. However, the commission ended up concluding that s 106 should remain intact. In particular, a clear majority of politicians entertained doubts as regards any extension of the scope of judicial review. See also Government Bill HE 60/2010 on the revision of the Constitution.

intensified through the significant impact of international human rights treaties on the reform of the constitutional catalogue of fundamental rights in 1995, as well as through the influence of international human rights norms. This is seen in the light of the practice of international treaty bodies, on the interpretation of constitutional provisions on fundamental rights, including domestic constitutional principles and doctrines pertaining to fundamental rights.[21]

The Constitutional Law Committee is one of the 16 permanent committees of Parliament. As with other parliamentary committees, the Constitutional Committee is composed of members of Parliament in accordance with the relative strength of the parliamentary groups. As a committee of Parliament, the Constitutional Law Committee also acts as an integral part in the political process of legislative action.[22] As with other committees, the Constitutional Law Committee is appointed for the electoral period, which is four years. Currently, the Constitutional Law Committee has 17 members and nine alternate members.[23]

However, although the Constitutional Law Committee is a political organ, its review function is greatly shaped by a legal argumentation founded on the wording of constitutional provisions and their preparatory works, including the Committee's own interpretive practice. Indeed, there is a firmly rooted parliamentary tradition of over 100 years that the members of the Committee are expected to exercise a 'quasi-judicial function' whenever entering the meeting room of the Committee and reviewing legislative proposals for their compatibility with the Constitution and international human rights treaties. In addition, the Committee has a well-established tradition of regularly listening to university professors or other academic experts of constitutional law and international human rights law.[24] The scope of expert hearings varies

21 For an overview of the domestic status and effects of international human rights treaties in Finland, see T. Ojanen, *Human Rights in Nordic Constitutions and the Impact of International Obligations*, (in:) H. Krunke, B. Thorarensen (eds.), *The Nordic Constitutions: A Comparative and Contextual Study*, Hart Publishing 2018, p. 133.

22 A cautionary note for those readers who believe that the political organisation of constitutional review would result in unlegalistic and morally deep deliberation of rights issues as suggested, for instance, by Jeremy Waldron (Waldron supra note 1 at 1348): despite its political organisation, the practice of Finnish Constitutional Law Committee is characterised by formalistic argumentation and a search for interpretations that can be directly linked to the text of the Constitution or its preparatory works as well to its own precedents. Moreover, before issuing its Opinions or Reports, the Committee regularly hears experts in constitutional law, notably university professors, whose opinions have a significant impact on the Committee's interpretive framework.

23 Basic information on the Constitutional Law Committee is available in English on the www-pages of Parliament: https://www.eduskunta.fi/EN/valiokunnat/Pages/default.aspx (20.09.2022).

24 For instance, the Committee has heard the author of this article over 500 times on the constitutionality of legislative proposals or other matters brought to the Committee.

according to the issue at hand: in some cases, only two or three experts may be called, but in major legislative projects the committee may hear more than ten experts. These experts provide an important source of interpretive expertise and legitimacy for the Committee. The legal expertise of the Committee is bolstered by its secretariat and by the parliamentary practice of trying to select to the Committee MPs who are lawyers by education. It is also important to note that, unlike other committees of Parliament, the Constitutional Law Committee does not hear interest groups and lobbying organisations. Instead, it only hears civil servants who have prepared a bill in addition to experts of constitutional law and international human rights law.

The Constitutional Law Committee is also on the same footing with other committees of Parliament insofar as its decision-making processes are concerned. While there is a strong tradition of trying to reach unanimity on the constitutionality of legislative proposals, there are also situations in which a committee has been unable to reach unanimity. If a matter is put to a vote, the issue of constitutionality can be decided by majority vote. A member can have a dissenting opinion or a protest appended to the opinion or report, together with the grounds and a motion for a resolution. They must be based on the view that the member has proclaimed during the decisive reading. In recent years, dissenting opinions have emerged from the maze of the Committee's decisions more often than in previous years, thereby giving rise to public speculation over the politicisation of constitutional review by the Committee.[25]

The threshold of sending a matter to the Constitutional Law Committee is quite low as is also the threshold of finding constitutional problems in matters brought to the Committee. During the current parliamentary term of 2019–2022, the Committee has so far given 155 Opinions and 51 Reports. Several of them include observations by the Committee that a legislative proposal or other matters brought to Committee's consideration include incompatibilities with the Constitution and/or with international human rights treaties binding on Finland. As a result, the Committee has also demanded changes to be made

25 A recent example is Opinion 37/2022 on amendments to the Border Guard Act. These amendments aimed at the temporary closing of a border crossing point, restricting cross-border traffic and concentration of applications for international protection. Three members of the Committee – all from the current Government coalition – dissented because they considered that the amendment violated the Constitution and Finland's obligations under EU law and international human rights treaties. Another quite recent example is the Committee's Opinion 14/2021 on the EU's Own Resources Decision dealing with the so-called Next Generation EU package of 750 billion EUR relating to the COVID-19 crisis. The Committee concluded by a close 9-8 majority vote that the ORD entails a transfer of authority to the EU that is of significance with regard to Finland's authority within the meaning of s 94.2 of the Constitution and, accordingly, acceptance of the ORD by Parliament shall be made by at least two-thirds of the votes cast. It is interesting to note that the distribution of votes was not in accordance with the government-opposition divide as three members from the government coalition were among the majority while the other members from the government coalition dissented.

in these bills for the purpose of achieving harmony with the Constitution and/or human rights treaties. As these amendments required by the Committee are also almost invariably *de facto* made by other parliamentary committees, constitutional review of legislative proposals by the Committee do have a real impact on legislative proceedings. It is significant to note that *ex ante* review of legislative proposals by the Committee also extends to cover the review of the constitutionality of proposals for EU legislative measures such as directives and regulations. This also explains why Finland has sometimes been the first Member State of the European Union expressing constitutional concerns over proposals for various EU or EMU measures.[26]

While the Committee quite often finds a Government Bill to be unconstitutional in one or more ways, it is very seldom that the bill is totally quashed and dropped in Parliament due to its constitutional problems. Instead, the practical outcome of the Committee finding incompatibilities with the Constitution is usually that the Committee requires amendments to be made to the bill by the parliamentary Committee charged with the task of preparing a report on the bill. If the Committee has decided that a government proposal for the enactment of an Act of Parliament should be amended for the purpose of achieving compliance with the Constitution, the Committee may also make concrete proposals how inconsistencies with the Constitution can be solved. Sometimes, the Committee also requires that amendments by the parliamentary Committee charged with the task of preparing a report on the bill are resubmitted to the Constitutional Law Committee for its re-examination of the constitutionality of amendments. However, it is important to add for the sake of clarity that the Constitutional Law Committee cannot declare a bill null or void or invalid. Instead, the formal decision that the bill is overturned in Parliament is made by other Committees or by plenary. It is also possible that the Government may withdraw the bill from Parliament if the Constitutional Law Committee finds it to be in conflict with the Constitution.

The Constitutional Law Committee of Parliament is the main authority of constitutional review and interpretation in Finland. Its views on the constitutionality of legislative proposals are regarded as binding on other parliamentary committees and Parliament in general. This is also shown by s 42(2) of the Constitution, which regulates how a difference of views between the Speaker and a plenary session on the constitutionality of a matter should be resolved. According to this provision, the Speaker cannot refuse to include a matter on

26 For instance, the Constitutional Law Committee has reviewed *ex ante* often the constitutionality of various proposals for the so-called euro crisis measures since the late 2000s. See, e.g., K. Tuori, K. Tuori, *The Eurozone Crisis, A Constitutional Analysis*, Cambridge University Press 2013, and P. Leino, J. Salminen, *The Euro Crisis and Its Constitutional Consequences for Finland: Is There Room for National Politics in EU Decision-Making?*, "European Constitutional Law Review" 2013, pp. 451–479. See also T. Ojanen, *Finland*, (in:) S. Griller, E. Lentsch (eds.), *EMU Integration and Member States' Constitutions*, Hart: Bloomsbury 2021, pp. 649–670.

the agenda or a motion in a vote, unless he or she considers it to be contrary to the Constitution, another Act, or a prior decision of Parliament. In this event, the Speaker must be able to explain the reasons for the refusal. If Parliament does not accept the decision of the Speaker, the matter is referred to the Constitutional Law Committee, which shall without delay rule whether the action of the Speaker has been correct or not. The decision of the Committee is final.

13.5 Taking stock of the major strengths and pitfalls of the Finnish model of constitutional review

The Finnish system of constitutional review stands out from the systems of constitutional review as a highly original way of institutionalising and structuring constitutional review of legislation.

The first strength of this peculiar review system is that it is essentially pluralist and decentralised. It includes a number of organs from both the legislative, executive and judicial branches of the state charged with tasks of *ex ante* preview or *ex post* review of the constitutionality of ordinary legislation. In particular, it combines the proactive preview of legislative proposals by a parliamentary committee with the retroactive judicial review of legislative provisions for their compatibility with the Constitution in concrete cases. These features bring about at least some degree of democratic legitimacy to the Finnish way of securing the compatibility of legislation with the Constitution.

The other main strength of the Finnish system is closely related to the former. There is a relatively good case to argue that *ex ante* preview of the constitutionality of legislative proposals by the Constitutional Law Committee is a constructive way of achieving compliance with the Constitution since this ultimately allows the acceptance of the bill by Parliament while simultaneously accomplishing compatibility with the Constitution. This can be contrasted with constitutional review systems of full-fledged judicial review in which a constitutional court has competence to invalidate, often with retroactive effect *ex tunc*, those law that are deemed to be in conflict with the Constitution. Accordingly, in the Finnish review system, the democratically elected legislature has the last word on legislation and this can be seen as funneling democratic legitimacy to *ex ante* preview by the Constitutional Law Committee in addition to the Committee's composition.

Yet another virtue may originate in the form of judicial review under s 106. While it is certainly quite strange and arguably problematic as well in shrinking judicial review to almost nothing, it nonetheless maintains the important difference between legislative and judicial powers by confining the competence of the courts to declare provisions of Acts of Parliament inapplicable in concrete cases. Hence, s 106 does not allow courts to declare null and void such Acts of Parliament that they consider incompatible with the Constitution. Again, the legislature possesses the final word, including the ultimate competence to assess whether and how exactly the constitutional problem discerned by a court will be remedied for the purpose of future cases.

The most vulnerable part of the Finnish system of constitutional review can be traced to the central role of the Constitutional Law Committee of Parliament. It does indeed constitute a potential Achilles heel of the Finnish system that the main authority of constitutional review and interpretation is a parliamentary committee which is composed of members of Parliament in accordance with the relative strength of the parliamentary groups and which can make its decisions by a majority vote if it cannot reach unanimity. Thus, the Committee is inevitably an inherently political organ consisting of democratically elected politicians working as an integral part of the parliamentary decision-making system but simultaneously entrusted with a constitutional mandate to review the constitutionality of the legislative proposals and other matters brought to its consideration. While in most cases over the years and decades the opinions of the Committee on the constitutionality of legislative proposals have been strikingly legal-dogmatic, unanimous and free from the impression that its findings are defined by daily or party politics, there have also been accusations of the politicisation of the Committee over the years. In recent years, these accusations have become more common, which may be indicative of turbulent transformations of Finnish constitutional and political culture that have even started eroding such long-standing patterns and traditions as those pertaining to constitutional review by the Constitutional Law Committee. It is impossible to assess at this stage where the *changes may be leading but the fact is that there has been increasingly discussion and debate* over the role of the Constitutional Law Committee in recent years. The fact is also that the Finnish political landscape has become more polarised in recent years. While earlier, 'consensual pathos' has strongly characterised Finnish political and constitutional culture, and there has also been a lack of significant ethnic, cultural, political or religious controversies that would have split Finnish society into factions or would have involved severe conflicts of interest and competing right claims and diverse conceptions of good, recent years have witnessed the emergence of these kinds of controversies and competitions. As with other Nordic countries, Finland has also confronted the rise of populism, including neo-Nazi and anti-immigration movements, which may at worst even mutate into such authoritarianism and illiberal constitutional amendments that could eventually endanger the very foundations of the Nordic constitutions based on democracy, the rule of law and the protection of fundamental and human rights. While the constitutional-political culture has so far been resilient to counter these tendencies, they have nonetheless entered the scene of Finnish constitutionalism and political life. Besides, it cannot escape attention that an organ like the Constitutional Law Committee would be a titbit for absolutist or authoritarian regimes if they gained a parliamentary majority. Luckily, Finland has a strong multi-party system tradition where even the biggest parties are at best middle-sized with at most around 20 per cent backing by voters.

While the role of the Constitutional Law Committee clearly stands out as the main weak spot of the Finnish system, another pitfall relates to overtly restricted judicial review under s 106. Judicial review under s 106 is much too curtailed to be able to provide a real and credible counterbalance and guarantee of constitutional compliance in cases in which *ex ante* preview by the Constitutional Law Committee fails or forfeits its credibility due to the politicisation of the Committee. A particular problem is that the evident conflict criterion creates a grey area at the juncture of judicial competencies under the 'constitutional-oriented interpretation approach' and judicial mandate under s 106. Within that grey area, there are cases involving a 'mere' conflict between the Constitution and a provision of an Act of Parliament. In such cases, courts have no effective judicial powers to guarantee the observance of the Constitution. This can be contrasted with power granted to Finnish courts to review all national law for its compatibility with EU law. As a matter of EU law, the primacy of EU law covers *all* conflicting national law, irrespective of the *lex posterior* nature or the hierarchical status of the latter, and a mere conflict of domestic legislation with EU law triggers the primacy of EU law. The other distinct problem relates to the unquestioned authority of the views of the Constitutional Law Committee in the Finnish constitutional system. Given judicial deference to the views of the Constitutional Law Committee, courts may simply accept the Committee's assurance that no constitutional problems remain and *a fortiori* ignore the existence of an evident conflict between an Act of Parliament and the Constitution. If daily or party politics direct and start shaping *ex ante* review by the Constitutional Law Committee, judicial deference to the views of the Committee on the constitutionality of legislation with the Constitution entails that politics may also start gaining, at least tacitly and by implication, the upper hand over judicial review under s 106 of the Constitution.[27]

As already noted, there have been steady calls to abolish the criterion of manifest conflict in s 106, in this way bolstering *ex post* judicial review by courts, but so far these calls have been in vain. Perhaps it is telling that proposals to strengthen the role of courts in constitutional review have met with strongest resistance from politicians, who have been eager to preserve the Constitutional Law Committee as the centre stage of the Finnish system of constitutional review.

The above observations certainly do not exhaust the spectrum of pitfalls of the Finnish system of constitutional review, but they do draw one's attention to the major ones. The other problems relate to the lack of regular constitutional dialogue between the Constitutional Law Committee and the courts, as well as to the excessive emphasis by the Committee and the Courts on the ECHR, including the case law by the ECtHR. This has come at the expense

27 On these problems, see especially Lavapuro et al. (2011).

of other human rights treaties and domestic constitutional provisions on fundamental rights. However, as these problems are discussed in more detail elsewhere, it is sufficient to merely refer to them here.[28]

13.6 Concluding remarks

The Finnish system of constitutional review is certainly extraordinary in that it places a political organ, the Constitutional Law Committee, centre stage. It is impossible to assess exactly to what extent the Finnish system of constitutional review can be positively correlated with Finland's compliance with the rule of law, democracy and the protection of fundamental and human rights. However, there is a relatively strong case to argue that this review system is among those many legal, political and economic factors that have combined to safeguard and promote constitutional compliance by Finland with the rule of law, democracy and fundamental and human rights until now. In doing so, the Finnish system of constitutional review with only weak judicial review also effectively challenges some widely held assumptions of modern constitutionalism, such as those about the necessity of strong forms of judicial review as an essential condition of constitutional compliance with the rule of law, fundamental and human rights and democracy. Indeed, many European or Latin American countries have adopted the system of centralized constitutional review by constitutional courts, but this has not prevented several of them from backsliding into authoritarianism and illiberal constitutionalism, eroding such essentials of modern constitutionalism as the rule of law and the protection of fundamental and human rights.

Could the Finnish system of constitutional review be exported to other European countries? The answer is a straightforward no. While some elements of the Finnish system of constitutional review may provide sources of inspiration for elaborating systems of constitutional review in other European countries, there would certainly be unsurmountable difficulties in transplanting this model in its entirety into workable practice elsewhere, except perhaps in other Nordic countries. To be sure, the Finnish system of constitutional review can at most do only reasonably well in the Nordic countries as they currently are. And even up here in the North the very fundamentals of Nordic constitutionalism have become subject to turbulent transformations that may eventually warrant the framing of new modes of constitutional review.

References

Follesdal A., Wind M., *Introduction: Nordic Reluctance towards Judicial Review under Siege*, "Nordic Journal of Human Rights" 2009, vol. 27(2), 131–142.

Hallberg P. et al., *Perusoikeudet [Fundamental Rights]*, Werner Söderström Lakitieto Oy, Helsinki 1999.

28 See especially, Lavapuro et al. (2011) and Lavapuro et al. (2016).

Hirschl R., *The Nordic Counternarrative: Democracy, Human Development, and Judicial Review*, "International Journal of Constitutional Law" 2011, vol. 9(2), 449–469.

Jyränki A., *Lakien laki [Law of the Laws]*, Lakimiesliiton kustannus, Jyväskylä 1989.

Länsineva P., *Perusoikeudet ja varallisuussuhteet [System of Basic Rights and Property]*, Suomalainen lakimiesyhdistys, Vammala 2002.

Lavapuro J., Ojanen T., Scheinin M., *Intermediate Constitutional Review in Finland: Promising in Theory, Problematic in Practice*, (in:) J. Bell, M.-L. Paris (eds.), *Rights-Based Constitutional Review: Constitutional Courts in a Changing Landscape*, Edward Elgar Publishing 2016.

Lavapuro J., Ojanen T., Scheinin M., *Rights-Based Constitutionalism in Finland and the Development of Pluralist Constitutional Review*, "International Journal of Constitutional Law" 2011, Cheltenham UK, vol. 9.

Leino P., Salminen J., *The Euro Crisis and Its Constitutional Consequences for Finland: Is There Room for National Politics in EU Decision-Making?*, "European Constitutional Law Review" 2013.

Nergelius J., *The Nordic States and Continental Europe: A Two-Fold Story*, (in:) J. Nergelius (ed.), *Nordic and Other European Constitutional Traditions*, Martinus Nijhoff 2006.

Ojanen T., *Finland*, (in:) L. Burgorgue-Larsen (ed.), *La Chartre des droits fondamentaux de l'Union européenne saisie par les juges en Europe/The EU Charter of Fundamental Rights as Apprehended by National Judges*, Pedone, Paris 2017.

Ojanen T., *Finland*, (in:) S. Griller, E. Lentsch (eds.), *EMU Integration and Member States' Constitutions*, Bloomsbury, Hart 2021.

Ojanen T., *From Constitutional Periphery toward the Center: Transformations of Judicial Review in Finland*, "Nordic Journal of Human Rights / Nordisk Tidsskrift for Menneskerettigheter" 2009, vol. 27(2), pp. 194–207.

Ojanen T., *Human Rights in Nordic Constitutions and the Impact of International Obligations*, (in:) H. Krunke, B. Thorarensen (eds.), *The Nordic Constitutions: A Comparative and Contextual Study*, Hart Publishing, Oxford 2018.

Ojanen T., *The Europeanization of Finnish Law*, (in:) P. Luif (Hrsg.), *Österreich, Schweden, Finnland – Zehn Jahre Mitgliedschaft in der Europäischen Union*, Böhlau Verlag, Wien 2007.

Rytter J.E., Wind M., *In Need of Juristocracy? The Silence of Denmark in the Development of European legal norms*, "International Journal of Constitutional Law" 2011, vol. 9(2), 470–504.

Scheinin A.M., *Constitutionalism and Approaches to Rights in the Nordic Countries*, (in:) J. Nergelius (ed.), *Constitutionalism: New Challenges: European Law from a Nordic Perspective*, Martinus Nijhoff 2008.

Scheinin A.M., *Finland*, (in:) A.M. Scheinin (ed.), *International Human Rights Norms in the Nordic and Baltic Countries*, Martinus Nijhoff Publishers, The Hague-London-Boston 1996.

Scheinin A.M., *Ihmisoikeudet Suomen oikeudessa [Human Rights in Finnish Law]*, Suomalainen Lakimiesyhdistys, Vammala 1991.

Scheinin A.M., *Protection of Economic, Social and Cultural Rights in Finland: A Rights-Based Variant of the Welfare State?*, (in:) A.M. Scheinin (ed.), *Constitutionalism and the Welfare State*, Nordic Perspectives, København 2001.

Tuori K., Tuori K., *The Eurozone Crisis, A Constitutional Analysis*, Cambridge University Press, Cambridge 2013.

14 Conclusion

Mirosław Granat

14.1 Conclusion: What next?

The present book does not propose a ready answer to 'what next?' – after the crisis of the constitutional courts in Central and Eastern Europe. Providing ready answers is not an option. It is extremely difficult to make statements about the future of the constitutionality of law in our part of Europe. The answer to the question of 'what next?' is complex and has two dimensions: a legal and a political one. The former entails considerations concerning institutions in one form or another. Restoring constitutional courts in the form in which they had existed since the 1990s until the beginning of the 21st century seems rather improbable. Recreating them exactly as they were is rather unrealistic. They have lost their authority and are dependent on the legislature and the executive, both of which they once monitored. Even the strongest of the courts, like the Hungarian or the Polish one, could not protect the young democracies against the wave of populism. The latter dimension mentioned above consists in following the constitutionalisms that function in Europe and around the globe. Their rivalries (for instance between liberal constitutionalism and its varieties, such as court or political constitutionalism, and illiberal constitutionalism) appear to be the subject of distant debates held by experts, but in reality, in the wake of the constitutional courts' crisis, we are right in the centre of those disputes. We follow how constitutionalisms are being 'tested', which can have various results. We are unable to predict which one of them will prevail in our part of Europe, as this depends on political processes. Thus, the matter of establishing specific review bodies is contingent upon the resolution of major political and ideological disputes over constitutionalism.

Asking 'what next?', we can consider solutions employed by those countries which have no constitutional courts and yet observe the rule of law. This is related to the discussion carried out in the book on entrusting constitutional review to common and administrative courts. This is the concept of dispersed review, according to which review should be performed by all judges. It demonstrates our intention to develop towards liberal constitutionalism, and more precisely, the type that we refer to as 'judicial' constitutionalism. For it seems that it is the judges who are best placed to ensure that the constitution

DOI: 10.4324/9781003355793-17

is complied with and that it is protected from populism. The experience of post-communist countries shows that a constitution without courts becomes chiefly a dummy, and is unable to protect its primacy on its own. Curbing the strong position of the constitutional court is a price worth paying to maintain the rule of law. The rule of law is a more important value than this or any other institution. At the same time, an analysis of the experiences of Finland and the Netherlands reveals that bare institutions such as courts or parliamentary committees will not suffice to defend the rule of law. In these countries, safety valves of democracy are at work: the political culture, the particular shape of the party system and the politicians' ability to reach a compromise. These are the prerequisites for effective constitutional review performed by 'weak courts' and parliamentary bodies, but ensuring human rights (in reference to the title of one of M. Tushnet's publications). Under such conditions, the onslaught of populism can be counterbalanced not only by institutions, but by tradition, culture and customs, as well. These prerequisites for ensuring the constitutionality of law, characteristic of Finland and the Netherlands, are difficult to transfer to other countries. Yet it is another matter to take advantage of the opportunities offered by the Europeanisation and internationalisation of law taking place in the legal systems of the two countries mentioned, and which has also occurred in Central and Eastern European states. As the book demonstrates, the principle of loyal cooperation between the European Union and the member states or the procedure of questions referred for a preliminary ruling are used in constitutional review and provide opportunities to strengthen the rule of law.

It is clear from the articles published in the book that we see no alternative to the rule of law in the states we write about. Consequently, we need to be responsible when speaking of specific changes to the form of constitutional review. It is not possible to abruptly transition from the Kelsenian to another model of review. That would be a radical change, akin to cutting the Gordian knot in constitutional law. If we are inclined to support dispersed constitutional review of law, in this or any other country, such a proposal must be carefully considered. For example, in the case of Poland, the exercise of review by judges is favoured by the principle of direct application of the constitution. This is a small loophole left by the authors of the constitution, but it opens up great possibilities for discussion of dispersed review. As it follows from our considerations, the boundary conditions are that this review should rather be complementary to centralised review and cannot be a kind of American-style judicial review. We do not resolve whether it should be a permanent solution or one used now, in a period when the rule of law is being undermined. However, we believe that it can be effective at least in times of populist constitutionalism.

Central and Eastern European countries are in the avant-garde of the struggle against populism. From our perspective, the dilemmas facing constitutionalism can be seen more clearly. Hence, the experience of the crisis of the constitutional courts and the efforts to maintain the review of the constitutionality of law may be relevant not only for our region of Europe but for other countries, as well.

Index

Note: References following "n" refer endnotes.

FSC
www.fsc.org
MIX
Papier | Fördert gute Waldnutzung
FSC® C083411

Kolibri 360 GmbH
Ferdinand-Jühlke-Straße 7
99095 Erfurt, Deutschland
produktsicherheit@kolibri360.de